LEIBNIZING

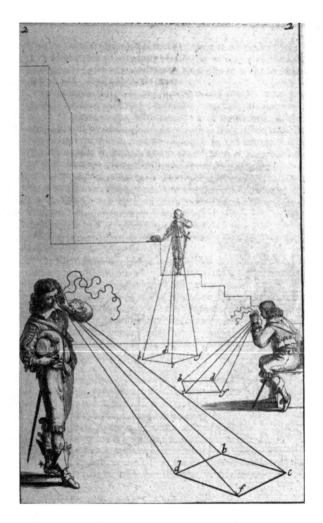

Abraham Bosse, *Manière Universelle de Mr. Desargues pour praticquer la Perspective* (Paris, 1647), p. 61.

LEIBNIZING

A Philosopher in Motion

RICHARD HALPERN

Columbia University Press

New York

Columbia University Press
Publishers Since 1893
New York   Chichester, West Sussex
cup.columbia.edu

Library of Congress Cataloging-in-Publication Data
Names: Halpern, Richard, 1954– author.
Title: Leibnizing : a philosopher in motion / Richard Halpern.
Description: New York : Columbia University Press, [2023] | Includes index. |
    Includes bibliographical references and index.
Identifiers: LCCN 2022060256 | ISBN 9780231211147 (hardback) |
    ISBN 9780231211154 (trade paperback) | ISBN 9780231558761 (ebook)
Subjects: LCSH: Leibniz, Gottfried Wilhelm, Freiherr von, 1646–1716.
Classification: LCC B2598 .H35 2023 | DDC 193—dc23/eng/20230124
LC record available at https://lccn.loc.gov/2022060256

Printed in the United States of America

Cover image: © imageBROKER / Alamy Stock Photo

The name [Leibniz] names the presence of a thinking whose strength has not yet been experienced, a presence that still awaits to encounter us.

—Martin Heidegger

Every philosophy is tinged with the colouring of some secret imaginative background, which never emerges explicitly into its trains of reasoning.

—Alfred North Whitehead

Contents

Preface

Leibniz Among the Disciplines

Why read Leibniz today? For what kinds of problems and issues can we turn to him for illumination? These questions are thrown into embarrassing relief by the ease with which they could be answered, were they asked not of Leibniz but of his great contemporary, Spinoza. Political philosophers, environmental thinkers, affect theorists, cognitive scientists, and others find Spinoza to be a continuing source of inspiration for thinking through a variety of questions and issues, some of great contemporary urgency. Leibniz, by contrast, has had a hard time gaining purchase outside the circle of Leibniz specialists and scholars of early modern philosophy more generally.[1] And for them, it is not necessary that Leibniz should achieve present-day relevance. If Spinoza is in some sense "our contemporary" (as his advocates never tire of claiming),[2] Leibniz seems a baroque clockwork by comparison, fascinating for the complexity of its mechanism but ultimately destined to be a dusty museum piece, not a practical method for keeping time.

Some clues to this situation may be offered by my first epigraph, from Martin Heidegger: "The name [Leibniz] names the presence of a thinking whose strength has not yet been experienced, a presence that still awaits to encounter us." This was published in 1957, when modern Leibniz scholarship was already well established. Its guiding principles had been erected upon studies by Bertrand Russell and Louis Couturat, both of whom argued that Leibniz's metaphysics was grounded in his logic.[3] Their Leibniz was a system-builder, and the system was to be judged by its logical coherence and consistency. Heidegger appears then to suggest, if only indirectly, that the then-extant body of academic work done on Leibniz had not led us to what is essential in him—that it had delayed, rather than enabled, the kind of philosophical encounter Heidegger has in mind. Leibniz the system-builder (who has a long afterlife in Anglophone scholarship) may be a phantom who diverts us from the real one in much the same way that the phantom Helen, in Euripides's play, takes the place of the true one for the hoodwinked Paris. A different approach may therefore be required to unlock what is most fundamental in Leibniz. I propose that we read his work, not through the stasis of the system but through the movement of his writing, and that we attend to its stylistic, rhetorical, and even poetic dimensions, not just the logical and conceptual ones.[4] From this Leibniz, read differently, different concerns and possibilities will arise. This book will argue that Leibniz offers valuable guidance on a number of issues, many of them involving aesthetic matters and perspectives; but that he also, and perhaps more fundamentally, provides a powerful *model* for thinking in general, one that we can follow and that a number of innovative modern thinkers have already followed. Leibniz's value to us, therefore, is not circumscribed entirely by the kinds of questions he can help answer.

Leibniz is particularly generative on the relation between thought and aesthetic experience, and this in a way that runs in two directions. He offers an early version of a cognitive aesthetics—one in which aesthetic experience involves conceptual thought as well as feeling. Of course, it is in part the robustness with which he asserts this relation that garners his aesthetic the somewhat diminishing label, "pre-Kantian." Yet such an approach might prove stimulating for fields such as literary criticism and art history, which often evince a certain awkwardness in handling the facts of aesthetic experience, and in which aesthetic judgment as such is often discouraged in favor of a generalized and nonhierarchical aesthetic openness.[5] This situation can be instructively contrasted with the one that obtains in mathematics and in highly mathematical sciences such as physics and computer science, which regularly apply aesthetic considerations in their ordinary work.[6] For physics, the elegance of a theory isn't just a nice bonus but a serious criterion to be brought to bear in deciding whether it is *true*. Indeed, as one physicist has recently argued, the astronomically high expense of devising experiments to provide empirical confirmation of recent theories has encouraged a dangerous degree of reliance on aesthetic criteria alone.[7] Leibnizian aesthetics likewise attempts to account for purely intellectual as well as sensuous modes of beauty. For Leibniz, a mathematical equation, a theory in physics, or a philosophical concept can be just as beautiful as an artwork or a natural landscape. Leibniz's disciplinary reach (of which, more anon) results in a widely encompassing account of the aesthetic.

German aesthetic theory of the early Enlightenment, along with its Leibnizian orientation, was eclipsed by the appearance of Immanuel Kant's Third Critique. This was probably both inevitable and salutary in many respects. One of the apparent advantages of a Kantian aesthetics was that it required much less in the way of metaphysical presuppositions. With Kant, one need only accept the existence of a few mental faculties such as understanding, sensibility, and imagination. Leibniz's aesthetics, by contrast, relies on numerous (and, in Kant's view, "dogmatic") assumptions about the structure of the entire universe, including the fact that it houses an infinite number of entities, each of which is in perceptual contact with all the others, no matter how distant or tiny. However, I believe that the gist of a Leibnizian aesthetic can be maintained while making only relatively minor modifications to its underlying metaphysic. Indeed, early German aesthetic theorists did precisely that. And one of the compensations for the effort is a concept of aesthetic experience that can tell us something about the nature of the world, and vice versa. I do not, in any case, harbor the unreasonable expectation that a Leibnizian aesthetic can or should be revived in its canonical form. But it can serve as an inspirational starting point for rethinking issues of aesthetics, perception, and the structures of the real.

Leibniz is not often regarded as a major aesthetic theorist partly because he never published a treatise devoted exclusively to aesthetic matters, in which he expounds his theories of beauty, nature, and the fine arts in a systematic and continuous way.[8] His aesthetic principles tend instead to emerge piecemeal, often in the context of discussing other topics: human perception, say, or the physical and moral design of the universe. For this reason, I think, even Leibniz scholars have tended to underestimate the importance of aesthetic considerations to his thought. For Leibniz, the aesthetic infiltrates other matters, and other matters infiltrate the aesthetic. But I think we can see this as a virtue rather than a flaw. The fact that Leibnizian aesthetics doesn't receive treatment in a work of its own reflects the fact that the aesthetic does not, for Leibniz, occupy a self-enclosed or exclusive realm but rather suffuses all of existence. This elevates its importance rather than diminishing it, while also rendering it more readily "usable."

Accordingly, this book will not attempt to isolate Leibnizian aesthetics in a way that Leibniz himself declined to do. It does not, in other words, aim to be the treatise on aesthetics that Leibniz either chose not to or could not write. (One might argue that Alexander Gottlieb Baumgarten composed that treatise in the eighteenth century.) Rather, this is a broad and revisionary account of

Leibnizian *metaphysics*—one that takes a new approach to this topic by accentuating its aesthetic and stylistic dimensions, but also ranges widely beyond them. It is in relation to the metaphysics that the aesthetic thinking achieves its full resonance, and so to separate them would be a mistake. Moreover, that metaphysics is incredibly generative, engrossing, and worthy of attention on its own merits.

If Leibniz insists on the role of thought in aesthetic experience, he also insists on the role of aesthetic experience in thought. And this should be of interest even to those whose academic specialties do not focus specifically on aesthetic issues. In contrast to the logical Leibniz set in place by Russell and Couturat, the Leibniz presented in this book also allows considerable scope for "confused" thinking. What Leibniz means by that term will require further explication; but his attachment to it involves not policing the line between concept on the one hand and image and metaphor on the other; and it means that while he extols clear and distinct thoughts, he also values mental zones that trail off into less well-defined, cloudlike aggregates of microperceptions. More generally, Leibniz classes even logical thought as a *form* of perception, which allows for easier interchange with other kinds of experience. While Leibniz's intellectual rigor is of course to be respected, I shall argue that his immense philosophical originality results in part from "confused" processes in which disparate intellectual realms are allowed to seep into one another. Even the philosophical imperative to render thoughts ever more clear and distinct runs into both a limit and a counter-imperative in the form of confused thoughts and perceptions, because these are both ineradicable from philosophical practice and crucial to its success. Attending properly to the role of the confused in Leibnizian thinking entails shifting attention from an exclusive focus on concepts to include his philosophical *style* and the way this informs his writing practices. Style mediates between the conceptual and the aesthetic, and thus serves as a conduit for Leibniz's cognitive aesthetics (and aestheticized cognition). What Leibniz habitually does on the page is as important as what he habitually says, and indeed the two are intimately related.

In part, this is a book about the virtues of confused thinking, as Leibniz understood it. For Leibniz, confused thought is not the opposite of clear but a variety of it, and one that has fertilizing effects on cognition. As I shall go on to argue, the fundamental movement of Leibnizian philosophizing involves mapping different forms of knowledge and discourse onto one another, thereby producing what cognitive linguists call blended conceptual spaces, from which creative solutions to problems can arise. Sometimes this mapping is deliberate and explicit; at other times it is implicit, even spontaneous; and it can also take place in ways that occupy the margins of consciousness rather than its clear and distinct zones. But all contribute to the work of thought. Leibnizian confusion entails cognitive blending in which emergent conceptual spaces arise from the meeting of component discourses, fomenting novel and unpredictable ideas.

Leibniz was called the "last universal genius," and he did substantial work in what today would seem an inconceivable range of fields, including (but not limited to) mathematics, physics, philosophy, theology, geology, biology, logic, history, and law. And his work in each of these fields invigorated the others, often by bleeding over into them in subtle but informing ways. (This image of fluidity is not incidental. Leibniz compared knowledge to an ocean, into which various disciplinary rivers flow and are intermingled.) As I have already claimed, for example, one point in favor of a Leibnizian aesthetic is that he embraces what a mathematician or a physicist would consider beautiful as well as what a humanist would, and tries to bring these into meaningful relation. Here as elsewhere, his thought is enriched by occupying multiple disciplinary positions at once or by toggling among them. As I shall argue, Leibniz invented a distinctive and productive *style* of interdisciplinarity that continues to inform the work of more contemporary thinkers. Leibniz occupies a crucial place in the early histories of both disciplinarity and interdisciplinarity.

On the one hand, Leibniz is an important precursor of what we might call normative, canonical, or institutional interdisciplinarity. This is most readily visible in his having served as founding president of the Berlin Society of Sciences in 1700. A counterpart to royal societies in England and France, Leibniz's sought to foster the work of natural scientists and mathematicians along with that of historians, philosophers, and other humanists. And this institutional dimension of Leibniz's thinking lives on, if only as a namesake, in the Wissenschaftsgemeinschaft Gottfried Wilhelm Leibniz, an important collection of interdisciplinary research centers located in present-day Germany. In this book, however, I am less interested in Leibniz's contributions to normative interdisciplinarity than I am in his embodiment of what the philosopher Steve Fuller calls its "deviant" kin.[9]

Fuller describes deviant interdisciplinarity as a "persistent and persistently abnormal" strain within the Western intellectual tradition.[10] Normal interdisciplinarity is, for Fuller, personified by the interdisciplinary research team in which representatives of individual disciplines each contribute well-defined and delimited areas of expertise. By contrast, "deviant interdisciplinarity assumes that the differences in disciplinary expertise themselves pose an obstacle to the completion of the project."[11] "The deviant tends to treat the very presence of different disciplines as *prima facie* pathological" and instead "aims to recover a lost sense of intellectual unity, typically by advancing a heterodox sense of intellectual history that questions the soundness of our normal understanding of how the disciplines come to be as they are."[12] In effect, the deviant rebels against the fact that in the division of interdisciplinary labor, there is no overarching subject of knowledge but merely a distributive grouping of delimited forms of expertise. In response, the deviant attempts to "know everything" herself—to be a "universal genius." Deviants are generally regarded as "eclectic" or "arbitrary" by their normative peers, and in consequence, deviant interdisciplinarities often "struggled for legitimacy within the university but commanded a considerable following outside the academy."[13] Fuller constructs his own anti-canon of deviant interdisciplinarians from Duns Scotus and William of Ockham to Giordano Bruno, Francis Bacon, and René Descartes, Johann Wolfgang von Goethe, Jean-Baptiste Lamarck, Gustav Fechner, William James, and others; as well as whole fields of deviant interdisciplinarity from dialectical materialism and psychoanalysis to neo-Thomism, general semantics, and general systems theory. Leibniz does not play more than an incidental role in Fuller's exposition, but Leibniz is nevertheless a paradigmatic case of deviant interdisciplinarity, and this book will explore some of the ways in which this is so.

Fuller thus provides a useful class into which Leibniz can be inserted; but to grasp the distinctive flavor or style of interdisciplinarity he represents will require supplementing Fuller's account. To do so I shall borrow—indeed, kidnap—a different term, "transdisciplinary," which I shall modify to suit my purposes.[14] By interdisciplinary, I mean the "clear and distinct" version of a meeting between two or more disciplinary areas. To do responsible interdisciplinary work means not only borrowing content from different disciplines but also understanding and respecting their distinctive methodologies and norms. Interdisciplinary work is orderly, and it holds its component discourses at a respectful distance even while enabling conversation between them.[15] This book is an example of interdisciplinary work, and I have made such efforts as I can to respect (while also prodding in some respects) the disciplinary norms of philosophers, especially the Anglophone philosophers whose invaluable scholarship on Leibniz underwrites much of what I say.

By "transdisciplinary," I mean something like a penumbra that extends outward from the interdisciplinary. In the transdisciplinary, relations between disciplines can become fluid and "confused"—implicit, intuitive, even subconscious. In some sense I am simply drawing attention to a fact about interdisciplinarity. But transdisciplinary currents can inform work that does not announce itself as or even at first blush appear to be interdisciplinary. If interdisciplinarity makes the communication between disciplines orderly and respectful, transdisciplinarity makes it creative, spontaneous, and unpredictable.[16] In my view, Leibniz's philosophical style becomes a conduit for a radically transdisciplinary way of thinking, and this fact is crucial to his originality as a thinker. It might be helpful when trying to assess Leibniz's transdisciplinary style to remind ourselves that in addition to pursuing the intellectual fields listed above, Leibniz also wrote poetry, although his high estimate of his accomplishments in this area were not always shared by others. But as we shall see, Johann Gottfried von Herder regarded Leibniz as a kind of poet, and Leibniz's philosophical style does indeed harbor "poetic" elements that help carry out his transdisciplinary work. In Friedrich Schlegel's view, Leibniz's transdisciplinary thinking produced explicitly *aesthetic* effects he called "chemical wit." It is my contention that Leibniz is a brilliantly original transdisciplinary thinker, and that his own philosophy allows one to grasp the essential mechanisms of transdisciplinary thought, not least via the aesthetic dimensions Leibniz assigns to all thinking. Leibniz is both the premier theorist and the premier practitioner of transdisciplinarity.

The transdisciplinary often plays its greatest role in what might be called the initial, "workshop" stage of thinking, when ideas are being tried out or experimented with. Conceptual blends of different disciplines can serve a function analogous to that of a catalyst in a chemical reaction, sparking change or providing inspiration but then often not appearing in the final product, which can be reabsorbed into the terms of the "home" discipline. Leibnizian metaphysics remains metaphysics and not some interdisciplinary hybrid despite incorporating any number of other forms of proto-disciplinary knowledge. The final results of transdisciplinary thinking need not necessarily look interdisciplinary, then, despite being so in a covert way. But transdisciplinary processes can also leave visible traces as well. The workshop phase of thinking, that is, can survive into its more advanced, elaborated phases. In Leibniz's case, as we shall see, a taste for tinkering will tend to extend the workshop phase of thought indefinitely. And this is something he shares with the "strong" transdisciplinary thinkers, to be examined later, who follow in his wake.

Interdisciplinarity often envisions some collaborative reorganization or even consolidation of the current disciplinary regime. Writing and thinking between disciplines is a prelude to conjoining or subordinating them. In the case of the humanities, calls for interdisciplinary consolidation often entail a plan to bring them under the control of the natural sciences. E. O. Wilson's notion of "consilience" is a well-known example, as are attempts to place literary criticism, for example, under the wing of neuroscience or evolutionary psychology.[17] But the transdisciplinary thrives precisely on the conceptual distances among the kinds of knowledge it brings together. For transdisciplinarity, the more disciplines (and the more different and separate they are), the better. What Leibniz calls "combinatorial genius" works best when multiple, variegated disciplinary knowledges converge in unexpected ways. Transdisciplinarity allows borrowing across disciplinary areas without attempting to subsume one discipline under another.

I should pause here and acknowledge that my argument relies on "hard" binaries that need to be softened: normal versus deviant interdisciplinarity, and the interdisciplinary versus the transdisciplinary. In fact, the transdisciplinary is best regarded as a subspecies of the interdisciplinary with its own peculiar (deviant) characteristics or even as an omnipresent dimension inherent to the interdisciplinary as such. Likewise, even the most normative interdisciplinarian probably harbors a deviant one somewhere within. I am employing these terms to provide preliminary coordinates for mapping Leibniz's interdisciplinary style. It is a question of the degree and manner in which these categories orient Leibniz's thought.

It might further be objected that terms such as "interdisciplinary" and "transdisciplinary" are anachronistic when applied to Leibniz, and that he is rather predisciplinary. A widely held view maintains that the modern system of academic disciplines would not begin to take form until the Enlightenment and would not become fully institutionalized until the nineteenth century.[18] Conversations among areas of intellectual specialization were in Leibniz's day more readily possible than they would subsequently become, as was the figure of the polymath. Specialization, knowledge production, and the formation of distinctive methodologies had not yet reached a point where it was practically impossible for anyone to understand more than a few knowledge domains reasonably well and to become really expert in more than one. Leibniz was "the *last* universal genius," not because his capacities necessarily exceeded those of any future thinker, but precisely because the progress of knowledge would soon make it impossible for anyone to know more or less everything.

I want to both acknowledge the force of this objection and contest it. Even granting that Leibniz is in some sense predisciplinary, I would argue that in the predisciplinary we can find an anticipatory image of the postdisciplinary, and so Leibniz's present-day relevance as intellectual model is not necessarily compromised by historical distance. Moreover, the standard timeline for the birth and development of disciplinarity is not without its (deviant?) dissidents. Some would extend it back to the early modern or even the classical period.[19] If Leibniz's world did not include disciplines in quite the modern sense, it certainly contained proto-disciplines. Intellectual fields were both multiplying in his day and in some cases—mathematics, for instance—undergoing internal differentiation into subfields, though these were not yet worked exclusively by specialists. The "flavor" of Leibnizian thinking is a product partly of the cognitive processes already mentioned but also of the state and institutions of knowledge production that were emerging in his era. Later modules of this book will go on to show that a recognizably Leibnizian style of thought is at work even among twentieth-century and twenty-first-century figures who write when the modern disciplinary system is fully in place. That Leibniz exhibits a transdisciplinary style of thinking even before the disciplines are fully formed may seem paradoxical, but it is not self-contradictory. The domains and institutions of knowledge production in his day are not quite the modern ones. But they are modern enough, and he has mastered enough of them to produce the distinctive effects described in this book, given the fact that my approach is cognitive rather than historical and institutional. If one prefers, out of historical fastidiousness, to describe Leibniz's cognitive style as transdiscursive rather than transdisciplinary, I won't object. But I think that by the end of this book, my use of the term "transdisciplinary" will be seen as justified.

The sources of my own interest in Leibniz are multiple and complex. But I am drawn to his transdisciplinary dimensions in no small part because of the current state of my own discipline, literary criticism, which is currently undergoing a crisis of hyperprofessionalization—a crisis that it shares with at least some other fields in the humanities. The historian of science Steven Shapin defines hyperprofessionalism as a "pathological form" of disciplinary professionalism "whose symptoms include self-referentiality, self-absorption, and a narrowing of intellectual focus."[20] Hyperprofessionalism is a form of disciplinary "deviance" running in the opposite direction from Fuller's. While Shapin focuses primarily on his own field, the history of science, he opines that hyperprofessionalism afflicts other disciplines, including "much of philosophy and much of sociology,"[21] and that it contributes to a shrinking of readership in such fields. Interdisciplinary work would seem, on the face of it, to contest hyperprofessional brands of intellectual narrowness. But as Jerry A. Jacobs observes, "[T]he tacit assumption that interdisciplinary work is broad and synthetic is often not the case."[22] A Leibnizian brand of deviant transdisciplinarity is, however, spectacularly broad and synthetic.

In an age of disciplinary hyperprofessionalism, Leibniz's brand of transdisciplinary thinking reminds us that other ways of intellectual being are possible—that thought can still be vastly ambitious while also being experimental, playful, adventurous. Leibniz performs this service not by being "our contemporary," in Spinoza's fashion, but precisely by being untimely in the Nietzschean sense—out of tune with our times, and hence both a rebuke to them and a reminder of lost possibilities. Some of the central qualities I will go on to attribute to Leibniz's philosophical style—"tinkering," for instance, and "intellectual sprawl"—are very much at odds with the demands of productivity, academic polish, and intellectual narrowness that prevail at present. Later in my book, I will look at more recent figures who carry on a Leibnizian style of thinking, and in every case they fit awkwardly in their disciplinary niches. But in so doing they also show the durability and continuing fecundity of a Leibnizian style of thinking. Even though the disciplines themselves have evolved considerably since Leibniz's day, thus altering and perhaps diminishing the possibilities for creative interchange among them, these thinkers show that a Leibnizian style of deviant transdisciplinarity is still possible.

I began by asking why we should read Leibniz today, and thus far I have offered two answers. He enables us to think about the relation between aesthetic experience and intellection; and he models for us a particularly generative style of interdisciplinary thinking I am calling (with a nod to Steve Fuller) deviant transdisciplinarity. But in pursuing the second of these topics I seem to have drifted away from the first, and I now want to show that this drift is merely apparent. Let's return to Fuller's portrait of the deviant interdisciplinarian and examine it more closely. As we have seen, Fuller argues that in the context of an interdisciplinary project, "deviant interdisciplinarity assumes that the differences in disciplinary expertise themselves pose an obstacle to the completion of the project."[23] In this formulation, the deviant disciplinarian shares the same practical goals as the normal one; she dissents only as to the means, insisting that a more unified grasp of the intellectual field is better suited to problem-solving than a gathering of narrow specialists. But in this case, "deviant" seems a rather aggrandizing term for what is in fact a simple disagreement. Fuller's deviant interdisciplinarian is in some sense insufficiently deviant. But at the same time, Fuller sketches in an alternative, and less clearly defined, portrait of the deviant as someone who values a unifying view of the intellectual field for its own sake; and it is here, I would argue, that a genuine sort of deviance begins to emerge. The truly deviant interdisciplinarian acknowledges that specialized, disciplinary knowledge is often superior for purposes of problem-solving, perhaps especially when organized into "normal" interdisciplinary groupings. But *despite* this she insists on a unifying grasp of the totality of thought, finding it intrinsically more satisfying. The genuinely deviant interdisciplinarian doesn't want to organize a colloquy among disciplines but rather to de-discipline knowledge; and she pursues her vision from an essentially aesthetic motive—for the sake of the intellectual pleasure it confers, irrespective of its practical applications.

The portrait of Leibniz that will emerge in this book is deviant in this second, stronger sense. And this may be surprising to Leibniz specialists because, as is well known, Leibniz often insisted that philosophical thought should have a practical orientation. The motto of the Berlin Society for which he served as founding president was *theoria cum praxi*—theory with practice. But as I shall show, Leibniz's involvement in practical projects rarely if ever yielded useful results and more often than not devolved into a kind of aimless tinkering pursued for its own pleasurable sake. Moreover, Leibniz's view of philosophy as something devoted to the public good was balanced by an apparently antithetical notion of philosophy as aesthetic object, both devoted to the production of "beautiful" truths and also beautiful in itself.

Leibnizian aesthetics is grounded on the notion of harmony as unity-in-variety. The baroque harmony of his day included a good deal of dissonance as well; more broadly, baroque aesthetics pushed unity-in-variety toward a kind of breaking point where the centripetal pull of unity is set unstably against an equally powerful centrifugal pull of variety. Leibnizian metaphysics attempts an intellectual counterpart to this aesthetic, forcing the viewpoints of the numerous proto-disciplines in which Leibniz was expert into a unified intellectual vision. In other words, the transdisciplinary deviance I have been ascribing to Leibniz may be redescribed as a kind of baroque artwork, executed in the medium of the concept. Thus does philosophy become beautiful, and Leibniz insists that the beauty of philosophical truths must be valued independent of any practical goods they can yield us.

But this play of the beautiful and the practical must not harden into that stark opposition that is part of the Kantian legacy. For Leibniz, beauty can derive from the perfection of a being—in effect from its heightened functionality, as when we find the sleek lines of a panther beautiful. Conversely, the useful can supervene on the aesthetic. Theoretical physics is on the verge of yielding powerful quantum computers, but that practical benefit results in large part from physics pursuing its own interests and applying its own aesthetic criteria to them (while also ensuring experimentally that its theories are *correct*; but correctness is not the same as practicality). In effect, the achievement of the practical is wagered on the abandonment of the practical in pursuit of other criteria, including aesthetic ones. Metaphysics is a similarly *impractical* discourse devoted to providing an intellectually satisfying overview of the world without any specific useful applications in mind. And indeed, it is difficult to guess what *praxis* can be immediately derived from Leibniz's metaphysical *theoria*. But as the example of physics shows, sometimes the practical can be achieved only by turning away from practice, though there are never any guarantees that this will be so. The philosopher is not an engineer, but Leibniz took on both roles and did not see them as incompatible.

What Leibniz can help us get at is a fundamental duality to thought, and to philosophical thought in particular. On the one hand, thought is good for problem-solving, and in this sense is end-directed. But philosophers (and intellectuals in general) also feel the appeal of thinking as a pleasurable end in itself. Here thought is endless, in the double sense of lacking immediate ends or goals and of thereby becoming interminable.[24] Leibniz feels the tug of both of these, and of the ways in which one can insensibly transform into the other. Thought has both practical and aesthetic yields, which are opposed in some regards and mutually supportive in others. This is what I mean when I state that Leibniz's thinking about thought and aesthetic experience should not be of interest solely to those concerned with artworks. Leibniz's cognitive aesthetic helps us to think about why and how we think.

And here we should grasp that my initial question has been transformed somewhat. I began by asking what questions Leibniz can answer for us. What, in other words, might be the practical benefit of reading him? How can Leibniz contribute to our preexisting intellectual projects? I have provided some suggestions, but now we must also say that he may (or may not—there are no guarantees) contribute to these in ways that cannot be anticipated and which require us to plunge into the intrinsic interest and beauty of Leibniz's philosophical vision. Fortunately, these provide their own, ample rewards.

LEIBNIZING

CHAPTER 1

Leibniz in Motion

---

une Monade . . . dont moi j'en suis une . . .[1]

Positing Leibniz as an aesthetic philosopher may well strike some Leibniz scholars as a curious exaggeration if not an outright anachronism. The term "aesthetics" did not even exist in Leibniz's day, though it was coined by the Leibnizian acolyte Alexander Gottlieb Baumgarten, who, along with Christian Wolff, set early German Enlightenment aesthetics on a firmly Leibnizian basis.[2] Leibniz did have theories of beauty, but one might then argue that "aesthetic philosopher" is just one of many intellectual hats that he wore, and a relatively petite one compared to those of metaphysician, mathematician, etc. Part of my task, then, will be to argue for the centrality of aesthetic matters to Leibnizian thinking.

Certainly, Leibniz made paintings, music, novels, etc., into frequent points of reference when discussing metaphysical matters. Moreover, he attempted to formulate principles that would unify the aesthetic effects produced by these different artistic forms. Hence, for instance, he held that dissonance in music is like chiaroscuro in painting, which is also like the distressing plot developments in novels—all forms of aesthetic tension or stress that lead to ultimate resolution. It is in this synthesizing movement, and in his widespread concern with questions of beauty, that Leibniz formulates an early aesthetics rather than, say, a late-Renaissance poetics.[3] Leibniz was hardly alone among seventeenth-century thinkers in undertaking such a project, but he made what he regarded as a significant contribution by explaining the *je ne sais quoi* of the artwork by way of confused perceptions.

Aesthetic matters play a broad role in Leibnizian thinking. Ours is, in Leibniz's notorious phrase, "the best of all possible worlds," in large part because it is a beautiful one. Its beauty is sensuous but also architectural, moral, and intellectual. Hence Leibniz will not infrequently compare the world to a painting or other work of art. In line with this, some key terms of Leibnizian metaphysics, such as "perspective" and "expression," have distinct (if oddly underexamined) connections to the artwork. Moreover, if monads are essentially a sequence of perceptions strung together in sequence by appetition (more on this later), and if—a possibility Leibniz entertains more consistently in his later years—there may possibly be nothing *but* monads and their perceptions, with no nonmental entities corresponding to them, then in some sense the world consists of nothing but aesthesis, taken in its broader sense as perception or sensation. Monads also think and reason, of course, but it is telling that Leibniz's description of a monad as a series of perceptions implicitly classes even higher-level, abstract thought as perceptual.[4] In all these regards, aesthetic experience may be more central to Leibniz's philosophy than is usually acknowledged.

While Leibniz certainly evinces an interest in art, his aesthetic thinking arises as well from mathematical models. What can this tell us? And what can humanists learn from the notion of intellectual, as opposed to merely sensuous, beauty? Artists themselves (if not necessarily the people studying them) are often inspired by mathematical thinking.[5] This was certainly so during the baroque period when Leibniz lived and worked.[6] Leibniz himself famously observed that "Music is a secret exercise of arithmetic where the mind is unaware that it is counting."[7] The apparent opposition of the mathematical and the aesthetic is more a function of current disciplinary boundaries than it is of the nature of mathematics and art themselves.

In a letter to Duke Johann Friedrich, Leibniz described his life's work as aiming at "the glory of God and the advancement of the public good by means of useful works and beautiful discoveries."[8] I shall have more to say about the dichotomy of the useful and the beautiful a bit further on. Here I want to draw attention to Leibniz's use of an aesthetic qualifier to characterize his own intellectual accomplishments. Why not rather describe his theories and ideas as original, or profound, or even correct? Why beautiful? Because if the world is beautiful, the ideas that analyze its structures will be likewise beautiful. For Leibniz, as for today's physicists, the fact that his ideas are beautiful is a sign of their truth. Moreover, I find Leibniz's assessment of his own thinking and writing (if not necessarily the veridical conclusions he draws from them) to be correct. His philosophical vision *is* beautiful, often bewitchingly so. The late, monadic version of it in particular has a kind of chilly gorgeousness that I hope to convey. In both his theory and his philosophical practice, Leibniz anticipates Nietzsche's claim in *The Birth of Tragedy* that "the existence of the world is *justified* only as an aesthetic phenomenon."[9] Leibniz influenced Nietzsche's perspectival vision, and while he is not quite the master stylist that Nietzsche would later become, he does, like Nietzsche, understand that the aesthetic as well as the logical or argumentative plays a role in philosophical discourse. Another, perhaps excessively provocative, way to put this is to claim that Leibniz is not only a philosopher but an early science-fiction writer. Certainly, his work has the kind of dense intellectual beauty that characterizes the writings of a Stanisław Lem or a Philip K. Dick or a Cixin Liu. Conversely, Leibniz took occasional philosophical inspiration from the science fiction of his day.[10]

Gaining full access to Leibniz the aesthetic philosopher, as well as the transdisciplinary Leibniz described in my preface, will require approaching him from an unaccustomed angle—one that attends to his writing practices as well as his philosophical doctrine. This will be a pleasurable undertaking, however, because Leibniz is as exceptional a writer as he is a philosopher. Moreover, his literary brilliance is not a mere flourish added onto his philosophical accomplishments but is in many ways constitutive of them. The literary Leibniz therefore is—or at least, should be—of as much interest to philosophers as it is to literary critics. Leibniz produced not only a novel philosophical "system" (I'll explain the scare quotes later) but a novel style or manner of doing philosophy, and it can be argued that it was the style rather than the system that ultimately survived him, though in sometimes unexpected guises.

When I speak of Leibniz as writer, I mean more than the fact that his works have come down to us as written texts. Even here, though, it is worth noting a lifelong commitment to writing so prolific as to border on the compulsive. Leibniz left behind some two hundred thousand pages in a variety of fields and a corresponding variety of forms—treatises, letters, philosophical dialogues, project descriptions, histories, sketches, and so forth—the vast bulk of it unpublished during his lifetime. Perhaps every philosopher is perpetually thinking, but not all of them feel compelled to commit every thought to paper. Leibniz apparently did.

When considering Leibniz's writing, it is especially important to keep in mind that the word "writing" is at once a verbal noun and a participial verb.

I am interested in the writings or texts that Leibniz produced but also in the ongoing process or activity of writing that produced them, and to which Leibniz demonstrated an unwavering commitment. Writing as final product is seemingly static—a set of unchanging words recorded and arranged on a page. But writing as process is dynamic, unfolding in time. Even the apparent stasis of the written product is somewhat deceptive, since when taken up by the reader its words are once again set in motion through the process of reading. In this respect, the stasis of writing is at best temporary—less like the shell or corpse of the writing process than the temporary idling in neutral gear of a still-running machine. My book's title, *Leibnizing: A Philosopher in Motion*, refers in part to my belief that Leibniz is more productively grasped through what Heidegger calls "the restless movement of Leibnizian thought"[11] than through the relative stasis of the philosophical system.[12]

I can perhaps clarify by taking up Spinoza's distinction (which he borrowed in turn from the Scholastic philosophers) between *natura naturans* and *natura naturata*. The latter term, "nature natured," refers to nature grasped as a sum of created entities or things: earth, stones, birds, plants, people, stars, and so forth. The former term, "nature naturing," grasps nature now not as being but as becoming—not as product or thing but as a dynamic, creative process that brings those natural things into existence. *Natura naturans* is not something that happens just once, leaving us henceforth merely with *natura naturata* as its residue. It is rather the same nature grasped through a different perspective. Neither dimension can subsist without the other.

By analogy, I wish to distinguish between *Leibnitius Leibnitians* and *Leibnitius Leibnitiatus*—"Leibniz Leibnizing" and "Leibniz Leibnized." The latter, by analogy to *natura naturata*, is the set of propositions, theories, claims, beliefs, discoveries, scholarship, etc., that we associate with Leibniz. In their totality, these elements seem to organize themselves into a system, just as the objects that constitute nature can organize themselves into a landscape. *Leibnitius Leibnitiatus* is the thing that has received the most attention from academic philosophers. I by no means intend to ignore it, but I do intend to place it back into relation with *Leibnitius Leibnitians*—the dynamic process of thinking and writing that creates these philosophical elements and which, I would argue, imbues them with an inextinguishable vitality or movement that tends to prevent them from congealing into a system, just as the movement of living (and even unliving) things on Earth can disrupt the putative stasis of landscape.

My claim that Leibniz is a great writer may come as a surprise to many Leibniz scholars, among whom it is apparently a widespread but usually unstated assumption that Leibniz is a great philosopher but *not* a particularly elegant or accomplished stylist. To be sure, Leibniz's prose does not display any great verbal panache. There are very few striking aphorisms, or memorable phrases, or artful balancing of parallel and antithesis in the construction of clauses, or graceful diction. In other words, few signs of what would have been regarded in his age as a conventionally "literary" style. At the same time, philosophers as distinguished as Johann Gottfried von Herder and Friedrich Schlegel expressed admiration for Leibniz's style of writing, and Herder even regarded him as a "poet" (see module 04). The French philosopher and encyclopedist Denis Diderot praised Leibniz's "most sublime eloquence," which he ranked second among philosophers only to Plato's.[13] The twentieth-century poet Wallace Stevens was a bit less hyperbolic and perhaps closer to the mark when he described Leibniz as a "poet without flash."[14] And as we shall see, Leibniz's handling of simile and metaphor is not only complex—indeed, profound—but also central to his philosophical project. In this book I am employing the word "style" in an expanded sense that includes prose style but also attempts to relate this to Leibniz's style of thinking or philosophizing and even, sometimes, to his style of being in the world (if this does not seem too grandiose a term). I do hold that some of Leibniz's most fundamental habits as a philosopher also manifest themselves at the level of the sentence, as I'll try to demonstrate later.

Because my topic is *Leibniz's* philosophical style, I am construing style as something essentially individual. But style has collective and institutional dimensions as well. The historian of science Ludwik Fleck develops these latter in his concept of the "thought style" (*Denkstil*),[15] which he assigns to "thought collectives," including academic disciplines.[16] For Fleck, every discipline has its distinctive thought style that consists in part of formal elements such as methodology, epistemology, standards of evidence and argument, etc., but also of informal and even subliminal habits of thinking, expression, and attention. And it welds all of these into a totality. A given performance will be judged intellectually satisfying by disciplinary peers only if it conforms to the reigning thought style of the discipline. Fleck is primarily interested in epistemological matters, not aesthetic ones, but the term "thought style" appears to imply an aesthetic charge, even if sometimes an unacknowledged one. In disciplines such as physics or mathematics, the aesthetic dimensions of thought style can become explicit.[17] As I argued in my preface, Leibnizian metaphysics exhibits a baroque aesthetics of unity-in-variety.

The aesthetic dimensions inherent to Fleck's concept remain largely—though not entirely—undeveloped by him;[18] they inhere largely in the semantics of the term itself. And Fleck's work has, in any case, not played a significant role in the debates over disciplinarity and interdisciplinarity that have simmered for several decades now.[19] I find both of these facts unfortunate and believe that attending to the aesthetic components of disciplinary and interdisciplinary thought styles can be productive. In any case, I feel justified in drawing on Fleck's work to argue for a Leibnizian *style* of deviant transdisciplinarity. Some of the sources for this style are of course inherited and reworked by Leibniz. Each of the different proto-disciplines he attempts to unite within his metaphysics has its own thought style, as for that matter does metaphysics itself. And the various genres in which Leibniz writes—epistles, dialogues, treatises, etc., contribute their own elements of thought style, as does Leibniz's status as courtier-philosopher, with its codes of deference, flattery, and so forth. But at the same time, Leibniz gives a distinctive and transformative turn to these inherited styles.

Leibniz made pronouncements about what a good philosophical style should look like, and the few extant studies that address his prose style tend to take these as a starting point.[20] But I believe that Leibniz's stylistic practice cannot be fully accounted for by his stated principles, which are in any case fairly anodyne: the philosopher's writing should be clear, it should be publicly accessible, it should use words in their generally accepted sense, etc. This will not get us terribly far in understanding Leibniz's philosophical project. Hence I will take as my guide what Leibniz habitually does on the page as opposed to his declarations about what should take place there. The former usually includes the latter but also goes well beyond it. In trying to grasp Leibniz's philosophical style, I am driven to employ terms that do not at first blush appear particularly stylistic—terms such as "intellectual sprawl," "tinkering," "cognitive mapping," and "chemical wit" (the last of these borrowed from Schlegel). But together—and they do indeed form a nexus—they can help us get at something fundamental to Leibniz's manner of philosophizing.

A related strand of my argument has to do with Leibniz's legacy or philosophical afterlife. I am particularly interested in thinkers who inherit his transdisciplinary style, thus demonstrating the latter's durability and ongoing productivity. I am devoted less to cataloguing the direct influence of Leibnizian ideas, therefore, than to tracing the sometimes uncanny ways in which Leibnizian intuitions and even philosophical impasses get played out in contemporary philosophy and science. For instance, the mind-body problem as formulated by Leibniz (I shall argue that he, rather than Descartes, is the first to present this problem in a truly intractable form) reemerges in the work of contemporary philosophers of mind such as David Chalmers and Galen Strawson. Likewise, a good deal of Leibnizian physics and metaphysics finds answering echoes in contemporary quantum theory. This is often not a question of direct or even indirect influence but of reemergences that are all the more striking for being contingent.

I am interested above all by writers who reproduce not Leibniz's ideas but rather his intellectual style or manner. What I mean by this will necessarily remain abstract until we see what exactly this style consists of. But it will not be surprising to learn that the figures I have in mind tend to breach the barriers between mathematics and science on the one side and philosophy and art on the other. And they tend to be highly original thinkers but also eccentric in that their work does not fit cleanly into established traditions, and for that reason their influence is sometimes accordingly muted compared to what it might otherwise have been: I refer to the philosopher Alfred North Whitehead, the cognitive scientist Douglas Hofstadter, the Chilean neuroanatomists Humberto Maturana and Francisco Varela, and the physicist David Bohm. My book's title indicates not only the dynamic movement of Leibniz's writing, then, but also the way that this movement of writing then propagates itself through intellectual history, often in unpredictable and indirect ways.

Having briefly outlined the book's main argumentative strands, I now want to say more about its intended audiences, because at least two of them are somewhat at odds. Obviously, this book is aimed in part at specialists in Leibniz and early modern philosophy more generally. These are the people doing the bulk of the work on Leibniz, and they are generally housed in philosophy departments, not departments of literature. Having read at least desultorily in the recent bibliography, I think I can say that the Leibniz industry appears to be flourishing, and that Leibniz himself, could he be somehow aware of it, would count himself happy in both the quantity and the quality of commentary he has attracted. Which raises the question of why philosophers should bother with the work of an interloping literary critic. It is my hope that an outsider's perspective may prove stimulating. In particular, one of the things I have noticed as an outsider is that the recent work I have read on Leibniz's philosophy is various in many respects but largely unanimous in at least one. And this is its assumption that the underlying aim of studying Leibniz is to contribute to a more capacious and detailed grasp of his philosophical system.

Now, there are ample reasons to regard Leibniz as a system-builder.[21] He repeatedly refers to his philosophy as "my system."[22] In 1695 he published his "New System of the Nature of Substances and Their Communication"; other titles, without employing the word "system," nonetheless imply systematic organization, such as "Principles of Nature and Grace" (1714). Leibniz viewed the universe as a system, and described it as such, which implies that any metaphysical account of it must likewise be systematic. And then there is his interest in logic, already mentioned, which would likewise conduce to logical and conceptual coherence.

And yet, Leibniz never presented his system in a single, comprehensive form; there is no magnum opus corresponding to Spinoza's *Ethics*. Rather, the system is scattered and ceaselessly elaborated across innumerable writings and reams of correspondence. Not only does it evolve over time, but also its principles are reiterated in ways that introduce significant, sometimes unruly variation, and even contradiction. The system never appears as such, in its totality, but is reconstructed by the community of scholars, not without debates and differences arising along the way. If there is, indeed, a Leibnizian system, then it seems odd to me that such fundamental questions as whether Leibniz has an idealist or realist account of bodies does not appear to be generating anything close to a consensus. The mirage of a definitive or even progressive grasp of Leibniz's system beckons but somehow is never fully actualized—which may be a good thing with regard to providing employment for ever new generations of Leibniz specialists but a less good thing in other respects. As I shall argue shortly, this state of affairs reflects the fact that Leibniz displays both systematic and anti-systematic tendencies. He gestures toward system but then frustrates his own systematicity. Or as Michel Serres puts it, the system can be glimpsed but never grasped.[23] And this may be not the result of inattention or incapacity on Leibniz's part but rather a conscious strategy, the nature of which I shall explore a bit later on. In any case, the fact remains that the Leibnizian system is never anything more than virtual and thus incompletely available, while the individual writings are real and quite available. This fact alone might invite a more rigorously textual approach.

Now, in one sense it is hardly news that Leibniz may not in fact be the system-builder he was once thought to be. No less prominent a Leibnizian than Daniel Garber has stated this explicitly, and Catherine Wilson published an article back in 1999 titled "The Illusory Nature of Leibniz's System."[24] So in some sense everyone already knows what I am claiming. And yet, the disciplinary norms of philosophy are such that this knowledge is often disavowed in practice, and so when writing about Leibniz, his systematic coherence tends to be assumed, at least as an ideal.[25] The hypothesis of a Leibnizian system, moreover, determines which kinds of questions about Leibniz are important and are therefore worth working on, and which are not. Questions concerning Leibniz's conception of substance, for example, or the nature and degree of his logical nominalism, or the relations between Leibniz's geometry and his metaphysics, are philosophically respectable issues. But as far as I can tell, activities such as doing close readings of Leibnizian metaphors—the kinds of things a literary critic might do—are generally not, at least among Anglophone Leibniz scholars. Even if they were to be regarded with a kind of bemused interest, they would not be seen as germane to the central undertaking of explicating Leibniz's philosophy. *That* entails not embedding the philosophy in its local, textual particulars but, to the contrary, extracting and abstracting philosophical themes *from* the writings. Thus is the virtuality of the philosophical system purified of the messy textual or rhetorical or stylistic details through which it happens to be expressed. But what if, as I have suggested, there is no philosophical system? There are just the texts, open in front of you, in all their literary murkiness and richness as well as their philosophical splendor—texts that move toward but also, maddeningly, away from systematicity. What if there is only the ceaseless movement of Leibnizian thought and writing? Leibniz's own conception of the monad would seem to support such a view. What is a monad, after all, but an endless series of perceptions, driven by appetition from one to the next? The monad is itself in perpetual motion and change as it processes a world that is likewise in endless flux. There is no final, consummative grasp of the world available to a monad, even if that monad happens to be a philosopher who wants to achieve such a definitive view.

All of this is not to deny that Leibniz's writings do manage to create an impressive, if still incomplete, degree of coherence. If they did not, he would not have something we could call a philosophy at all. Moreover, Leibniz himself nursed dreams of radical systematicity. In a 1715 letter to a Polish diplomat called Biber, he confessed his wish to write work in the style of Spinoza's *Ethics*: "if God will grant me more free time, I will attempt by means of well-formed demonstrations to impart to a good portion of my views the certainty of Euclid's *Elements*."[26] In addition, a lifelong project of Leibniz's was his general characteristic, which would put all concepts into a form from which indisputable truths could be produced by means of an infallible predicative calculus. And yet, his writing never fulfills these ideals, and as often as not blatantly contradicts them. It might be argued that the fundamental fault line within Leibniz's corpus is not a conceptual one, exactly, but rather that between the dream of systematicity and his actual writing practice.

Now, my willingness to jettison at least the goal of reconstructing a coherent system is going to strike some Leibniz scholars as being rather blithe if not positively dangerous. Indeed, it will probably strike them as embodying just the kind of floppy epistemological anarchy one might have expected from a literary critic. For one thing, it appears to violate the so-called principle of charity when approaching Leibniz. In the face of apparent inconsistencies or contradictions in the writings, the principle of charity demands that we make at least some attempt to reconcile or synthesize them—and thus to assume that Leibniz was not merely a sloppy thinker—rather than simply shrugging our shoulders and moving on. The Leibnizian system should therefore exist as an interpretive ideal, even if it can't ever be fully realized. And in its absence, it might be hard to say how progress in the project of understanding Leibniz's work can be judged. Moreover, scholars can rightly point to the ways in which this approach has both enriched and refined our grasp of Leibniz. Commentators disagree, but from their clashes, progress is made. Or so at least the story goes. But as an outsider, it seems to me that Leibniz studies are progressing nicely in many respects but less so with regard to the one ideal of producing a unified, coherent account of his system. What I propose is that there are ways of reading Leibniz that are charitable without adopting the ideal of logical consistency as the sole criterion of charity. Such consistency is indeed a philosophical good for Leibniz, and he often pursues it strenuously. But it is not the only good, and too exclusive a focus on it might blind us to other goods he is seeking. There is simply too much inconsistency, contradiction, and, above all, *variation* in Leibniz's various pronouncements to allow perfect synthesis. The trick is to see the variations not simply as lapses from consistency but as productive in themselves.[27]

At the same time I should also admit that, for all my plumping on behalf of a nonsystematic reading of Leibniz, I will myself display plenty of systematizing moves in my own reading practices. For instance, I don't always explicitly observe the evolution of Leibniz's thought over time, and so I (for example) apply the term "monad" when discussing texts that predate it. In general, I privilege

Leibniz's later formulations over earlier ones. When pursuing a given topic, I cherry-pick passages that best fit the point I wish to make without in every case drawing attention to other passages that differ from or even contradict them. I am hardly alone among Leibniz commentators in doing the last two of these things in particular, but I do them. In part, this reflects the kinds of simplification unavoidable in any book of this sort that intends, among other things, to provide a general introduction to Leibniz's thought in a relatively short span. It reflects the additional fact that I am not, in the end, a trained Leibnizian but only an interested amateur, with all the weaknesses and lapses that this will entail. But it additionally reflects the inescapable gravitational pull exerted by the ideal of the Leibnizian system, even for a reader who wants to escape it in some respects. And I don't want to escape it entirely. What I aim at rather is a kind of "charitable" reading that regards Leibniz's apparent lapses in consistency as something more than mere lapses.

In section 36 of the *Monadology*, Leibniz suddenly and momentarily shifts his view to himself in the act of writing: "There are an infinite number of shapes and of motions, present and past, which play a part in the efficient cause of my present writing; and there are an infinite number of tiny inclinations and dispositions of my soul, which play a part in its final cause."[28] For those unfamiliar with Leibniz, this brief passage will require some unpacking. First of all, he divides himself into bodily and mental components that do not interact and each of which therefore obeys a different order of causation. (Events in the physical and mental realms are independently coordinated by means of what Leibniz calls preestablished harmony.) The act of writing is therefore distributed between the actions of the writing body and the movements of the writing mind. The writer's body is caught in the same web of causes and effects that governs all physical bodies. If it picks up a pen and writes, this is not because the mind tells it to but because of purely physical interactions between it and other bodies. But these physical causes are not exclusively the local, obvious ones because in Leibniz's view, every physical body in the world, no matter how tiny or how distant, impinges upon and thus exerts causative influence on every other body. Hence the writing body's act of writing results from an infinity of causative relations, most of them so minute as to be untraceable.

The writing soul or mind, though unconnected with the body, experiences a set of perceptions that correspond to, but in no way influence or are influenced by, the motions of the body. As a result, we perceive everything in the universe, no matter how tiny or far away, though the vast bulk of these are microperceptions (*petites perceptions*) that fall beneath the threshold of consciousness. So, just as the writing body's motions answer to some obvious, local causes but also to an infinity of untraceable microcauses, the mental process of writing involves an area of clear and distinct perceptions that enable things such as logic and philosophical reasoning to occur, but these are afloat on clouds of confused or obscure microperceptions that exert their own causative force. As a result, we cannot know with any fullness or certainty how or why we write what we are writing. "My present writing" of this apparently systematic treatise called the *Monadology*, Leibniz informs us, is subject to an infinity of microcauses from which the philosophical argument cannot be disentangled. Even when writing about monads, I cannot extricate myself from the condition of being a monad, and that means that my attempted system-building is traversed by subtle currents I cannot know or understand.

More generally, Leibniz believes that thought operates according to spiritual mechanisms that we do not control or even, in many cases, perceive:

> What necessity is there for one always to be aware how that which is done is done? Are salts, metals, plants, animals and a thousand other animate or inanimate bodies aware how that which they do is done, and need they be aware? Must a drop of oil or of fat understand geometry in order to become round on the surface of water? Sewing stitches is another matter: one acts for an end, one must be aware of the means. But we do not form our ideas because we will to do so, they form themselves within us, they form themselves through us, not in consequence of our will, but in accordance with our nature and that of things.[29]

As we shall see, the only sure way of escaping this condition is by exteriorizing thought. One of Leibniz's lifelong undertakings was a "general characteristic" that could manipulate symbols automatically and "blindly" and thereby escape the confusions of everyday thinking.[30] Short of this, the philosopher who employs ordinary language finds himself in an ambiguous situation in which clear and distinct ideas achieve at best a relative autonomy from confused ones. And the enterprise of writing reflects these ambiguities of the situation. On the one hand, writing is something we plan and control. We have an idea of what we want to say, and we plot out how and in what order to say it. But at the same time, as anyone who has actually written expository prose understands, the process of writing seems to have a will of its own. When beginning a paragraph, we don't always know for certain exactly how it will end, and the longer writing goes on, the more it can lead in unanticipated directions. There is an argument to be made, and a plan, but the plan and the argument are not all there is. Obscure currents both animate and frustrate the process of writing. Leibniz's brief turning of the mirror on his writing self betrays his awareness that what he is doing when he writes philosophy cannot be reduced entirely to its official aims.

Leibniz returns to the topic of his writing in a letter to Bartholomew Des Bosses:

> Forgive the fact that I write in fits and starts, and for that reason do not, perhaps, always satisfy, for I cannot go back to what I wrote earlier. Because of that, perhaps certain sorts of contradiction will arise from time to time. But once the matter is examined, the contradiction will be more in the way that I express myself than in the account. I don't know whether, when, or in what I might have said that the modification of a nonextended thing produces an extended thing.[31]

At first glance, this will seem to give comfort to the extractive method. Yes, Leibniz says, my *writings* may contradict each other, but the underlying matter is not contradictory—or at least, not *as* contradictory as the writings. It is the latter that are principally at fault. In any case, I can't go back to the past. In fact, I can't remember if or when or where I said the thing you attribute to me. But (he implies) believe me when I say that what I tell you *now* is not contradictory.

The longer one looks at these reassurances, however, the less reassuring they are. How can Leibniz know that what he says right now is not contradictory, and with respect to what, since this judgment can be made only by comparing it with what he had said in the past and with what he will say in the future? And the past is already succumbing to the confusions of memory such that it can never be fully retrieved. As Leibniz says, he cannot go back to past writings.[32] Like the monad, he moves ever forward (though in "fits and starts"), endlessly generating new thoughts and writings. Better keep up and don't pay too much attention to the fact that I contradict myself. (I am infinite, I contain multitudes.) Writing is, at best, a brief moment of at least somewhat clear and distinct thoughts trailing off into the confused microperceptions that constitute memory of the past and anticipation of the future.

If the obscure currents that traverse writing could be reduced entirely to an inert, ineffectual background, Leibniz would not bother accounting for them. But, anticipating the so-called butterfly effect, he holds that tiny or distant causes can produce results out of all proportion to their scale.[33] Moreover, as we shall see, Leibniz believes that these unconscious microcauses are not only unavoidable but actually beneficial to the philosopher's work. Perhaps a literary reading is better attuned, then, to the confused elements that, in Leibniz's own view, permeate his writing. As I will later argue, for example, Leibniz's use of illustrative metaphor and simile is not meant to "clarify" his philosophical arguments. By introducing concrete images into an otherwise abstract, conceptual discourse, these metaphors actually plunge what was a relatively clear and distinct set of thoughts back into the realm of the confused and the microperceptual, and they are meant to do so. In this as in other regards, Leibniz's writings actively resist the extractive process that attempts to separate a system from its textual basis. The moral of this story is not that philosophers should try to become literary critics. It is simply that a literary critical reading of Leibniz might have serious philosophical import because Leibniz's writerly flourishes are not philosophically superfluous. My guess is that at least some Leibniz specialists would accede to this view without too much resistance, at least on a theoretical level. But this seems to have had little effect on the kinds of work actually being done. Hence the available space (I hope) for an investigation of this kind.

This book is in part a study of Leibniz's philosophical style. But Leibniz is an especially felicitous subject for a focus of this kind. Not only does he display an interesting and distinctive manner of philosophizing, but also his conceptions of writing and the writing self are conducive to the development of a modern understanding of style, including philosophical style. For classical rhetoricians, style was a broad marker of different *levels* of discourse—there were high, middle, and low styles—and a good deal of cultural evolution had to occur before we arrive at a more contemporary understanding of style as the expression of a writer's distinctive selfhood or manner.[34] But Leibniz helps lead us to this modern understanding in a couple of ways. First, as we shall see, the fact that an individual monad is marked by an infinity of subtle determinations grants it a *haecceity*, or "thisness," that distinguishes it from all others. Leibniz's philosophy is highly sensitive to, indeed theorizes, the sometimes elusive marks of the individuated self. In addition, his understanding of writing as a process not entirely controlled by the writer but shaped by ungraspable micro-determinations helps us see style, not as a technical rhetorical device—something artfully and intentionally deployed—but rather as something closer to a *symptom* that emerges of its own will, as it were. Leibniz's conception of writing makes the notion of style meaningful in philosophical as well as literary terms.

------◆------

If my first intended audience consists of academic philosophers, the second, it will naturally be assumed, consists of those of my own kind—literary critics. This is correct in a sense, but to those literary critics, my book will be apprehended as a work of "theory," and this is the trickier category. The vexing fact is that defining theory in any precise way is extremely difficult, despite the fact that the people conversant with it know it when they see it. For our purposes, I will offer the incomplete and inadequate definition of theory as a set of philosophically inflected discourses, prevalent in fields such as literary criticism, art history, sociology, and political science (though not, notably, in Anglophone philosophy itself), designed to address large, general issues rather than local, practical ones. "Theory" is an agglomerative truncation of what used to be more precisely defined subsets such as French theory, literary theory, etc., as well as the Critical Theory of the Frankfurt School.[35]

Now for at least a certain brand of theorist, my argument that philosophical texts should be read like literary texts will be so unexceptionable as to go without saying. Their problem will be not with my method, but with Leibniz himself. While philosophy departments display a continuing and healthy interest in Leibniz, theorists, generally, do not. Really, only two works on Leibniz have been produced by major (in this case, French) theorists: Michel Serres's book *Le système de Leibniz et ses modèles mathématiques* (1968) and Gilles Deleuze's book *Le pli: Leibniz et le baroque* (1988; Eng. trans. 1993). Neither has had any substantial influence, as far as I can tell, on Leibniz's reputation in the realms of either philosophy or theory. Deleuze's book has, to be sure, attracted the attention of people interested in Deleuze, and it has sparked further work on the baroque, but it hasn't to all appearances broadened the appeal of Leibniz himself, who remains a hard sell to theorists.

I probably won't help my case with readers from the theory camp by announcing that I do not in this book much engage with major figures in theory. I will not, for instance, directly take up *Le pli*, though I happily acknowledge my indebtedness to it. Nor will I examine, for instance, the monadological elements in the Epistemo-Critical Prologue to Walter Benjamin's *The Origins of German Tragic Drama*. The things about Leibniz that interest me simply do not lead me back to the usual suspects in the theory canon. They have taken me instead to areas such as cognitive linguistics, philosophy of mind, and computer science—areas that don't have as much purchase as yet within the realm of theory. While I adore the usual suspects as much as anyone, in this case I found it profitable to look elsewhere, and I hope this will count as a possible source of piquancy rather than a demerit.

If theorists aren't much interested in Leibniz, Leibniz specialists in philosophy departments display a corresponding lack of interest in those few theorists who do write on him. Deleuze's book will get an occasional offhand reference in a footnote, and Serres's book usually not even that.[36] This saddens me in that both books are brilliant and generative. But it doesn't surprise me. It is a predictable if probably insoluble product of disciplinary formations and boundaries. The *style* of Deleuze's book rather than its content is probably what many Leibniz specialists in Anglophone philosophy departments find off-putting or, at least, unassimilable to their ongoing work of Leibniz scholarship.

I am dwelling on these issues to prepare readers for what lies ahead. This book doesn't look quite like either the usual sort of Leibniz commentary or the usual kind of theory. I have included elements that I hope will appeal to both camps, however, and to a third (alas, probably mythical) set of intended readers as well: the so-called general reader. For her, this book aims to offer an introduction to Leibniz that, while somewhat unorthodox and hardly methodical, aims at least to spark interest. For all potential readers, I will try to make a case for why Leibniz is still worth reading and thinking about.

Finally, a word on form. This book does not consist of chapters but of shorter units I'll call modules. Some of these are only a few pages long, others more extensive. They occur in a deliberate order, but the immediate connections between one and the next will not always be equally obvious. They can probably be read out of order or even selectively without undue ill effects. Taken together, they do not provide anything like an encompassing or synthetic view of Leibniz; they are rather like strategically placed core samples, often located at key terms of his philosophical vocabulary. My choice of this structure was born not out of any desire to be (or appear) experimental but out of the fact that the traditional form of the chapter did not seem to answer well to my subject matter. In particular, Leibnizian transdisciplinarity cannot be apprehended via one royal and unswerving pathway. It will emerge in its full complexity only from a tangle of approaches apprehended in their convergence. The modules are therefore meant to resonate with one another, in the manner of a network. Moreover, I will admit that this form was inspired in part by a well-known passage from the *Discourse on Metaphysics*: "Suppose, for example, that someone puts a number of completely haphazard points on paper, as people do who practice the ridiculous art of geomancy. I say that it is possible to find a geometrical line whose notion is constant and uniform according to a certain rule, such that the line passes through all the points, and in the same order as they were drawn."[37]

CHAPTER 2

Tinkering

The notion of system is of no use to us, for system is the end product of tinkering and not its point of departure.

—Bruno Latour[1]

As quoted in the introduction, Leibniz describes his intellectual contributions as consisting of "useful works and beautiful discoveries." I want now to focus on the first of these two: useful works. Leibniz always believed that the intellectual should try to contribute to the public good, and that philosophical thought should therefore have a practical orientation. The motto of the Berlin Society of Sciences, for which Leibniz served as first president when it was founded in 1700, was *theoria cum praxi*: "theory with practice." And Leibniz continually engaged in projects that would yield some kind of perceived public benefit, sometimes technological (he worked for decades on a calculating machine, for example, attempted to desalinate water, and tried to devise a new method for removing water from the silver mines in the Harz mountains), sometimes social and religious (he hoped, for instance, that his metaphysics could help reunite the Protestant and Catholic faiths, and he attempted to automate the process of human thought so as to produce irrefutable results and thereby avoid religious controversy).

Leibniz's ambitions, however, often exceeded his capacities or available resources in a way that frustrated the practical aims of his work. The plan to remove water from the mines in the Harz mountains by means of windmills never succeeded and ended up infuriating the mining officials.[2] A plan to foster employment in Hanover by growing silkworms and harvesting silk likewise came to naught. The various "characteristics" that were meant to automate thought did foreshadow far-off developments in computer science and artificial intelligence but could not be achieved with the means available in Leibniz's day. Even his famed calculating machine, which he worked on improving until his death, never achieved full functionality. Undaunted, however, he tended to persist in his impracticable plans.

What I want to suggest is that these repeated failures were not without compensating rewards, because the founding of a practical project that became stuck in a state of permanent incompletion allowed Leibniz to do something he clearly loved: to tinker. Indeed, the pleasures of tinkering did not merely sustain Leibniz as he worked indefatigably toward practical aims. I would argue that they sometimes supplanted those aims, which thus became mere alibis to enable endless tinkering. Perhaps the clearest example of this is the extended history of the Guelf family that Leibniz undertook for his patrons the Dukes of Hanover. This was a massive scholarly project in the course of which Leibniz made substantive discoveries. But he also kept expanding the framework of the project in a way that progressively postponed its completion. For instance, Leibniz decided that the history of the Guelfs could not adequately be narrated without an account of the geologic conditions of the region in which they ruled. And he then decided that *that* could not be accomplished without undertaking the geologic history of Earth itself. The result was a prefatory work known as the *Protogaea*. Researching and writing the Guelf history stretched on for decades; Leibniz managed to make just enough progress to prevent his patrons from shutting the project down entirely while keeping them perpetually on the cusp of exasperation. At his death, it was still not completed.[3]

A key motive for delay in this case was financial; support for the Guelf history allowed Leibniz the freedom to do other kinds of intellectual work on the side. But this financial motive is not necessarily exhaustive, given his more general propensity for tinkering. Conversely, this one clear instance of inflating a supposedly practical project *in order that* it would not be completed, only endlessly tinkered with, should cast some doubt on the many other instances in which Leibniz failed to finish impossibly ambitious undertakings. I am not arguing that Leibniz was indifferent to the success of his practical projects; he often pursued them vigorously, less out of some vague commitment to the public good than from hopes of increased reputation, influence, and (in the case of the silver mines project, for example) income. Regardless, out of what was initially a practical endeavor, a different kind of impulse would repeatedly emerge: the impulse to tinker.

In stating this, I am not claiming that Leibniz possessed any artisanal or mechanical skills. In the case of projects such as the calculating machine or the windmills designed to remove water from the Hartz Mountains, he hired artisans and their workshops to try to turn his design ideas into workable realities. This involved not merely executing Leibniz's instructions but specifying, modifying, and testing them as well. For the calculating machine, he engaged the Parisian master clockmaker Ollivier, with whom he collaborated but with whom he was also sometimes at odds.[4] While Leibniz learned from his collaborative endeavors with artisans, and respected their practical knowledge, he maintained a strict division between intellectual and manual labor. Leibniz tinkered with his pen alone—"thinkering."[5]

The tinkerer is an interesting figure: practical in some respects, he purportedly knows how to build or fix things but tends to do so in an imperfect way. He is practical to a degree but also a kind of dilettante or hobbyist who likes to occupy himself with the act of building or repairing. Hence his projects can linger and turn into mere puttering about. For the tinkerer, utilitarian aims tend to dissolve into a kind of purposiveness without purpose yet without disappearing completely. End-directed activity turns at least partly autotelic—something pursued for its own sake, at which point the practical ends are partially bracketed. And as my invocation of the well-known Kantian formula suggests, tinkering tends to invert the practical into a kind of proto-aesthetic activity.

It should not be difficult to see where this is leading. Leibniz's greatest, lifelong tinkering project, I would claim, is nothing other than his philosophical system itself. The system manages to be somehow always under construction: apparently nearly done, there are always a few loose ends (often rather substantial) that need attending to. And if there aren't enough of these, new ones can always be created. In the correspondence with Des Bosses, Leibniz miracles up an entirely unprecedented concept—the substantial bond—that would require a significant modification of his metaphysical system in order to be accommodated. As laid out in the letters, it is largely incoherent. And then when the correspondence with Des Bosses ends, the concept of the substantial bond simply disappears and is never mentioned again.

In a way, metaphysics is the perfect medium for tinkering because metaphysics has no immediate practical application anyway. It can therefore become a space for making what Leibniz calls "beautiful discoveries." He elaborates on this notion in a letter:

> Beautiful truths deserve to be sought out, even when they bring no profit, and [. . .] it is to dishonor them to measure them by the yardstick of our interest.
>
> It is the nature of beautiful things in general, like diamonds and excellent paintings, that they should be valued because of the pleasure that their beauty gives.[6]

The opposition between beauty and utility expressed in this letter is not so stark as may appear in this one brief excerpt, and even here, Leibniz leaves open the possibility that truths may be both beautiful and profitable. The point he eventually makes is that the utility of truth is supervenient on its beauty; one should pursue the truth for its own beautiful sake, and utility will naturally follow. But this is a kind of high-aesthetic version of the tinkerer's logic that does not quite lose sight of practical aims while also insisting on the pursuit of activity for its own sake.

If we reconceive of Leibniz's philosophical activity as a form of tinkering, we can also reconceive its various contradictions, inconsistencies, and equivocations that so bedevil commentators. From the perspective of the system, these are, without question, bugs. But from the perspective of the tinkerer, they are features in that they allow the process of philosophizing to continue indefinitely. Leibniz's philosophy is never fully functional. There is always something more to be done, additional contrivances to introduce or, at least, to test out and then possibly reject. Thus does Leibnitius Leibnitians refuse to subside entirely into Leibnitius Leibnitiatus.

My use of the figure of the tinkerer will inevitably recall Claude Lévi-Strauss's invocation of the *bricoleur* to describe the workings of mythical thought. Contrasting the *bricoleur* with the engineer, Lévi-Strauss depicts the former as someone who makes use of whatever materials are at hand, as opposed to the engineer, the parts of whose constructions are themselves preformed with their purposes in mind. The engineer is a strategic designer while the *bricoleur* improvises with what happens to be lying around.[7] At the risk (and also the intent) of appearing somewhat facetious, I would like to suggest that Leibniz is a philosophical *bricoleur* in Lévi-Strauss's sense while Spinoza is closer to a philosophical engineer. Here I am referring to the patchwork quality of Leibniz's philosophy, which makes use of materials philosophically "at hand." As Leibniz puts it, his thought "appears to unite Plato with Democritus, Aristotle with Descartes, the Scholastics with the moderns, theology and morality with reason."[8] The term "monad" is picked up from Neoplatonic and kabbalistic circles.[9] Then there is Leibniz's perspectivalism (of which, more later), which construes the same phenomenon from multiple points of view, not all of which are immediately translatable into the others. Leibniz would also adapt his style to different audiences so as to appeal to their philosophical prejudices, sometimes employing the language of Cartesianism and sometimes that of Scholasticism.[10] And this is to say nothing of the broad variety of intellectual fields that Leibniz contributes to and sometimes combines. By contrast, Spinoza is pretty much exclusively a philosopher.[11] Certainly, he makes no substantial contribution to any other field. For the *Ethics*, Spinoza borrows a few foundational philosophical terms such as substance, attribute, and mode but then retools them beyond recognition for specific functions within his system. And from these preformed elements he builds a meticulously constructed edifice of argument, its parts perfectly fitted and arranged. (Perhaps it is telling that in his work as lens grinder he likewise produced highly polished, preformed elements for use in larger constructions.) Definitions, axioms, propositions, demonstrations, corollaries, scholia: everything in its proper and immutable order. Spinoza's system gives an impression (at least, relatively) of highly patterned conceptual homogeneity, whereas Leibniz's "system" is unembarrassedly heterogeneous and accommodates more than a little intellectual sprawl. Again, I am not employing this contrast to privilege either thinker but simply to bring to the fore some distinctive aspects of the Leibnizian style of thought.

The idea of "intellectual sprawl," by the way, often finds a kind of literal embodiment on Leibniz's manuscript pages, which display a distinctive degree of chaos: along with the usual crossings out and rewritings and emendations, Leibnizian writing sometimes drifts away from the imaginary grid that orders a page and takes off at oblique angles, mixes in drawings or figures, establishes autonomous zones (see figure 2.1). Perhaps the graphic counterpart to sprawl is scrawl. (I wish I could produce a Spinozan page written in a contrastingly neat and orderly hand, but unfortunately, no Spinozan autographs appear to have survived.)

2.1 G. W. Leibniz, mathematical manuscripts LH 35.8.21.1 r. With permission of the Gottfried Wilhelm Leibniz Bibliothek—Niedersäschsische Landesbibliothek, Hannover.

While the heterogeneity of Leibniz's thinking might be disconcerting to some, it accords with his own intellectual aesthetic. Part of what makes the world beautiful for Leibniz is its variety. The world accommodates as many things as it can, and as many *kinds* of things as it can, short of violating its harmony and optimality. This "more the merrier" quality is accordingly reflected in the texture of his discourse. The variousness of its irregular surface should therefore be appreciated as a virtue rather than a fault.

When Leibniz took a demonstration model of his calculator to show the Royal Society in London, Robert Hooke opened the back, briefly inspected the inner workings, and within a very short period of time produced a calculator superior to the one Leibniz had been working on for years. This was partly a matter of Hooke's having better access to networks of local artisans and partly to his greater knack as a practical inventor. His criticisms of Leibniz's model are telling: "It seemed to me soe complicated with wheeles pinnions Cantrights springs screws stops and Truckles that I could not perceive it ever to be of any great use especially common use.... It could onely be fitt for great persons to purchase and for great force to remove and manage and for great witts to understand and comprehend."[12] Leibniz's designs for a calculator perpetually frustrated the efforts of even master artisans to instantiate them in a working model. And Hooke's critique points to a baroque love of complexity in Leibniz's design that tended to impede its practical aims. I quote him, though, because his criticisms of the calculator could serve almost word for word if applied to Leibnizian metaphysics, stuffed as it is with what the members of the Royal Society would have regarded as an excess of philosophical mechanism.

Perhaps it is telling that, while it could never do the practical work of multiplying or dividing numbers on its own, Leibniz's calculator did end up in a work of art—admittedly, of a low-end sort. The 1710 *Miscellanea Berolinensia*, which included an essay by Leibniz on his calculator, had for the occasion (this was the inaugural issue) a frontispiece that rendered selected items and topic areas included in the table of contents into a baroque allegory (see figure 2.2).

Sharing a scene with Minerva, Urania, a skeleton representing medicine/ anatomy, winged Time looking into an hourglass, and a putto writing history/ philology on a book supported by Time's back, Leibniz's calculator sits on the ground by the lower corner of the writing putto's massive tome. That the calculator has been converted into allegorical furniture serves, perhaps inadvertently

2.2 *Miscellanea Berolinensia ad Incrementum Scientiarum* (Berlin, 1710), frontispiece and title page.

and at a more abstract level, to represent the evaporation of the practical into the aesthetic that perpetually haunts Leibnizian invention.

It is telling that Leibniz never published a philosophical magnum opus on the scale of the *Ethics*. (The *Theodicy* has the size but not the philosophical heft.) His best-known works are shorter, somewhat more elliptical, and less definitively structured than Spinoza's. The vast majority of his writings were unpublished in his day, and these often take the form of proposals or sketches of projects to be fleshed out later. (He once described himself in a letter as being "too distracted myself to cultivate sufficiently the seeds of all the thoughts I have conceived.")[13] A significant portion of his writing consist of long streams of correspondence that incorporate an ongoing, unfinished quality into their very nature—a potentially endless back-and-forth of written conversation, perpetually inviting further response and debate, with multiple correspondents. Leibniz the tinkerer thereby ensures that he always has something at hand to work on.

All this being said, I should admit that the engineering/bricolage binary is suggestive but oversimplifying, both in itself and as applied to Leibniz. For one thing, Lévi-Strauss's account of engineering is tendentious. Engineering is not simply "strategic design" but necessarily includes improvisatory, experimental, and empirical elements, not to mention a good deal of working with what is at hand, and can therefore approximate to forms of tinkering.[14] For another, some of Leibniz's projects, such as the calculating machine, obviously involved pre-cisely preformed elements that were created and fitted together according to a pre-given design, though these obviously had to be subjected to adjustments and modifications under the pressure of trial and error. In other words, this is engineering, as Lévi-Strauss would have it.[15] Calculating machines can't be built out of whatever is lying around. Rather than two opposing forms of enterprise, engineering and tinkering might better be thought of as conceptual poles that organize overlapping forms of activity. Leibniz's philosophical system displays elements of both engineering and tinkering—as does Spinoza's, for that matter. What distinguishes them is a matter of relative emphasis. I want to highlight, though, the continuities between intellectual and manual-material forms of pro-duction in both thinkers.

Writing is an apt medium for tinkering—and nowhere more so than in the genre of the essay as practiced by Michel de Montaigne. The very word "essay," meaning an attempt or endeavor, places the author in a relation of non-mastery with respect to his subject matter. The essayist is in no position to offer a definitive exposition and so does his best by cobbling together what is lying about. Montaigne's essays famously resist coming to conclusions or even staying on topic. They meander and contradict themselves, most often illustrating the difficulty or even impossibility of coming to grips with the question at hand. Brimming with quotations, they thereby incorporate heterogeneous materials and perspectives into their texture. Indeed, the perspectivalism of Montaigne's *Essays* might serve as a deep source for Leibniz's. Above all, Montaigne's habit of perpetual self-revision betrays the tinkerer's ethic. Each new edition of the *Essays* incorporates new passages, additional quotations, second (or third or fourth) thoughts on whatever the topic happens to be. The *Essays* are incomplete by design, a monument to the endlessness of meditative thought.

At the same time, in Montaigne's hands the form of the essay undertakes serious philosophical work, and moreover shows how literary and philosophical projects can complement each other.[16] Montaigne's example remained influential throughout the seventeenth century. As Christia Mercer has shown, titles from the period that employ the plural form "essays" advertise Montaigne's influence in a particularly unmistakable fashion.[17] And as it happens, Leibniz's two longest works do just this: the *New Essays on Human Understanding* (composed 1704–1705) and the *Essays on Theodicy* (1710).[18] The latter, especially, betrays Montaigne's influence in its sometimes meandering arguments, autobiographical asides, and variety of perspectives.[19] While Leibniz lacks Montaigne's epistemological modesty, the presence of this most anti-systematic of philosophers in Leibniz's work should give pause.[20] I am not, of course, arguing that Montaigne is a governing presence in Leibniz's work. In some sense he is just another gizmo for Leibniz the philosophical tinkerer to add to his assemblages. But he is also a manual for tinkering or, at least, a brilliant model to follow. His very presence bespeaks and gives form to the drive to tinker that suffuses Leibniz's work.

Tinkering is a foundational element of Leibniz's intellectual style. Somewhat later, I will identify another, equally foundational element: the metaphorical mapping of discursive areas onto one another. While different, these two elements are highly compatible. Leibnizian mapping aims at multiplying perspectives on a problem and on forming conceptual blends from which new ideas can arise. It is undertaken with the aim not of generating definitive formulations but rather with probing the contours of a problem, trying out new approaches, looking for unexpected insights or inspirations—in short, with tinkering. One (doubtless oversimplified) way of describing Leibniz's style would be to say that mapping is a principal means and tinkering a principal end. But if tinkering is a crucial component of Leibniz's intellectual style, it is also, conversely, something that allows style as such to flourish—something that provides a space for style by partially suspending the work of philosophy or by infiltrating it with an element of play or, at least, with a provisional, experimental quality.[21] Style does philosophical work, of course, but it may do so most interestingly and variously when the philosopher is not in a hurry to reach conclusions; that is, when philosophizing becomes something of an end in itself, as it does spectacularly for Montaigne and somewhat more subtly for Leibniz.

CHAPTER 3

How to Read a Leibnizian Sentence

What happens if we approach Leibniz not from the macroperspective of the system but from the microperspective of the sentence? What if we follow the movement of his words as they unfold themselves, one by one—linking together into phrases and clauses and thereby creating meaning? What if we overturn the massive rock of thought to see what's crawling beneath?

Following is a sentence from Leibniz's debates with the German physician Georg Ernst Stahl over issues relating to medicine and organic life. I will not claim that it is typical in any statistical sense, but I do think that what goes on there is not anomalous in kind, though perhaps unusual in degree:

> Et *perceptio* quidem figuratio, ut sic dicam, seu representatio est compositi in simplice multitudinis [in monade]: ut angulus jam representatur in centro seu inclinatione exeuntium linearum.

> "And perception is indeed a figuration, so to speak, or a representation of the composite in the simple, that is, of a multitude in the monad: just as an angle is already represented in the center by the inclination of lines issuing from it."[1]

This sentence begins with something of a surprise. Leibniz is in the habit of describing perception as the *expression* or *representation* of the many in the one (i.e., of the multiplicity of the world in the unity of the monad or mind). But here he unexpectedly depicts perception as *figuration*, and this choice of words produces some conceptual tensions. *Perceptio* means, literally, a taking, receiving, or gathering in. To perceive something (in the ordinary sense of the word if not the Leibnizian one) is to reach out and take it from the outside world and store it in one's inner world. *Figuratio*, by contrast, is an act of forming or fashioning. Leibniz emphasizes the transformative nature of *figuratio* when he posits it elsewhere as synonymous with *modificatio*, and hence with alteration or change.[2] *Figuratio* can suggest artisanal fashioning but is also associated with the power of imagination and of course with figurative language.

Figuratio is not a term that Leibniz employs frequently and certainly not with respect to perception. But the term was much more central to a possible influence on Leibniz in his earlier years—the Italian philosopher Giordano Bruno.[3] Indeed, it appeared in the title of one of Bruno's works, the *Figuratio Aristotelici Physici Auditus* of 1586. There as elsewhere, Bruno had attempted "to translate abstract concepts into figurative language, that is, into a *figuratio*, in which he combined things, concepts, images, and words."[4] Leibniz eventually repudiated Bruno, and there's no reason to think he is employing figuration in any technically Brunonian sense here. But Bruno's enthusiasm for *figuratio* may nevertheless peek through Leibniz's use of it. If so, it would reinforce the word's transformational or translational valence.

The word "*figura*" embedded in "*figuratio*" might well produce another kind of echo, especially given the topic of Leibniz's sentence, by recalling the role of *figurae* in Descartes's theory of perception. For Descartes, *figurae* are the abstract outlines of objects that light etches onto the retina. From there, the nerves transfer them to the pineal gland, where the soul "sees" (really, reads) them. The Cartesian theory of perception is at odds with the Leibnizian one in some fundamental ways. But for Descartes, the optical focusing of *figurae* toward an ideal point in the eye provides a paradigm for the *res cogitans* as dimensionless, unextended "point."[5] And the final simile in our sample Leibnizian sentence, which compares perception to the convergence of geometric rays toward a point, seems to gesture at something similar. Hence Cartesian as well as Brunonian residues may well adhere to Leibniz's *figuratio*, both enriching and complicating its meaning.

In any case, the original tension produced by the sentence remains: perception is an act of receiving or introjecting something already made (or at least already in existence), but figuration is an act of making or at least remaking something. So the equivalence is not immediately obvious. But this may be Leibniz's point, since he regards perception *not* as the taking in of external objects but as something that mind produces for itself. In any case, having for better or worse connected perception to figuration, Leibniz then adds "so to speak." Perception is figuration, but only *so to speak*. Hence this is not an identity after all but a trope or metaphor. When Leibniz speaks of figuration, he does so *figuratively*.[6] Figuration is a *figure* for perception. We proceed: "or representation (*seu representatio*)." The *seu* or *sive* indicates an alternative as equivalent—an "id est" or "that is to say," or "in other words," as in Spinoza's famous "*Deus sive Natura.*" So now we have a short chain of equivalences or comparisons: perception is figuration, which in turn is representation. Figuration serves as a link or hinge between the other two terms. But is to figure something the same as to represent it? This might reproduce the original tension between perception and figuration. In fact, the statement "Perception is representation" would have appeared relatively unproblematic if "figuration" hadn't been jammed between them. But it is that insertion that makes Leibniz Leibniz.

There's a kind of performative redoubling here. Figuration as *word or concept* complicates what would otherwise have been a fairly transparent equivalence between perception and representation. But also, figuration as Leibniz's rhetorical *practice* of using figurative language is doing this. His habit of speaking figuratively makes his statement much more complicated and contradictory but also much more interesting and suggestive. Language's capacity to passively and accurately *represent* concepts gets blurred by its active capacity to *figure* them: to fashion, refashion, invent, and forge things.

The next phrase, "of the composite in the simple," modifies and thereby specifies what precedes it. Perception is like a figuration or representation *of the composite in the simple*. But the grammatical and hence conceptual linkage isn't entirely unambiguous. Does the "or" equate "figuration" and "representation"? Or does it equate "figuration" and "representation of the composite in the simple"? Is Leibniz saying: (A) "Perception is figuration (that is, representation) of the composite in the simple"? Or is he saying: (B) "Perception is figuration, that is (representation of the composite in the simple)"? Representing the composite in the simple would indeed seem to entail a transformation or conversion in the act of representation, which would make it more like figuration. And Leibniz frequently describes perception as the representation of the composite in the simple.[7] So there's much to be said for option B. But the unusual presence of "figuration" here renders option A difficult to rule out completely, especially because the placement of the "est" seems slightly to favor it. We thus have an additional ambiguity.

Next phrase: "that is, of a multitude in the monad." So here we have a second (actually third) equivalence or pairing. "Figuration *or* representation" is balanced by "the composite in the simple *or* the multitude in the monad" (though the second instance works by apposition rather than a conjunction). This is less vexing, for monadic perception does indeed represent the complex in the simple. But there are other ways of representing the composite in the simple that do not involve monadic perception (Leibniz will offer one directly), so here the relation between the two terms is that between species and genus or example and paradigm. In any case, the sentence thus far is just a series of ramifying juxtapositions or comparisons. Its conceptual work (such as it is) is conducted by way of figurative or rhetorical work.

But don't worry: if we're confused by this array of comparisons, Leibniz will offer to clarify it through *yet another comparison*—this one a figure that will be similar to the entire series of ambiguously conjoined similarities that is the sentence thus far: "just as an angle is already represented in the center by the inclination of lines issuing from it." The *ut* or "as" delivers us officially into the hands of the rhetorical device known as the simile, though of course we've been there all along without saying so, and thus this *soi-disant* simile just extends the series already in place. Actually, this simile is also an analogy, since what it compares are relationships: a mathematical angle is to its vertex as the multiplicity of the universe is to its representation in the metaphysical "point" known as the monad.[8] The comparison makes sense at least insofar as both monads and mathematical points are both dimensionless and indestructible unities. Still, the purpose of the analogy, and even its meaning, are by no means a given. Let's try to decode it. An angle is a mathematical figure formed when two rays emerge from a point or vertex. In figure 3.1, the vertex is the point marked B.

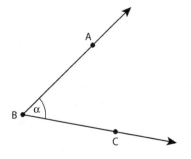

3.1 Angle with rays.

Leibniz is saying that the angle is "represented" in that vertex. But what does this mean, exactly? That point is just a point—the very same point it would be if two rays didn't diverge there. A point by itself cannot constitute an angle, and indeed the angle depicted in this illustration ceases to exist precisely when it reaches the vertex, since at that moment there would be no more rays.[9]

Still, there are a couple of ways we can try to make sense of Leibniz's claim. During his Paris period, Leibniz held that points were not dimensionless but rather infinitesimally extended in space. Moreover, Leibniz understood infinitesimals not as infinitely small quantities but rather as mathematical limits: something that can be made arbitrarily small by defining it as smaller than any quantitative measure one gives. So if we regard point B, not as dimensionless but as an infinitesimal limit as we approach the vertex along the two rays, the angle would be preserved throughout the approach and hence in the vertex "point." Awkwardly for our purposes, Leibniz had abandoned his view of geometric points as infinitesimally extended decades before his response to Stahl.[10] However, in a later work, the "Justification of the Infinitesimal Calculus by that of Ordinary Algebra" (1702), the ratio of the sections of two sides of a triangle converging on a vertex remain constant even as those two sections become infinitesimally small, and indeed even when they reach the vertex itself.[11] So this is one interpretive possibility. That Leibniz writes of lines exiting the vertex (and hence in its immediate neighborhood) speaks in favor of this reading.

Another approach would be to say that the vertex B is *defined* by the fact that it is the convergent endpoint of two rays that are themselves defined by sharing this endpoint and diverging by the angle α. This approach draws on two different elements of Leibniz's thinking: first, that all spatial positions (*situs*) are definitionally relative to other positions; and second, that entities are constituted by a complete description that entails all of their predicates. In this sense the angle would be "represented" in the point by way of the latter's complete concept or description or definition, which would involve the two rays and their angle. Moreover, Leibniz might well regard this second, definitional explanation as complementary to the first, mathematical one. Nevertheless, the two approaches are not identical.

We therefore find ourselves again faced with more than one possible interpretation, neither of which can be proffered with complete confidence. Moreover, the meaning of "representation" appears to be very different in each case, and one is faced with the further task of relating these two meanings both to one another and to the way the word is used earlier in the sentence, when "representation" refers not to mathematical angles but to the way that monads perceive the world. It only remains to be pointed out that this mathematical simile or analogy is also a meta-analogy. What I mean by this is that an analogy is meant to bring two different things into conceptual relation to each other. But this function is also "represented" by the particular mathematical figure chosen here, since two different entities (in this case, rays) meet at one point. In effect, spatial convergence figures conceptual convergence. This analogy, which supposedly effects convergence, is also about convergence. Only it fails to converge definitively with its analogical target because it fails to converge definitively even with *itself*.

What appears at first to be a simple declarative sentence of some kind thus dissolves, upon attentive reading, into a superfetating mass of metaphors, analogies, allusions, and interpretive pathways with no very clear or univocal meaning. Note, moreover, that this figurative work is conducted by a variety of means. It doesn't always announce itself through a formal rhetorical device such as simile, which doesn't arrive until halfway through the sentence. Before that, we have an intensifying adverb *quidem*, the conjunction *seu*, and mere apposition. All that being said, I am not making the standard deconstructionist point that attempts at conceptual closure in Leibniz are undone by the text's rhetoricity. Our sample sentence is not, in other words, what Stanley Fish called a "self-consuming artifact" back in 1972.[12] The work of metaphor in Leibniz is not to undo or subvert meaning because in my view Leibniz is not aiming at conceptual closure in the first place. To the contrary, he is trying out a series of formulations—experimenting or tinkering with thought as he varies his metaphoric expressions. What we get here is thinking in its "molten" state before it has hardened into a definitive form. And the sentence becomes thereby an *act* of thinking rather than the recitation of the already-thought. Nor is this unusual in Leibniz. Anyone who reads his work will discover that he is quite repetitive. But at the same time, these repetitions usually also involve some degree of variation, with the result that Leibniz is rarely repeating exactly the same thing but rather proposing some new formulation of it.

In any case, this way of reading Leibniz suggests that his sentences are in some respects ill suited to their ordinary use in Leibniz scholarship. When trying to reconstruct Leibniz's "system," commentators will cull sentences or phrases from the works and arrange them into a conceptual edifice. But this activity assumes a kind of geometric regularity and consistency to those excerpts, which can be securely piled one on another like bricks. But what if they aren't bricks at all, but masses of wriggling worms? What kind of edifice can be built from that? You can only treat them as bricks if you don't inspect them too closely and thereby ignore all the wriggling. But in the case of this particular sentence, *there's nothing but the wriggling.*

Now, this way of putting things may suggest—wrongly—that I consider the normal sort of Leibniz commentary to be based on some sort of category error. But there's no way to talk about Leibniz without extracting passages from the work and fitting them together in some fashion. And this is not very different in some respects from the practice in my own field of extracting passages from a literary work in order to construct a reading. I myself will be doing this with Leibniz passages later on. There's really no alternative to arranging blocks of worms. But it is good to be aware of this, not only because it imposes useful limits to one's expectations for systematic coherence, but also because ultimately it can enrich rather than encumber one's reading practices.

Let me convert this dilemma into more recognizably Leibnizian terms, though, in fact, I have already been doing so with the image of the worms, which Leibniz himself often employs. In his view, physical bodies are made up of organic entities, which are themselves made up of smaller organic entities, folded one into the other ad infinitum. Leibniz will therefore sometimes compare a body to a cheese filled with worms or invoke the fact that actual worms are often found in the digestive systems of animals. Worms are what you find if you start looking at a body very closely, just as Anton van Leeuwenhoek discovered tiny infusoria when he inspected a drop of pond water under a microscope. And what is true of the physical body, I would suggest, is true of the textual body of Leibniz's writings. The practice of close reading is like a microscope through which we can glimpse the microbiome of Leibnizian thought.

This in turn raises a problem of *perspective*, which is central for Leibniz (see module 08). In this case, the perspectives are attached to scale: if you view the macrostructure of something, you tend to miss the microstructure (we don't see the infusoria when we behold the pond from a distance), and conversely when you look at the microstructure, you lose sight of the macrostructure (viewing the infusoria through the microscope, you can no longer see the pond). But Leibniz is committed to the multiplication of perspectives, which increase the perceptual richness of the world. So not only do his sentences exhibit fascinating, teeming movements of figurative language, but also his "system" would seem to insist that we pay at least some attention to them.

Leibniz argues that when we look at a circle, it appears circular to us only because we don't notice the tiny imperfections that pit its outer surface and render it completely irregular if inspected closely enough. In other words, we can see the circle as circular—as a geometric figure rather than as an infinitely irregular thing—only if we perceive it *confusedly*. Likewise, we perceive his sentences as geometrically regular crystals of philosophical doctrine only if we see them confusedly. There is nothing inherently wrong with doing this, of course. It is valuable to be able to see a circle as a circle, and our world would be impoverished both conceptually and visually if we could not. Likewise it is valuable to be able to apprehend the various philosophical positions that Leibniz elaborates with his sentences. But it is also important not to reify these latter in a way that takes them for all there is or prevents us from grasping the perspectival effects that result from switching between levels. There is therefore a philosophical point to *reading* Leibniz closely—to turning the microscope of literary and rhetorical analysis upon him.

CHAPTER 4

Metaphorical Clumping

Disciplinary training in the humanities involves, to a large degree, learning techniques of reading designed to sharpen the eye in ways that matter to the discipline in question. To borrow Leibnizian terms, they render distinct what might otherwise be glimpsed only confusedly or perhaps not noticed at all. This is part of the process of producing what Ludwik Fleck calls a "thought style." But not everything can be brought into focus at once, and so the very practices that highlight some things inevitably throw others into shadow. For many philosophical readers of Leibniz, the attention focused on conceptual and logical matters nurtures a corresponding inattention to the figurative, rhetorical, and literary dimensions of his writing. There are exceptions, of course, but they appear to have had little influence on Leibniz scholarship in the Anglophone world.[1]

This particular bias sometimes finds direct expression in ways of construing Leibniz's philosophical project. A striking example, to my mind, is a recent article by John Whipple that traces and elaborates a distinction made by Leibniz between esoteric and exoteric writing.[2] Esoteric writing proceeds along the lines of geometric demonstration and is designed for an audience accomplished in philosophical ways of thought; exoteric writing is meant to convey philosophical ideas to a broader audience, one that is less rational and more prey to common prejudices. For such audiences, abstract arguments that depart from commonly received ideas will be off-putting. Therefore, the philosopher must employ the language of the senses, along with rhetorical figures and colors. But these are always elements in a heuristic strategy meant to prepare readers for an esoteric presentation and thus lead them away from the exoteric world of images, analogy, and rhetoric.

Whipple's article has the effect of both explaining the rhetorical elements in Leibniz's prose and explaining them away. They are there, but they are secondary, provisional, even temporary with respect to the essential, esoteric, and decidedly non-figurative core of the philosophy. They can therefore (and this is not stated by Whipple but may be inferred) be more or less ignored as mere exoteric accommodations by those interested in weightier philosophical matters. Whipple makes a strong evidentiary case that Leibniz maintains a theoretical distinction between esoteric and exoteric writing and values the former more highly. Moreover, the ideal of a purely demonstrative, non-figurative writing accords with Leibniz's dream of a general characteristic that would reduce thought to blind calculation. In fact, the only objection I can find to Whipple's argument is that Leibniz never once engages in esoteric writing—not even in his private correspondence with learned figures such as Antoine Arnauld and Burchard De Volder.[3] If these do not constitute an appropriate audience for an esoteric presentation of ideas, one is left wondering who would. And yet we possess exoteric writings by Leibniz in abundance.

This is not to say that audience does not matter for Leibniz. It clearly does. He often adjusts his philosophical vocabulary to cater to the predilections of individual correspondents. He presents his ideas in more philosophically precise and technical terms when writing to fellow intellectuals. He does indeed make more abundant use of figures and images in works intended for publication, and hence for a broader audience, or when writing to less philosophically adept correspondents. But the differences are of degree, not of kind. As they would have to be since, as I shall argue later, analogical thinking is foundational for Leibniz.

While Whipple merely implies that philosophical readers can ignore Leibniz's figurative language, Donald Rutherford enjoins them to do so, so as not to be seduced into fantastic misconstructions:

First-time readers of Leibniz's popular works such as the *Monadology* are often struck by the vivid imagery of his philosophical writing. We read that every monadic substance is a "mirror" of the universe, and the "center" of a bodily mass; moreover, soul-like monads are located everywhere "within" matter, with the result that nature is everywhere "alive." It is easy to be misled by language like this and to conclude that Leibniz's metaphysics is far stranger, and far less credible, than it actually is. Now and then we are given signs to indicate that expressions such as these are not to be taken literally; but for the most part, in Leibniz's more popular writings, we are left to interpret them as we will. His confidence that we will treat them solely as helpful indicators of a deeper underlying truth has all too seldom been borne out by the habits of his readers. They have misread the figurative for the literal, and in so doing have transformed a metaphysics of reason into an implausible fantasy.[4]

Rutherford warns against taking Leibniz's figurative language *literally*, which seems like good enough advice, though sometimes impossible to follow. But one cannot come away from this passage without also feeling that figurative language is not to be taken *seriously*, either. The real content of Leibniz's philosophy lies elsewhere.

On the one hand, such views trivialize the role of figurative language in Leibniz. Rhetorical tropes are like pretty little shells strewn across a beach, whose very abundance makes them not worth stooping to gather. But at the same time, and somewhat contradictorily, these harmless baubles exert a dangerous power to distract and even seduce the unwary reader. At no point, however, are sound methodological principles offered for deciding that some things on the Leibnizian page deserve careful attention while others safely can, and indeed should, be demoted if not ignored. What seems to underlie this position is therefore not so much reason as an anti-rhetorical prejudice on the part of philosophy that stretches back at least to Plato's dismissal of the Sophists.

Given current attitudes such as this, it is salubrious to recall that, once upon a time, Leibniz was admired as much for his writing as for his system, and that his use of rhetorical language was celebrated rather than dismissed. The Enlightenment philosopher, poet, and aesthetic theorist Johann Gottfried von Herder declared that Leibniz "was always a poet in his system: a metaphor of his gave the whole doctrine of the soul a different form." Leibniz was "a witty thinker, for whom at most a metaphor, an image, a simile casually let fall produced the theories which he jotted down on a quarto sheet and from which the weaver's guilds [Christian Wolff and his pupils] wrote thick volumes after him." The *Monadology* is, in Herder's view, a "monad-poem," and the *Theodicy* is "the finest poem ever written by a human mind."[5] Herder, admittedly, had a habit of dubbing thinkers poets. But Friedrich Schlegel also praised Leibniz as a "witty" writer and ranked him among "the chief representatives of scholastic prose."[6]

I would argue that the yawning chasm between Schlegel and Herder, on the one hand, and Whipple and Rutherford on the other, is not merely a chronological one. In addition, it reflects a significant discrepancy between the ways in which Leibniz talks about the language of philosophy and the way he practices philosophy. If one attends solely to Leibniz's statements about how philosophical language should ideally work, he often (though not always) supports Whipple's and Rutherford's views. But if one attends instead to the rhetorical texture of what he habitually puts down on paper, then Herder and Schlegel have the edge. As an antidote to the current, anti-rhetorical biases of Leibniz commentators, therefore, a useful exercise might be to choose just about any piece of Leibniz's metaphysical prose and take the time to notice how densely figurative it is. By this I mean partly his use of formal rhetorical devices, particularly those involving comparison or similitude: metaphor, simile, analogy. But it also involves noticing how frequently his argumentative strategies likewise proceed by way of analogy, either announced or unannounced, and how deeply his metaphysics is structured by isomorphisms that are in essence metaphors writ large. This is to say nothing of the many rhetorical figures sometimes silently embedded in the very structures of his sentences, as we saw in the previous module. Leibnizian prose is teeming with figuration, at various levels of specificity and generality, both when Leibniz is writing for a more general readership and in the correspondence, where, it is generally agreed, he often presents a more philosophically rigorous version of his thinking. I am therefore tempted to flip Whipple's argument on its head and claim that Leibniz attempts to put a demonstrative, esoteric sheen on a mode of thinking that is essentially analogical and figurative. If this is the case, rhetorical figures such as metaphor can offer a useful starting point in approaching his work rather than a mere afterthought. Leibniz argues through imagery and metaphor as much as he does through concept and logic, and not merely as a sop to popular tastes. Synthesizing these two dimensions of his work will take some doing, and I will attempt this later on.

For Anglophone philosophers, my claims may bring to mind unhappy memories of a disciplinary coup d'état attempted by French theory in the 1960s and 1970s—one that attempted to deconstruct philosophical discourse by appealing to its rhetoricity. It is worth noting, however, that many of the themes announced in a sly, playful, and sometimes elusive manner by the likes of Jacques Derrida have since been taken up in much more sober, lucid, and empirical fashion by cognitive linguists. And it is on them rather than on poststructuralist theory that I shall principally draw in this study. Among cognitive linguists there are, of course, lively arguments about how metaphor works, including the question whether it involves similarity at all. (Some insist that metaphor is rather a class-inclusion claim in disguise or else involves "experiential correlations and not similarities."[7]) Widely agreed upon, however, is that concepts, no matter how crisply they appear to be defined and how autonomously they appear to operate, are actually imperfect, partial crystallizations of ongoing metaphorical and analogical activity, often proceeding unnoticed in the background of consciousness.[8] Here I think it is important to preserve the notions of activity and movement evoked by the etymology of "metaphor," and to contrast them with the relative solidity and stasis traditionally associated with the concept. To grasp Leibniz in motion, then, involves tracking his "mobile army of metaphors," to borrow Nietzsche's well-known phrase.[9] More specifically, I want here to examine Leibniz's distinctive *manner* with metaphor—and its cousins, simile and analogy. (I should say that I will not distinguish sharply among metaphor, simile, and analogy, in preparation for subsuming all three later, along with isomorphism, under the more general category of cognitive mapping. In fact, I will sometimes use the generic term "figures of similitude" to indicate all of them.)

I'll begin with a set of similes that will be familiar to any reader of Leibniz, since he trots them out repeatedly when discussing the aggregation problem: the fact that bodies are, in his view, mere collections of parts without anything that can effectively unify them. Here is a small sampling:

> Such masses can only be thought of as like an army or a flock, or like a pond full of fish, or like a watch composed of springs and wheels.[10]
>   . . . every body as found in the world is, in fact, like an army of creatures, a flock, or a confluence like a cheese made of worms, . . . [11]
>   I would say that they are united perhaps *per aggregationem*, like a heap of stones.[12] [Elsewhere he mentions piles of logs or firewood or bricks.[13]]

Before getting into specifics, the first thing to note is Leibniz's predilection to multiply comparisons. I'll call this "metaphorical clumping." Sometimes he pairs metaphors, as when he almost invariably describes "well-founded phenomena" as being like both rainbows and parhelia. And sometimes the clumpings become massier and more elaborate. Moreover, the individual lists are subject to continuous variation. When discussing aggregation, Leibniz rarely repeats exactly the same terms in the same order.

One effect of metaphorical clumping is the establishment of implicit, lateral connections among the metaphorical sources that supplement the explicit one between sources and target. Not only are flocks, sheep, watches, rocks, worms, logs, and armies all like aggregated bodies, but because of this they are also, in at least one respect, like one another. But otherwise, these various terms seem conspicuously heterogeneous. Some are living things (fish, sheep), some are inanimate objects (rocks), some are inanimate objects that were once living things (logs), some are products of nature and others are products of human design, some are stationary and some are in motion, some are chaotic and others are highly ordered. Indeed, some are so ordered that they seem to press against the boundaries of the merely aggregated. A flock is not just a bunch of individual sheep: flocks exhibit emergent, self-organized behaviors that cannot be engaged in by individual sheep, and even if Leibniz lacked this specific concept, he had certainly observed flocks of sheep.[14] Even more striking is the mention of armies, which engage in coordinated, intentional activities organized by lines of command. Is an army an aggregate in the same sense that a pile of stones is one? Leibniz would ultimately say "yes," and yet his collection of metaphors is not only heterogeneous but somewhat unruly. It doesn't merely exemplify the category of the aggregate but raises questions about it and renders it a bit fuzzy around the edges. Rather than merely solidifying or reinforcing or illustrating the concept of the aggregate, it sets it into motion (like a flock or an army?).

It is worth noting that Leibniz does, at least once, place the ambiguities I have been discussing into philosophically "doctrinal" form. Here he is in a letter to Arnauld:

> I agree that there are degrees of accidental unity: that a regulated society has more unity than a confused throng, and that an organized body, or a machine, has more unity than a society. That is, it is more appropriate to conceive them as a single thing, because there is more relation among the ingredients. But in the end all these unities are made complete only by thoughts and appearances, like colors and other phenomena that are still called real.[15]

Admittedly, Leibniz is in a concessive mode here, and in the end he insists that an element of the phenomenal is needed to "complete" the inherent but partial unity of the listed groupings. Nevertheless, he does recognize meaningful "degrees of accidental unity" within what he otherwise regards as aggregates. But one would probably not know this without happening upon this one particular passage in this one letter—unless, that is, one paid attention to the similes of flocks and armies scattered throughout Leibniz's writings, where he repeatedly suggests the same idea by way of literary figures. Why, then, is a phrase such as "degrees of accidental unity" meaningful to philosophical commentators, while the image of a flock or an army is not? As I have already suggested, it is a consequence of ingrained disciplinary reading practices that overlook as much as they reveal.

But let us return to our collection of clumped similitudes. In addition to the lateral connections among metaphorical sources, there is also a self-referential dimension to the clumpings as a whole. Indeed, I have chosen the term "clumping" in part because of its conceptual proximity to "aggregation," which is the concept Leibniz is trying to illustrate. The question then becomes: Are these metaphors randomly stacked one on the other, like a pile of stones, or are they organized in some fashion, either like a clockwork or like a flock or like an army (each structured in ways very different from the others). Is this simply a case of an army being used as a metaphorical basis of comparison or is this Nietzsche's "mobile army of metaphors?" Note that we saw a comparable "meta-" dimension in the simile of the rays and the vertex, and we will see it again repeatedly. Self-reference is another way in which metaphors become "unruly"—in which they diverge from their ostensible task of illuminating the target concept and begin to take on a life of their own.

And there is yet a third way (beyond lateral reference and self-reference) in which Leibniz's metaphors do this: by establishing connections between images and metaphors that have nothing to do with the immediate context of comparison and can even occur across different works. So, for instance, the pond of fish, which appears so often in the context of aggregation, also makes a cameo in the *Monadology* under somewhat different auspices:

> 67. Every portion of matter can be thought of as a garden full of plants, or as a pond full of fish. But every branch of the plant, every part of the animal, and every drop of its vital fluids, is another such garden, or another such pond.
>
> 68. And although the earth and the air in between the plants in the garden, and the water in between the fish in the pond, are not themselves plants or fish, they do nevertheless contain others, though usually they are so tiny as to be imperceptible to us.

Now the pond of fish is paired with a garden, which it never is when aggregation is the primary topic. The latter is in this context merely residual, and the primary role of the fish and pond are to image forth, not contiguity but inclusion or containment—a mise-en-abyme of fish within ponds within fish within ponds. Moreover, the pond full of fish, in which solid (indeed living) creatures float in a liquid medium, connects to yet other, and in this context merely implicit, elements of Leibniz's worldview. For Leibniz indeed saw the universe as a liquid in which solids are suspended (see module 15). The metaphor of the fish in the pond is therefore somewhat promiscuous, forming networks of associative chains well outside of its immediate context. Rather than providing a pat "illustration" of a pre-given concept, it and the other clumped metaphors serve as provocations to thought that are moreover inclined to drift from their immediate contexts, like sheep wandering from their fold.

Part of this unruly process results from Leibniz's manner with metaphor, and part results from the nature of metaphor itself. The basic notion that metaphor establishes resemblances between two concepts is true but obviously reductive, because the terms brought into contact inevitably include not only points of similarity but also points of difference, and it is sometimes hard to say where the one ends and the other begins. Hence what at first seems a fairly straightforward comparison can become, upon further reflection, something more like an open question. To put this in Leibnizian terms, metaphor establishes some relatively clear and distinct connections between concepts, but also a confused penumbra of partial or strained similarities trailing off into increasingly strong differences. This contributes to the suggestive richness of metaphor but also to a fuzziness of boundaries that may make it frustrating for a discipline that prizes conceptual tidiness. Leibniz's clumping together of heterogeneous metaphors brings this sometimes dizzying play of similarity and difference to the fore.

Here is another interesting set of clumped similes, this time from a letter to the Electress Sophie:

> For the machines of nature are superior to artificial machines in that they have that wondrous quality of being indestructible, which is because their author, who is himself infinite, made them resistant to all accidents and gave them an infinity of organs and members enveloped one inside the other, rather like the skins in onions and in pearls, and like Harlequin's great number of clothes— I saw him take off one set immediately after the others so often that I started

to wonder whether he would ever finish. So as life and apparent death are only envelopments and developments of one true and continual life, animals thought to have been destroyed have in fact only become compressed.[16]

Leibniz holds that the bodies of living creatures are preformed as tiny, folded seeds that unfold into their mature living forms. Upon death, the body is not entirely destroyed; part of it enfolds itself once more into a microscopic form wherein the monad or mind of the creature persists, though now invisible to the naked eye. And he illustrates this with a series of similes comparing the body to various items composed of enveloped layers. An onion can shed its outer layers and still remain an onion. Pearls grow by means of accreted layers but of course cannot subsequently shed them, which makes the analogy a bit shakier. And then there is Harlequin, who sheds his clothes in performance.

This instance of clumping exhibits many of the qualities of the previous one. The metaphorical sources are heterogeneous: a gem, a root vegetable, and a dramatic performance. There is also a self-referential dimension, which will require some unpacking. Leibniz paints himself into the scene as an audience member astounded at Harlequin's apparently endless series of garments. But Leibniz also displays a tendency to identify with Harlequin. As he states in another letter to Sophie: "my great principle of natural things is that of Harlequin, Emperor of the Moon (whom I did not, however, do the honor of quoting)—*that it is always and everywhere in all things just as it is here.*"[17] Leibniz, a man always careful not to offend his social superiors, might well be fascinated by this servant, who is also a trickster-figure, repeatedly subverting the will of his master to pursue his own interests. In this particular context, there seems to be a rhetorical and performative identification as well, since Harlequin's act of shedding successive sets of clothes to reveal new layers resembles Leibniz's production of similes one after the other. The dramatic character's theatrical dexterity finds a counterpart in Leibniz's seemingly inexhaustible rhetorical creativity.

As I am already beginning to suggest, Harlequin's presence in this rhetorical clumping cannot be restricted to his official role of illustrating a multiplicity of layers. Harlequin, that is to say, is not merely an onion in human form. Given his context, he converts death itself into a theatrical performance, one in which the dying person does not succumb to dissolution but instead effects a miraculous sleight of hand. One is reminded of Guil's final, dying lines in Tom Stoppard's *Rosencrantz and Guildenstern Are Dead*: "Well, we'll know better next time. Now you see me, now you (*and disappears*)."[18] Death, the most tragic event, becomes a comic, indeed burlesque bit of stagecraft. This might not seem to be of any great philosophical import, but in fact Leibniz repeatedly uses theatrical language of passing between smaller and larger stages to depict the transitions from preformed seed to developed creature, and then once again from living creature to (apparently, but not really) dead one. "And so, throwing off their cloak or tattered clothing, they merely return to a more subtle stage on which nevertheless they can be just as perceptible and orderly as they were on the larger one."[19] It is because death involves only a change of scale rather than a dissolution of order that it is no real loss: indeed, it is a kind of trompe l'oeil or trick that presents the spectator's eye with a falsely tragic face. As I shall argue later, it is of philosophical import that these microworlds, as well as ours, exhibit the characteristics of a theater. But this notion never receives the armature of a well-formed philosophical concept. It exists *only* as image or metaphor. And in the case of the specific metaphorical clumping at issue here, the suggestiveness of the metaphor results from properties within the source image (Harlequin) that exceed its official role of illustrating multi-layeredness. Not only as servant but also as simile, Harlequin is a human instrument who nevertheless throws off his instrumentality to display a manic, unexpected autonomy. If Harlequin embodies a certain unquenchable vitality within all living organisms, then he also represents the anarchic potential within figurative language itself—a rhetorical instrument that nevertheless displays extravagant, unruly qualities. These can both enrich and unsettle philosophical arguments that are based on concept and logic. Rhetoric, like Harlequin, is an untrustworthy servant in philosophical contexts.

As we have already seen, Leibniz's metaphors repeatedly exhibit a self-referential dimension. Aside from displaying his literary artfulness, this speaks to the fact that his use of metaphor, far from being casual, is carefully thought-out. Metaphor is a means of thinking for Leibniz, but clearly also something he thinks *about*. His metaphors do important intellectual work while simultaneously reflecting on their own figurative and cognitive capacities.

Let us proceed to a final metaphorical clumping that is extravagant in a somewhat different way, and for different purposes. This one comes from the *Discourse on Metaphysics*, where Leibniz is extolling the economy of God's act of creation:

> We can say that someone who behaves perfectly is like an expert geometer who finds the best construction for a problem; or like a good architect who

utilizes the location and the ground for his building in the most advantageous way, leaving nothing discordant, or which doesn't have the beauty of which it is capable; or like a good head of a household, who manages his property in such a way that there is no ground left uncultivated or barren; or like a clever stage-manager who produces his effects by the least awkward means that could be found; or like a learned author, who gets the most reality into the least space he can. Now, the most perfect of all beings, and which occupy the least space, that is to say that which obstruct each other the least, are minds, whose perfections are virtues. That is why there is no doubt that the happiness of minds is the main aim of God, which he carries out as far as the general harmony will permit. We will say more about this later. As to the simplicity of God's ways, it properly relates to means, whereas on the other hand, their variety, richness, or abundance relate to ends or effects. The one should be balanced against the other, as the expenses allowed for a building are balanced against its desired size and beauty. It is true that things cost God nothing, less indeed than it costs a philosopher to invent theories as he constructs his imaginary world, since God has only to make a decree for a real world to be produced; but in regard to wisdom, decrees or theories function as costs in proportion to their independence from each other—for reason requires that multiplicity of hypotheses or principles be avoided, rather as the most simple system is always preferred in astronomy.[20]

This extraordinary passage exhibits metaphorical clumping with a vengeance. By the time it is through, divine creation has been compared to no fewer than seven kinds of activity: that of the geometer, architect, head of household, stage manager, author, philosopher, and astronomer. Here metaphorical clumping exhibits a self-consciously bravura quality as Leibniz reels off comparison after comparison. Even more than in the previous passage, he exhibits the inexhaustible figurative energy of a Harlequin. And the simile of the stage manager provides an associative train to lead us back to the topic of the theatrical, should we choose to follow it. This passage is very much a virtuosic rhetorical *performance* or production on Leibniz's part.

But what is its purpose, exactly? The reader can be forgiven for wondering whether all of these similes are strictly necessary, even while marveling at their variety. After all, they all seem to make more or less the same point about achieving a profusion of effect while employing an economy of means. Wouldn't one or two or even three have sufficed? But of course, an almost excessive profusion is precisely the point here. Because just as Leibniz compares God's worldmaking with that of the philosopher, so is he, as philosopher, here emulating the abundance of divine creation. In this respect, the similes are important primarily for their performative dimension.

While it is not possible, obviously, for a philosopher to imitate divine creation in matters of scale or ontological gravity, what is at question here is rather the formal, economic criteria behind creation; that is, the achievement of profuse, variegated effects with limited means. This is something Leibniz *can* emulate, if only on a rhetorical and figurative plane. But I don't think we should regard this as merely a passing fancy on his part—a mood or whim momentarily indulged in before he returns to the serious work of philosophizing. Rather, Leibniz here reveals a capacious set of discursive aims that, I think, operates more widely in his work. Two of these are the related principles of abundance and variety, which are evident in any number of ways—from the sheer number of pages that Leibniz produces, to the variety of disciplines in which he works, to the fact that his metaphysics exhibits a kind of hodgepodge quality that accommodates concepts from different and sometimes opposed philosophical schools. Abundance and variety are not merely side effects of Leibniz's philosophical activity: they are aims, and hence values that coexist with, but cannot be entirely reduced to, that of philosophical rigor. The examples of the architect, who aims to produce buildings of "size and beauty," and that of the stage manager, who likewise aims at an aesthetic effect, reminds us that variety in unity is the Leibnizian formula for harmony and thus for beauty. Leibniz aims at producing intellectual beauty but also, I would argue, writerly beauty. His metaphysics aspires to generate a maximum of interconnected philosophical conclusions from a minimum of postulates; but his writing does not restrict itself to the sole means of a priori demonstrations. Its figurative copiousness is the complement to its conceptual copiousness. Indeed, it is sometimes the achievement of intellectual copiousness by other means. This final instance of metaphorical clumping, in other words, is a defense or rationalization of metaphorical clumping, and of the figurative language that pervades Leibniz's writing, like veins through marble. Metaphors can be beautiful or striking, but they can also *think*. They think differently from, but no less consequentially than, concepts or arguments. Just as Leibniz holds that creation is densely packed with variegated creatures, with no patches left idle or empty, so he makes certain that no writerly instrument lies idle if it can contribute to the variegated orchestra of thought.

As I shall go on to argue later, the fundamental movement of Leibnizian thought involves the analogical mapping of different proto-disciplinary forms of knowledge onto one another. Metaphor is neither a local exception to nor a mere embellishment upon Leibniz's more ordinary way of proceeding, then, but rather a surface manifestation of deeper processes fundamental to his manner of philosophizing. Metaphors function as portals that allow us to peer into the engine-room of Leibnizian thought. There is an important cognitive dimension to metaphorical clumping, then, but simultaneously an aesthetic one, and the two are related. The very profusion of Leibnizian metaphors—their tendency to aggregate into "clumps"—multiplies the number of images and thought-objects brought into contact with one another. It thereby produces the variety-in-unity that constitutes harmonious beauty for Leibniz, and moreover raises the tension between variety and unity to baroque levels. Via metaphor, the cognitive and the aesthetic become mutually reinforcing, challenging, and enriching.

CHAPTER 5

The Mathematics of Resemblance

There is one Leibnizian analogy that deserves a module of its own, because it raises issues central to this study. It is one that Leibniz has recourse to frequently. Here it is in two versions:

As for the sixth supposition, it isn't necessary that what we understand of things outside ourselves should resemble them perfectly, but only that it should express them; in the way that an ellipse expresses a circle seen from an angle, so that each point on the circle corresponds to one on the ellipse and vice versa in accordance with a certain law of correspondence, for, as I have already said, each individual substance expresses the universe in its way, rather like the way the same town is differently expressed according to different points of view.[1]

It is true that the same thing may be represented in different ways; but there must always be an exact relation between the representation and the thing, and consequently between the different representations of one and the same thing. The projections in perspective of the conic sections of the circle show that one and the same circle may be represented by an ellipse, a parabola and a hyperbola, and even by another circle, a straight line and a point. Nothing appears so different nor so dissimilar as these figures; and yet there is an exact relation between each point and every other point. Thus one must allow that each soul represents the universe to itself according to its point of view, and through a relation which is peculiar to it; but a perfect harmony subsists therein.[2]

The topic here is the relation between objects out in the world and their representation—or expression—within the mental field of the monad. Leibniz's point is that things in themselves and the ideas we have of them do not exactly correspond, but that an invariant law allows one to be transformed into the other in a consistent way. Perception alters its objects, but in a regular, predictable fashion. We thus return to the idea of perception as figuration explored in module 03.

To illustrate this process, Leibniz refers to the mathematics of conic sections; that is, the geometric figures created when a plane intersects a cone at different angles (see figure 5.1).

Two important treatises on the mathematics of conic section had been published in the seventeenth century: one by Pascal (now lost except for some sections transcribed by Leibniz) and one by the French mathematician Gérard Desargues. Both demonstrated, using different procedures, how a circle could be mathematically transformed into the different conic sections.[3] Leibniz is comparing the mathematical laws that govern this process to the metaphysical law that governs the transformation of external objects into internal monadic perceptions. His point is that our ideas of things may be quite dissimilar to the things themselves but that this does not matter so long as the conversion is carried out consistently.

More broadly, this analogy is about apparently dissimilar things that reveal deeper similarities. It is therefore also "about" simile itself, or analogy, which

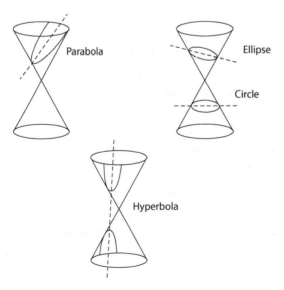

5.1 Conic sections.

establishes connections between things that are dissimilar in some respect. So again, this Leibnizian analogy has a self-referential dimension. The different conic sections—circles, ellipses, parabolas, etc.—are at some level "alike." So the simile doesn't just establish an explicit analogical relation between the mathematical transformation of conic sections and the metaphysical transformation of objects into ideas. It also establishes an implicit analogical relation between the mathematical transformation of conic sections and the conceptual transformation carried out by the rhetorical figures of similitude. Conceptual and mathematical mappings are analogical.[4]

In the examples I gave, Leibniz employs the mathematics of conic sections to explain three terms: expression, perspective, and representation. These three are themselves roughly synonymous: different but similar, they can be converted into one another, just as objects can be converted into ideas of them, or ellipses into circles. "Expression" and "perspective" are so central to Leibniz's thinking that they will receive modules of their own a bit further on. Here, though, we should note that the geometry of conic sections is also the geometry of perspective. The vertex of the cone is the place of the eye, and the cone itself corresponds to the cone of vision. The ellipse produced when a plane cuts the cone at an angle is the ellipse we see when we hold a circular object at the same angle. The projective geometry that described conical sections made it into treatises on perspective for artists in the seventeenth century, and Leibniz was familiar with both. But "perspective" is also not a bad description for what the rhetorical figures of similitude provide. A metaphor or simile distances the target concept from itself and views it from the place of the source concept. As with perspective, the rhetorical figures of similitude illustrate their target concept from a particular angle or point of view—turning it, as it were, within our conceptual field of vision so as to see it in a new way. As often in Leibniz, then, here in his similitudes involving conic sections, the field of analogy does not limit itself to the official or explicit comparison being drawn. It extends itself to every term being discussed in these passages and converts them into a network of analogical relations, each with its own forms of similarity and difference. But I want to argue that this use of conic sections is not quite like the other examples of rhetorical similitude examined in the previous module. And that is because mathematics offers Leibniz a privileged model for thinking about relations of similitude.

What I have in mind here is an approach to geometry invented by Leibniz but one that never got beyond the embryonic stage. Leibniz sometimes called it the *characteristica geometrica* and sometimes (especially in the 1690s) the *analysis situs*.[5] The first of the two names indicates its role in one of Leibniz's larger intellectual projects: the dream of founding a "general characteristic" that would reduce thought to calculations that could be done "blindly" and without any chance of error. *Characteristica geometrica* is a subfield of this larger project that would enable geometric discoveries and proofs via a formalism that had no direct reference to geometric figures; hence the imagination would no longer have to burden itself with drawing diagrams, imagining circles and triangles, etc., but could simply manipulate a set of symbols according to rule. Now as it happened, this was already possible to do, and in fact many of the advances in geometry during this period could dispense with diagrams. It was Descartes who had successfully converted geometric problems into an algebraic form and solved them with algebraic methods. So, for instance, a circle could be represented by the equation $x^2 + y^2 = r^2$, where r is the radius of the circle. But Leibniz hoped to avoid the detour though algebra and solve geometric problems through a characteristic that was itself geometric. And the basis for this method was situatedness, or *situs*. A point in geometric space has no absolute location; it is simply situated with respect to other points, and so it is defined by its spatial relations to those other points. *Analysis situs* attempted to establish a geometry that is based purely on situatedness and hence on spatial relation. As a project, this didn't get very far, and Leibniz never managed to prove anything with his *analysis situs* beyond the most trivial and self-evident facts of geometry.[6] But the aspirations and method of the project are important.

Analysis situs is based entirely on the principles of geometric similarity and congruence. To review: geometric figures are *similar* if they have the same shape. All circles are similar, being round, even if they are of different sizes. The same is true of squares and of triangles that have the same angles. Figures are *congruent* if they are similar *and* have the same magnitude. Hence all circles with a radius of 2 are congruent (and similar as well). Congruent figures, having both the same shape and the same magnitude, are identical, except that they may be differently oriented and situated in space. To get a sense of the flavor of *analysis situs*, consider its ways of defining a circle, a sphere, and a plane. We'll start with the circle, though in fact I'll be cheating here. Let's take a circle with center point Q and point R on the circumference. The line QR is the radius, as shown in figure 5.2.

One way to define a circle is to say that it is the set of endpoints of all radii with endpoint R whose other endpoint is the center Q. So if QR is a straight

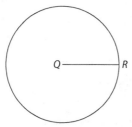

5.2 Circle with radius.

line, and all straight lines of equal length are congruent, a circle would be the complete set of endpoints of other radii of the circle, i.e., of all straight lines of equal length with endpoint Q (you can produce these other lines by imaginarily moving the radius QR around the center Q as if it were the hand of a clock). Now the circle is defined not by roundness but by the congruence of rays emerging from Q—hence by their relative positions or situations in space. (The reason I'm cheating is that since we live in three-dimensional space, the set of all congruent rays centered on Q will be a sphere, not a circle. Additional specifications will be needed to produce a circle. Leibniz requires triangles to do that.) A plane is defined by taking two points A and B that are separated in space, and drawing straight lines from those points such that the lines are congruent (i.e., of equal length) when they intersect (figure 5.3).

So, AX will be congruent with BX, and AX' will be congruent with BX'. If you take the complete set of intersecting, congruent straight lines emanating from points A and B, the result will be a plane. Again, a plane can now be *defined* as the set of intersection points of congruent lines running from points A and B, without invoking a figure or image directly. Similar procedures can be used to define lines, points, etc., through relations of situatedness and congruence. Moving from congruence to similarity, Leibniz can demonstrate that, for instance, if

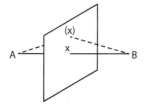

5.3 Plane as set of intersection points of congruent lines radiating from two fixed points. Image from G. W. Leibniz, *Philosophical Papers and Letters*, 2nd ed., trans. and ed. Leroy E. Loemker (Dordrecht: Reidel, 1969), p. 252.

the sides of triangles are proportional, the triangles are similar, or that circles are to each other as the squares of their diameters.

Although the accomplishments of *analysis situs* were minimal, its influence on Leibniz's thought was extensive. Transferring the notion of *situs* from geometric space to the real world, Leibniz challenged Newton's notion of space, claiming that both position and movement are only relative between entities, which have *situs* but no absolute position. More broadly, as Vincenzo De Risi has shown, *analysis situs* had wide-ranging effects on Leibniz's metaphysics, including his concepts of expression and spatiotemporal phenomenology.[7]

Here I want to see what *analysis situs* can tell us about Leibniz's style of thinking, by focusing on its concept of similarity. As Leibniz states in "Metaphysical Foundations of Mathematics": "*Equals* are things having the same quantity. *Similars* are things having the same quality."[8] He elaborates in "Studies in a Geometry of Situation":

> Besides quantity, figure in general includes also quality or form. And as those figures are *equal* whose magnitude is the same, so those are *similar* whose form is the same. The theory of similarities or of forms lies beyond mathematics and must be sought in metaphysics. Yet it has many uses in mathematics also, being of use even in the algebraic calculus itself. But *similarity* is seen best of all in the *situations* or figures of geometry.[9]

The equal sign (=) in algebraic equations indicates a merely quantitative equivalence between the expressions on either side and therefore tells us nothing about them qualitatively. But similarity is based on formal or qualitative elements inherent to the things being compared and therefore gets at something more specific and fundamental about them. The assumption here is that a circle's being circular, which makes it similar to other circles, matters more than the size of the circle because the circle's qualitative form is what makes it what it is and can be described without reference to magnitude. Indeed, Leibniz viewed the magnitude of geometric figures as somehow less substantial than their forms. Magnitude is something merely comparative (Leibniz claimed) and can be grasped only by beholding two figures in each other's presence, while the formal, qualitative features are definitionally inherent to each.

When Leibniz states that "the theory of similarities or forms lies beyond mathematics and must be sought in metaphysics," he is drawing a connection between geometric form and the role of substantial form in his metaphysics. That being said, the translation from geometric to metaphysical similarity cannot be a direct one, because Leibniz's metaphysics insists that every monad is different from every other, just as every physical body is different from every other. Geometric similarity in any literal sense is therefore not to be found in nature. As Leibniz never tired of repeating, no two leaves are exactly alike. He appears rather to be thinking about the fact that in both metaphysics and geometry, form is what makes a thing what it is. So another analogical similarity has been drawn, this time on the topic of formal similarity itself.

What I have been sidling up to is the fact that Leibniz's *analysis situs*, with its insistence on a world constructed from pure relationality, is congenial with his general style of thinking, which is consistently analogical. In establishing relations of similarity between the qualitative aspects of things, the demonstrations of *analysis situs* conduct a kind of conceptual work in which Leibniz is more broadly engaged, including his use of the rhetorical figures of similitude. The mathematics of resemblance resembles the figurations of resemblance, and this analogy is itself the product of a mind devoted to analogical thinking.

It also upends our casual notions about the nature of analogy. Often, we construe similarity as a pale, incomplete version of identity, and we tend therefore to denigrate analogical or metaphorical statements by employing phrases such as "merely analogical" or "just a metaphor," as if the resemblances established there were mere imperfect gesturings toward some unstated but more fundamental identity or equality. But in Leibnizian mathematics, the "is like" of the geometrically similar trumps the "is" (the same) of the quantitatively equal, and therefore to resemble something is more fundamental than to be the equivalent of it. And Leibniz applies this lesson to metaphysical thinking as well, which should cause us to hesitate in constructing hierarchies of assertion that privilege logical statements of identity or inclusion over metaphorical ones. Mathematics is (like) figuration, and figuration is (like) mathematics.[10] And because of this, the priority of "is" over "is like" in Leibniz's writings cannot simply be assumed.

CHAPTER 6

Cognitive Mapping and Blended Spaces

I have thus far been exploring the role of analogy on the microlevels of rhetorical figure and sentence-production. But they are also fully operative on the macrolevels of Leibnizian thought. Sometimes they work explicitly and play crucial roles in his metaphysical "system." Thus, for example, the physical world expresses (and is in turn expressed by) the monadic one, such that each is isomorphic to the other. But sometimes—more often, in fact—isomorphisms operate unannounced, as Leibniz models one area of his thinking on another. Analogy plays a significant role in Leibniz's metaphysics, that is to say, but it plays an even larger role in the process of producing that metaphysics. Mathematical models abound there, but aesthetic, theological, and others do as well. Analogy and isomorphism connect the diverse discursive realms in which Leibniz works, such that each one fertilizes the others.

It has become increasingly apparent over recent decades that analogy is central to human thought as such. In 1992, David Chalmers, Robert French, and Douglas Hofstadter wrote:

One gets the impression from the work of most researchers that analogy-making is conceived of as a special tool in reasoning or problem-solving, a heavy weapon wheeled out now and then to deal with especially tough problems. Our view, by contrast, is that analogy-making is going on constantly in the background of the mind, helping to shape our perceptions of everyday situations. In our view, analogy is not separate from perception: analogy-making itself is a perceptual process.[1]

Or, as Gilles Fauconnier puts it:

> Our conceptual networks are intricately structured by analogical and met-
> aphorical mappings, which play a key role in the synchronic construction
> of meaning and in its diachronic evolution. Parts of such mappings are so
> entrenched in everyday thought and language that we do not consciously
> notice them; other parts strike us as novel and creative. The term *metaphor* is
> often applied to the latter, highlighting the literary and poetic aspects of the
> phenomenon. But the general cognitive principles at work are the same, and
> they play a key role in thought and language at all levels.[2]

Leibniz himself remarks in the *New Essays on Human Understanding* that "In so far
as you conceive the similarities among things, you are conceiving something in
addition [to the things themselves], and that is all that universality is."[3] While this
statement demotes similarities ontologically (they are not themselves real things),
it simultaneously installs them at the foundation of thinking by making them the
basis of concept-formation.

I have focused hitherto on rhetorical figures of similitude (metaphor, simile,
analogy), but now I want us to see these as the outcroppings of a vast under-
ground system of analogical processes, often implicit, at work in Leibniz's
philosophizing. I also want to gather these rhetorical elements together with the
structural isomorphisms discussed above and fold them into an umbrella term:
cognitive mapping.[4] The term "cognitive map" was coined by the cognitive psychologist Edward C. Tolman in 1948 and has been widely employed since then in
a variety of fields.[5] Here I shall focus on the work of the cognitive linguist Gilles
Fauconnier.[6] Fauconnier notes that "mapping, in the most general mathematical
sense, is a correspondence between two sets that assigns to each element in the
first a counterpart in the second."[7] Although Leibniz predated set theory, his
analogy comparing the relation between external objects and their mental representations with that between different conic sections offers a striking anticipation, since he notes that each point on one section finds an answering point
on the other. In Leibniz's analogy, mental mapping takes place between the mind
and the world, whereas for Fauconnier it occurs within the mind, between different cognitive domains or "spaces." Thought largely involves the mapping of one
cognitive domain or space (the "source") onto another (the "target"). Mapping

transfers individual elements from the source domain onto the target and, in the case of projective mapping, elements of the organizing structures of the source domain as well:

> The general (and deep) idea is that, in order to talk and think about some domains (*target* domains) we use the structure of other domains (*source* domains) and the corresponding vocabulary. Some of these mappings are used by all members of a culture—for instance, in English, TIME AS SPACE. We use structure from our everyday conception of space and motion to organize our everyday conception of time, as when we say: *Christmas is approaching; The weeks go by; Summer is around the corner; The long day stretched out with no end in sight.*[8]

Cognitive mapping enables the most basic, quotidian forms of human thinking as well as the most advanced, sophisticated ones. One of its most interesting variants, and one especially pertinent to our purposes, is "conceptual blending," in which one space is not simply mapped onto another but the two blend or merge into a third, composite space. "*The blend inherits partial structure* from the input spaces and *has emergent structure* of its own."[9] The emergent properties of conceptually blended spaces are conducive to creativity and discovery because they cannot be predicted in advance. It has been argued that in the field of mathematics, conceptual blending played a role in the discovery of, for instance, imaginary numbers and hyperbolic geometry; in physics, the diaries of James Clerk Maxwell likewise provide evidence of conceptual blending at work.[10]

If my book has any one central thesis, it is that Leibniz's work is marked by especially complex, creative, and insistent acts of cognitive mapping. These can take many forms and occur on various levels. Sometimes they are patent and sometimes they hum quietly in the background, but their informing power is no less powerful for that. Whatever Leibniz may be saying at a given moment, what he is usually *doing* (not always exclusively, but as part of the mix) involves cognitive mapping. His work is therefore marked primarily not by a particular set of positions, much less by a system, but by a characteristic *trait*. His analogies, metaphors, isomorphisms, and acts of modeling are all variants of this one activity.

In putting the matter this way, I invite comparison with Gilles Deleuze's reading of Leibniz and the baroque, in which both are likewise marked by a dominant trait: that of folding. It seems to me that the conceit of folding works especially well (or at least, has been most influential) when applied to the material realm and becomes somewhat more nebulous when applied to the mental, monadic realm. So if someone wants to say that my reading of Leibniz through cognitive mapping is, among other things, a way of reconceptualizing Deleuze's concept of folding, I will not object in the least.[11]

Leibniz himself appears to endorse cognitive mapping, if not in so many words, in the following passage: "One who deals with only a limited field rarely discovers anything new, since he soon exhausts his subject. But from those who investigate many different things and are gifted with a combinatorial genius we may expect many new and useful interconnections of things."[12] Leibniz possessed nothing if not "combinatorial genius," the capacity to produce blended conceptual spaces from which new discoveries would emerge. A few pages later in the same essay ("On the Elements of Natural Science"), he observes:

> The hypothetical method a posteriori, which proceeds from experiments, rests for the most part upon analogies. For instance, seeing that many terrestrial phenomena agree with magnetic phenomena, some men teach that the earth is a great magnet, that the structure of the earth corresponds to this, and that heavy bodies are drawn to earth as a magnet draws iron. Others explain everything by fermentation, even the ebb and flow of the tides. Still others, seeing that lye fights against acids, reduce all corporeal conflicts to those of acid and alkali. We must guard against the abuse of analogies. Yet they can be of exceedingly great use in making inductions and in setting up aphorisms from inductions by means of which we can also make predictions about matters of which we as yet have little experience. This too is useful in investigating the true causes of things, for it is always easier to discover the cause of a phenomenon which several things have in common.[13]

While Leibniz warns against "the abuse of analogies," this seems to involve totalizing the reach of any single one, resulting in explanations that are both impoverished and overextended. The point appears to be not that one shouldn't analogize, but rather that one should have a variety of analogical perspectives at the ready. An abundance of knowledge, and a multiplicity of analogical frameworks, are prerequisites for productive scientific thought—and more specifically, for Leibniz's own transdisciplinary style. That style works, not only by incorporating a diversity of disciplinary perspectives and objects, but also by ensuring that none of these achieves either explanatory or methodological dominance over the others, thus reducing a plurality of perspectives to a single, master discourse.

I invoke the notion of transdisciplinary style because I think it can further enrich Fauconnier's notion of cognitive mapping and help us get at something distinctively Leibnizian. Cognitive mapping involves the transfer of individual concepts or thought objects from one cognitive realm to another, and also of the conceptual relations in which those objects are already inevitably embedded. But if we now think of these cognitive spaces as disciplinary, then intellectual objects are likewise embedded in—and to some degree produced by—the "thought styles" peculiar to each of those disciplines.[14] When we speak of cognitive mappings and conceptual blends in Leibniz, then, I propose that these notions should include *stylistic* transfers and blendings among disciplines as well. The philosopher Friedrich Schlegel employs the term "chemical wit" (the subject of module 07) to describe Leibniz's distinctive transdisciplinary style, and in so doing ascribes aesthetic as well as cognitive effects to it. We shall see later on how this style is perpetuated by some notable twentieth-century thinkers.

Mathematical modeling may well be Leibniz's most widespread form of cognitive mapping.[15] The mathematics of infinitesimals contributes, for example, to Leibniz's conception of material bodies as composed of ever-smaller, nested creatures as well as to his treatment of *petites perceptions*. But in the former, elements of contemporary biology and microscopy also come into play; and in the latter, the proto-aesthetic category of the *je ne sais quoi*. Multiple models generally converge in Leibniz's thought without any one establishing dominance, thereby producing blended conceptual spaces. The premier example of this is his most celebrated term, the monad. Just consider the number of descriptions, and associated discursive fields, that converge there: monads are perceptions driven by appetition (biology, psychology); they are perspectives (optics, painting, projective geometry); they are arrays of forces (physics); they are infinite series (mathematics—see module 10); they are complete individual concepts built from articulated sets of predicates (logic); they are mirrors of God (theology), etc. In fact, the word "monad" does not name a *concept* at all; it names a blended conceptual space where Leibniz's "combinatorial genius" endlessly weaves concepts and structures borrowed from elsewhere. And the variously blended components never quite congeal into a self-consistent concept, which is why Leibniz's notion lends itself to endless exposition and debate. Likewise, the various perspectives that Leibniz brings to bear do not congeal into a self-consistent system; at least, the ideal of systematicity does not prevent Leibniz from multiplying analogical perspectives for their fertilizing effects, even if they cannot immediately be reconciled.

There is a passage in the *New Essays on Human Understanding* where this process is given a striking figurative expression.

> PHIL. §17. "The understanding is not much unlike a closet wholly shut from light, with only some little openings left, to let in external visible [images]; would the [images] coming into such a dark room but stay there, and lie so orderly as to be found upon occasion, it would very much resemble the understanding of a man."

> THEO. To increase the resemblance we should have to postulate that there is a screen in this dark room to receive the species, and that it is not uniform but is diversified by folds representing items of innate knowledge; and, what is more, that this screen or membrane, being under tension, has a kind of elasticity or active force, and indeed that it acts (or reacts) in ways which are adapted both to past folds and to new ones coming from impressions of the species. This action would consist in certain vibrations or oscillations, like those we see when a cord under tension is plucked and gives off something of a musical sound. For not only do we receive images and traces in the brain, but we form new ones from them when we bring "complex ideas" to mind; and so the screen which represents our brain must be active and elastic. This analogy would explain reasonably well what goes on in the brain. As for the soul, which is a simple substance or "monad": without being extended it represents these various extended masses and has perceptions of them.[16]

Philalethes, who represents Locke in this dialogue, repeats from book II, chapter xi of the *Essay Concerning Human Understanding*, where Locke compares the understanding to a *camera obscura*. Theophilus, who represents Leibniz, responds with some modifications. Locke's analogy is already a suggestive one, but Leibniz alters it almost beyond recognition. Putting aside for the moment the changes to the source analogy itself, one should note first that Leibniz changes its target, which in Locke is the understanding and in Leibniz is the brain. Locke, that is to say, describes the passage from the external to the mental world, while Leibniz converts this to a process occurring entirely within the external, physical world.

The monad's act of perception will express these physical changes, which adds another layer of analogical mediation. This passage attempts to depict monadic perception by way of its physical correlates in the brain.

Leibniz adds a screen to the dark room, which would serve the same image-receiving function as Locke's wall, only the screen is also "diversified by folds representing items of innate knowledge." These folds both make the screen more like a brain in appearance and render it less obviously suitable for projecting images onto. They represent the fact that the mind is not, in Leibniz's view, a *tabula rasa* for the reception of knowledge from without but has its knowledge preprogrammed into it. The brain's folds would therefore be the physical expression of this innate knowledge, which transforms what impinges on it.

While the brain is, in fact, folded, it also here invokes the fact that for Leibniz, organic bodies as such are folded—or rather, are the unfolding of a folded seed—a notion entailed by the preformationist biology of Anton van Leeuwenhoek and Jan Swammerdam.[17] At the same time, as Deleuze appears to suggest, Leibniz could have absorbed the concept of the fold from the visual culture of the baroque. This latter association might be invoked here by the fact that the *camera obscura* was employed as an aid by baroque painters such as Johannes Vermeer. And then Leibniz's folded screen emits a musical note. That it references both biology and the artwork suggests that it is already the product of a blended conceptual space.

The folded screen is further folded by the visual species that impinge upon it; or rather, it acts in response to that impingement. Here Leibniz is drawing on his physics of forces. Elasticity is the active force in physical bodies. In Leibniz's view, a billiard ball struck by another is not passively sent on its way by the force of the ball that strikes it. Rather, the billiard ball's own active force, in the form of elasticity, acts in response to the "occasion" offered by its being struck. But derivative forces are merely the physical expression of the primary forces in monads. Since the screen in Leibniz's analogy serves as the physical expression of the primary force in a perceiving monad, it too must be elastic. If I am reading the image correctly (and I by no means feel confident here), the elasticity of the folded, vibrating screen transforms the visual folds in the incoming visual species into musical waves. And some mental counterpart to this convoluted physical process—i.e., its expression—is occurring in the monad.

I don't think that the logic of this image can be worked out to any great degree of specificity. Rather, it seems to me the result of a kind of figurational overload entailed by Leibniz's attempt to give visual form to the process of monadic perception. There are so many descriptions of monadic activity available from so many domains that the attempt to integrate them into a single image breaks down. In a sense, Leibniz's screen is "folded" by the multiplicity of discourses that contribute to the monad as blended conceptual space and that cannot be given a coherent visual expression because they cannot be fully reconciled with one another. The attempt to do so results in an uncanny, overdetermined, somewhat monstrous image. At once screen and musical string, not-quite-animate but not-quite-dead, either, this folding, humming entity is not necessarily something you want to meet with in a dark room. But it pulses with the creative energy of the blended space to which it tries in vain to give shape.

This visual experiment gone awry manifests another important aspect of Leibniz's blended spaces: they are the cognitive workshops in which he tinkers. The emergent properties of conceptually blended spaces enable creative problem-solving to occur. But they can also be cultivated for their own sake, as perpetual sources of experimentation, innovation, and delight. Leibniz employs blended spaces for purposes of philosophical problem-solving, to be sure. But he also employs them to tinker—to fuel the endless processes of thinking and writing, the ceaseless reformulations and rejiggerings that he so enjoys. In his case, blended spaces are not transitional but perpetual. They are nurtured both for philosophical ends and as things to be valued in themselves.

CHAPTER 7

Chemical Wit

Viewing Leibniz's philosophical style through cognitive mapping and conceptual blends has the advantage of connecting it to some very fundamental elements of human cognition. The corresponding disadvantage is that by doing so, one risks dissolving Leibniz's particularity into a shared generality. The best I could do in the previous module was to state that Leibniz's cognitive mappings are "especially complex, creative, and insistent." But this does not tell us much about the flavor of Leibniz's philosophical style; in fact, it tells us very little at all.

A potentially more promising approach is offered by Friedrich Schlegel in his *Athenaeum Fragments*:

> If wit in all its manifestations is the principle and the organ of universal philosophy, and if all philosophy is nothing but the spirit of universality, the science of all the eternally dividing and uniting sciences, a logical chemistry; then the value and importance of that absolute, enthusiastic, thoroughly material wit is infinite, that wit wherein Bacon and Leibniz, the chief representatives of scholastic prose, were masters, the former among the first, chronologically speaking, the latter among the greatest. The most important scientific discoveries are *bon mot* of this sort—are so because of the surprising contingency of their origin, the unifying force of their thought, and the baroqueness of their casual expression. The best ones are *échappées de vue* into the infinite. Leibniz's whole philosophy consists of a few fragments and projects that are witty in this sense. (fragment 220)[1]

Several elements in Schlegel's take on Leibniz recommend themselves: he recognizes Leibniz's greatness as a writer; he identifies Leibniz's style as baroque; and his take on Leibniz's philosophy is radically anti-systematic. In fact, not only radically but suspiciously so. By making Leibniz into a producer of witty fragments, the author of the *Athenaeum Fragments* also converts him into a mirror of himself. One should therefore approach Schlegel's characterization with at least some caution. That being acknowledged, Schlegel's depiction of Leibniz as a *witty* writer, though perhaps not immediately intuitive, has a good deal to be said for it. Herder, as we have seen, preceded Schlegel in describing Leibniz as witty.

The concept of wit is variously inflected by different writers and national traditions. But all share a common core: wit is the ability to grasp resemblances and connections, usually of an unexpected and surprising sort, between apparently unlike things. It is a capacity frequently (though by no means exclusively) attributed to poets in the seventeenth and eighteenth centuries. One *locus classicus* is Samuel Johnson's critique of the metaphysical poets:

> Wit . . . may be more rigorously and philosophically considered as a kind of *discordia concors*; a combination of dissimilar images, or discovery of occult resemblances in things apparently unlike. Of wit, thus defined, they [the metaphysical poets] have more than enough. The most heterogeneous ideas are yoked by violence together; nature and art are ransacked for illustrations, comparisons, and allusions; their learning instructs, and their subtlety surprises; but the reader thinks his improvement dearly bought, and, though he sometimes admires, is seldom pleased.[2]

Johnson depicts wit as an unstable equilibrium of forces—a binding together of things that of their own natures desperately wish to fly apart. This metaphorical energetics is picked up by Schlegel when he describes wit as a "logical chemistry." In fragment 336, he elaborates: "Understanding is mechanical, wit is chemical, and genius is organic spirit."[3] For Schlegel, the conceptual bond between ideas effected by wit is like the chemical bond formed between elements. Antoine Lavoisier's chemistry, which would have been the most current at the moment of the *Athenaeum Fragments*, held that particles exerted an inherently attractive force, while heat (or as Lavoisier called it, caloric) exerted a repulsive one upon chemical substances. It hardly needs pointing out that Schlegel's notion of "chemical wit" is an example of what it describes, since it bonds concepts from the scientific realm of chemistry and the cultural realm of *belles lettres* in a surprising manner. It radiates intellectual energy in the same way that forming a chemical bond can give off heat. One of the things that Schlegel's formulation suggests is that mapping can have an affective or indeed aesthetic dimension as well as a cognitive one. The blended conceptual space is a kind of cognitive laboratory in which new insights and connections are generated. But this intellectual process is also productive of the pleasurable aesthetic shocks associated with "wit"—shocks that result when the mind unexpectedly apprehends connections among elements previously thought to be widely separated. Chemical wit is a transdisciplinary aesthetic, juxtaposing unlike intellectual objects often garnered from distant disciplinary areas. Its energy is generated not merely by juxtaposing unlikely intellectual objects but also by juxtaposing the different "thought styles" in which those objects are inevitably embedded.

In ascribing chemical wit to Leibniz, Schlegel regards him not as a builder of systems but as someone whose unexpected mappings of concepts onto one another produce flashes of insight. This anti-systematic reading is, moreover, something that Schlegel has in common with Herder. As we saw, Herder's Leibniz is a spontaneous poet whose fecund rhetorical figures are bound up into a system only by his less-talented epigones. By insisting on a "witty" Leibniz, Herder and Schlegel seem to be placing him not in the usual company of Spinoza and Descartes but rather with metaphysical poets such as John Donne and George Herbert, who likewise surprised with their juxtapositions. Donne's famous comparison of the souls of two lovers to "stiff twin compasses" exemplifies Schlegel's notion of a chemical (or, as he also calls it, "material") wit, bringing the embodied and the disembodied together in striking fashion. And doesn't Leibniz do something of the same when he brings concepts from physics or logic to bear on the notion of the monad? While juxtaposing Leibniz with the metaphysical poets might itself seem like a (merely) "witty" conceit—a violent yoking together of opposites—I think it can also be productive of new, unexpected insights into Leibniz's philosophical manner. I am not suggesting that Herder's and Schlegel's versions of Leibniz are the only *correct* ones. I am suggesting that they produce *another* Leibniz, Leibniz as viewed from a different perspective that might further enrich and energize the more usual ones. In any case, the notion of wit has something suggestive to say about Leibniz's *manner* of mapping, and about the intellectual sparks it strikes off. Leibniz is a witty mapper, a violent yoker together of opposites, and a mad chemist.

CHAPTER 8

Perspective

L eibniz's modernity is perhaps nowhere so evident as in the radically perspectival nature of his metaphysics. Nietzsche is his heir in this above all else. Leibniz's perspectivalism is partly a matter of content: substances or monads are, for him, points of view on the universe. But the perspectivalism of content entails a corresponding perspectivalism of method as well. Perspective is Leibniz's way of thinking relation and transformation and their roles in knowledge. As such, it is also his way of conceptualizing his central activity of cognitive mapping, and thus of transdisciplinary insight. To understand a phenomenon means, for Leibniz, to multiply perspectives upon it—to see it from various points of view, which is just another way of saying that multiple models are mapped onto it.

The notion of perspective is itself a product of mapping since it occupies a point where three different discourses and practices converge, imperfectly. One is optics, or *perspectiva naturalis*, as it was known in the Middle Ages. A second is Renaissance painting, which is more or less defined by its discovery of perspective, or *perspectiva artificialis*. Third is the mathematical art of perspective, which grew from projective geometry. The imperfections of convergence among these three, as well as the convergences themselves, are of interest. Projective geometry, principally the work of the French mathematician Gérard Desargues, finally (or at least apparently) completed a project that Renaissance painters had aimed at for centuries: providing a secure set of mathematical procedures governing the ways that objects in space appear in the human field of vision. Mathematical perspective rationalized visual space, and with it the relative scale of objects in space, their lines of recession or diminution, and their transformations as point of view shifts. In so doing it also provided a model for perspective as practiced by artists. The French artist Abraham Bosse incorporated Desargues's work into his various treatises on perspective, going so far as to directly reproduce sections of Desargues's paper on projective geometry in his *Manière Universelle de Mr Desargues, Pour Pratiquer la Perspective* (1648). Leibniz was familiar with the work of both Bosse and Desargues, the latter of whom influenced Leibniz's own unpublished works on mathematical perspective.[1] Mathematical space, optical space, and painterly space are unified under the concept of perspective.

Only they aren't, completely. As Erwin Panofsky famously pointed out in *Perspective as Symbolic Form*, the mathematics of linear perspective only approximates the realities of visual perception:

> In a sense, perspective transforms psychophysiological space into mathematical space. It negates the differences between front and back, between right and left, between bodies and intervening space ("empty" space), so that the sum of all the parts of space and all its contents are absorbed into a single "quantum continuum." It forgets that we see not with a single fixed eye but with two constantly moving eyes, resulting in a spheroidal field of vision. . . . Perspectival construction [also] ignores the crucial circumstance that this retinal image—entirely apart from its subsequent psychological "interpretation," and even apart from the fact that the eyes move—is a projection not on a flat but on a concave surface.[2]

That being said, Panofsky held that painterly perspective in the Renaissance "succeeded in mathematically fully rationalizing an image of space which had already earlier been aesthetically unified."[3] In other words, while linear mathematics and the psychophysiology of optics may have been at variance, mathematics and painterly space were at one during the Renaissance. But this latter assumption has in turn been subject to critique by James Elkins, who argues persuasively that Renaissance painting did not incorporate mathematically rationalized space and often not even a single, unified point of view; that the mathematics of Renaissance treatises on perspective represented *ad hoc* improvisation; and that Renaissance painters were not interested in depicting space at all but rather objects and their relations.[4] It is rather during the baroque period that mathematical and painterly perspective begin seriously to converge and that the artistic representation of space becomes a goal. Baroque practices of trompe l'oeil, anamorphosis, and forced perspective (in all of which Leibniz demonstrates interest, as we shall see) trumpet a more secure technical mastery of the geometry of perspective. Optical, painterly, and mathematical spaces do tend to converge in Leibniz's era, without ever quite perfectly coinciding.

I shall focus on the aesthetic rather than the mathematical dimensions of Leibnizian perspective, in part because the former have received less attention.[5] But the mathematics of perspective does offer an important lesson. In transforming objects while retaining their properties, projective geometry makes clear that perspective is not "subjective" and not merely distorting. It thus supports Deleuze's claim that baroque perspective "is not a variation of the truth according to the subject, but the condition in which the truth of a variation appears to the subject."[6]

According to Leibniz, "each soul is a mirror of the entire world, from its own point of view."[7] A soul mirrors the world in perceiving it; its perceptions redouble the universe as a mirror would—and, like a mirror, it reflects the universe back to itself from the particular place it occupies, its point of view. But how does a soul perceive the whole world at once? Not visually, to be sure, since the eye's cone of vision encompasses only a fraction of three-dimensional space at a given moment, even if we extend the cone indefinitely. Likewise, a mirror cannot reflect what is behind it. Perhaps Leibniz has a spherical mirror in mind, but he never says so. This problem provides the first indication that visual perspective is to be understood figuratively, not literally. As Leibniz states, "monads in themselves do not even have situation with respect to each other—at least one that is real, which extends beyond the order of phenomena."[8] Monads do not exist in space, and hence their relations with one another are not spatial. The phenomenon of visual position in space therefore represents or expresses something else.

Here Leibniz gives an initial sense of that something else:

Moreover it is no wonder that a mind perceives what is going on in the whole world, since there is no body so minute that it will not, given the plenitude of the world, sense all others. And so there arises in this way a wonderful variety, for there are as many different relations in the universe as there are minds—just as when the same town is looked at from different locations. So, by creating a plurality of minds, God wanted to bring about for the universe what some painter does for a large town, when he wants to display delineations of its various aspects or projections: the painter does on canvas what God does in the mind.[9]

The human body perceives the universe because the universe is a plenum. When any physical body moves, therefore, it impinges on the bodies around it; and even if it doesn't move, it resists bodies that push against it. And because of the plenum, that movement or presence is passed along from body to contiguous body in its environs, and from there throughout the entire universe. Hence the existence and movement of everything in the world presses upon, and is at some level registered by, our bodies. Most of this will be perceived confusedly, indeed unconsciously. But some things, in the vicinity of our bodies, will be registered more distinctly by our sense organs. And mental counterparts to all of this physical activity will occur in our minds, thus constituting perception of the whole world. What Leibniz means by "point of view" in perception is thus not a visual positioning but the array of distinct and confused perceptions available to a monad, many of them tactile—an array determined in part, but not wholly, by the physical locations of our bodies in space.

In this passage, Leibniz adds two elements that recur frequently: comparing the point of view of minds upon the universe with visual points of view upon a town, and comparing optical and painterly perspective. Indeed, these are here condensed, so that perception is compared directly to painting, or to multiple paintings. We will return to this point. First, though, there is more to say about the metaphysics of point of view. The whole point of multiplying perspectives is to create a "wonderful variety." In a sense, there are as many universes as there are minds to perceive it in different ways. Indeed, since ordered variety is an imperative of divine creation, God must make as many minds, and hence perspectives, as the universe will conveniently hold.[10] And these are not solely human minds, either. "It is to have a very impoverished idea of the author of nature (who multiplies as far as he can, his *little worlds*, or *indivisible active mirrors*) to accord them only to human bodies: it is in fact impossible that they are not everywhere."[11] Point of view is thus determined, not only by the spatial locations of bodies but also by their different sensoria. A grasshopper perceives differently from the way you or I do, not only because it is perched on a blade of grass and we are not, but also because it sees through grasshopper eyes and with a grasshopper mind.[12] Likewise, at a less drastic level of difference, you and I perceive differently because of our different sensibilities, experiences, and kinds of knowledge. All of these things are figured by visual positioning but clearly go well beyond it.

The imperatives of abundance and variety that govern divine creation dictate that God must pack as many perspectives as possible into the world, and thus create as many minds as possible. At the same time, there are limits: "It follows from the perfection of the Supreme Maker not only that the order of the universe is the most perfect that could be, but also that every living mirror which represents the universe according to its own point of view, that is to say every monad, every substantial centre, must have its perceptions and its appetites ordered in the best way that remains compatible with all the rest."[13] Here we encounter Leibniz's doctrine of compossibility, in which only those creatures achieve being that are compatible with one another so as to ensure the optimality of the whole. Say I am running a graduate seminar on Leibniz. That seminar generates many different, interesting perspectives by way of the participating students, and thus contributes to the perceptual variety of the universe. God could increase that diversity of perspectives still further by placing a Bengal tiger in the classroom. Its view of the proceedings would be refreshingly different from ours. But the presence of the Bengal tiger is not compossible with the continued conduct of the seminar, so God must choose.

Moreover, potential (and potentially incompatible) perspectives are constantly straining toward actualization:

> From the very fact that something exists rather than nothing, there is a certain urgency [*exigentia*] toward existence in possible things or in possibility or essence itself—a pre-tension to exist, so to speak—and, in a word, that essence in itself tends to exist. From this it follows further that all possible things, or things expressing an essence or possible reality, tend toward existence with equal right in proportion to the quantity of essence or reality, or to the degree of perfection which they involve; for perfection is nothing but quantity of essence.
>
> Hence it is very clearly understood that out of the infinite combinations and series of possible things, one exists through which the greatest amount of essence or possibility is brought into existence.[14]

In light of this, it is not sufficient to say that every entity has its own perspective (a banal enough observation, in any case). Rather, for Leibniz, the privilege of becoming a real entity at all results from the quality of perspective it can bring to bear and from how that enriches the whole. Perspective is ontologically prior to existence, and hence existence is merely a vehicle for perspective. A vast multiplicity of perspectives aches to be, and God must choose an array such that they do not block one another's view when actualized. The town exists for the array of perspectives it yields.

Leibniz's philosophical intuition takes striking artistic form in David Hockney's photomontages (figure 8.1). With a nod to cubism's "view from everywhere" (and perhaps to Francis Bacon as well), these works deconstruct not so much the visual object as perspective itself.[15] Or rather, they create a space of pure potentiality in which possible perspectives swarm and interfere with one another and

8.1 David Hockney, "Mother I, Yorkshire Moors, August 1985," photographic collage, © David Hockney, photo by Richard Schmidt.

compete for realization. Abjuring—or perhaps simply prior to—God's work of choosing "the best," and thus freed from the imperatives of coherence and optimality, Hockney allows a multiplicity of perspectives to coexist. The effect is of a visual plenum in which every possible space is filled with perspectival beings.

Leibniz's perspectivism accords with his notion of *situs* or relative position. Entities have location only with respect to one another, and so both position and movement are radically perspectival:

> A remarkable fact: motion is something relative, and one cannot distinguish exactly which of the bodies is moving. Thus if motion is an affection, its subject will not be any one individual body, but the whole world. Hence all its effects must also necessarily be relative. The absolute motion we imagine to ourselves, however, is nothing but an affection of our soul while we consider ourselves or other things as immobile, since we are able to understand everything more easily when these things are considered as immobile.[16]

We falsely imagine that other bodies are moving and that we are at rest because we absolutize our own perspective, whereas from another reference frame the apparently moving body would appear to be at rest and we would be seen to be in motion. Neither reference frame is correct in any absolute sense, and so motion is merely perspectival. Leibniz's relativism seems in some respects to anticipate the equivalence of non-inertial reference frames in Einstein's special theory of relativity. And it had consequences for Leibniz's understanding of contemporary issues in astronomy. For instance, it was unnecessary—indeed, impossible—to decide between the Copernican and Ptolemaic systems in any absolute sense if motion was merely relative. And as Michel Serres argues, this position is more radical than the Copernican revolution itself. Copernicus displaced Earth from the center of the cosmos, but Leibniz removed the very possibility of a center.[17] For Leibniz there is only relative position and relative movement, with nothing to center or ground them. In other words, there is nothing but perspectives.

This relativism extends to metaphysical issues as well: "To reinforce the distinction between essence and definition, bear in mind that although a thing has only one essence, this can be expressed by several definitions, just as the same structure or the same town can be represented by different drawings in perspective depending on the direction from which it is viewed."[18] A multiplicity of definitions is a sign of conceptual blending, which Leibniz here understands via perspective. Take the monad, again: it is, from one perspective, a set of forces; from another, a complete individuated concept; from yet another, a law of the series, and so forth. Every definition is a way of viewing the monad from the place of a different discourse. (It is as if Hockney's photomontages took conceptual form.) And Leibniz's invocation of drawings in perspective undergirds the epistemological relativism of his stance. There is no one "right" way to depict a town but rather a multiplicity of rewarding views, and likewise there is no one right definition of something like the monad. Different perspectives simply bring different aspects of it into focus. Leibniz's perspectivalism thus feeds the anti-systematic component of his thought. While Leibniz sometimes (and rather tentatively) attempts to synthesize the various perspectival descriptions of the monad, he also understands them *as perspectives* that are mutually exclusive in the sense that the viewer can occupy no more than one point of view at once. When a given facet of the monad comes into view, another has turned away from us. We lack a "view from everywhere" that can see the monad from all sides at once. Perspective therefore imputes a certain untotalizable dimension to complex concepts—for us, if not for God. Only God can see by way of ichnography—a direct, ground-plan view of things. Lesser beings must content themselves with scenographies, or perspectival views.[19] Perspectival vision is part of the human condition, even for philosophers.

The relativity of different perspectives does not necessarily imply equality, however. Regarding the Copernican and Ptolemaic systems, and despite the relativity of motion, Leibniz states:

> On this matter we must reply that one should choose the more intelligible hypothesis, and that the truth of a hypothesis is nothing but its intelligibility. Now, from a different point of view, not with respect to people and their opinions, but with respect to the very things we need to deal with, one hypothesis might be more intelligible than another and more appropriate for a given purpose. And so, from different points of view, the one might be true and the other false. Thus, for a hypothesis to be true is just for it to be properly used. So, although a painter can present the same palace through drawings that use different perspectives, we would judge that he made the wrong choice if he brought forward the one which covers or hides parts that are important to know for a matter at hand. In just the same way, an astronomer makes no greater mistake by explaining the theory of the planets in

accordance with the Tychonic hypothesis than he would make by using the Copernican hypothesis in teaching spherical astronomy and explaining day and night, thereby burdening the student with unnecessary difficulties.[20]

This passage sets forth an intriguingly pragmatic and perspectival theory of truth. The competing world systems each make a valid claim, not only because of the relativity of motion, but because of a relativity of application. For some limited purposes (spherical astronomy), the Ptolemaic system is simpler, more intelligible, and more useful, and for others, Copernicus's system prevails. Thus perspectivalism can ground a theory of truth, but of truth that is itself perspectival.

It is the case, of course, that political equivocation plays a role here. Leibniz, always the diplomat, offers the Church authorities the option of endorsing Copernicanism based on its superior intelligibility and intellectual beauty while dangling the relativity of motion as a means of withholding final assent. In effect, Leibniz substitutes epistemological for ontological truth. But this rhetorical context is no reason for dismissing his conclusions. Leibniz frequently inflects his system to suit the prejudices and interests of particular interlocutors. And this is itself another form of perspectivalism on his part, in a performative rather than a thematic vein. To try to extract the "real" system from its multiple inflections, to substitute a (nonexistent) ichnographic ground plan for the multiple scenographies Leibniz furnishes, is to flatten his philosophical practice in ways that can only impoverish it. Even if Leibniz did not himself produce differently inflected versions of his thought, we as readers necessarily would—bringing, as we do, our own sensibilities, agendas, and interests to the work and thereby producing different perspectives upon it. Is it any wonder that these never manage fully to coalesce?

In the course of this discussion I have quoted several iterations of a simile that Leibniz invokes repeatedly and in a variety of contexts: that of a town viewed from multiple angles. Sometimes there is an actual town observed by actual people, and sometimes there are multiple paintings of a town from different perspectives. Sometimes Leibniz employs the word "perspective," which invokes the world of the artwork more strongly than the alternative, but just as frequently (if not more frequently) employs the term "point of view." This might suggest that the two versions are essentially synonymous, in which case we might ask: What, if anything, do the versions involving paintings add to those that involve actual observers? How does painterly perspective differ from optical perspective, and how does it enrich Leibniz's metaphysics?

Panofsky offers the following definition of perspective:

We shall speak of a fully "perspectival" view of space not when mere isolated objects, such as houses or furniture, are represented in "foreshort-
ening," but rather only when the entire picture has been transformed—to
cite another Renaissance theoretician—into a "window," and when we are
meant to believe we are looking through this window into a space. The
material surface upon which the individual figures or objects are drawn
or painted or carved is thus negated, and instead reinterpreted as a mere
"picture plane." Upon this picture plane is projected the spatial continuum
which is seen through it and which is understood to contain all the various
individual objects.[21]

The figure of the window is omnipresent in early modern treatises on perspective, while actual window devices were used as aids in painting (figure 8.2).

To view a perspectival painting is to observe a three-dimensional space
through a window; only there is no space and there is no window. There is instead
a representation that creates the illusion of an "outside" world from the formal
relations internal to the canvas. Likewise, "Monads have no windows, through
which anything could come in or go out."[22] Perceptions are instead pre-inscribed
onto the monad itself—onto, that is, the mental counterpart to the bizarrely
folded and vibrating canvas that Leibniz describes in the *New Essays*. The ontology of the perspectival painting is the ontology of the monad and may even serve
as one model for it. Especially insofar as Leibniz comes to see space and time as

8.2 Artist drawing through a window. Albrecht Dürer, *The Painter's Manual*, ed. Walter L.
Strauss (New York: Abaris, 1977), p. 434.

"expressions" of intermonadic relations that have nothing to do themselves with either space or time.

Much of this is made explicit in the following passage from the *New Essays*:

> THEO. That is perfectly true: this is how a painting can deceive us, by means of an artful use of perspective. . . . So when we are deceived by a painting our judgments are doubly in error. First, we substitute the cause for the effect, and believe that we immediately see the thing that causes the image, rather like a dog barking at a mirror. For strictly we see only the image, and are affected only by rays of light. Since rays of light need time—however little— to reach us, it is possible that the object should be destroyed during the interval and no longer exist when the light reaches the eye; and something which no longer exists cannot be the present object of our sight. Secondly, we are further deceived when we substitute one cause for another and believe that what comes merely from a flat painting actually comes from a body. In such cases our judgments involve both metonymy and metaphor (for even figures of rhetoric turn into sophisms when they mislead us). This confusion of the effect with the real or the putative cause frequently occurs with other sorts of judgments too. This is how we come to believe that it is by an immediate real influence that we sense our bodies and the things which touch them, and move our arms, taking this influence to constitute the interaction between the soul and the body; whereas really all that we sense or alter in that way is what is within us.[23]

To think that we perceive bodies outside of us is as naïve as to believe that the objects depicted in a painting are real. Likewise for the space in which they appear to exist. If not fully imaginary, space is the projection or "expression" (see module 09) of things that are not themselves spatial, just as the perspectival space of the painting expresses a geometry that is mathematical and ideal. Here I am especially interested in Leibniz's account of pictorial deception as figurative, involving both metonymy (in this case, substitution of cause for effect) and metaphor (confusions of similar things). Whether or not Leibniz was aware of the humanist traditions that saw painterly and rhetorical forms as akin, this analogy casts some retrospective illumination on his equating of perception and figuration in our specimen sentence of module 03.[24] It is worth noting too that the dialogue form, which Leibniz employs here, engages in its own version of painterly deception, since in reality there are no persons named Theophilus and Philalethes having a conversation but only words on a page, with their internal relations generating an illusion of an outside world. *Ut pictura poesis.*

Leibniz's interest in painting extends to advanced perspectival techniques such as trompe l'oeil and anamorphosis that proliferated during the baroque period. He invokes these specifically in the context of distinct and confused perceptions. For instance:

> So what matters are not names but the *distinct properties* which the idea must be found to contain when one has brought order into its confusion. It is sometimes hard to find the key to the confusion—the way of viewing the object which shows one its intelligible properties; rather like those pictures which Father Niceron has shown how to construct, which must be viewed from a special position or by means of a special mirror if one is to see what the artist was aiming at.[25]

"Father Niceron" is Jean-Franc-cedillaois Niceron, a mathematician and author of *La perspective curieuse* (1638), an influential treatise on perspective and anamorphosis. Leibniz here compares the confused perception of an object (i.e., perception of its sensory qualia alone) to the confusedly distorted anamorphic image that is restored to coherence when viewed in a cylindrical mirror (corresponding to the distinct or conceptual grasp of the same object). The criterion of superior intelligibility that Leibniz applied to perspective in the Copernican debate reemerges here as a way of judging perspectives. But the whole point of anamorphic art is not simply to produce a coherent image by roundabout means but rather to hold it in tension with the distorted one and to enable a shuttling between the two views. One can occupy either perspective point with respect to the image but not both simultaneously. A similar issue arises in a discussion of the color green, which, Leibniz observes, is composed of blue and yellow mixed confusedly so that we cannot distinguish them. We can know conceptually that green is composed of two colors, but if we were to perceive it visually, the green would disappear:

> For it is self-contradictory to want these confused images to persist while wanting their components to be perceived by the imagination itself. It is like wanting to be deceived by some charming perspective and wanting to see through the deception at the same time—which would spoil the effect.[26]

Here again, one perspective cancels the other, and to want to experience both is self-contradictory. Different perspectives complement each other but also exclude each other. They cannot be synthesized or superimposed. A perspectival approach to knowledge will have to accept this limitation as a price to pay for the variety it can produce.

Leibniz's attraction to trompe l'oeil and anamorphosis bespeaks his interest in extreme forms of perspectival art that, to an unusual degree, determine a specific viewing position. For the most part, Renaissance perspective does not require the eye of the viewer to occupy the painting's center of projection, nor were artworks necessarily displayed so as to render this convenient. James Elkins points out that "Not a single surviving relief work of Donatello, for example, can be seen from a position approximating its center of projection."[27] Moreover, as Elkins observes, the

> connection between the painted surface and a point in front of it, hovering in space, was not part of the Renaissance imagination. . . . The lack of correspondence between viewer and perspective in Renaissance paintings and reliefs springs, I think, from the Renaissance understanding of perspective as a thing *in* a painting rather than vice versa. Even the most acute theorists, such as Leonardo, did not think the invisible construction in front of a painting shared ontological status with what happened in the painting or on its surface.[28]

With baroque perspectival techniques such as anamorphosis and trompe l'oeil, however, this is no longer the case. The anamorphic artwork demands to be viewed from a certain point—a *punto stabile* rather than a *punto mobile*—though it is still a virtual point that exists even if no viewer is there to occupy it. And such viewing points are determined by quite technical applications of geometric rules. This is an *objectivized* perspective with a vengeance, conveying what Deleuze calls "the truth of a variation."

That being said, the issue of truth becomes a complicated one in this context. In both of the final two Leibniz passages quoted in this module, perspectival art serves as a figure for different kinds of knowledge. But the purport of each is somewhat different. In the first, it is a question of finding the one correct perspective that will turn visual turbulence into coherence, and thus enable a passage from confused to distinct knowledge. But in the second, the emphasis shifts to maintaining a charming deception, since if we could attain a sufficiently distinct visual impression of green, it would resolve into blue and yellow components and the green would disappear. The first envisions the transcendence of confusion in the name of knowledge, while the second insists on maintaining it in the name of visual delight or enjoyment. This discrepancy gets at some complicated issues in Leibniz's theory of knowledge, which we will address in due course. But it also gets at a certain tension between the aesthetic and epistemological dimensions of perspective as Leibniz conceives it. On the one hand, a variety of perspectives is itself a good, regardless of how confused they are. Perspectives enrich the perceptual richness and multiplicity of the world. On the other, perspectives must be sifted through to choose the right ones for purposes of understanding. In this case they are ranked, and the insufficient ones are discarded. There is no way to resolve this tension, but nor is there any need to. It results from the fact that perspectives can be variously employed, as a result of which there is more than one perspective on perspective, as there is on everything else.

CHAPTER 9

Expression

As important as perspective is for Leibniz, it is but a subset of a still more encompassing category: expression.[1] It is no exaggeration to say that for Leibniz, every relation among entities is expressive. The Leibnizian universe is held together by a network of expressive relations—which, as it turns out, are at bottom relations of analogy. If, as I have been arguing, Leibnizian thinking is fundamentally analogical, the ceaseless process of mapping distinct mental spaces onto one another, it should be no surprise that the world it conceives is likewise analogical in its structure: an outward projection, or expression, of the mapping that produced it in the first place.

The *locus classicus* for Leibniz's understanding of "expression" occurs in his essay "What Is an Idea?":

> That is said to express a thing in which there are relations [*habitudines*] which correspond to the relations of the thing expressed. But there are various kinds of expression; for example, the model of a machine expresses the machine itself, the projective delineation on a plane expresses a solid, speech expresses thoughts and truths, characters express numbers, and an algebraic equation expresses a circle or some other figure. What is common to all these expressions is that we can pass from a consideration of the relations in the expression to a knowledge of the corresponding properties of the thing expressed. Hence it is clearly not necessary for that which expresses to be similar to the thing expressed, if only a certain analogy is maintained between the relations.[2]

Expression establishes relations between relations: the relations internal to the thing being expressed are matched by the relations internal to the thing expressing it. This correspondence of *relations* is somewhat different from the correspondence of *elements* entailed when Leibniz compared expression to conic sections in the passage examined in module 05. There, every point on a circle found a corresponding point on an ellipse. But here it is not elements but rather the relation between elements that is carried over. It seems to be the case that Leibnizian expression always involves a mapping of relations and sometimes (but not necessarily) elements as well. But the similarity or mapping across *relations* is what gives expression the character of analogy, as Leibniz makes explicit toward the end of the passage. To express something is to be analogical to it. It is worth noting here that for Fauconnier as well, what gets mapped in cognitive mapping is primarily the relational structures of mental spaces, rather than their individual elements. So again, the analogical structure of Leibniz's world reflects the analogical structure of the thinking that generates it.

Leibniz's passage on expression continues:

It is also clear that some expressions have a basis in nature, while others are arbitrary, at least in part, such as the expressions which consist of words or characters. Those which are founded in nature either require some similarity, such as that between a large and a small circle or that between a geographic region and a map of the region, or require some connection such as that between a circle and the ellipse which represents it optically, since any point whatever on the ellipse corresponds to some point on the circle according to a definite law. Indeed, a circle would be poorly represented by any other figure more similar to it in such a case. Similarly every entire effect represents the whole cause, for I can always pass from the knowledge of such an effect to a knowledge of its cause. So, too, the deeds of each one represent his mind, and in a way the world itself represents God. It may also happen that the effects which arise from the same cause express each other mutually as, for example, gesture and speech. So deaf people understand speakers, not by sound, but by the motion of the mouth.[3]

Without attempting to unpack everything in this rich passage, it is worth noting a few points. First, the fact that expression involves a mapping of relations means that it can work even when the elements that compose those relations are unlike. Words are not like things, but relations internal to language can express or map onto relations between things—hence (among other developments) philosophy.

Second, expression requires difference as well as resemblance. An ellipse can express a circle, but another circle would do poorly at this task. Something cannot be expressed by something else identical to it or even too similar. The more extensive the difference that an expression traverses, the more vivid it is. Sometimes this necessary difference involves a change of medium, as with the map and the territory it represents, or as with words and ideas, or as with an algebraic equation and the geometric shape it describes. Finally, it is worth noting how much, in a short space, has been accommodated within the category of expression: language, mathematics, cause and effect, and the relationship between God and the world. One item not mentioned here is perspective. But in a letter to Arnauld, Leibniz observes that "a perspectival projection expresses its Ground plan."[4] Perspective thus joins the above list in embodying the similarity-in-difference that marks all expression.

In fact, like perception, expression unites everything there is. In a letter to De Volder, Leibniz writes: "You seem to have grasped beautifully my doctrine of how every body whatsoever expresses everything else, and how any soul or entelechy whatsoever expresses both its own body and, through it, everything else."[5] Just as every entity has a perspective on every other, so it expresses every other. Indeed, by "express" Leibniz means in part "perceive" and in part the fact that the perceptions of individual monads are mutually accommodated according to the principle of compossibility. In some unpublished remarks on Pierre Bayle, Leibniz observes that "In God the universe is not only concentrated, but perfectly expressed; but in each created monad there is expressed only one part, which is larger or smaller according as the soul is more or less excellent, and all the infinite remainder is expressed only confusedly."[6] Confused and distinct expression is here more or less synonymous with confused and distinct perception.

Indeed, "Leibniz *defines* perception as the expression or representation of the many in the one, or of the composite in the simple (G II, 121, 311; G III, 69, 574–75; G VI, 598, 608; G VII, 317, 529)."[7] In a letter to Des Bosses, for instance, he writes that "Since perception is nothing but the expression of many things in one, it is necessary that all entelechies or monads be endowed with expression."[8] And in accordance with the logic of expression, the way we perceive things need not accurately reproduce the things themselves. To quote once more the passage from module 05:

> It isn't necessary that what we understand of things outside ourselves should resemble them perfectly, but only that it should express them; in the way that

an ellipse expresses a circle seen from an angle, so that each point on the circle corresponds to one on the ellipse and vice versa in accordance with a certain law of correspondence, for, as I have already said, each individual substance expresses the universe in its way, rather like the way the same town is differently expressed according to different points of view.

This is the sort of thing that could have but (typically for Leibniz) does not produce epistemological anxiety of a Cartesian flavor. It simply doesn't *matter* to Leibniz whether things themselves and our images of them match perfectly as long as the transformation follows an invariant rule, thus coordinating the relations in each. "But it must not be thought that, when I speak of [the soul as] a mirror, I mean that external things are always depicted in the organs and in the soul itself. For it is sufficient for the expression of one thing in another that there should be a certain constant relational law . . . "[9]

One reason why perceptions differ from the things perceived is that perception is mediated by the way those things interact with or impinge upon our bodies: "The soul nevertheless is still the form of its body, because it expresses the phenomena of all other bodies following the relation to its own."[10] Since each body is different, it produces a unique translation or transformation or expression of other bodies. And all bodies impinge on our own, owing to the plenum that connects them. Our bodies express other bodies, and our minds express our bodies. Things that are in some proximity to our bodies express themselves in relatively distinct ways while things that are spatially or temporally distant express themselves in more confused fashion. Hence our bodies help define perceptual zones of clarity and obscurity.

Expression is representation, but representation that entails transformation, refracting representational content by passing it through another medium or by viewing it through a particular, oblique perspective. In the case of perception, the perspective is that of the monad's associated body. But if perception is simply a subset of expression, assimilable to all the other kinds that Leibniz lists, it is the one through which the primary forms of metaphysical work performed by the latter become visible. In the first of these, expression mediates between the worlds of mind and body, the monadic universe and the physical one, and does so in such a way as to occupy the place that would otherwise be taken by causality. No causal relations pierce the barrier between the mental and bodily worlds. Rather, these worlds or "kingdoms" operate in a parallelism that Leibniz calls preestablished harmony. In the act of creation, God programs the universe of physical things to execute a planned sequence purely through relations of cause and effect immanent to that world. If your body picks up a pen and writes, this is not because your mind "told" it to do so but because of the properties of its component parts as they interact causally with one another and with other, external bodies. But in parallel with this preplanned sequence, God creates another in the realm of thought, no less determined and no less causal than the physical series, but operating according to different laws that will be spelled out more fully in module 10. Because the two series operate in parallel, the thought of picking up a pen and writing happens at the same time that the body picks up a pen and writes. And what binds these two series together, apart from mere simultaneity, is the fact that the two *express each other*. The mutuality is crucial. As Serres observes, " 'analogical' relations are biunivocal: that is to say, the thing expressed expresses in turn its expression."[11] If an algebraic formula expresses a circle, the circle expresses the algebraic formula; if a map expresses a territory, the territory expresses the map; if the universe expresses God, God expresses the universe; and, crucially, if the mind expresses the body, the body expresses the mind. It is the scrupulousness with which Leibniz maintains this mutuality that keeps expression from devolving into a kind of crypto-causality (something that happens, for instance, in Spinoza's treatment of mind-body relations).

The second, and even more important, metaphysical role of expression is to mediate the relations between monads. If we ask what monads perceive—that is, express—one answer is "the universe" and an additional answer is "one another." As Leibniz writes to Des Bosses, "since a monad always expresses within itself its relation to all other monads, it will perceive very different things when it is in a horse from when it is in a dog."[12] And again in the *Monadology*: "Now, this *interconnection*, or this adapting of all created things to each one, and of each one to all the others, means that each simple substance expresses all the others, and that it is therefore a perpetual living mirror of the universe."[13] As these two passages show, monads express one another both insofar as they perceive one another and insofar as their internal constitutions are accommodated to one another via the principle of compossibility. Not only what they see but their capacity to see reflects their relations to other monads. These two modes of interrelation are, moreover, bound together.

But let us step back from this proposition for a moment and try to grasp it concretely. What does it mean to say that monads perceive other monads?

Monads are purely mental entities, after all. To perceive other monads therefore involves perceiving something invisible and disembodied—those monads'
internal perceptual states. But we are all monads, and it is difficult to grasp how
this idea accords in any way with our empirical experience of perception. What
we perceive, for the most part, are not mental entities but physical ones: the
visual and auditory and tactile qualities, the sounds and smells of bodies. We can
sometimes perceive other minds as well, but not directly, because access to other
minds is necessarily mediated by the words people speak or write, along with
the expressions on their faces, and the acts their bodies perform. Even the most
abstract kinds of thought must be materially mediated:

> For it is an admirable arrangement on the part of nature that we cannot have
> abstract thoughts which have no need of something sensible, even if it be
> merely symbols such as the shapes of letters, or sounds; though there is no
> necessary connection between such arbitrary symbols and such thoughts. If
> sensible traces were not required, the pre-established harmony between body
> and soul . . . would not obtain.[14]

We have not fully grasped the audacity of Leibniz's stance on monadic perception
until we see that the privileged object of that perception is precisely the thing
no one can perceive directly, the one thing that is *hidden* from perception: the
internal mental states of other people.

Leibniz's philosophical reasoning lands him in a bit of a dilemma. On the
one hand, monads are the most important components of the universe—possibly,
the only ones there are. If the business of monads is perception, then other
monads offer the most worthwhile objects. A system of monadic perception
wouldn't count for much if monads couldn't perceive each other, and thereby
constitute a kind of society. On the other hand, Leibniz's business as philosopher
is to describe the world as it is—not to substitute another, made-up world for
it. Much as we might like to, we simply can't perceive other minds directly. And
thus we arrive at the primary metaphysical function of expression. Monads can
perceive other monads *only by way of an expressive detour*. We can know other
minds solely via bodies of some kind, be they human bodies or written letters or
spoken words, etc. We can call this a detour through the physical. But it would
be more accurate to call it a detour through the phenomenal, thus preserving the
fact that the same perceptual problem remains whether physical bodies actually

exist or whether they are merely well-founded phenomena. Vincenzo De Risi has employed the Kantian terms noumenal and phenomenal to describe the difference between internal monadic states and what monads can perceive, and this terminological distinction points to the need for the expressive detour. As De Risi argues, compellingly, not only the things of the world but also space and time, the dimensions in which these things are arrayed, are phenomenological expressions of intermonadic relations that themselves do not pertain to space or time.[15] The situation of bodies in space gives phenomenal expression to relations between monads that inherently involve neither bodies nor space.

I am tempted to call the expressive detour *aesthetic*. Insofar as the word can refer to sensual perception in general, "aesthetic" is roughly synonymous with "phenomenal." But I employ it as well to bring out some etymological implications of "expression." *Expressio* comes from the verb *exprimo*, which can mean to mold or form something, often in imitation of something else. The word bears within it connotations of artistic or artisanal expression—connotations that, I think, should be activated when we think of the phenomenal world as expressing the noumenal, monadic one. Let us recall Leibniz's habit, explored in module 08, of comparing the act of perception to the act of looking at a painting. Paintings, indeed artworks in general, are both perceptually and ideationally rich. Their sensual, representational content is also a vehicle for abstract, nonsensual meaning, and in this way they embody, in a particularly intense and concentrated fashion, some fundamental aspects of monadic perception in general. Indeed, the world as a whole is a kind of artwork for Leibniz, insofar as it is both sensually and intellectually beautiful. The expressive/aesthetic detour required by monadic perception is not only unavoidable, then, but also, fortuitously, enriching. Without it, existence would be poorer. The enjoyment is in the detours.

CHAPTER 10

How to Build a Monad

"**M**onad" is probably the best-known entry in the Leibnizian lexicon. But what is a monad? A monad is a mind, but mind as understood in a particular way.[1] Or rather, it is mind as understood in a multiplicity of distinct though related ways. In the spirit of Leibnizian tinkering, we shall learn to grasp the concept of the monad through the practical process of trying to build one. What follows, then, is a set of assembly instructions. Fortunately, monads can be constructed with materials easily found around the home. In fact, all you need is pencil, paper, and an infinite, godlike intelligence. Let's get started!

First, though, some terminological decluttering. In his middle years, Leibniz uses the term "monad" to mean the unity of a mind and its associated body. Later, as he comes to believe more consistently that bodies may not be material things after all but only what he calls "well-founded phenomena," "monad" often comes to mean mind alone, which may or may not be accompanied by a material body. Moreover, Leibniz employs a series of other terms that are rough synonyms for "monad": "substance," "formal substance," and "entelechy."[2] All refer to the same general idea but bring out different aspects of it, and Leibniz's use of one or the other often (though not always) traces the preoccupations that dominate in different stages of his thinking or else answers to the contours of a specific intellectual problem or context.

Leibniz's terminological variations reflect the fact that he has multiple ways of understanding monads or minds that provide different perspectives on the topic. But they are also compatible and thus mutually mappable or convertible. At the same time, the process of conversion is not trivial, for if it were, the different perspectives wouldn't add much to the richness and complexity of the concept. They would be thinly disguised repetitions of one another rather than sources of novel, variegated insight.

One way to understand monads or minds—the way with which Leibniz begins the *Monadology*—is as perceptions strung together by appetitions.[3] A "perception" (of the universe, of other monads) is an instantaneous, snapshot view, but these are strung together into a kind of cinematic sequence we recognize as consciousness or mind, and the means for this is "appetition."[4] Sometimes appetition can take the form of conscious desire or appetite. But the term should be understood more generally in its etymological sense: "appetition" derives from the Latin *ad-peto*, to head toward. Appetition is therefore the underlying law or force or logic that leads from one perception to another.[5] If perceptions are beads, appetition is the string (as well as the choice of how to sequence the beads).

So: monads can be understood as perceptions sequenced by appetitions. They can be understood as perspectives. They can also be understood as expressions (of the universe and especially of their bodies). But Leibniz has other descriptive languages available. Monads can be understood as combinations of active and passive forces; as endless, logically articulated lists of predicates; and as infinite series, in the mathematical sense. In building our monad, we shall privilege this last and relatively underexamined sense. Among other virtues, it will provide a much better and more detailed sense of what Leibniz means by "appetition." All of these descriptions, however, enrich the concept of the monad, and each can be mapped onto the others.

If the notion of monad as infinite series is relatively unexplored compared to the others, one principal reason for this is that it is never quite stated expressly and unequivocally. In fact, it has to be reconstructed from scattered evidence. Before we can use the mathematical conception of the monad to help build one, I will therefore have to construct—or reconstruct—the mathematical conception itself. Or rather, I will have to reconstruct this particular one, since multiple mathematical models undergird the monad.[6]

One more proviso before we begin. Building just one monad considerably—indeed, infinitely—simplifies the actual task. For as difficult as it will be to make one, this is as nothing compared to the fact that God makes an infinity of monads, and that they not merely perceive or express one another (this will be a feature of ours) but are internally accommodated to one another, via the principle of compossibility. Hence one must have all the other monads and their internal states constantly in mind when designing the areas of confused and distinct

perceptions for any one. But we'll imagine building an isolated, unaccommo-
dated demonstration model that produces perceptions ordered by appetitions.
Now, it will probably not count as a spoiler if I reveal that even this simplified
task is impossible and that our attempts to build a monad will not go well. The
point of the exercise (apart from the intrinsic pleasures of tinkering) is therefore
to isolate and identify breakdown points that can illuminate aspects of the Leibnizian monad and of his philosophy more generally.

In the *Discourse on Metaphysics*, Leibniz sets forth the notion of substance as an
infinite, logically coherent set of predicates, exemplified by Alexander the Great:

> The nature of an individual substance or of a complete being is to have a
> notion so complete that it is sufficient to include, and to allow the deduc-
> tion of, all the predicates of the subject to which the notion is attributed. . . .
> Thus, the quality of being a king, which belongs to Alexander the Great, is
> an abstraction from the subject, and so is not sufficiently determinate to the
> individual, and does not involve the other qualities of the same subject, nor
> everything to which the notion of that prince includes; whereas God, who
> sees the individual notion or haecceity of Alexander, sees in it at the same
> time the foundation and the reason for all the predicates which can truly
> be said to belong to it, such as, for example, that he would conquer Darius
> and Porus, even to the extent of knowing a priori (and not by experience)
> whether he dies a natural death or by poison, something which we can know
> only by history. And, moreover, if we consider carefully the interconnected-
> ness of things, we can say that in the soul of Alexander there are for all time
> remnants of everything that has happened to him, and marks of everything
> that will happen to him—and even traces of everything that happens in the
> universe, although it is only God who can recognize them all.[7]

Alexander's substance is understood in relation to his complete individual concept: a collection of every predicate that can be correctly attached to him. Here
Leibniz lists only those kinds of predicates we might call "life events": things that
Alexander did or that happened to him.[8] For ordinary human purposes it is sufficient to enumerate a few of these predicated life-events in order to identify the
person under discussion as Alexander: say, "the Macedonian king who conquered
Darius and Porus." For a more detailed understanding, we would want to include
more of these events and consider how they might fit together into a unified

portrait of the person. In so doing, we would be constructing a more refined and differentiated conception of Alexander. As finite creatures with finite mental capacities, however, we will nevertheless fall short of grasping his full haecceity, or "thisness": the mysterious supplement of rich individuality that distinguishes Alexander from any other person.[9]

Now, the failure of this process might lead one to conclude that the act of predication is simply not a very good way of accessing haecceity—that someone's "thisness" cannot be grasped by multiplying attributes. In one sense, Leibniz assumes the opposite: the failure results rather from not listing enough of them. In fact, the list of predicates that constitutes Alexander is infinite, since it includes not only everything that ever happened to him but also the relation between those events and the rest of the universe. Only God can have access to the total account of Alexander's predicates.

But even if we listed every predicate that attaches to Alexander, we would still fall short, because the very form of the list cannot do anything more than pile up events and occurrences. The aggregation problem that attaches to physical bodies thus plagues the act of predication as well. Just as a physical body is for Leibniz a mere heap of smaller bodies—like a pile of stones or a flock of sheep—so even a full list of predicates is merely an act of conceptual aggregation. The aggregated body cannot achieve unity without the aid of a dominant monad, and likewise the jumble of attributes that constitute Alexander cannot achieve unity without his total concept. One cannot, therefore, construct the latter inductively by assembling Alexander's predicates. Rather, the predicates must be *deducible* from his concept, such that they are logically entailed by it, and in a given order. As human beings who cannot have access to or comprehend this unifying concept, we perceive Alexander's life as a series of historical events, some of which might seem connected and others contingent or random. Only God, who forms the concept of Alexander, can see the mutual logical entailment of everything that goes into him. It is this timeless, unifying concept that constitutes his haecceity.

As Leibniz states, "the nature of an individual substance or of a being is to have a [complete] notion." Now in the *Discourse* as elsewhere, "substance" denotes a purely mental entity—a Cartesian *res cogitans*. But then what does it mean to say that this "has" a notion? One mental entity apparently "has" another. Is Alexander's notion—the complete concept that God has of him—a blueprint for his soul or *is* it his soul?[10] I want to argue that it is in some sense both. The "is" might seem to take us perilously close to a Spinozan ontology. If Alexander and the rest of us are just God's thoughts, then maybe there is only one divine substance of which we are merely modes. A couple of things insulate against this. First, the Alexander-concept, like all divine ideas, answers to criteria of logical noncontradiction, optimality, etc., that grant it a kind of quasi-autonomy, in the same way that Newton's inverse square law for gravity exists as a legitimate abstract object even when Newton isn't thinking of it. Its correctness and coherence are inherent to it, and so the law exists independently of its creator.[11] And likewise for the Alexander-concept. But then why not simply say that Alexander's substance *is* this concept rather than merely *having* it? Perhaps because in the concept, all the various attributes are connected by timeless, logico-conceptual relations, whereas in the case of Alexander's substance, these relations play out temporally as well as logically. If the Alexander-concept were a computer program, Alexander's substance would be the running of that program. (The situation is actually more complex than this, but let's leave it here for now.)

A couple of pages prior to the passage on Alexander, Leibniz employs a mathematical analogy to show how God is never haphazard or random in his creative acts, despite occasional appearances to the contrary:

> Suppose, for example, that someone puts a number of completely haphazard points on paper, as do those who practice the ridiculous art of geomancy. I say that it is possible to find a geometrical line whose notion is constant and uniform according to a certain rule, such that the line passes through all the points, and in the same order as they were drawn.[12]

Just as the predicates that attach to Alexander find their logical unity in the complete notion that God has of him, so the points on the piece of paper—randomly distributed, or so it seems—find their mathematical unity in the line that passes through them, in order. And this line is not just drawn ad hoc: its "notion is constant and uniform," i.e., it is a smooth, continuous mathematical function whose graph is the curving line in question. No matter how irregular or numerous the array of points, a linear function can *always* be found, Leibniz claims, to plot all of them on a single, curving line. The function unifies the points in the same way that Alexander's notion unifies his predicates. Only now the notion is mathematical rather than logical. If we apply this passage to the later one, Alexander's life appears as a curvilinear function connecting its component events.[13] I want to suggest that this mapping is unstable, as Leibniz's often are. It may be that the analogy of the mathematical function is just that—a way of conceptualizing or illustrating the unifying powers of God's complete notions of things. Or maybe the logical and mathematical concepts are simply different perspectives on the same reality. A logical concept from one point of view, substance is a mathematical function from another.

In a 1704 letter to De Volder, Leibniz writes that "all individual things are successive, i.e. subject to a succession. . . . For me, nothing is permanent in those things except the very law that involves the continual succession." And he goes on:

> You say that "in a series" (of numbers, say), "nothing is conceived of as successive." So what? I do not say that a series is a succession but that a succession is a series, and that it has this in common with other series, namely that the law of the series shows where it must reach by continuing its progression, i.e., that, with the starting point and the law of progression given, the terms will be produced in order whether the order or priority is of nature only or also of time.[14]

Just as the series of events that constitute Alexander's life is determined by the (complete, hence unchanging) Alexander-notion formulated by God, and just as the movement of the line connecting the dots on the piece of paper is determined by the (unchanging) mathematical function, so here the succession of ever-new perceptions in the monad is governed by the unchanging "law of the series." Monads experience a never-ending sequence of perceptions, and these are not only ordered but, I shall suggest, generated by the law of the series.

In quoting De Volder on series and succession, it is *Leibniz* who adds "(of numbers, say [*qualis numerorum*])." De Volder never explicitly mentions numbers, though the notion silently undergirds the entire exchange. Conversely, in his mathematical papers, Leibniz speaks of "the law of the series" (*lex progressionis*) and, more often, of the "rule" (*regula*) of the series.[15] In the letter to De Volder, the *qualis* ("as in") suggests that numerical series are simply one example of a larger type, but in fact, the whole conception is clearly derived from mathematical series and borrows any kind of precise meaning only from that. It is equally clear that the kind of mathematical series Leibniz has in mind is the infinite series—the subject of some of his earliest work when he was mastering mathematics in Paris, and a crucial step in his ultimate formulation of the calculus.

In a response to Simon Foucher's comments in 1676, Leibniz writes that "the essence of substances consist in the primitive force of acting, or in the law of the series of changes, like the nature of a series in numbers."[16] Here he offers the mathematical series as an *analogy* to the monad's law of the series. But the line between analogy and identity can be fuzzy in Leibniz, as we have seen, and this is especially the case when he discusses the different ways of describing a monad. Thus, for instance, Leibniz states in one letter to De Volder that "primitive force is like the law of the series" (*vis primitiva sit velut lex serei*) thereby presenting an analogy. But in the above-quoted comment on Foucher, he speaks of the primitive force and the law of the series as if they were synonymous.[17] I propose that a comparable ambiguity pertains to the relation between the mathematical infinite series and the monadic law of the series. In constructing this mathematical analogy. Leibniz is actually revealing the model on which the law of the monadic series is based.

An infinite series is, as the name suggests, an endless sequence of numbers generated by a rule. In 1672, Leibniz discovered a "method of differences" that allowed him to calculate the sums of infinite series, including that of the reciprocals of the so-called triangular numbers $\frac{1}{1} + \frac{1}{3} + \frac{1}{6} + \frac{1}{10} + \ldots + \frac{2}{n(n+1)} + \ldots$.[18] Here (as often) the infinite series is in the form of a sum, and Leibniz was able to show that the sum of the terms when added up is 2. Like the monad, the infinite series has a beginning but no end: there is a first term but no final one, just as the monad is created but then never stops generating perceptions. (Leibniz, incidentally, was the first to show that infinite series work in this way. Previously, they were thought to have a final term.)[19] And like the monad, the infinite series incorporates both change and fixity: succeeding terms are always different, but they are generated by an unvarying law or rule. Thus to state that a substance or monad is an infinite series is as legitimate as to state that it is a force, or a perspective, or a complete notion. But this particular formulation will provide a blueprint as we go about trying to build our monad. The trick will be in getting from a series of numbers to a series of perceptions, thus constituting a mind. Leibniz will not show us the way here, nor could he—in part because he lacked, for historical reasons, the requisite intellectual machinery and in part because (of course) the project is an impossible one. In fact, our attempt to build a monad is really just a thought-experiment meant to show its very high degree of impossibility (if that phrase even makes sense) even while trying to think through a way in which it might conceivably be imagined. How would one go about constructing a mind from mathematics alone—and more specifically, from an infinite series?

Let's start by looking at a very simple infinite series: the one known as the harmonic series. Its mathematical expression is $\sum\limits_{1}^{\infty}\dfrac{1}{n} = \dfrac{1}{1} + \dfrac{1}{2} + \dfrac{1}{3} + \dfrac{1}{4} + \ldots$ This series happens to be divergent, meaning that adding up all the terms on the right-hand side of the equation will result in an infinitely large sum. It is called the "harmonic series" because it describes the overtones of a vibrating string. When a violin is bowed or plucked, it produces a fundamental wavelength or tone but also a set of overtones that will be $\dfrac{1}{2}, \dfrac{1}{3}, \dfrac{1}{4}$, etc., of this fundamental wavelength. Figure 10.1 shows a diagram of what that looks like.

As is apparent, this simple sequence produces a complex set of interference patterns that contributes to the richness of tone of the violin (or guitar, or whatever).

The harmonic series provides a (partial) mathematical description of what a violin string does when it vibrates. But I want to suggest that in doing so, it

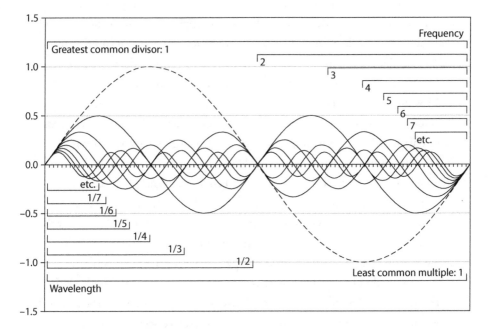

10.1 Harmonic series.

also describes the *monad* of that string. That is to say, the harmonic series is the ideal, abstract, and in some sense "mental" counterpart to what the violin string is doing physically in vibrating. The equation doesn't *cause* the string to vibrate, because it occupies a mathematical realm, not a material one. Rather, it *expresses* the movement of the string, and the movement of the string conversely expresses the harmonic series. It is thus a mathematical counterpart to the complete "Alexander-concept" that constitutes Alexander's substance. And like that concept, it can be thought by God but also has an autonomous (mathematical) existence, even if no one happens to be actively thinking about it. Just as Alexander's life is the running of his "program," so the vibrating string is the running of the harmonic series.

In providing a (partial) description of a bowed violin string, then, the harmonic series also constitutes (part of) the *monad* of that string. But are violin strings the kinds of things that have monads? I suspect that most Leibniz scholars—indeed, Leibniz himself—would respond with a resounding "No!," and for pretty good but not quite airtight reasons. I want to spend some time on this point, though, because the question of what can "have" a monad is relevant to the problem of building one. Technically, the question is whether something like a violin string can have a *dominant* monad, since it, like any material thing, is constituted of parts within parts that are posited by Leibniz as organic and that therefore have associated monads. The question is whether a violin string *as a whole* can have a dominant monad. Here as often, Leibniz does not provide a crystal-clear answer because different parts of his "system" are in tension. Often, and I would say fairly consistently in the latter phases of his career, he assigns dominant monads only to animal bodies.[20] But occasionally he affords even inorganic entities what he calls simple or "bare" monads—monads that exhibit a very rudimentary, intermittent, and confused kind of perception that lacks memory.[21] (For Leibniz, inorganic objects are like small children asleep in the back seat of a car who are momentarily and very partially roused when the car turns or brakes.) Even more to the point, violin strings are elastic. For Leibniz, elasticity is the paradigm of what he calls "derivative active force." The elasticity of the violin string means that it vibrates not as the passive consequence of being plucked by another body (a finger) but because its own elastic force responds actively to this occasion. And for Leibniz, derivative active force is always the physical expression of primary active force—another way of conceiving the appetitive drive of the monad. This is why Leibniz employs the analogy of a vibrating string (or rather, of a folded canvas that vibrates like a string) to describe the mind in the *New Essays*.[22] Basically, when biology comes to the fore, Leibniz assigns dominant monads only to organic bodies, but when the physics of forces comes to the fore, it is more difficult to say that inorganic bodies do not have dominant monads as well. Thus in the *Specimen Dynamicum* of 1695, Leibniz's most systematic exposition of his theory of forces, he equates force with entelechy and assigns to *all* bodies with mass, including inanimate ones, "primitive entelechies" that "correspond" to souls.[23] I will therefore take the liberty, for heuristic purposes, of positing that the violin string can be considered as having a primitive kind of monad, or something like one, especially since Leibniz employs vibration as a figure for the workings of the *human* mind. The string's dominant monad converts it from a mere aggregate of smaller parts into a unified, elastic, active thing.

Even so, we seem to have a bit of a haecceity problem here, because the harmonic series provides a description not of the action of a particular violin string but that of all violin strings. But of course, it provides only a very *partial* and incomplete description. The full description of the vibration of a particular violin string would be different from the description of the vibrating of any other string. Every string has its own unique mathematical description and hence its own monad.[24]

When the violin string is plucked or bowed, the harmonic series that governs the vibration of the violin string will necessarily also constitute part of the monad of the person *listening* to the violin string. "Listening," of course, should not be understood here to imply direct communication. Our monadic perceptions are preprogrammed within us, and they merely correspond to things that happen in the external world without being caused by them. So when a violin string is bowed, and vibrates according to the harmonic series, the monad within the listener will likewise have to produce the harmonic series (unconsciously, of course) as part of its preprogrammed "hearing" of the note.

In fact, the mathematical concept of an infinite series is especially helpful in trying to grasp precisely the preprogrammed nature of the monad. The infinite series is a kind of perpetual-motion machine that, once set going, generates term after term governed by its founding law. And this is what monads do as well. Having been created, they unleash a perpetual series of terms that in this case are not mere arithmetical fractions but rather perceptions. And this series of perceptions follows an underlying law or logic, just as does each subsequent term of the infinite series. So the infinite series gives us a good way of understanding what

Leibniz means by "appetition." Appetition is the law of the series, specifically of the infinite mathematical series.[25] It is in part because they are modeled on mathematical series that monads do not die. Even if their bodies are destroyed, they retreat to a tiny, enfolded fragment of their original body and continue to crank out new perceptual terms, forever.

In one sense, then, our task is, if not done then at least modeled for us. In building the harmonic series, we have produced a very simple kind of monad—one that suffices (in part) for a vibrating violin string. For higher-level monads, the task is rather more complex, because simple fractions will not do a very good job of representing what goes on in our heads. To begin to grasp the dimensions of this larger problem, let's think of monadic life as one in which, instead of viewing the external world directly, we just watch a movie version or streaming video of it instead. Everyone has their own streaming video, and they are coordinated so that we "see" the same things, but from our own perspective. An even better analogy might be a video game, since there the entire environment is created from scratch rather than recorded from a preexistent reality and then processed into digital form. And then our own bodies/avatars as well as everything else we see are the "well-founded phenomena" described by Leibniz in his late phase.

But what is a video game? Well, in the end it is just a string of digital code that produces a fictional world when run on the proper device, just as the harmonic series is a mathematical function (one that could be transformed into an algorithm and thence to a string of code) that plays when "run" on a violin string. To make our video game, a degree in computer science and some experience in engineering video games would doubtless help, but we don't yet need an infinite, godlike intelligence. Or so it seems. But there are a couple of complicating factors. One is that monads don't just perceive their immediate environments. They perceive every entity in the universe, no matter how tiny or distant. Moreover, every physical entity is composed of smaller entities, and those in turn are composed of still smaller ones, ad infinitum. And all of them must be perceived, if only fuzzily. So this is an awful lot of information to encode—indeed, an infinite amount. On top of that, a video game is engineered in a kind of ad hoc fashion, with different subroutines stitched together to make it work.[26] But in the case of the monad, we need *a single mathematical function* that, as it unspools, will produce a code and a resulting perceptual detail and complexity infinitely beyond what is merely pieced together by game developers. For the latter, that is, there is a merely aggregative element in what they do. At some level, their creations are the equivalent of listing an infinite number of predicates in order to try to grasp Alexander's haecceity. But that haecceity is secured only by a unified concept or notion from which the predicates can be derived or deduced. And in the case of our monadic video game, the various elements of the game must likewise derive their complex variety from a master algorithm or function that imparts a corresponding unity to the monad. A monad, after all, cannot have "parts."

And if this were not enough, there's another problem. I have been describing a monad as if it were a video game. But strictly speaking, that's not right. A monad is not like a video game; it is like the *viewing* or *perception* of—or really, the *playing* of—such a game.[27] To produce this, it would help if consciousness were at least the same kind or class of entity as the imaginary video game we have produced thus far: that is to say, something that is computable/programmable in the same way as the game is. Recent developments in artificial intelligence have, in fact, prompted some philosophers of mind to describe consciousness as a highly complex information state that is "substrate independent"—it happens to be embodied in the neural networks of our brains but is in principle independent of them or indeed of any given instantiating medium, and therefore could be run on a sufficiently sophisticated computer, instead.[28] But if this is the case, we builders of monads are not merely programming an endless, infinitely detailed video game; we are programming the vastly more complex information structure that is our consciousness playing such a video game. And again, all of this is generated by one single (unimaginably complex) mathematical function. I hope you left your weekend free and have lots of scratch paper![29]

Let's take a moment and catch our breath. Some physicists and computer scientists, working from different premises, have speculated that not only individual minds but also the universe as a whole (including all the minds it contains) is computable, and most likely by means of a relatively short algorithm.[30] Stephen Wolfram is probably the best-known, if controversial, exponent of this view, which draws on the model of cellular automata that can produce patterns of immense complexity from simple instructions.[31] From a Leibnizian perspective, this would seem to deliver us much closer to where we want to go. Why engineer individual monads from massively complex algorithms when we can create a whole universe of them from a simple one? Here it is worth noting that Leibniz often describes not only individual monads but also the universe as a whole as if it were a continuous mathematical function or series (individual monads then presumably being folds nested within this megafold but still part of its linear windings).[32] However, the behavior of the more promising classes of cellular automata are unpredictable, which means that one cannot program them to achieve a particular end but can only observe the results of the process as they unfold. This would militate against the "clockmaker" God that Leibniz presupposes—one who preordains the entire sequence of the universe's states, or even the states within an individual monad, with an eye toward optimality. It would better suit Alfred North Whitehead's God, whose "unity of conceptual operations is a free creative act, untrammeled by reference to any particular course of things."[33]

Putting all this aside, and returning for a moment our dream of building a monad, we are faced with another challenge: every algorithm requires a Turing machine to run it. More concretely, a video game is run on a physical device that includes not only an operating system but also hardware that executes the game's code and converts it into images, etc., just as the information state of our mind is "run" on the neural networks of the brain. But there is no physical device on which we can run our massively complex algorithm, since monads do not interact with the physical world. It must therefore be somehow self-executing. And this is indicative of a still-deeper problem. I've been pretending that the notion of a "substrate-independent information state" means a state independent of any substrate whatsoever and thus a free-floating, ideal entity. But in fact, the phrase merely indicates independence of any *particular, given* substrate. As the physicist Rolf Landauer famously declared in 1961, "information is physical," and must be materially encoded, either with pencil on paper or in the neural networks of our brains, or *somehow*. So even if we were able to program the evolving information state of the brain as a vastly complex algorithm, we would still need to encode that information, and then run it.

Now in one sense, this problem is solved simply by regarding the monad from another perspective—as force. Leibniz states that the primitive force that drives real entities is supplied by God's ongoing concurrence in their existence—the "continual fulgurations" colorfully invoked in the *Monadology*. God, in effect, supplies everything with a metaphysical battery-pack in the form of his approval; and as Ohad Nachtomy points out, this battery is of a very peculiar kind, since it never runs down.[34] But this peculiarity disappears when we recall that the monadic realm is not physical and that its "force" is simply the law of the series that assigns one perceptual state after another. From a mathematical point of view, there is no difficulty because, *mathematically speaking*, infinite series *are* self-executing. In the physical world, we have to take the time and trouble to calculate successive terms and write them down: $\frac{1}{2}$, $\frac{1}{3}$, $\frac{1}{4}$, etc. But mathematically, they are already implicit in the left-hand term. Infinite series "run themselves," which was doubtless another quality that made them an appealing means for thinking the concept of the monad.

But is a mathematical object ontologically sufficient to serve as the engine for a monad? How can such an object "run" the thoughts of a monad if it is itself no more than an object of thought? In the classical world, Plato granted numbers and geometric shapes an independent existence, while Aristotle demoted them to mere abstractions made by the human mind from material things and their relations. Leibniz split the difference, regarding numbers as relational but real.[35] Indeed, Leibniz insists on numerous occasions that mathematical objects have intrinsic qualities that derive from immanent necessity and that even God cannot alter them by an act of divine will.[36] A number of prominent modern philosophers, including Willard Van Orman Quine, Hilary Putnam, Kurt Gödel, and more recently, Alain Badiou (though in a very different fashion), have likewise endorsed the ontological reality of mathematical objects.[37] Gödel may even have been influenced by Leibniz's thinking and language on this count.[38]

Leibniz not only grants mathematical objects at least some degree of ontological self-sufficiency; he also assigns them something like a regulative force with respect to other kinds of entities. As he remarks in the *New System*, "The utility of mathematical meditations is not in any way diminished by their being ideal, because actual things could never go against their rules; and in fact we can say that this is what the reality of phenomena consists in, and what distinguishes them from dreams."[39] Here mathematical objects do not merely *describe* actual beings. They lay down rules that such beings must follow. And indeed, actual beings derive their reality *only from following these mathematical rules*. Compare this evocative passage: "Number is thus a basic metaphysical figure, as it were, and arithmetic a kind of statics of the universe by which the powers of things are discovered."[40] Mathematics spills over, of its own accord, into both physics and metaphysics; and quantities, into force. The perspective that sees the monad as infinite mathematical series thus calls for its own mapping onto the perspective that sees the monad as an array of active and passive forces. Mathematics is a monadic engine, with its own power supply.[41] When writing about force in a letter to De Volder, Leibniz states that "one must pass though this door [i.e., that of force] from mathematics to metaphysics."[42] In a sense, what is the monad but a perpetual passing through the door from mathematics to metaphysics?

And here an even more radical ontological question poses itself: if the perceptions in a monad are a result of its underlying algorithm, which of the two is more "real" or fundamental: the perceptual product or the mathematical machinery that generates it? In one respect, we should have to choose the perceptions. Certainly, these are what is real to the monad itself. The monad's status as algorithm is necessarily barred from its own consciousness (though Leibniz's metaphysics makes it apparent to us in a general way). It is not aware of its own mathematical machinery, and that machinery is there *in order to produce* the perceptions. The monad experiences only its perceptions and in some sense *is* nothing more than those perceptions. To re-borrow Leibniz's borrowing of Aristotelian terms, the distinction here is between final and efficient causality. The perceptions are the final cause—the reason the whole mechanism exists in the first place— while the algorithm is the efficient cause, or the way of bringing it about.[43] And since Leibniz argues that the physical kingdom operates mainly via efficient causes while the spiritual or monadic kingdom ultimately answers to final causes (even if efficient ones can be found there), we have yet another reason for granting priority to the perceptions.[44] And yet. . . . Despite all this, an alternative, mathematical ontology sometimes emerges. Leibniz declares that "the essence of the substance *consists in* the law of the sequence of changes," and again, "this law of order . . . constitutes the individuality of each particular substance."[45] In this more radical version, mathematical objects are not merely real. They are, if not the only real things, at least the most real ones.[46] Mathematical ontologies of this kind are not unprecedented, of course. One can find different versions running back from Descartes and Galileo all the way to Plato and Pythagoras, and then forward to Alain Badiou.[47]

But the nature of a mathematical ontology also changes along with the specific mathematics on which it is based. A Platonic ontology draws on mathematical objects that are essentially static: numbers and geometric figures. The unchangeable nature of such objects grounds that of Platonic forms in general and locates reality in what is rather than what becomes. But the mathematical series is an object that is also a process, indeed an unending one. It rescues becoming from the merely aleatory by subjecting it to a law. It thereby, in effect, reconciles being and becoming. The monad is a process of perpetual movement from one perception to another, an endless becoming that is the expression of its being. The notion of the infinite series enables Leibniz to found not only the physical, natural world but also the subjective, mental one on a mathematical basis and to grasp the latter as a dynamic process. At some level, nothing exists but infinite series. Everything else is epiphenomenal.

This mathematical ontology is, I would suggest, a deep ancestor of the informational ontology at work in some versions of contemporary physics. Nowhere is this ontology more directly and canonically stated than by the eminent physicist John A. Wheeler as the principle of "It from Bit":

> Otherwise put, every it—every particle, every field of force, even the space-time continuum itself—derives its function, its meaning, its very existence entirely—even if in some contexts indirectly—from the apparatus-elicited answers to yes or no questions, binary choices, bits.
>
> It from bit symbolizes the idea that every item of the physical world has at bottom—at a very deep bottom, in most instances—an immaterial source and explanation; that what we call reality arises in the last analysis from the posing of yes-no questions and the registering of equipment-evoked responses; in short, that all things physical are information-theoretic in origin and this is a participatory universe.[48]

It is worth noting that Wheeler cites Leibniz twice in the above-quoted article—once to the effect that the universe is real even if only phenomenal, and once on the unreality of space and time.[49] Conversely, Leibniz himself describes all created things as "different combinations of unity and zero"—in other words, as a string of binary code.[50]

The reality of mathematical objects would seem to solve some basic problems for our project of building a monad. But at the same time, it creates others. The working ontology of mathematicians leads them to describe their labors, not as acts of creation but as acts of discovery. One "discovers" a mathematical proof, one does not invent it. That is to say, mathematical objects and their truths are held to exist in a timeless, Platonic realm. We can progressively come to know them, but we do not cause them to be in any way. We come upon them as explorers come upon preexisting land masses. But if this is the case, in what sense can we be said to "build" a monad, even if we were to hit upon the (impossible) algorithm that would produce one? We would simply have become aware of a mathematical object that was there all along without our previously having noticed it.

But this problem is a productive one that can lead us even deeper into Leibnizian metaphysics. For Leibniz, there is an infinite number of possible universes, each of which contains a different array of monads and monadic relations. God chooses the optimal one to actualize, which means that the laws of the (infinite) series for those monads in the chosen universe are somehow realized in a way that the others are not. This is the arena of the battery pack or "divine fulgurations" of God's approval, discussed earlier. If mathematical ontology were all that was involved, the unrealized monadic series would be just as real as the actualized ones, since their underlying algorithms are ontologically indistinguishable from the chosen ones. Hence some kind of supplement must intervene. A useful analogy for grasping this fact might run as follows: a chosen (i.e., realized) series is to an unrealized one as an infinite series that is actually calculated is to one that is not. If I take, say, the harmonic series and actually start calculating and adding up the terms, I convert what is otherwise an ideal mathematical object into a real *event*—the event of calculation. In effect, I am making myself into the hardware upon which the algorithm of the series is run. My choice to calculate a given infinite series and not others is like God's choice to realize certain monads and not others. Of course, this choice to calculate can never be completed by us, precisely because infinite series are infinite. Only God is the mathematician who can do these calculations. We shall return to this point later.

Having laid out a case for viewing (and building) a monad as a mathematical series, I will now apply the concept to a couple of issues. One is that of time, with which the monad has a complex and seemingly contradictory relationship. On the one hand, the monad seems tied to temporal sequence in that appetition leads from one perception to the next, just as a film or streaming video plays out in time. But on the other hand, Leibniz holds that time, like space, has something imaginary about it. It is a way of ordering events, just as spatial position is, but it has no ultimate foundation in being. At a deep level the monad has no more to do with time than it does with space. Indeed, one of the reasons that an infinite series is "like" a monad (or "is" a monad) is that, as a mathematical object, it exists in neither time nor space.

Here again the infinite series is illuminating. In the case of the harmonic series, the sequence of fractions seems to imply a temporal order: since we read from left to right, we think "first take $\frac{1}{1}$, and then add $\frac{1}{2}$, and then add $\frac{1}{3}$, etc." But mathematically, there is no "and then." There is simply the plus sign of addition. *We* spontaneously turn a mathematical operator into a temporal sequence because we experience everything temporally. We write out the figures, or read them, one after the other. Hence we project temporality onto what is strictly speaking nontemporal. This is what Leibniz means when, in the above-quoted letter to De Volder, he insists that succession is a series but that a series is not necessarily a succession. But perhaps the mistake of confusing series with succession is metaphysically significant. Simply put, we can think of time or temporal succession itself as an *expression* of the mathematical or monadic series: a way of converting it into a physical (or phenomenal) medium. Time expresses the essentially nontemporal relations among perceptions within a monad, and among monads as well.[51] It is also a way of rendering them phenomenally compossible internally, since one can't experience more than one perceptual state at a time. In a sense, then, the act of calculating a series is what converts a mathematical operation into a temporal one, thus "realizing" what would otherwise be an ideal order *as* a temporal one.

I want to turn next to one of most problematic dimensions of the monad: the crushingly deterministic worldview seemingly implied by its preprogrammed nature. This was at least as disturbing to Leibniz's contemporaries as it is to us, and Leibniz accordingly felt compelled to return repeatedly to the issue of human freedom.[52] Much of what he has to say on the topic is, however, incompatible with his conception of the monad as preprogrammed "spiritual automaton"—not so much a solution of the problem as a way of pretending it doesn't exist. In the *Critique of Practical Reason*, Kant remarked acidly that Leibniz's metaphysics assigned to human beings "the freedom of a turnspit, which when once wound up also carries out its motions of itself."[53] but I would like to suggest that it assigns to them instead the freedom of an infinite series.

How is freedom to be conceived here? Not, certainly, in the sense that such a series could spontaneously "decide" to change the order or nature of the sums it spits out. The harmonic series, for instance, is not free to produce $\frac{1}{\pi}$ as one of its terms, however much it might like to. But the terms it *does* produce are the product *of its own law* and hence of its own "nature," so to speak. Nothing outside of the infinite series can intervene in or divert its workings.[54] The unalterable nature of the series is the sign of its autonomy. Were any of its terms as encountered unexpectedly different, *that* would be the sign that an outside hand had altered the series to suit itself—the sign, that is, of determinism. In its absence, the infinite series spontaneously unfolds its own nature.

In his book *Gödel, Escher, Bach*, where Douglas Hofstadter promotes an algorithmic model of consciousness, he offers an idea of human freedom comparable in some ways to Leibniz's. "We *feel* self-programmed," he argues, because we experience only the self-looping software of our brains, not the deterministic neural hardware that underlies it.[55] The mind "cannot monitor its own processes in complete detail, and therefore has a sort of *intuitive* sense of its workings, without full understanding. From this balance between self-knowledge and self-ignorance comes the feeling of free will." We are very complicated sorts of computer programs, but they are *our* programs and we are blissfully unaware of them, which provides us with the effect of freedom.[56]

Leibniz compares freedom to an irrational number, an idea deserving of some consideration in this context.[57] An irrational number is a real number that cannot be made by dividing two integers. Indeed, its name means "without ratio." As in the case of (most famously) π, irrational numbers can be represented decimally as infinitely long strings of numerals that are not repeating or predictable but are, in at least some instances, calculable.[58] One of Leibniz's notable mathematical discoveries, in fact, was an infinite series that could calculate the value of π—

or, more precisely, of $\frac{\pi}{4}$, to any degree of accuracy. The sequence of an irrational

yet calculable number cannot be predicted in advance of being calculated.[59] And so here is another difference between an infinite series and Kant's turnspit: the latter is monotonously repetitive, while the former can produce endless, unpredictable novelty *even while adhering unwaveringly to the "law of the series."*[60]

Another, related way in which mathematics opens a door onto the possibility of freedom is by way of infinite analysis. Necessary truths, Leibniz claims, are those that can be demonstrated within a finite series of steps. But contingent truths are those that require an infinite number of steps to be proved, with the result that determinism is endlessly deferred. Entities such as we, who are implicated in an infinity of relations with other beings, therefore fall under the aegis of the contingent as infinite analysis.[61]

The wit of Kant's "freedom of turnspit" remark derives from the fact that a turnspit does indeed have its own "law of the series," however circular and monotonous that might be. In that respect, at least, it displays in debased form the autonomy of a Leibnizian monad. But the Kantian turnspit is also heteronomous in the sense that it is mere instrument. Its functioning serves another—the turnspit does not get to enjoy the meat it roasts. Leibniz insists, by contrast, that we are programmed so as to experience a maximally possible happiness—or at least such happiness as is compatible with the optimality of the universe as a whole. We are therefore ends and not means—not mere instruments of God. We are preprogrammed, it is true, and while this removes the spontaneity that would arise from a genuinely contingent world, or even one in which we enjoyed freedom of a more conventional sort, we are at least free to unfold our natures without interference and even to experience what appear to us (wrongly) to be genuine moments of spontaneity or free choice. One could do worse than to enjoy the freedom of an infinite series.

If one wants nevertheless to retain a more traditional, "absolute" notion of freedom, one must therefore turn from human beings to God. Leibniz never describes God as a monad, and he never implies that there is an underlying "law of the series" to God's actions. Indeed, such a notion would be flagrantly contradictory. A more traditional notion of freedom is therefore not entirely excluded from Leibniz's system but rather transferred from the human to the divine realm. And yet, divine freedom is not entirely unconditioned, either. First of all, the criteria by which God judges the optimality of the best, chosen universe are themselves of objective validity and hence independent of divine volition. Tellingly, Leibniz expresses this fact by comparing these criteria to mathematical truths that are likewise independent of God's will.[62] Moreover, God's status as infinitely good and wise means that he cannot but choose the objectively best universe to realize. God does not therefore so much "choose" the best universe, then, as simply *acknowledge* the preexisting superiority of the best, as he must do given his own nature. In acknowledging an independent truth, God finds himself in a position rather like that of the mathematician who discovers rather than creates a proof.

Leibniz was interested in the mathematical problem of the limit, and I think we are approaching a limit here as well. From the realm of the mathematical, we seem to be passing over into the theological. It is not as though mathematics ceases to play a role here, but it appears unable to resolve all of the problems that the theological sphere generates. At some point, our mathematical model exhausts itself by raising questions it cannot answer on its own terms. If thought is to proceed, then, a change of perspective is required. Or, to phrase it otherwise, different threads from the transdisciplinary fabric must come into play and take over for the mathematical.

So, this is the second, more consequential, and more instructive way in which our project of building a monad fails. The first, more local way involves the impossibility (indeed, incoherence) of it as a mathematical project. But this second way involves the inadequacy of any one model, any one descriptive method, for approaching the monad. A mathematical perspective enriches our understanding of the monad but reaches its own internal limits and must then be supplemented by others. Those in turn reach their limits and must give way to others still. In module 11, we shall approach the problem of the monad via another, little explored pathway—the political. What we discover there will converge with our mathematical themes in some respects but cannot be reduced to them. Both the mathematical and the political, along with the biological, the optical, the aesthetic, the theological, etc., converge in the transdisciplinary blend from which the monad is thought and ceaselessly rethought.

CHAPTER 11

Monadic Politics

The snowball is a model for the soul because billions of souls are embedded in it, though none can dominate or even characterize it.

—John Ashbery

D o monads have politics? And if so, what might the politics of a monadic world look like? In posing this question, I am not attempting to bring Leibniz's metaphysics into line with his political writings, where he emerges as a constitutional monarchist of a liberal and tolerationist bent—one who understands the benefits of a republic but does not ultimately endorse it as a form of government.[1] Rather, I want to explore the forms of political potential inherent to, or implied by, that metaphysics, which may or may not align with Leibniz's avowed political stances. Before commencing, it must be observed that one thing Leibnizian metaphysics does is devalue the actual political world. This is because political bodies of whatever type count for Leibniz as mere aggregations lacking the true unity of substance, hence to be classed with flocks of sheep or piles of rocks. Indeed, in a letter to Arnauld, he explicitly compares the difference between unified substances and a flock of sheep with that between "a man and a community, like a people, army, society or college, which are moral beings in which there is something imaginary, and dependent on the fiction of our mind."[2] Individual human beings possess substantial unity, but gatherings of them do not, however organized they may be. Hence the latter are less real than the former. A kind of antipolitical flavor inheres as well in Leibniz's view that monads do not interact, and in the way his nominalism denies even logical relations among them. One could be forgiven for thinking that Leibnizian metaphysics is structured in part by a studious avoidance, and denigration, of politics, lest anyone should draw unwelcome political conclusions from his thinking.

Nevertheless, political or at least proto-political themes do occasionally sound, albeit faintly, through Leibniz's metaphysical realms. Perhaps the most suggestive of these is his notion of a dominant monad (*monas dominans* or *monas dominatrix*).[3] Because bodies are simply aggregates or compounds of other bodies, a dominant monad is required in order to confer unity upon them. Organic bodies, in particular, exhibit degrees of unity and functional organization that inorganic ones do not. A mouse's body is made of parts (and, as Leibniz holds, those parts have parts and those parts have parts . . .), but its various organs and systems cooperate in such a way that the mouse's body perceives and moves and feeds as one thing—a mouse. And this higher degree of functional organization must of necessity express a different level of organization among the monads associated with the mouse's component bodies. All of those monads appear to be organized under the aegis of the mouse's mind—its dominant monad, which confers unity upon the whole. But the division of monads into dominant and dominated also appears to cast the structure of organic bodies as a proto-political order.

Why describe the organizing or unifying function of the monad as domination? The term can be taken to imply a monarchical system in which one monad "rules" over an infinity of others, in which case one is tempted to borrow Abraham Bosse's famous frontispiece to Thomas Hobbes's *Leviathan* and apply it to the structure of a corporeal body for Leibniz (figure 11.1).

An intriguing literary parallel to this notion, and a possible inspiration for Leibniz's concept of the dominant monad, occurs in Cyrano de Bergerac's *Histoire comique des États et Empires du soleil*. There the narrator encounters a tree composed of tiny creatures who then dissolve the form of the tree, engage in a dance, and form into a human body that comes to life when the "King" of the little people enters the body through its mouth and animates it.[4]

We can initially temper suggestions of monadic absolutism by recalling that the Latin *dominus* can also mean "host" or "master of a feast." However, such meanings can expand but not displace the more usual understanding of domination as mastery, lordship, or possession. Some further questions associated with monadic domination then include: How can one monad "dominate" others when monads do not interact? How exactly does a dominant monad do the work

11.1 Thomas Hobbes, *Leviathan* (London, 1651), frontispiece (detail).

of unifying its body? Does the dominance relation obtain between the dominant monad and its body or between the dominant monad and the subordinate monads associated with its bodily parts?

The secondary literature on monadic dominance, which is not extensive, advances several proposals for what constitutes dominance for Leibniz: (1) the dominant monad perceives its associated body more clearly than do the dominated monads;[5] (2) the dominant monad is more "perfect" than the dominated monads;[6] (3) the dominant monad offers a better reason for the nature and existence of the body than do the dominated monads;[7] (4) the dominant monad synthesizes the perceptions of the dominated monads;[8] (5) the dominant monad functionally organizes the dominant monads.[9] With the exception of item 4 in the list, all of these can find some direct or indirect textual support within Leibniz's writings.[10] They clearly overlap to some degree, but at the same time they cannot be fully synthesized under the aegis of one master concept. In other words, they exhibit the practice of cognitive mapping or conceptual perspectivalism in which

Leibniz habitually engages when faced with complex issues. The various commentators advance their own favorites and criticize the alternatives as problematic, but the fact is that they are all problematic in different ways. This is a demerit only if one demands a degree of systematicity that Leibniz does not deliver. Perhaps it is fitting that there is no "dominant concept" in the debate over dominant monads.

In a letter to Des Bosses, Leibniz offers the following remarks on monadic domination:

> I believe that monads have a full existence, and that they cannot be conceived of as parts that are said to be potentially in a whole. Nor do I see what a dominant monad takes away from the existence of other monads, since there is, in fact, no communication between them but only an agreement. The unity of corporeal substance in a horse does not arise from any refraction of monads but from a superadded substantial bond, through which nothing at all is changed in the monads themselves. Some worm can be a part of my body and subject to my soul as its dominant monad, and the same worm can have other little animals in its body subject to its dominant monad. But considered in terms of monads themselves, domination and subordination consist only in degrees of perception.[11]

This particular passage invokes the concept of the substantial bond that appears only in the correspondence with Des Bosses and can be set aside for present purposes. Doing so, the following points emerge: (1) Monadic domination works through agreement or consensus among noncommunicating monads. The dominant monad does not issue orders or exert any causal force on the dominated monads. It is not the metaphysical counterpart to a Hobbesian monarch, though even the latter rules by unanimous contractual consent of his subjects. (2) All dominated monads are also dominant monads. While they play a subordinate role within the body in which they are embedded and over which a dominant monad presides, *they* are the dominant monad with respect to their own bodies and hence with respect to the infinity of infinities of monads embedded within them. And since the structure of bodies nested within bodies goes on forever, there is no "last monad" that is merely dominated and lacks an infinity of monads over which it in turn presides. As a result of this, the question of whether a given monad is to be described as dominant or dominated becomes largely perspectival. Dominated or dominant *with respect to what?* (3) All monads have complete existences and cannot be reduced to a merely functional role as "parts" of another monad. (4) The dominant monad is distinguished from the dominated ones only through a greater clarity of perception. It seems reasonable to interpret this last along the lines suggested by Bertrand Russell and say that it means greater perception specifically of the body in which they all participate rather than a general superiority of perceptual capacities. This is, then, a version of domination so modest as to render it difficult to say of what exactly it consists or even why Leibniz employs that particular term. It is as if his choice of "domination" were designed to empty it of all its usual associations. And because of this, it is likewise difficult to say how exactly the dominant monad accomplishes the work of converting its nested individuals into a unity.

Here I want to look more closely at one attempt to resolve this dilemma. Ohad Nachtomy interprets the role of the dominant monad as involving functional organization of its nested individuals. I quote him here at length:

Animals and plants vividly exemplify a functional hierarchy, which is particularly evident in the Aristotelian notion of final causality ascribed to their activities and endorsed by Leibniz. It is also consistent with Aristotle's notion of a hierarchy of ends. For example, an acorn develops into a mature oak through the activation of matter by its entelechy in accordance with the acorn's final form. In such organic examples, the various functions of the constituents comprising the animal or plant may be seen as serving the telos and executing its natural development. In turn, the telos of an individual can be viewed as a program of action consisting of numerous sub-programs of action. All the sub-structures that make up an oak tree—branches, leaves, cells, subcellular constituents, etc.—are organized by a single program and directed towards a single end, which gives the tree its unity. At the same time, each constituent is fully organized (and in turn organizes its sub-structures) towards the fulfillment of its function. A leaf is a unit whose function is to produce sugar which provides energy for the tree's growth. The leaf itself may be seen as a fully organized unit whose constituents are organized and activated in order to perform their functions (e.g., one of chlorophyll's functions is to provide color) and thereby to contribute to the function of the leaf. In turn, their constituents, such as cells, are themselves entirely organized towards performing their function in the overall program of the leaf, which in turn is organized towards performing its function in the program of the oak.[12]

Understanding dominance through final rather than efficient causality is appealing in that the dominant monad doesn't "make" the others do anything. Rather, the same goal or telos, expressed more clearly in the dominant monad, is shared by each subordinate monad as well. This would seem to accord with the consensus model set forth in the letter to Des Bosses. Nachtomy elaborates this model to include nested *teloi* programmed into nested individuals. Smaller units have their own subprograms and embedded teloi that enable them to carry out functions necessary for the next higher level, all of them hierarchically coordinated to the functioning of the whole.

While there is much to be said in its favor, however, Nachtomy's account leaves some issues unresolved. First, Leibniz's insistence to Des Bosses that monads cannot be considered as mere parts of larger wholes seems to rub against the grain of the functionalist model Nachtomy presents. Something Leibniz says in his controversies with Stahl is also interesting in this context:

> But it is not the case that any given part of an organic body is an organic body: thus, although a heart retains its motion for a certain amount of time after it has been torn out of the body, it is not proved from this that the heart is an animated body, for a mere mechanism suffices for some continuation of this motion, even if perception and appetite are wanting.[13]

The heart and other organs perform functions within the body, but they are not themselves organic bodies because they lack perception and appetite. There is no dominant monad for a heart, which is a mere machine made of meat. For the same reason, the leaf in Nachtomy's plant model would not seem to have a dominant monad either. There are entire structural levels in the organism that are functional but not monadic. One would have to descend to the cells, which are both functional and also autonomous entities, to reach the next monadic level. Conversely, in the letter to Des Bosses, a parasitic worm living in an organism is considered subject to the dominant monad but is not particularly functional and not part of the substance of the monad. So we can have functionality without monadic subjection and monadic subjection without functionality.[14] The notion of functional organization is appealing because, after all, that is how bodies actually work. If dominant monads do anything concrete, they would presumably oversee this organization. And yet, the autonomy of monads appears to be at odds with their functionality. They are more adequately and consistently conceived as ends rather than means.

To elaborate this theme, it will be worthwhile to pursue Leibniz's views of the microscopic world more generally, apart from the specific issue of monadic dominance, because what we learn of the former will condition possibilities for the latter. Leibniz, it seems fair to say, possessed a microscopic rather than a telescopic imagination. The discoveries of Leeuwenhoek and Hooke spark his theorizing more than do those of Galileo and Kepler. His mathematical, scientific, and metaphysical attention is drawn more to the infinitesimal than to the infinite. (And for what it is worth, the myopic Leibniz even preferred reading small writing, and wrote in a small hand himself.)[15]

In a letter to the mathematician Johann Bernoulli, Leibniz writes:

Besides, it is no jest, but a firm conviction of mine, that there are animals in the world as much greater than ours as ours are greater than the animalcules of the microscope. Nature knows no limits. And so it is possible on the other hand—indeed, it is necessary—that there should be worlds not inferior to our own in beauty and variety, in the smallest bits of dust, in fact, in atoms. And though this may seem even more wonderful, nothing prevents animals from passing over into such worlds when they die. For I am of the opinion that death is nothing but the contraction of an animal, as generation is nothing but its unfolding [*evolutio*].[16]

It is characteristic of Leibniz's perspectivalism that our observation of animals so much smaller than we are that they are unaware of us raises the possibility—though this seems much closer to a certainty—that there are animals as much larger than we are as we are larger than the animalcules, and as invisible to us as we are to the latter. (And why not so forth, ad infinitum?) Nor is this a one-off; Leibniz postulates immense animals on at least two other occasions.[17]

Microscopic animals occupy a world "not inferior to ours in beauty and variety." Is this because they themselves are not as individuals inferior in these qualities or because the microcosm they produce and inhabit is not? Leibniz seems to imply both. It should not be surprising that for Leibniz, a vast reduction in spatial scale does not necessarily entail a loss of complexity. For one thing, as we have seen, quantity—including size—is, for him, relatively imaginary compared to quality. Moreover, the mathematics of infinity comes into play here—as Leibniz's correspondent Bernoulli would have been acutely aware. No matter how far one goes down the microscopic rabbit hole, the creatures one encounters still have an infinity of creatures within them, over which their dominant monads preside. And since finite quantities subtracted from infinite ones do not reduce the latter even a little, those tiny creatures are every bit as complex as we are. In the draft of a 1699 letter to Thomas Burnet, Leibniz declares that "nothing prevents" the microscopic substances embedded in matter "from being elevated to the degree of perception that we call thought."[18] Correspondingly, the immense creatures inhabiting a world in which we are mere dust motes by comparison are not assumed by Leibniz to be correspondingly more intelligent. Presumably they are less so, since he restricts souls and reason to human beings. So moving upward likewise reinforces the lesson that scale and internal complexity are independent.

When Leibniz insists that the microscopic world is not inferior in beauty to our own, is this a beauty that only we can perceive or one available to its own inhabitants? Here his use of the word "world" (*mundus*) comes into play. Not only are there creatures much smaller than we, but also there are worlds much smaller than ours:

> For it should be recognized, as those celebrated *Micrographers, Kircher* and *Hooke* have observed, that most of the qualities that we are sensible of in larger things, a sharp-eyed observer will detect in proportion in smaller things. And if this proceeds to infinity—which is certainly possible, since the continuum is divisible to infinity—any atom will be of infinite species, like a sort of world, and there will be *worlds within worlds to infinity*. And those who consider this more profoundly will be unable to stop themselves being carried away by a certain ecstasy of admiration, which should be transferred to the Author of things.[19]

The notion of worlds within worlds enhances Leibniz's perspectivalism by suggesting that something vast and even immeasurable in extent exists within the confines of the incredibly tiny, if only we occupy the latter's point of view. The "ecstasy of admiration" mentioned by Leibniz seems to result, in part, from superimposing these seemingly antithetical spatial experiences. Indeed, it can be argued that Leibniz theorizes here and elsewhere a kind of microscopic sublime.[20]

In addition, the term "world" suggests not merely a distribution of beings in physical space but also a perceptible, habitable, and even cohabitable realm—an environment for being and for being with others. Leibniz's use of the term "world" should therefore be placed in juxtaposition with his use of "stage" or "theater" to describe the movement of beings from the microscopic to the macroscopic worlds, and back again, in the processes of birth and death (see module 03). "Stage" amplifies the senses of spectatorship and even fellowship inherent in "world," and suggests that microscopic beings do not exist in stupefied isolation but enjoy their own richness of perceptual existence. Indeed, there would be a problematic moral economy in condemning infinities upon infinities of creatures to an eternity of relative perceptual impoverishment in order to bring a single fly or mouse into existence. As Leibniz notes, "our body is a kind of world full of an infinity of creatures *which also deserved to exist*" (my emphasis). Every monad is an end in itself, even those participating in the functional organization of larger entities.[21] They are not merely parts engineered to serve a purpose.

I therefore think we are pushing Leibniz's conception only a little if we see monadic worlds as sociable, perceptually rewarding spaces in which monads can flourish to the degree compatible with the optimality of the whole, including their functions in the service of dominant monads at higher tiers. At the same time, "world" suggests that these spaces, complete unto themselves, are also largely sealed off from the others. Each tier or level affords clear perceptions only of entities within that world. Monads at a given tier do not distinctly perceive bodies that are either vastly larger or vastly smaller than they are but live the clear zones of their existence only within their own tier. If they have a functional role to play with respect to the dominant monad of a much larger creature, then they presumably fulfill it unconsciously, since that larger creature is undetectable to their perceptive capacities.[22] Again, think of the microbiome in our gut. The populations of bacteria there perform functions crucial for our physical and even psychological well-being, yet those bacteria are unaware of these functions or even of us. They live their bacterial lives, reacting only to entities relevant to their world.[23] Their natures simply happen to harmonize with our own. Of course, the Leibnizian inhabitants of his counterpart to our microbiome would be infinitely more complex than bacteria and thus presumably capable of more complex and differentiated perceptions. And their worlds would presumably offer a correspondingly rewarding landscape for their perceptual capacities, at least insofar as this is compossible with their functional roles.

Leibniz was not alone among seventeenth-century thinkers in imagining microscopic worlds. The poet, fiction writer, and natural philosopher Margaret Cavendish, for instance, adopted this notion more than once as a theme for lyric treatment. In her poem "A World in an Earring," the lady's earring in question encompasses an entire miniature cosmos invisible to its wearer: stars, planets, a sun and moon, landscapes with pastures and cattle, towns and buildings, human societies with our habits and foibles. Like Leibniz, Cavendish delights in imagining vast, cosmic spaces contained within minute ones. And, like Leibniz, she emphasizes the variety, richness, and beauty of her microscopic universe. Her world within an earring is a social one, the inhabitants of which interact much as we do. In fact, as the poem proceeds, it picks up a satirical flavor by reducing the characteristic activities of gallants and ladies to Lilliputian—indeed, microbial—scale. Leibniz, of course, does not imagine creatures who are necessarily "like us" in his endless succession of smaller worlds and stages. Indeed, the imperative of maximal variety within order that governs divine creation demands that such creatures should be very different from us, with correspondingly different sensoria and kinds of perceptual experience—as the microscope appeared to confirm.

My overarching point is that any notion of monadic dominance as functional subordination in which the component entities are reduced to dull vassals carrying out delimited roles rubs against the grain of a competing vision that emphasizes the richness, variety, beauty, and complexity of the microscopic world. It is certainly possible to see in Leibniz's understanding of monadic dominance and the microscopic world a refracted version of his own constitutional monarchist views. But it seems to me that his metaphysics offers a vision potentially more radical than his explicitly political one. Just as Leibniz produces a version of causality emptied of anything recognizable as causation, so he produces a version of dominance emptied of anything resembling domination. Of course, the apparent unanimity or consensus of monads within a given organism is antipolitical, but the variety of the microscopic world tugs against this.

As an indication of the political potential inherent in Leibnizian metaphysics, I would point to a fascinating passage in a letter to the Electress Sophie:

A seemingly small thing can change the whole course of general affairs. A lead bullet travelling low enough will encounter the head of an able general, and this will ensure that the battle is lost. A melon eaten at the wrong time will kill a King. A certain prince will not be able to sleep one night because of the food he ate in the evening; this will give him despondent thoughts and will lead him to take a violent resolution on matters of state. A spark will jump to a shop, and that will lead to Belgrade or Nice being lost. There is no devil or angel who can foresee all these small things which give rise to such great events, because nothing is so small which does not arise from a great variety of even smaller circumstances, and these circumstances from others again, and so on to infinity. Microscopes show us that the smallest things are enriched with variety in proportion to the great. Moreover, all the things of the universe have such a close and remarkable connection between themselves that nothing happens here which does not have some insensible dependency on things which are a hundred thousand leagues from here. For every corporeal action or passion, in some small part of its effect, depends on the impressions of the air and of other neighbouring bodies, and these again on their neighbours further away, and this carries on through a continuous chain, irrespective of distance.[24]

This passage exhibits Leibniz's anticipative version of the "butterfly effect" that amplifies tiny perturbations in chaotic systems. The causative force of an event is not proportional to its magnitude and can therefore escape from its own tier or level to affect things above it—at least, if a vast swarm of other microscopic entities somehow gets drawn into its force field. Causation, that is to say, is not exclusively top-down but can be bottom-up as well, such that even the infinitesimal can wreak havoc upon the macroscopic world. That Leibniz's regicide melon dispatches a king rather than an ordinary citizen multiplies its effects still more, but it also reveals a somewhat anarchic political imagination at work in this fantasy.[25] The prince whose ill-timed meal results in political disaster bespeaks the fact that his "dominant monad" is subject to the body it supposedly organizes. Political and military authorities succumb repeatedly to the seething mass of microcauses in which they find themselves inevitably immersed. It is hard to resist the thought that Leibniz, so careful never to offend his patrons and political superiors, here enjoys a brief revenge fantasy hosted by his metaphysics. It is as if one of the tiny subjects in the body politic of Bosse's frontispiece to Hobbes were somehow to leap up, grab the monarch's scepter, and crush his skull with it. Of course, the enabling condition for this fantasy is that natural causes rather than political ones are at work. A melon and not a rebel dispatches the king. But this crossing of the metaphysical and the political, while neutering Leibniz's fantasy enough to render it safe for consumption by the Electress Sophie, does not quite eliminate its volatility. Political impulses of various and contradictory kinds traverse Leibnizian metaphysics. In the cited passage, obscure, anarchic currents from within Leibniz's own microlevels appear to surge up and disturb the rule of his sovereign authorial self.

Another instance in which political language infiltrates Leibniz's thinking is his concept of the republic of souls:

> *Those souls, finally, are immortal which are receptive of laws.*
>
> These alone are to be considered citizens of the universe, i.e. of the Republic, of which God is King. To these are destined punishments, to these rewards.[26]

Only human souls are capable of moral action and hence they form an elite grouping among monads, enjoying a privileged relationship both with God and with one another. Leibniz describes this as a republic and moreover refers to its inhabitants as citizens rather than subjects. Despite the fact that God rules over this republic as king, Leibniz intends to reduce, not enlarge, the distinction between this divine monarch and the citizens of his republic: "And it is this general Republic or Society of minds under this supreme Monarch that is the most elevated part of the universe, composed of so many little Gods under this great God. For it may be said that created spirits differ from God only as more differs from less, as finite differs from infinite."[27] Moreover, "universal right is the same for God as for men."[28] The just and the good are not arbitrary postulates of the divine will but objectively valid ideas, "founded in the immutable nature of things," to which God voluntarily subjects himself no less than do human beings.[29] Heaven and earth answer to a common moral law. Leibniz appears to have something like a constitutional monarchy in mind, but he did not need to draw on the language of republicanism in order to invoke it, and that he does so is telling. At the same time, and characteristically, this republic of souls is kept at a safe distance from any actual political order, and Leibniz does not draw any conclusions from it about the best form of secular government. And yet, here again, metaphysics appears to be engaged in political thinking by other means. What lessons readers derive from it is up to them. It would be foolhardy, in any case, to assume that the political implications of Leibnizian metaphysics are necessarily conservative.

Some of the themes I have been pursuing here find an answering voice in the visionary book *Monadology and Sociology* (1893) by the French sociologist Gabriel Tarde. Tarde, a startlingly original and even poetic thinker, was ultimately eclipsed in the field of sociology by his contemporary Émile Durkheim, with whose approach he was profoundly at odds. He fared better at the hands of French philosophy and theory—praised by Henri Bergson, revived by Gilles Deleuze, and anointed by Bruno Latour as the intellectual forebearer of the latter's actor network theory.[30] In *Monadology and Sociology*, Tarde does what Leibniz would not—convert a monadological metaphysics into an explicit theory of social and political organization. In so doing, he also modifies Leibniz's system in ways that accentuate the more radical strains of potential within it.

Monadology and Sociology begins by declaring that modern science has vindicated Leibniz's monadological views. The atom in physics, the cell in biology, and the increasing applications of calculus to the sciences bespeak the universal role of the infinitesimal in the constitution of all things. These micro-constituents are inherently diverse and various. They are also necessarily conscious, as Tarde attempts to prove through arguments similar to those of today's panpsychists (see the following module). Physical, biological, and social bodies alike are aggregates of aware, active, microscopic entities. In place of Leibniz's perception and appetition, Tarde equips his monads with belief and desire. Tardeian desire or avidity is the drive within each monad to realize and universalize its belief or point of view: "it is the case that an immense sphere of light spread through space is due to the unique vibration, multiplied by contagion, of one central atom of ether,—that the entire population of a species originates from the prodigious multiplication of one unique first ovulary cell, in a kind of generative radiation,—that the presence of the correct astronomical theory in millions of human brains is due to the multiplied repetition of an idea which appeared one day in a cerebral cell of Newton's brain."[31] Whereas the Leibnizian monad merely *perceives* the universe around it, the Tardeian monad strives to remake the universe in its own image, to impose its belief on all the others, be it through conquest, persuasion, or simply "the contagion of the example."[32] Since all other monads wish to do the same, a Darwinian struggle ensues in which one infinitesimal point manages to propagate its perspective and recruit all the others to it—though always only partially. Thus is Tarde's counterpart to the Leibnizian dominant monad formed, whether as the ego in the self, the social order of a population, or the structure of a cell or a star. Tarde's monadic sociology posits that *"everything is a society*, that every phenomenon is a social fact."[33] His sociology aspires to explain not only the social world but the natural one as well; it exhibits an avid, unbounded drive toward explanatory mastery that exemplifies the very process it describes. "All sciences seem destined to become branches of sociology."[34]

Tarde inherits several premises from Leibniz, which together structure his universal sociology. One is the absence of a final term or lowest level to the hierarchy of monads: "There is no way to call a halt to this descent to the infinitesimal, which, most unexpectedly, becomes the key to the entire universe."[35] A second is a commitment to maximal diversity: "To exist is to differ; difference is, in a sense, the truly substantial side of things; it is at once their ownmost possession and that which they hold most in common."[36] This is Tarde's version of Leibniz's law of the identity of indiscernibles: if two things did not differ in at least some respect, they would be the same thing. Third, Tarde shares with Leibniz the conviction that the monads at every level of organization are every bit as complex and diverse as those above it.[37]

Despite these similarities, there are crucial differences between Leibniz's notion of monadic organization and Tarde's. For Leibniz, diversity is always recouped within unity. The whole point of the dominant monad is to unify its constituent monads; and the principle of harmony, which structures the Leibnizian universe, accommodates maximal diversity *within unity*. But for Tarde, "diversity and not unity is at the heart of things."[38] Thus a kind of Empedoclean Strife replaces Leibniz's preestablished harmony. For Leibniz, the dominant monad is primary both logically and actually, and the subordinate monads serve functional roles within it. For Tarde, the dominant monad is not appointed from above but emerges from the struggles among monads. Higher-order phenomena arise from lower-level ones rather than serving as their presupposition. In contrast to present-day theories of emergence, however, in which the emergent property is usually something more complex than that from which it arises (say, consciousness from neurons), Tarde rejects the "widespread prejudice according to which the result is always more complex than its conditions, and the action more differentiated than its agents, whence it follows that universal evolution is necessarily a movement from the homogenous to the heterogeneous, in a progressive and constant process of differentiation."[39] Looking at societies, for example, "we see agents, men, much more differentiated and more sharply characterized as individuals, and richer in continual variations, than are the mechanisms of government or the systems of laws or of beliefs, or even dictionaries or grammars, and this differentiation is maintained by their competition."[40] Moreover in Tarde's view, social evolution is almost always in the direction of increasing uniformity, though that process also serves as the precondition for new and unprecedented forms of diversity.[41]

For higher-order phenomena to emerge from lower, a diverse array of monads must be recruited to join the project of the dominant one. But this recruitment is always necessarily partial and provisional. The dominant monad's

> constitutive elements, the soldiers of these diverse regiments, the temporary incarnation of their laws, always belong only by one aspect of their being to the world they constitute, and by other aspects escape it. This world would not exist without them; without the world, conversely, the elements would still be something. The attributes which each element possesses in virtue of its incorporation into its regiment do not form the whole of its nature; it has other tendencies and other instincts which come to it from its other regimentations; and, moreover (we will shortly see the necessity of this corollary), still others which come to it from its basic nature, from itself, from its own fundamental substance which is the basis of its struggle against the collective power of which it forms a part.[42]

For Tarde, the subordinated monads are actually more ontologically substantial than the dominant one, since the former would continue to exist even if the emergent order to which they contribute were to dissolve. Moreover, the subordinated monads have secondary affiliations as well as their own innate inclinations that resist incorporation into the dominant order, which as a result is inherently volatile. No matter how solid and stable they may appear, all social groupings have the potential for instantaneous, revolutionary transformation—what Tarde calls "evolution by leaps or crises."[43] Indeed:

> Forms are only brakes and laws are only dykes erected in vain against the overflowing of revolutionary differences and civil dissensions, in which the laws and forms of tomorrow secretly take shape, and which, in spite of the yokes upon yokes they bear, in spite of chemical and vital discipline, in spite of reason, in spite of celestial mechanics, will one distant day, like the people of a nation, sweep away all barriers and from their very wreckage construct the instrument of a still higher diversity.[44]

Unlike the orderly, harmonious dance that is Leibnizian progression, Tarde envisions an unpredictable, nonlinear and chaotic series of breaks in which subordinate monads defect from their commander and suddenly form new assemblages, instigating both novel uniformities and novel diversities.

It is important, to note, however, that this process is not anarchic. One dominant monad is always replaced by another, and it is only by forming a (partial, provisional) allegiance to the latter that the component monads desert the former. In human societies, this might seem at first to underwrite a "Great Man" theory of history, and Tarde does acknowledge the important role played by a Caesar or Napoleon I in effecting cataclysmic change.[45] On a cosmic scale, Tarde even goes so far as to posit certain dominant monads as having imposed the laws of physics on all the others.[46] At the same time, Tarde undercuts such a "Great Man" view in fundamental ways. Take the case of scientific revolutions:

> The obscure labourers who, by the accumulation of tiny facts, prepare the appearance of a great scientific theory formulated by a Newton, a Cuvier, or a Darwin, compose in some sense the organism of which this genius is the soul; and their labours are the cerebral vibrations of which this theory is the consciousness. Consciousness means in some sense the cerebral glory of the brain's most influential and powerful element. Thus, left to its own devices, a monad can achieve nothing. This is the crucial fact, and it immediately explains another, the tendency of monads to assemble.

Tarde adds that

> the obscure labourers I mentioned above may sometimes have as much merit, erudition, and force of thought, as the celebrated beneficiary of their labours, or indeed even more. I make this remark in passing, to address the prejudice which leads us to judge all external monads inferior to ourselves. If the ego is only a director monad among the myriads of commensal monads in the same skull, why, fundamentally, should we believe the latter to be inferior? Is a monarch necessarily more intelligent than his ministers or his subjects?[47]

A Newton merely reorganizes and reframes the work of innumerable other scientists who may be as intelligent as he. At the same time, it is not Newton but Newton's brain or actually just "a cerebral cell of Newton's brain" that has effected this change. The mind of a Newton is itself an assemblage created under the dominance of one of its components, which in turn may have been organized by one of *its* components, ad infinitum. The scientific "Great Man" thus dissolves into both the myriad of other scientific workers and into his own component parts. Hence, in the end, *it is impossible to locate exactly whence or why dominance emerges*, just as it is impossible to predict when and under what conditions it will do so. There is always a set of microscopic instabilities simmering beneath the surface of the apparently solid and enduring.

Obviously, Tarde takes Leibniz's monadology in directions the latter would be hesitant to go. He (or perhaps a single cell in his brain) does not adopt the Leibnizian system wholesale but reorganizes it under the aegis of his own thinking. But this is inevitable; if one wants to use Leibniz productively rather than simply elucidate or endlessly repeat him, his work must be subject to some retooling and transformation. At the same time, Tarde's thinking accords with some of Leibniz's most fundamental intuitions about the microscopic world, not to mention the volatile political imagination exhibited in the passage from the letter to the Electress Sophie. If Tarde effects an intellectual coup d'état, it is in some sense an authorized one. Tarde's sociological theory elaborates certain strains of political potential already present within Leibniz's metaphysics—strains whose implications and outcomes are no more easily predictable than the fate of a given social formation in Tarde's vision. Certainly, things more interesting than constitutional monarchism can be made of them.

CHAPTER 12

The Mind-Body Problem

Leibniz bequeathed many things to contemporary philosophy. One of the most consequential may be neither a concept nor a methodology but a problem: the mind-body problem. How can mind and body interact if they are of fundamentally different natures? How can consciousness and thought, apparently nonmaterial themselves, arise from the physical organ that is the brain? These are questions hotly debated in contemporary philosophy of mind. If it is an overstatement to grant Leibniz sole credit for originating this problem, he can at least be said to have brought to completion a process begun by Descartes. Cartesian dualism, the division of entities into extended substance and thinking substance, lays the groundwork for the modern mind-body problem. But Descartes's theories of perception and passion somewhat neutralize the force of this dualism by allowing causal interaction between body and mind despite their different natures.

Spinoza's theory of attributes officially denies any such interaction: "The body cannot determine the mind to thinking, nor can the mind determine the body to motion or rest, or to anything else" (*Ethics*, part III, prop. 2), and hence mind and body run in parallel.[1] Here we seem to arrive at something that looks more like the modern mind-body problem. But Spinoza commentators have had some difficulty reconciling Spinoza's apparently clear declaration with his equally clear insistence that "thinking substance and extended substance is one and the same substance, which is understood now under this and now under that attribute" (*Ethics*, part II, prop. 7, scholium).[2] This is turn gets drawn into debates over subjective versus objective interpretations of the attributes.[3] Because the relation between mind and body is a crux—perhaps, *the* crux—of the *Ethics*, Spinoza's non-interactionism is beset with interpretive difficulties. Perhaps chief among these is the fact that Spinoza lends himself to materialist readings in which mind is both ontologically and explanatorily dependent on body.[4] His supposed non-interactionism can therefore end up looking like an unacknowledged interactionism, and moreover an interactionism that moves in one direction, from body to mind. This susceptibility to a materialist reading, far from being seen as a problem, constitutes one of Spinoza's chief attractions for contemporary thinkers examining the relation between mind and brain from the perspective of neuroscience, such as the psychologist Antonio Damasio and the philosopher Catherine Malabou. Spinoza, that is to say, exerts a notable influence on contemporary thinking about mind.[5] But the seemingly compromised nature of his non-interactionism makes him a poor antecedent for the mind-body problem as construed by contemporary philosophers of mind. In the end, Spinoza's mind-body problem is the problem of trying to construe what exactly Spinoza thought about relations between the two.

Leibniz's non-interactionist stance is pellucid by contrast. Mind and body run in parallel, their separate sequences coordinated by God in preestablished harmony. There is no causal interference between them, though they express one another. It is Leibniz, therefore, who completes Cartesian dualism by sealing body off from mind causally. And in so doing, it is Leibniz who establishes the terms of the modern mind-body problem. Leibniz, admittedly, is not a substance dualist as Descartes is. For Leibniz there is only one kind of substance and that is mind. But he is what we might call a descriptive dualist insofar as mind and body are of different natures and can be explained without reference to each other. It is on the question of what exactly body is that Leibniz himself can become fuzzy. But the bright line of non-interactionism remains whether the Leibnizian body is an extended if merely aggregated object or a well-founded phenomenon.[6]

Let us look more closely at Leibnizian non-interactionism and its consequences. One of the principal documents in which Leibniz presents his notion of preestablished harmony between mind and body is the "New System of the Nature of Substances and Their Communication" (1695):

> The body transmits nothing to the soul, nor the soul to the body, and neither is there any need to say that God does it for them. The soul was created from the outset in such a way that all that the body can provide appears in the soul, in virtue of the representative nature which was given to it with its being, for production at the relevant time.[7]

Despite their mutual non-transmission, there is nevertheless an asymmetry between body and soul. Body "appears in the soul" insofar as representations of the body are preprogrammed into it. But soul does not "appear in" body. Bodies operate according to the laws of efficient causality as these play out through the different kinds and quantities of force that each body possesses. Bodies, that is, react to one another (or appear to react), but the physical laws that govern their interactions make no reference to mind, and hence the world of bodies is effectively "blind" to the mental world, whereas the mind "perceives" bodies or at least the expressions or representations of bodies that are already within them.

One consequence of preestablished harmony is that the bodily world is a zombie world: "If minds were eliminated, leaving the laws of nature (which would be impossible), the same thing would happen as if there were minds: books would even be written and read by human machines, though they would understand nothing."[8] In this zombie world, bodies read and write books while understanding nothing because they lack consciousness. But despite Leibniz's use of the counterfactual (because there are minds or souls associated with every body), his physical world does work in precisely this way. Human bodies pick up books, move their eyes and turn pages not because the mind tells them to or because they know what they are doing, but only because a chain of mechanical interactions internal to the physical world make them go through certain sequences of movement. In fact, it can be argued that not only Leibniz's world but the actual world works in this way: our bodies look at books and turn pages, but our bodies do not read. Our minds read. Our bodies *are* zombies.

I invoke the notions of a zombie body and a zombie world because philosophers of mind employ them regularly when wrestling with the mind-body problem. Here is David Chalmers:

> The most obvious way (although not the only way) to investigate the logical supervenience of consciousness is to consider the logical possibility of a *zombie*: someone or something physically identical to me (or to any other conscious being), but lacking conscious experiences altogether. At the global level, we can consider the logical possibility of a *zombie world*: a world physically identical to ours, but in which there are no conscious experiences at all. In such a world, everybody is a zombie.[9]

Chalmers traces the notion of the philosopher's zombie back to the 1970s, but its real originator is Leibniz.[10] That being said, Chalmers's zombie is very different from a Leibnizian one. The former possesses every mental faculty except for conscious experience. Hence it can reproduce ordinary human behaviors without being aware of them. The latter lacks any trace of mind and is therefore a purely corporeal mechanism. The laws of physics alone propel it through the world. There is a mind having its thoughts, but that mind is not "in" the body. For Leibniz, rather, the zombie world, which is physically embodied but not conscious, is redoubled by a ghost world, which is conscious but disembodied. Zombies and ghosts never interact, however, nor can they.[11]

It is not enough for a body to execute what looks to a third party like commands from the mind. A body that picks up a book and scans it with its eyes when the mind wants to read maintains a body-mind parallel, but only in a rough way. Preestablished harmony requires that *every mental event* have a bodily correlate, and vice versa. It is the brain that receives inputs from the senses and converts them into traces, though Leibniz insists that what happens in the brain is not thought: "First of all, by the term *idea* we understand *something which is in our mind*. Traces impressed on the brain are therefore not ideas, for I take it as certain that the mind is something other than the brain or a more subtle part of the brain substance."[12] Brain traces are not thought, but the production of brain traces by way of the nervous and sensory systems is the bodily correlate to, or expression of, thought—or at least, the bodily correlate to sensory perception. What happens to the brain when the mind is having abstract, nonsensory thoughts is rather more difficult to say, since these don't have any obvious "trigger" from outside the body in the way that sensory perceptions do. One must assume that movements of bodies internal to the brain fold or inscribe it in ways that correspond to such thoughts, again responding to subtle networks of cause and effect in the brain matter itself. But the thoughts are not causing the folds, any more than the folds are causing the thoughts.

To claim that minds and bodies can causally interact assumes some questionable premises. First, there would have to be a mechanism whereby a physical entity could affect a nonphysical entity, and vice versa. Second, and even more fundamentally, the very notion of cause is derived from the physical realm and achieves its clearest expression there in the interactions of bodies (one billiard ball strikes another and sets it in motion). So there are questions about whether such a model can be applied to the relations between bodily and nonbodily entities. But even if it can (and here we get to the crux of the matter), Leibniz does not believe in causation even in the physical realm. That is to say, not only do bodies have no causal effects on minds, they do not have causal effects on one another: "Rigorously speaking, no force is transferred from one body to another, but every body moves by an innate force."[13] When one body strikes a second, this merely provides an occasion for the elastic force in the struck body to exert itself. Hence "what we call causes are only concurrent requisites, in metaphysical rigor."[14] There is no causality, only interactions that appear causal:

> However, that whose expression is more distinct is deemed to act, and that whose expression is more confused to be acted upon, since to act is a perfection, and to be acted upon is an imperfection. And that thing from whose state a reason for the changes is most readily provided is adjudged to be the cause. Thus if one person supposes that a solid moving in a fluid stirs up various waves, another can understand the same things to occur if, with the solid at rest in the middle of the fluid, one supposes certain equivalent motions of the fluid (in various waves); indeed, the same phenomena can be explained in infinitely many ways. And granted that motion is really a relative thing, nonetheless that hypothesis which attributes motion to the solid, and from this deduces the waves in the liquid, is infinitely simpler than the others, and for this reason the solid is adjudged to be the cause of the motion. Causes are not derived from a real influence, but from the providing of a reason.[15]

What we deem physical causation is merely the bodily expression of something that is nonbodily: the fact that, given two entities, one expresses their relation—or rather, the reason behind it—more clearly than another. The combined principles of sufficient reason and compossibility mean that some entities will be privileged over others. The privileged entities will express more clearly than others the reasons behind a given sequence of events, and that explanatory privilege will be expressed or represented as an apparent causal force exerted upon entities that express the reason for the sequence less clearly. But this means "cause" is the expression of something noncausal—an appearance or epiphenomenon.

Leibniz's noncausal causality grants to physical bodies an autonomy comparable to the perceptual autonomy of monads. Just as the latter have their perceptions preprogrammed within, so the latter have an immanent set of active and passive forces (elastic force is active, inertia and antitypy or impenetrability are passive) that govern their movements. Indeed, these derivative active and passive forces are the expressions of primary active and passive forces within the monad. Other bodies provide occasions for the exercise of a body's internal forces but do not actually cause changes in position or movement. The autonomy of bodies is just another way in which the monadic and bodily realms express each another. To an external observer, it will look as if minds communicate with minds and bodies cause movement in other bodies, but in neither case is that really happening.

In a sense, then, Leibniz's non-interactionism with respect to mind and body is simply the expression of a larger, indeed all-encompassing non-interactionism. Mind and body do not interact with each other because *nothing interacts with anything else* (except with God). Minds do not interact with other minds, bodies do not interact with other bodies, and bodies do not interact with minds. The question of mind-body interaction does not demand a special solution since it is just one instance of something more general. The problem is solved by being demoted.

One of the correlates of Leibniz's non-interactionism is that minds are not located *in* their associated bodies. But again, this simply manifests the larger fact that they do not exist in space at all:

> In this way of explaining things, space becomes the order of coexisting phenomena, as time is the order of successive phenomena, and there is no absolute or spatial nearness or distance between monads. To say that they are crowded together in a point or disseminated in space is to employ certain fictions of our mind when we willingly seek to imagine things that can only be understood.[16]

Monads will see the world from the perspective of their associated bodies but they are not actually located there, any more than the player of a virtual reality game actually occupies a point in the fictional gaming space.[17] This is one of the many counterintuitive elements of Leibniz's metaphysics, since we "know" that our minds are always "with" our brains. But a little reflection should begin to dislodge this certainty. First of all, our sensed position depends not on where our brain is but on where our perceptual organs are (they happen to be in the same neighborhood). But even so, the connection is not always secure. Think of the phrase "my mind was elsewhere." Well, where *was* it, exactly, if it wasn't where you were? Or where is your mind when you are engrossed in reading a novel? At Mansfield Park? And where is that, on the map? Brains are spatially located, but perhaps minds are not, and for the reason given by Leibniz that they are not physical entities and hence do not pertain to physical space.

Admittedly, there is a lot of "as if" to Leibniz's account. Minds perceive the world *as if* they were located in their associated bodies, although they are not. The sequences going on in minds and bodies are coordinated in such a way that it frequently appears *as if* they interact, although they do not. It would be simpler, surely, just to assume that these things are indeed happening and to begin one's theorizing there, as Leibniz's contemporaries not infrequently observed.[18] But as I have already pointed out, nothing interacts with anything in Leibniz's world. And even if things did, mind and body would still present an especially intractable case because they are of completely incommensurable natures. They can no more interact than my bicycle can interact with logical positivism. None of this is perceived as a problem by Leibniz, and so he does not have a mind-body problem. But he lays the basis for ours.

Obviously, current debates about the relation between mind and brain are too extensive and wide-ranging to admit of systematic discussion in this context. I shall therefore focus on a strain of argument within current philosophy of mind that has a marked relation to Leibniz's thinking. The principal figures here are David Chalmers and Galen Strawson, and while their respective positions do not align exactly, they have enough in common that they offer a relatively united front and have attracted a significant group of adherents as well as critics.[19] Chalmers and Strawson further elaborate and refine a set of arguments made as far back as the 1970s by Thomas Nagel and others. Without setting forth the relevant claims in detail, I shall simply state that they revolve around a fundamental problem: how conscious experience can arise from the workings of the brain. While neuroscientists claim that consciousness is somehow "emergent" from the brain's neural networks, and while most people who aren't engaged in the technicalities of the issue probably assume that this is how things work, Chalmers and Strawson claim to find significant logical and conceptual problems in explaining how conscious experience can arise from matter, however elaborately organized. There are many other forms of mental functioning that look more like computing and that do not require consciousness at all. These pose no problem. But something like the conscious experience of qualia does. As Strawson clams, other examples of physically emergent phenomena don't have to leap quite so wide a gap. Liquidity, for example, arises from conditions that are in some sense proto-liquid, but there is nothing visibly proto-conscious about matter.[20] Notably, one of Leibniz's better-known arguments about how mind cannot arise from brain or body follows a similar logic:

> As for thought, it is certain, as our author more than once acknowledges, that it cannot be an intelligible modification of matter and be comprehensible and explicable in terms of it. That is, a sentient or thinking being is not a mechanical thing like a watch or a mill: one cannot conceive of sizes and shapes and motions combining mechanically to produce something which thinks, and senses too, in a mass where [formerly] there was nothing of the kind—something which would likewise be extinguished by the machine's going out of order.[21]

Of course, there is a vast difference between a watch or mill and the brain's neural networks. But Chalmers and Strawson would endorse Leibniz's arguments. Nevertheless, Chalmers, who associates consciousness with information states, speculates that the former may exist wherever the latter is present, and even suggests (notoriously) that a thermostat may therefore have associated phenomenal states—not very interesting ones, to be sure.[22] But these states will arise from the information, not the hardware. In his view, then, Leibniz's watch or mill might give rise to a kind of proto-consciousness after all, though nothing so complex as the "thought" that Leibniz seeks.

While Strawson insists that consciousness (along with anything else that actually exists) must be a material phenomenon, Chalmers argues that it cannot be, though it still forms part of a natural order and follows natural laws. Strawson is a monist, while Chalmers is a dualist. Despite these differences, however, their shared belief that any materialist explanation of consciousness must fail leads them to the same position: panpsychism. Since consciousness cannot arise from matter, matter must already be conscious—including its most basic components, such as elementary particles, quarks, and whatever else physicists may someday discover. This provides a striking revival of Leibniz's view that bodies are composed of smaller bodies, ad infinitum, each of which has an associated monad or consciousness. Panpsychism and micropanpsychism (the view that the most elementary constituents of matter have protophenomenal states), are now widespread enough among philosophers of mind to constitute a perfectly respectable and even burgeoning (if still somewhat niche) position, generating multiple monographs and essay collections.[23]

Now, as readers of this book will discover, no one loves more than I do to find Leibniz's views, and particularly his more counterintuitive ones, confirmed by later thinkers. But in this case I must demur because contemporary panpsychism strikes me as hopelessly problematic. First of all, there's the issue of a complete lack of scientific evidence that elementary particles have phenomenal states of any kind. In response to this, Chalmers and Strawson both embrace the somewhat Kantian distinction made by another panpsychist, Bertrand Russell, between the "extrinsic" or relational qualities of matter, which are susceptible to scientific observation and measurement, and the "intrinsic" qualities, which are not, and which might include phenomenal states.[24] Declaring the mental life of electrons unobservable renders the panpsychist position conveniently unfalsifiable, at least empirically. It can only be argued out of existence. And then there is the "combination problem" of how the protoexperiential states of elementary particles can somehow be aggregated, articulated, or otherwise combined into the more complex macroexperiential states of, say, human beings.[25] As Philip Goff notes in a response to Strawson: "The emergence of novel macroexperiential properties from the coming together of microexperiential properties is as brute and miraculous as the emergence of experiential properties from non-experiential properties. Strawson's panpsychism is committed to the very kind of brute emergence which it was set up to avoid."[26] Nevertheless, there is a fair amount of work being done on the combination problem, in which Leibniz is not infrequently invoked (sometimes in grievously misinterpreted form).

As already stated, the emergence of micropanpsychism in contemporary philosophy of mind hardly counts for me as belated vindication of Leibniz. What it says, rather, is that some contemporary formulations of the mind-body problem have not advanced beyond what are essentially Leibnizian positions, as a result of which they are forced to revive elements of Leibnizian metaphysics as well. Like King Hamlet's ghost, Leibniz's mind-body problem still haunts our philosophical battlements.

CHAPTER 13

Microperceptions

Monads perceive everything in the universe, from objects as distant as the farthest star to the endlessly embedded creatures within creatures nested invisibly in everything; and from events far in the past to those far in the future. But this claim, taken alone, does not accord with our ordinary experience. To make sense of it, we must look more closely at Leibniz's understanding of perception, and particularly at his concept of *petites perceptions*, or "small perceptions." I shall take the liberty of translating Leibniz's term as "microperceptions" to convey the fact that they are not merely small but very small indeed—so small as to be noticeable only in the aggregate.

Leibniz's 1676 essay "On the Plenitude of the World" begins:

> It seems to me that every mind is omniscient, confusedly; and that any mind perceives simultaneously whatever happens in the whole world; and these perceptions, of infinite varieties fused together [*confusis*] at the same time, give rise to those sensations we have of colors, tastes, touches. For such perceptions do not consist in one act of the intellect, but in an aggregate of infinitely many acts; especially since some stretch of time is necessary for the sensation of a color or some other perceptible thing. Time, though, is infinitely divisible, and it is certain that at any moment the soul perceives many different things, but that out of all the infinitely many perceptions fused together into one arise the perceptions of sensible things.[1]

Perception in the ordinary sense of the word results from the aggregation of infinite, tiny acts of perception. That word, "aggregation," should give us pause, since when applied by Leibniz to bodies it always signals a kind of ontological deficiency, the state of being *merely* an aggregate or collection rather than a substantial unity. The perceptual counterpart to that ontological deficiency is one that Leibniz calls confusion. Perceptual confusion is, therefore, the phenomenal expression or correlate of how bodies are physically constructed. Since the latter are aggregates of smaller components, our perceptions of them are correspondingly aggregated from tiny acts or microperceptions. For Leibniz, *all* sensory perception is confused, though it admits of relative degrees of distinctness.

As often in Leibniz, a mathematical model is silently at work here. Integral calculus adds together, sums up, or aggregates infinitesimal quantities and can thereby calculate volumes, the areas under curves, and so forth. Through mathematical integration, the invisibly small is conjoined into the visible.[2] The difference is that integration adds up homogeneous quantities while perception adds up heterogeneous ones. Microperceptions may be tiny, but they are all different from one another. In order to produce the appearance of one thing, therefore, these perceptions must be not only aggregated but also blended together, or "confused." In other words, while they retain full specificity in their microform, this gets blurred to some degree in the aggregate, and the blurring creates relative homogeneity from the heterogeneous. In a metaphorical sense, microperceptions get liquified; this, at least, is the etymological sense of *confusus*, which derives from the verb *fundo*, "to pour." Confused perceptions are figuratively "poured together." As we shall see, the metaphorics of liquidity are not incidental here.

Leibniz subjects the topic of microperception to more extended treatment in the *New Essays*. I shall examine one passage closely and in sections:

> Besides, there are hundreds of indications leading us to conclude that at every
> moment there is in us an infinity of perceptions, unaccompanied by aware-
> ness or reflection; that is, of alterations in the soul itself, of which we are
> unaware because these impressions are either too minute and too numerous,
> or else too unvarying, so that they are not sufficiently distinctive on their
> own. But when they are combined with others they do nevertheless have their
> effect and make themselves felt, at least confusedly, within the whole. This
> is how we become so accustomed to the motion of a mill or a waterfall, after
> living beside it for a while, that we pay no heed to it. Not that this motion
> ceases to strike on our sense-organs, or that something corresponding to it
> does not still occur in the soul because of the harmony between the soul and

the body; but these impressions in the soul and the body, lacking the appeal of novelty, are not forceful enough to attract our attention and our memory, which are applied only to more compelling objects.[3]

Microperceptions become the object of awareness only in the aggregate; individually, they escape notice and are therefore unconscious, although they are enregistered in the soul. Leibniz therefore sometimes uses the term "insensible perceptions" (*perceptions insensibles*) as a synonym. Indeed, Leibniz comes to regard perception in general as unconscious, reserving the term "apperception" for the conscious awareness of perceptions.[4] Clearly, there is a threshold that must be passed for awareness to fasten onto microperceptual aggregates, but Leibniz does not make clear what that might be, beyond what he calls "the appeal of novelty." As the examples of the unheard mill and windmill make clear, what is at stake is not the absolute magnitude of the percept but rather the degree of difference from its spatiotemporal surround. As in Gregory Bateson's well-known formula for defining information, conscious awareness is attracted by "a difference that makes a difference."

The passage continues:

> Memory is needed for attention: when we are not alerted, so to speak, to pay heed to certain of our own present perceptions, we allow them to slip by unconsidered and even unnoticed. But if someone alerts us to them straight away, and makes us take note, for instance, of some noise which we have just heard, then we remember it and are aware of just having had some sense of it. Thus, we were not straight away aware of these perceptions, and we became aware of them only because we were alerted to them after an interval, however brief.[5]

"Memory is needed for attention." But rather than going on immediately to explain or illustrate this claim, Leibniz makes the inverse point that attention is required for memory. What we do not attend to is not remembered and so slips away in the moment. Just as it introduces the topic of memory and attention, then, Leibniz's prose performs a tiny lapse of attention—though the word "performs" should not inspire false confidence that Leibniz is merely *pretending* to lose his train of thought. In any case, he has provided a negative illustration, intentionally or not, of the relation between memory and attention.

In this passage, it is a third party who draws the mind's attention to what otherwise would drift by it unnoticed. "Wow, it must be hard to work in such a noisy mill!" And then we remember that we've been hearing that sound all along without noticing it. In most cases, it is the percept itself that must perform this function by producing a difference that makes a difference, thereby claiming our attention. It is as if, for Leibniz, a tendency toward oblivion is built into perception, and we must keep ourselves constantly awake in order to fight it. At one point he describes our inattention to certain microperceptions as being "selectively asleep."[6]

By the end of the passage, Leibniz finally gets around to explaining what he means when he claims that memory is needed for attention: we are not aware of perceptions at the instant they occur but only after a tiny interval. To be consciously aware of something *is* to remember it. Later, in book II of the *New Essays*, Leibniz refers to "the memory of what was taking place immediately before—or, in other words, the consciousness or reflection which accompanies inner activity."[7] Here the word "reflection" suggests that consciousness requires a reflective *distance* on its objects, and that the very immediacy of the present moment therefore renders it unavailable for apperception. It is only after an infinitesimal gap, when it has been absorbed into the continuity of the remembered, that it can become available for conscious awareness. Apperception therefore has a structure of deferral built into it. Apperception "is a perception of an earlier perception," As Robert B. Brandom puts it.[8] In the present moment, the mind is perceiving, unconsciously. Only retroactively can this unconscious perception be rendered conscious.

But there's a peculiarity in the story Leibniz tells. If we've truly forgotten unconscious perceptions, how can we retrieve them after the fact when someone tries to call our attention to them? Conscious memories are possible only because unconscious memories are already and permanently in place from the moment of perception. "Each soul retains all its previous impressions. . . . Memory is not necessary for this, however, and sometimes not even possible, because of the multitude of past and present impressions which jointly contribute to our present thoughts."[9] By "memory," Leibniz here means conscious memory or awareness. By "impressions" he means perceptions, which, though unconscious, have inscribed themselves onto the soul. The word "impressions" carries associations of printing and casts the soul as a text or archive of unconscious impressions, which are then "read" and retrieved by conscious memory.[10] Unconscious perceptions have a trace-structure that implies deferral.[11] In the present moment, unconscious perceptions engage in an act of writing that is only retroactively read or apperceived. It is worth pondering how this process reflects on Leibniz's own acts of writing.

Leibniz's notion of unconscious memory bears some interesting resemblances to Freud's. In *Beyond the Pleasure Principle* (1920), Freud declares that "becoming conscious and leaving behind a memory trace are processes incompatible with each other within one and the same system."[12] Because consciousness must always remain open for fresh perceptions, it cannot afford to have anything permanently engraved upon it, which for Freud meant that memories have to be inscribed in the unconscious instead. In "A Note upon the 'Mystic Writing Pad' " (1925), Freud elaborated on this idea by comparing the psychic apparatus to a recent invention (at that point apparently not primarily used as a child's toy) in which layers of cellophane and paper lay upon a wax tablet.[13] Writing on the top (cellophane) layer with a stylus would cause it to adhere to the wax below, thus causing visible writing to appear, which could then be erased by lifting the cellophane and paper. Freud saw the cellophane as analogous to consciousness, which always remained open to new writing. The wax tablet, which not only retained impressions of the most recent message but also was a dense palimpsest of everything that had ever been written there, was an image of the unconscious. For Freud, as for Leibniz, the unconscious never forgets and therefore retains impressions of everything—available, under certain circumstances, for retrieval by consciousness. Freud also makes manifest the metaphorics of writing that underlie Leibniz's notion of unconscious "impressions."[14] I shall pursue further connections between the Leibnizian and the Freudian unconscious in module 14.

In the meanwhile, let us pick up the thread of Leibniz's exposition once more:

> To give a clearer idea of these minute perceptions which we are unable to pick out from the crowd, I like to use the example of the roaring noise of the sea which impresses itself on us when we are standing on the shore. To hear this noise as we do, we must hear the parts which make up this whole, that is the noise of each wave, although each of these little noises makes itself known only when combined confusedly with all the others, and would not be noticed if the wave which made it were by itself. We must be affected slightly by the motion of this wave, and have some perception of each of these noises, however faint they may be; otherwise there would be no perception of a hundred thousand waves, since a hundred thousand nothings cannot make something.[15]

Leibniz's argument here is borrowed from Zeno of Elea.[16] Zeno, however, speaks of millet grains rather than waves, and insists that if a falling bushel of millet makes a sound, then so must a single grain, or even a ten-thousandth of a grain. By switching to waves and the sea, however, Leibniz moves us from a granular to a liquid milieu. The sea's fluidity literally embodies the confusion or "pouring together" that characterizes microperceptions en masse. It also replaces Zeno's single act of dropping a bushel with a state of seemingly self-driven, perpetual motion; and it replaces Zeno's feeble, falling grains with a dynamic, surging energy whose sound is a confused roar. As Leibniz's ocean example indirectly suggests, microperceptions come equipped with an individual and cumulative *force*. And that force is named appetition.

For Leibniz, appetition is the force, or law of the series, that carries a monad from one perception to the next. Accordingly, microperceptions are attended by microappetitions. In an exchange with Stahl, Leibniz writes:

> Since I have recently referred to perception, I here refer to appetite. I understand by this term the smaller and more obscure endeavors of the soul toward obtaining something that is agreeable to it or repelling what is not agreeable to it, which endeavors arise from perceptions that are no less confused. Therefore, we are no more aware of our entire appetites than we are of our entire perceptions, and in this sense I think also that the motions of the body of which we are aware correspond to appetites of the soul.[17]

Like microperceptions, microappetitions can be summed or aggregated, but whereas perceptions are added as scalars, appetitions are added as vectors.[18] And just as microperceptual aggregates, when they pass a certain threshold, can attract awareness and be apperceived, so too with the vectorial sum of microappetitions, which thereupon become conscious desire. One must be careful, however, in speaking of a threshold, if that is taken to mean a clearly defined boundary. Rather, "noticeable perceptions arise *by degrees* from ones which are too minute to be noticed. To think otherwise is to be ignorant of the immeasurable fineness of things, which always and everywhere involves an actual infinity" (my emphasis).[19] Leibniz, as always, insists on linear continuity and rejects leaps or breaks. A continuum of mental states thus spans the space between pure unconsciousness and pure consciousness. Consciousness is differentially attracted to (or repelled by) different aggregates, which accordingly exert a differential force on thinking and perception. This opens up a whole realm of things and forces only indistinctly felt yet potentially potent in their effects—all the more so because they are *not* clearly sensed or recognized. I will look at the strictly perceptual consequences of this situation later, but here I would like to note briefly some of the effects of microperceptions conjoined with microappetitions. They enable instinctual actions;[20] they aid in decision-making;[21] they produce feelings;[22] they help us integrate the present with the past and future;[23] and they provide the basis for aesthetic taste. Commenting on Shaftesbury's *Characteristics of Men, Manners, Opinions, Times*, Leibniz notes:

> Taste as distinguished from understanding consists of confused perceptions for which one cannot give an adequate reason. It is something like an instinct. Tastes are formed by nature and by habits. To have good taste, one must practice enjoying the good things which reason and experience have already authorized. Young people need guidance in this.[24]

As this passage suggests, confused perceptions, though they remain beyond the pale of reason, can be educated and perfected by it, as well as by practice. The same is true of the moral instincts. Basically, any form of human perception, thought, practice, or feeling that falls outside the control of what Leibniz calls "distinct ideas," i.e., those for which well-formed definitions and arguments can be given, fall within the arena of microperception and microappetition. In particular, those forms of thought that intermingle with emotion and operate to some degree autonomously of rational control, exerting subtle and sometimes invisible influence upon us, are confused and microperceptual. It is on this cloudy basis that German philosophical aesthetics (and, at a greater remove, the Freudian unconscious) will eventually be erected.

CHAPTER 14

The Je Ne Sais Quoi *and the Leibnizian Unconscious*

There is no reason to think that Sigmund Freud was either interested in or terribly conversant with Leibniz's writings. While the Leibnizian unconscious anticipates the Freudian one in certain respects, any formative role on the latter would have had to occur by way of intermediate figures in the German philosophical tradition, from Herder to Nietzsche, who were more demonstrably influenced by Leibniz. What is interesting is that this line of possible influences generally involves thinkers who were also deeply engaged with aesthetic matters. Leibniz's theory of *petites perceptions* was formative for both German aesthetic philosophy and, much more indirectly, psychoanalysis, and in ways that often intertwine. Leibnizian microperceptions help lay the basis for what the theorist Jacques Rancière calls an "aesthetic unconscious."[1] Leibniz did not do this work on his own, however. He draws on a line of thinking that had already begun to connect aesthetic experience and liminal or inscrutable states of awareness. That line of thinking often centered on the phrase *je ne sais quoi*.

In his extended treatment of microperceptions in the *New Essays*, Leibniz observes:

> These minute perceptions, then, are more effective in their results than has been recognized. They constitute that *je ne sais quoi*, those flavours, those images of sensible qualities, vivid in the aggregate but confused as to the parts; those impressions which are made on us by the bodies around us and which involve the infinite; that connection that each being has with all the rest of the universe.[2]

The modish term *je ne sais quoi* had come to be applied to a variety of phenomena in the seventeenth century, from the charms of art, to the vagaries of passionate desire, to the subtle notes of fine wine, to the mysterious force by which magnets attract iron, to the ineffable and unteachable polish of aristocratic manners.³ At once mysteriously powerful and inexplicable, the *je ne sais quoi* lent itself to the very kinds of liminal feelings and judgments that Leibniz sought to explain through microperceptions and microappetitions. While unable to unravel any given instance of the *je ne sais quoi* in detail, Leibniz's theory of microperceptions offers a general account of its mechanisms. Leibniz *did* "know what" was at work, in theory if not in practice. In asserting that he can explain the *je ne sais quoi*, Leibniz is making a philosophical claim of some ambition and reach that is belied by the offhand way in which he makes it.

For Leibniz, sensory qualia in general exemplify the *je ne sais quoi*. Although we can recognize the color blue, for instance, we cannot explain what blueness is. But Leibniz is also given to invoking the work of art, and artistic judgment, as vivid instances of this more general quality: "Likewise we sometimes see painters and other artists correctly judge what has been done well or done badly; yet they are often unable to give a reason for their judgment but tell the inquirer that the work which displeases them lacks 'something, I know not what.' "⁴ Of course, aesthetic judgment, like the ability to identify the color blue, involves cognition as well as vision—confused *ideas* (which we will examine later) as well as confused perceptions. But both are founded on microperceptions—as is, therefore, the *je ne sais quoi*, which asserts itself not just in aesthetic judgment but also in artistic creation:

> I do not believe that there is a mortal man who would not confess to me that there have often occurred to him while he dreamed, spontaneously and as if made in a moment, elegant visions and skilfully fashioned songs, verses, books, melodies, houses, gardens, depending upon his interests—visions which he could not have formed without effort while awake. . . . They are sought by the waker; they offer themselves to the sleeper. There must therefore necessarily be some architectural and harmonious principle, *I know not what*, in our mind, which, when freed from separating ideas by judgment, turns to compounding them.⁵ [my emphasis]

In this interesting passage, dreamers appear actually to be engaged in effortless artistic creation, not falsely imagining so. Otherwise, it is hard to make sense of Leibniz's remark that such creations "are sought by the waker; they offer themselves to the sleeper." Moreover, Leibniz depicts this kind of dream-creation as a universal experience. "Separating ideas by judgment" apparently refers to the work of producing *distinct* ideas, which Leibniz privileges in some respects over confused ones, so it is interesting to see him describe the state of the artistic dreamer as being "freed" from its yoke. The dreamer replaces the labor of separating images and ideas with the spontaneous activity of combining them, and thereby anticipates the activity of condensation (*Verdichtung*) that constitutes half of the Freudian dream-work. Here Leibniz attaches the *je ne sais quoi* not to the product of dreamed artistic activity but to the creative mind itself, the powers of which are beyond analysis. Contemporary writers applied the *je ne sais quoi* to the capacity of (non-dreaming) artists to produce work in a negligent, nonchalant, or spontaneous fashion.[6]

The *je ne sais quoi* is not merely something that happens not to be known or that could be but is not yet known. It actively resists or defeats attempts to know it and thus alerts consciousness to something not fully accessible. While it affects conscious thought, it also embodies something that cannot be drawn out of the shadows into plain view. In aesthetic and erotic contexts, moreover, this situation affords a certain surplus of enjoyment. The *je ne sais quoi* occupies an intermediate zone between the conscious and the unconscious—so subtle and diffuse in its workings that it refuses to deliver itself up to precise analysis. Along with this, it can often contain elements that should not afford pleasure but somehow, inexplicably, do. It thereby raises sometimes disquieting questions about desire and its objects. Unsurprisingly, then, it is associated in seventeenth-century aesthetics more often with the sublime than with the beautiful.[7] It reemerges later in Schlegel's praise of *das Unbestimmte* in *Lucinde* and in John Ruskin's aesthetics of the indefinite in *Modern Painters*. But it also, and particularly in philosophical contexts, anticipates certain elements of the Freudian unconscious.

Fragment 162 of Pascal's *Pensées* offers the following thoughts on desire:

> Whoever wishes to know fully the vanity of humankind has only to consider the causes and effects of love. Its cause is a *je ne sais quoi* (Corneille), and the effects are appalling. This *je ne sais quoi*, so slight a thing that it cannot be recognized, shakes all the earth, princes, armies, the whole world.

Cleopatra's nose: had it been shorter, the entire face of the earth would have changed.[8]

Like the Leibnizian *je ne sais quoi*, the Pascalian one arises from a cause so small that it cannot be recognized yet exerts an outsized effect. Although Cleopatra is a woman and not an artwork, she is still in some sense an aesthetic object, and one that charms all the more because she violates classical canons of beauty. That tiny surplus of nose elevates her from the merely beautiful into an object of obsession, and thereby reveals unexpected forces within the observer. Something like a Freudian unconscious peeks out of this passage; indeed, Pascal's language makes of Cleopatra's nose an anticipation of the Freudian fetish object; and it is therefore not surprising that Jacques Lacan invokes it in his essay "The Freudian Thing."[9]

Even more suggestive, in a similar vein, is a passage in one of Descartes's letters. There he describes falling in love with a squinty-eyed girl as a child and then, later in life, being attracted to women with a similar feature without knowing why. He cures himself of this tendency only by reasoning with himself that it is a defect. He concludes: "So when we are inclined to love someone, without knowing the cause, we may believe that it is because there is something in him similar to what was in another object we have loved before, though we do not know what it is (*encore que nous ne sachions pas ce que c'est*)."[10] Descartes draws the very Freudian conclusion that love is the repetition of an earlier love, and that the trigger for this transference may be a trait that is not in itself beautiful or lovable. But he does so via a very un-Freudian mechanism that would appeal to Leibniz: the first love folds the brain in a way that, even when the stimulus disappears and the fold is undone, leaves the area prone to refold in a similar way. The Cartesian unconscious involves a trace-structure not unlike that of unconscious memory in both Leibniz and Freud.

In a moment of keen frustration at having not yet carried out his promise to avenge his father, Shakespeare's Hamlet exclaims:

> *I do not know*
> *Why* yet I live to say this thing's to do,
> Sith I have cause and will and strength and means
> To do't.[11] [4.4.42–45, my emphasis]

Here the *je ne sais quoi* yields a surplus of angry remorse, not pleasure. It also marks the limit of a process of deep introspection carried out in deadly seriousness.

Hamlet admits that, despite his best attempts to do so, he simply does not know why he still has not fulfilled his promise to the ghost, since he has both the capacity and will to do it. For Freud, this *je ne sais quoi* signals the presence of inaccessible, Oedipal motives in Hamlet.

In all three of these examples, the *je ne sais quoi* allows the seventeenth century to name an intuition that both human thought and desire operate in ways beyond the reach of conscious understanding. Explaining the *je ne sais quoi* by way of microperceptions allows Leibniz to flex his intellectual muscle; but at the same time, the *je ne sais quoi* exerts a counter-pull on the theory of microperceptions. When Leibniz describes microperceptions as insensible or unconscious, he often means that they are too weak or too little differentiated to attract the attention of consciousness except in the aggregate—and sometimes, not even in the aggregate. They are merely subconscious rather than unconscious in a Freudian sense. But the *je ne sais quoi* connotes something that is powerful as well as subtle, and which can therefore both elude and challenge the sovereignty of reason. Through the *je ne sais quoi*, the microperceptual punches above its weight, as it were. It thus becomes the perceptual counterpart to, or expression of, the insurrectional capacity of dominated monads as suggested by Leibniz and developed more fully by Tarde.

In the *New Essays*, Leibniz observes:

> If we do not always notice the reason which determines us, or rather by which we determine ourselves, it is because we are as little able to be aware of all the workings of our mind and of its usually confused and imperceptible thoughts as we are to sort out all the mechanisms which nature puts to work in bodies.[12]

What is Leibniz doing here if not laying down the basis for a Psychopathology of Everyday Life? Not only decisions and judgments but presumably also omissions, mistakes, forgettings, obsessions, slips of the tongue, and so forth—even hysterical symptoms—can be explained through microperceptions. As with Freud, the apparently random or contingent turns out to be the product of a thoroughgoing determinism. In Freud, however, the unconscious is a psychic agency at odds with consciousness and displays a very different kind of logic. As Freud famously states in *The Interpretation of Dreams*, the dream-work "does not think." In accord with the nature of the *je ne sais quoi*, by contrast, the Leibnizian differential unconscious is fundamentally continuous with the nature of conscious thought, though inaccessible—or else partially accessible—to it. This continuity makes possible a range of liminal states that are neither fully conscious nor fully unconscious, including those involved in aesthetic experience. While a masterful interpreter of artworks, Freud had relatively little of comparable interest to say about their aesthetic dimension, and the bright line he draws between conscious and unconscious thought may have something to do with this. By contrast, Leibniz's theory of microperceptions lays the basis for almost all of German aesthetic philosophy prior to Kant. Leibniz does this largely by providing a rigorous philosophical explanation for the aesthetic *je ne sais quoi*. At the same time, the *je ne sais quoi* helps attract Leibniz's attention to a variety of mental phenomena demanding explanation. From this encounter a distinctively modern vision of the self emerges.

CHAPTER 15

Mid Is a Liquid

Throughout this book, tiny rivulets have been forming. They began with the image of fish in a pond, used to describe bodies as an aggregate. That image flowed away from its metaphorical target and toward another instance of the same image, used now to illustrate embeddedness rather than aggregation. Then perceptions turned out to be fluid; that is, confused or poured together. Perceptual fluidity evoked the image of the sea and its crashing waves. These rivulets will now meet and pool into a theory of general fluidity in Leibniz. Both the physical universe and mind itself are suffused by, and in some sense merely are, liquids.[1]

In "A Specimen of Discoveries" (ca. 1686?), Leibniz states: "The whole universe is one continuous fluid, whose parts have differing degrees of tenacity, as if someone were to make up a liquid out of water, oil, liquid pitch, and similar things variously stirred up together."[2] In a letter to Gilles Filleau Des Billetes (1696), he writes: "The whole world is like a pond of matter in which there are different currents and waves."[3] Both statements are striking in that they suggest the universe consists of nothing but fluids. The first posits solids as merely denser or more viscous kinds of fluid. And in the second, more radical statement, there is only one kind of fluid, and everything that exists, including solid matter, is merely waves or currents within it. Here Leibniz sounds a bit like a present-day quantum field theorist. In fact, he has a relatively clear or at least internally consistent idea of what liquids are and a fuzzier or more "confused" notion of what solids are, and of how they differ from liquids.

What is a liquid? We can start with Leibniz's notion of the plenum. Leibniz rejected the possibility of a vacuum; every nook and cranny of the physical universe had to be filled with creatures and hence with matter, leaving no empty spaces between.[4] His theory of the plenum accords with his general principle that divine creation should manifest a maximum of being—a principle incompatible with empty spaces between entities. Moreover, the plenum serves as a communicational medium among bodies, transferring both presence and movement from one body to the next, throughout the universe:

> With the universe being a kind of fluid, all of one piece and like an ocean without limits, all motions within it are conserved and propagated to infinity, albeit insensibly, just like the aforementioned circles, produced by a stone thrown in water, are visibly propagated for some distance, and although they become invisible in the end, the impression nonetheless continues and extends to infinity, as is quite clear from the laws of motion.[5]

It is because of the fluid plenum that the movement of every body in the universe is transmitted to, and registered by, our bodies. This is the physical counterpart to, or expression of, the fact that our minds perceive everything in the universe. And this isomorphism or expressive resemblance between mind and body provides our first hint that mind itself may have a fluid nature.

If the plenum is a fluid, the fluid is also a plenum. To imagine a fluid plenum, or a plenary fluid, we can start by envisioning a bowl filled with tiny metal ball bearings. Individually, the ball bearings are solid, but collectively they can move around one another, they assume the shape of their container, and they allow themselves to be displaced if you stick your hand into the bowl—all of which are fluid qualities. The problem is that ball bearings, being spheres, come into contact with each other only at a single point, and hence there is empty space left between them. The solution? Just fill the empty spaces with still smaller ball bearings (figure 15.1).[6]

There are now smaller empty spaces between the smaller ball bearings, but those can be filled with still smaller ball bearings, ad infinitum. No matter how small the remaining space, it can be filled with still smaller ball bearings, a process that approaches a perfect plenum as a mathematical limit and also retains the liquidity of the medium. Of course, this "liquid" is made up out of solids; its liquidity is an emergent phenomenon resulting from aggregation. But as we shall see, solids are also made up out of liquids; the two are mutually enfolded and in a sense are distinguished only perspectivally. It needs only be added that even the "largest" ball bearings in this model of a fluid mixture are imperceptibly small.

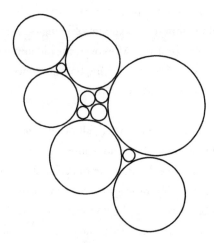

15.1 Leibnizian liquid. G. W. Leibniz, *The Labyrinth of the Continuum*, trans and ed. Richard W. Arthur (New Haven, CT: Yale University Press, 2001), p. 246.

Because of the plenum, all solid bodies are immersed in a perfectly fluid medium. But what are solid bodies, and how do they differ from the fluid that surrounds them? In the Paris Notes, Leibniz remarks:

> But above all we will prove that besides fluids there also exist solids, for these are more perfect than fluids, since they contain more essence. But not all things can be solid, for then they would impede each other. There are therefore solids mixed in with fluids. It does not seem possible to explain the origins of solids from the motion of fluids alone. All solids seem (if I may say so in passing) to be informed with a certain mind.[7]

Solids are "more perfect" than fluids because they can embody qualities that fluids cannot. They are differentiated and have shapes and colors; they display elasticity, and inertia, and antitypy; they possess an internal organization and coherence and relative permanence that fluids do not. Certainly, Leibniz's philosophical attention is drawn more often to solid bodies than it is to the fluid medium that surrounds them.

But what is it, exactly, that imparts all of these marvelous qualities to solids? In the above-quoted passage, Leibniz invokes "a certain mind" (*quadam mente*), by which he means what he will later call a "bare monad"—lacking memory and distinct perceptions but sufficient to confer a certain degree of unity upon an aggregate. Here we encounter Leibniz's minority position that all solid bodies, organic or not, are accompanied by monads—a position that tends to arise when physics rather than biology comes to the fore. At a much later point, he will attempt to distinguish between solids and liquids on purely physical grounds, without reference to mind:

> But since it is established on other grounds, by a general law of nature, that all bodies are agitated by internal motions, the conclusion is that bodies are firm insofar as these motions are concurrent, but remain fluid insofar as the motions are perturbed and not connected by any system. The result is that every body contains some degree of fluidity and some of firmness alike and that no body is so hard as not to have some flexibility, and the converse.[8]

Even here, though, something like Spinoza's *conatus* seems to lurk in the background of the terms "concurrent motions" and "system." Unlike liquids, solid bodies maintain consistent, enduring relations among their parts, despite internal motion, and Leibniz never quite explains what enables them to do that, once the obvious candidate that is the monad has been removed. In any case, what remains unchanged is the notion that solids are basically liquids with some organizational supplement added. Or, as Leibniz puts it in the *New Essays*: "hardness is not fundamental; on the contrary fluidity is the fundamental condition."[9]

Not only do solid bodies arise from liquid ones, but they remain permeated by liquid flows. In a letter to Des Bosses, Leibniz writes: "it is easy to . . . conceive the rarity and density of bodies (from which arises the force of tension, commonly called elastic force) on analogy with a sponge, through whose spaces flows a fluid that resists changes to its accustomed boundaries."[10] Since elasticity is derivative active force, the physical expression of primary active force, once again the presence of the monad hovers in the background. When, as in the passage quoted above, a body is distinguished from a liquid by maintaining a consistent shape (that is, when a more Cartesian notion of body as extension prevails), then solids are privileged and assigned monads. But when bodies are defined as bearers of *force* (a more specifically Leibnizian notion), then it is their liquid component that tends to imply a monadic dimension.

Summarizing the qualities of solid matter in Leibniz, Richard T. W. Arthur describes it as "at any instant not only infinitely divisible, but actually infinitely

divided by the diverse motions of its parts. Therefore no part of matter, however small, remains the same for longer than a moment; there are no motions
that do not contain other motions, and no enduring states; even shape is something evanescent, and a body with an enduring shape is something imaginary."[11]
In a sense, solid objects are nothing more than an especially slow and viscous
form of liquid. Putting this differently, the boundaries between the solid and
the fluid are themselves fluid. Nowhere is this clearer than in Leibniz's figure
of the fold:

> If a perfectly fluid body is assumed, a finest division, i.e. a division into min-
> ima, cannot be denied; but even a body that is everywhere flexible, but not
> without a certain and everywhere unequal resistance, still has cohering parts,
> although these are opened up and folded together in various ways. Accord-
> ingly the division of the continuum must not be considered to be like the
> division of sand into grains, but like that of a sheet of paper or tunic into
> folds. And so although there occur some folds smaller than others infinite
> in number, a body is never thereby dissolved into points or minima. On the
> contrary, every liquid has some tenacity, so that although it is torn into parts,
> not all the parts of the parts are so torn in their turn; instead they merely take
> shape for some time, and are transformed; and yet in this way there is no dis-
> solution all the way down into points, even though any point is distinguished
> from any other by motion. It is just as if we suppose a tunic to be scored with
> folds multiplied to infinity in such a way that there is no fold so small that it
> is not subdivided by a new fold: and yet in this way no point in the tunic will
> be assignable without its being moved in different directions by its neighbors,
> although it will not be torn apart by them. And the tunic cannot be said to
> be resolved all the way down into points; instead, although some folds are
> smaller than others to infinity, bodies are always extended and points never
> become parts but always remain mere extrema.[12]

I have quoted this passage from the dialogue *Placidus to Philalethes* at length
because it is a primary inspiration for Deleuze's study of Leibniz and the fold.
As Leibniz makes clear, the fold is enabled by a certain liquidity within solidity
that allows it to bend and flow without breaking. Elsewhere he puts this more
concisely: "All things seem in fact to be fluid but merely variously folded into
each other without a break in the continuity."[13] To borrow a Deleuzian locution,

the fold is the becoming-solid of the liquid or the becoming-liquid of the solid. The fold is where the liquid and the solid fold into each other.[14]

Among solid bodies, it is organic ones that most obviously incorporate a liquid element. And it is to organic bodies that Leibniz consistently and unambiguously assigns monads or minds. It should not be surprising, then, that Leibniz associates soul or mind or perception with the body's fluidity:

> I have believed that there is some fluid or, if you like, an ethereal substance, diffused in the whole body, and continuous; by which the soul senses: which inflates the nerves, which contracts itself, and which expands itself. It is by no means credible that each part of this substance is animated, for since something always flies away, also the souls would be multiplied and divided. [. . .] Therefore I would think that in this liquid itself there is some fount of motion and expansion, as in a burning candle. In fact, it seems that in the cavities of the brain all circular motion takes place and that the soul preserves its vortex. And that [sensible] species themselves are nothing other than waves impressed upon the liquid, and that each wave is preserved eternally, even if through the composition with others it becomes imperceptible. But that the soul itself agitates a vortex, is a true wonder. Nevertheless, it does so, since we do not act as simple machines, but out of those reflections, that is, actions on ourselves.[15]

Leibniz inherits his interest in vortices from Descartes, and he applies it in contexts ranging from planetary orbits to the nature of mind. Elsewhere, he states that "there are as many minds, or little worlds, or perceptions, as there are vortices in the world."[16] He likewise inherits from Descartes the notion that thoughts are connected to folds in the brain, though he converts this connection from a causal to an isomorphic one. The brain, that peculiarly gelatinous organ, can fold and refold because its solidity is so very liquid. And its folding motions are isomorphic to the motions of the soul. Mind, in short, is a liquid. It flows from perception to perception. And its perceptions are themselves confused, that is to say fluid, aggregations of unconscious microperceptions. The trick in moving from confused to distinct ideas will be to precipitate solid cognitive objects out of liquid ones.

Leaping from Leibniz's era to our own, it is notable how the metaphorics of liquidity continue to play a role in present-day cognitive science—particularly among scholars working on the problem of human creativity. In this book I draw on Fauconnier and Turner's notion of the "conceptual blend," which figuratively liquifies thought in considering how different discursive realms can combine or fuse. (Leibniz, too, depicted the supposedly separate realms of knowledge as a continuous ocean divided by name only in separate seas.[17]) Steven Mithen conjures the term "cognitive fluidity" for related purposes.[18] But no one is more attentive to the metaphorics of liquidity in describing human thought and creativeness than Douglas Hofstadter. His book *Fluid Concepts and Creative Analogies: Computer Models of the Fundamental Mechanisms of Thought*, co-written with the members of the Fluid Analogies Research Group, centers on a series of computer science projects Hofstadter ran in the 1980s that offered early versions of artificial intelligence and machine learning. Hofstadter's programs attempt to solve analogy puzzles (both numeric and alphabetic) and thereby cast light on the basic mechanisms of human creativity.[19] In order to solve challenging puzzles, these programs cannot follow the rigid procedures of serial processing. Rather, they generate large numbers of stochastically chosen "codelets" that nudge the program in subtle and flexible ways toward solutions (often more than one) of a given puzzle. Hoftstadter attaches the term "fluid" to "concepts" because it suggests "flexibility, mutability, nonrigidity, adaptability, subtlety, pliancy, continuousness, smoothness, slipperiness, suppleness."[20] While pondering the physics of fluidity, he writes:

> I recalled one of my favorite images and phrases from all of science—that of "flickering clusters." This poetic little phrase encapsulates a well-known theory of water according to which H_2O molecules continually make fleeting little associations, thanks to the very weak hydrogen bond that can form between the O of one and an H of another, if they happen to be passing close enough by each other [. . .]. If the flickering-clusters model of water is correct (and when I last read about it, this was somewhat unclear), then all throughout every tiny droplet of water, trillions of complex, randomly-shaped clusters of H_2O molecules are forming and then falling apart every microsecond, all completely silently and invisibly. And thanks to this fantastically unsuitable, unstable, dynamic, stochastic substrate, the familiar and utterly stable-seeming properties of wateriness emerge.
>
>   This image is ideal, I feel, for suggesting our philosophy, according to which the familiar and stable-seeming fluidlike properties of thought emerge

as a statistical consequence of a myriad of tiny, invisible, independent, sub-cognitive acts taking place in parallel. Concepts have this fluidity, and analogies are the quintessential manifestation of it. That is why we chose to call ourselves "FARG," and that is why this book's title is as it is.[21]

The apparent stability and regularity of concepts—which are necessary for thought, of course—is an emergent property of an ongoing background of analogical processes that imbues thinking with the requisite flexibility to problem-solve and innovate. As Hofstadter insists, the regularities of thought are those of a liquid, not a solid. Concepts can thus be blended and not merely stacked on top of one another, thereby enabling unexpected properties to emerge.

What is Hofstadter's "myriad of tiny, invisible, independent, subcognitive acts" if not a swarm of Leibnizian *petites perceptions*, reconfigured for an era of computer (and cognitive) science? Con-fused or blended or liquified thinking gives rise to the *je ne sais quoi* by which the artist carries out creative acts for which he cannot give a reason. Leibniz likewise confesses that microperceptions bubble up through his writing in ways that cannot be accounted for by logical process. Liquidity is not merely a quality of the kind of mind he theorizes; it is a quality of the kind of mind he exemplifies. The conceptual workshop of the Leibnizian tinker is filled with objects that are solid when need be but that can also liquify at the master's touch to enable forms of fluid, analogical thinking to gush forth.

Hofstadter can cast retrospective light on Leibniz not only because they both employ related figurative vocabularies but also because Hofstadter is a Leibnizian style of thinker. "Blending" the physics of water with the architecture of computer programs enables him to solve problems and arrive at novel insights. For Hofstadter, the fluid analogy is not just a rhetorical illustration but a tool for thinking, and he feels no need to hide its analogical character as some sort of embarrassment. Even the "hard" sciences must accommodate a liquid element.

CHAPTER 16

The Confused and the Distinct

As we have seen, confused perceptions play a wide and varied role in Leibniz's philosophy. But the category of the distinct is no less important, as it applies both to perception and to ideas. The relation between the confused and the distinct is a bit of a terminological tangle, however—and, to some degree, a conceptual one as well. But it requires sorting out, because the distinct will lead us in directions largely unanticipated to this point. I'll begin with the problem of perception, move on to that of ideas, and then return to perceptions.

Thus far, by the term "perception" I have meant mainly sensible perception: the work of the five senses in response to their relevant objects. For Leibniz, *all* sensible perceptions are confused, because all material entities contain microstructures that cannot be perceived clearly or even consciously. Nevertheless, Leibniz does sometimes speak of distinct perceptions, meaning distinct sensible perceptions. When he uses the term in this way, he does so to denote a perception that has become conscious and that can therefore distinguish itself from other conscious perceptions. As Robert McRae puts it, such a perception will be "distinct in terms of its external relations to other perceptions from which it is distinguished. It will be confused in terms of the infinitude of little perceptions of which it is composed."[1] Distinct perceptions, then, are a subclass of confused perceptions, not an alternative to them. All distinct perceptions are also confused, and all confused perceptions of which we are aware are distinct. The conceptual opposite of "distinct" in the context of perception is "unconscious" or "insensible," not "confused." And just as consciousness is a differential quality along a continuum, so therefore is distinctness. A perception can be more or less distinct, just as it can be more or less conscious.

A more elaborate and complex taxonomy emerges when we turn from perceptions to ideas. Here "confused" and "distinct" are subclasses of what Leibniz calls
"clear" ideas. I quote here from Leibniz's 1684 essay, "Meditations on Knowledge,
Truth, and Ideas":

> Knowledge is either obscure or *clear*; clear knowledge is either confused or
> *distinct*; distinct knowledge is either inadequate or *adequate*, and also either
> symbolic or *intuitive*. The most perfect knowledge is that which is both ade-
> quate and intuitive.
>
> A concept is obscure which does not suffice for recognizing the thing rep-
> resented, as when I merely remember some flower or animal which I have
> once seen but not well enough to recognize it when it is placed before me
> and to distinguish it from similar ones; or when I consider some term which
> the Scholastics had defined poorly, such as Aristotle's entelechy, or cause
> as a common term for material, formal, efficient, and final cause, or other
> such terms of which we have no sure definition. A proposition also becomes
> obscure when it contains such a concept.
>
> Knowledge is *clear*, therefore, when it makes it possible for me to recog-
> nize the thing represented. Clear knowledge, in turn, is either confused or
> distinct. It is *confused* when I cannot enumerate one by one the marks which
> are sufficient to distinguish the thing from others, even though the thing
> may in truth have such marks and constituents into which its concept can be
> resolved. Thus we know colors, odors, flavors, and other particular objects
> of the senses clearly enough and discern them from each other but only by
> the simple evidence of the senses and not by marks that can be expressed. . . .
>
> A *distinct* concept, however, is the kind of notion which assayers have
> of gold; one, namely, which enables them to distinguish gold from all other
> bodies by sufficient marks and observations. We usually have such concepts
> about objects common to many senses, such as number, magnitude, and fig-
> ure, and also about many affections of the mind such as hope and fear; in a
> word, about all concepts of which we have a *nominal definition*, which is noth-
> ing but the enumeration of sufficient marks.[2]

Before unpacking this passage in detail, I want to make a few general and perhaps obvious points about it. First, this taxonomy appears to be a hierarchy as
well; the movement from obscure to clear to distinct is also a movement toward

increased cognitive adequacy. Second, Leibniz's standard for assessing cognitive adequacy is object recognition. Sometimes these objects are bodies (flowers, a gold nugget), sometimes they are qualities (colors, flavors), and sometimes they are ideas (badly defined Scholastic concepts). The movement from obscure to distinct is a movement toward increased capacity to recognize objects, which for Leibniz means the ability to name the marks or characteristics that distinguish a particular object from others. A third and perhaps equally obvious point is that ideas are not sensible perceptions, and so different criteria apply, even though the terms "confused" and "distinct" reappear. Ideas do not admit of scale or size; there can be no such thing as a "micro-idea" to correspond to a microperception, and confused ideas are not conglomerates of micro-ideas. Ideas are confused for reasons other than those for which perceptions are confused. Although the examples of confused ideas that Leibniz gives are objects of the senses, hence perceived confusedly, the reasons for their ideational confusion are not directly identical to those for their perceptual confusion, although the two are not completely unrelated, either. An added wrinkle is that although ideas are not sensible perceptions, they can be percepts. We can perceive ideas, just as we can perceive flowers or colors.

Obscure ideas are those for which we lack virtually any identifying marks. Examples are a flower seen so long ago that one would not be able to recognize it now, and a concept so badly defined that one cannot say anything intelligible about it. In one case, the cause for obscurity is temporal distance, and in the other, inherent confusion. But one could presumably have an obscure idea of a distinct concept: a cosecant is a well-defined concept in trigonometry, but if you haven't thought about trigonometry since taking the subject in high school, you may not be able to say anything about cosecants that would distinguish them from other kinds of trigonometric functions or even remember what exactly a trigonometric function is.

Clear ideas are those that one can recognize and distinguish from other ideas. In the case of clear-but-confused ideas, one can recognize the thing to which the idea corresponds but cannot provide distinguishing marks, whereas in the case of distinct ideas, one can. Colors are confused because, while one can recognize the color blue when one sees it, and distinguish it from other colors, one cannot say what blueness consists of or identify blueness other than by pointing at it.[3] That is, one cannot list its conceptual ingredients, just as, perceptually, one cannot distinguish its microperceptual ingredients. Hence the term "confused" applies in both cases.[4] In the case of perceptual qualia, the difference between a perception and an idea is that the latter attaches a name and concept to the perception. The idea of the metal gold is distinct (or can be distinct) because, unlike the case with blueness, one can provide distinguishing marks: it is heavy, it has a gold color, it will not dissolve in aqua fortis (nitric acid), etc. Some of those distinguishing marks may themselves be confused; one does better with abstract objects, in which case the marks are themselves more likely to be distinct (as in the definition of a cosecant). A distinct idea for which all of the marks are themselves distinct counts for Leibniz as *adequate*.

One can, of course, provide physical explanations for sensory qualia, and hence give a distinct idea of them. The color blue results from light of a certain range of frequencies, which is different from the frequencies that produce other colors.[5] One can provide identifying marks for the color blue and thus have a distinct idea of it. But the distinct idea cannot supplant the confused idea because they are of different natures. Knowing what frequencies of light will produce the color blue cannot tell you anything about what the experience of seeing blue light is like; and vice versa. A spectrograph can identify blue light on the basis of its frequency but has no idea of what blueness is. Confused ideas are inherently confused; they cannot be further clarified into distinct ones because they are erected on a completely different basis.

The relation between confused and distinct perceptions is therefore very different from that between confused and distinct ideas. As we have seen, distinct perceptions are merely a subclass of confused ones. Confused perceptions are more or less distinct, along a continuum. But confused and distinct ideas are of utterly different natures. The former are based on sensory experience and the latter on attributes, reasons, definitions, and so forth. They attempt to provide a *conceptual* identification rather than a purely sensible one. Distinct ideas are of the kind with which mathematicians, scientists, and—not incidentally— philosophers work. Confused ideas are of the kind with which painters, chefs, and others concerned with sensory qualia and the *je ne sais quoi* of things work. (One can of course work with both.) It is possible to become expert in confused ideas no less than in distinct ones. Confused ideas are still a form of knowledge— indeed, an irreplaceable one. This is our first hint that Leibniz's hierarchy of knowledge forms may not be quite as hierarchical as at first appears.

Let us look at this hierarchy more closely. Because there is one, no doubt about it. Leibniz is sometimes positively dismissive of confused ideas, claiming that they embody ignorance more than knowledge: "It is commonly believed that we understand these *sensible qualities*, but they are precisely what we understand the least. For example, the color red and a bitter taste are things for which we have no explanation; they are an 'I know not what,' the reason for which we do not see at all."[6] The ability to process sensory data is something we share with animals; the ability to grasp and formulate distinct ideas is what makes us human: "But of all souls there are none more elevated than those which are capable of understanding the eternal truths, and of not only representing the universe in a confused manner, but also of understanding it and of having distinct ideas of the beauty and grandeur of the sovereign substance."[7] Distinct ideas allow the soul to be active and free; confused ones subject the soul to the body and render it passive: "The soul is free in its voluntary actions, when it has distinct thoughts and shows reason; but since confused perceptions are dependent on the body, they arise from preceding confused perceptions, without the soul's necessarily wanting them, or foreseeing them."[8] Reasoning with distinct ideas promotes true, reliable knowledge, fosters ethical freedom, and encourages appreciation of the divine order of the universe.

If this were all there is to say about the matter, things would be simple enough. But on this, as on many other topics, Leibniz often expresses contrary opinions. Although human reason makes us into a mirror of God and not merely of the universe, if not for physical bodies and confused thoughts, there would be no subject matter for us to think *about*:

> What would an intelligent creature do if there were no unintelligent things? What would it think of, if there were neither movement, nor matter, nor sense? If it had only distinct thoughts it would be a God, its wisdom would be without bounds: that is one of the results of my meditations. As soon as there is a mixture of confused thoughts, there is sense, there is matter. For these confused thoughts come from the relation of all things one to the other by way of duration and extent. Thus it is that in my philosophy there is no rational creature without some organic body, and there is no created spirit entirely detached from matter.[9]

If bodies and confused thoughts were not of value, Leibniz reasons, God would not have created them. Moreover, while he insists that reason and distinct ideas can free human beings from reliance on the body and its passions, he also recognizes that reason alone is often too pale and feeble to do this, and that confused thoughts are more powerful and vivid than distinct ones:

> Cicero somewhere makes the good remark that if our eyes could see the beauty of virtue we would love it ardently. Since neither that nor anything like it is the case, it is not surprising that, in the struggle between flesh and spirit, spirit so often loses, because it fails to make good use of its advantages. This struggle is nothing but the conflict between different endeavours—those that come from confused thoughts and those that come from distinct ones. Confused thoughts often make themselves vividly sensed, whereas distinct ones are usually only potentially vivid: they could be actually so, if we would only apply ourselves to getting through to the senses of the words or symbols; but since we do not do that, through lack of care or lack of time, what we oppose lively sentiments with are bare words or at best images which are too faint.[10]

In addition—and this is crucial for his practice as a philosopher—Leibniz insists that even the most distinct of ideas necessarily retains a residue of the confused and the imaginary, and that this fact enriches thought rather than merely encumbering it:

> The most abstract thoughts need some imagination: and when we consider what confused thoughts (which invariably accompany the most distinct that we can have) are, we realize that they always involve the infinite, and not only what happens in our body but also, by means of it, what happens elsewhere. Confused thoughts thus serve our purpose as the tool which seemed necessary for the functions I attribute to the soul much better than the legion of substances of which M. Bayle speaks. It is true that the soul does have these legions in its service, but not in its interior. It is, then, present perceptions, with an orderly tendency to change, that make up the musical score which tells the soul what to do.[11]

In a sense, distinct thoughts can be *too distinct*; their very well-defined and well-bounded properties cut them off from the infinity of connections that bind everything in the universe together, often in ways that elude distinct thought. I would therefore suggest that Leibniz's frequent use of visual imagery in metaphors and other figures of similitude is not intended solely to clarify his thinking for readers but also to confuse it—to drench distinct thinking periodically in the vivifying pools of the confused and the microperceptual in order to reinvigorate it. As we have seen, Leibniz's figurative language often demonstrates an autonomy that refuses to restrict itself to the delegated cognitive task of the moment and instead wanders off to pursue its own agendas or else (as in the case of illustrating the concept of the aggregate) renders conceptual borders fuzzy instead of clarifying them. Conceptual blending is another way in which distinct ideas are confused so as to have a fertilizing, liquifying, generative effect. These elements of Leibniz's writing are therefore no less important than are the distinctly defined concepts on which philosophical commentators tend to concentrate.

Leibniz insisted on maintaining a connection to the sensory, the imaginary, and the aesthetic even in those arenas where thought was at its most abstract and distinct. One of these was mathematics, where Leibniz held that mathematical symbolism should exhibit a certain "sensual beauty" and spoke of "painting" mathematical ideas.[12] Horst Bredekamp goes so far as to suggest a connection between the long "s" that Leibniz used as the sign of the integral and the *linea serpentinata* of mannerist aesthetics.[13] That Leibniz exhibits a concern with the visual and the aesthetic even here, in his mathematical writings, makes it difficult to argue that these are merely "exoteric" elements designed to appeal to lay readers. Even more striking, perhaps, is Leibniz's concern with aesthetic elements in his plans for a "general characteristic." The general characteristic aimed to represent concepts by numbers and to reduce thinking to numerical calculation. Leibniz's commitment to distinct concepts finds its apogee here. And yet in a paper of 1678, he devised a system whereby the numbers representing concepts in his system could then be converted to letters and words in an alphabetical language, imbued with phonetic flexibility that, Leibniz hoped, would aid in the composition of poetry and song.[14] If the distinct is so clearly superior to the confused, why does Leibniz insist on returning to the latter even in contexts where he appears to have thrown off its shackles?

No one has worked more assiduously to unsettle Leibniz's supposed privileging of the abstract, the logical, and the distinct over the visual, the sensory, and the confused than Horst Bredekamp. In his book *Die Fenster der Monade*, Bredekamp documents Leibniz's extensive engagements with visual culture and his considerable investments of intellectual energy into forms of visual learning such as picture atlases, encyclopedias, cabinets of wonders, physical models, and "theaters" of art and nature.[15] In addition, Bredekamp complicates the epistemological ladder that privileges distinct over confused ideas. It is worth noting in this context that for baroque art, confused perception becomes something to be both represented and elicited; the baroque raises confusion to an aesthetic value. Aside from specific techniques such as chiaroscuro, tenebrism, and trompe l'oeil, there is the general development in the direction of what Heinrich Wölfflin calls painterly and unclear styles, as opposed to the linear clarity dominant in Renaissance art.[16] Baroque painting understands perception as confused, and revels in it.

To pursue some of the themes raised by Bredekamp, let us return to the "Meditations on Knowledge, Truth, and Ideas," where Leibniz lays out the complexities of advanced thought.

> Yet for the most part, especially in a longer analysis, we do not intuit the entire nature of the subject matter at once but make use of signs instead of things, though we usually omit the explanation of these signs in any actually present thought for the sake of brevity, knowing or believing that we have the power to do it. Thus when I think of a chiliogon [sic], or a polygon of a thousand equal sides, I do not always consider the nature of a side and of equality and of a thousand (or the cube of ten), but I use these words, whose meaning appears obscurely and imperfectly to the mind, in place of the ideas which I have of them, because I remember that I know the meaning of the words but that their interpretation is not necessary for the present judgment. Such knowledge I usually call *blind* or *symbolic*; we use it in algebra and in arithmetic, and indeed almost everywhere. When a concept is very complex, we certainly cannot think simultaneously of all the concepts which compose it. But when this is possible, or at least insofar as it is possible, I call the knowledge *intuitive*. There is no other knowledge than intuitive of a distinct primitive concept, while for the most part we have only symbolic knowledge of composites.[17]

In complex demonstrations employing distinct ideas, we cannot keep everything in our mind at once, and so the stages of the demonstration must be carried out one at a time. In addition, we employ words in the case of a verbal argument or symbols in the case of a mathematical one, of whose complete meaning we are not always actively aware when we are using them in the demonstration, where they serve as a sort of shorthand. Our idea of them is therefore "obscure," which drops us to the bottom rung of the epistemological ladder. Distinct thought loses its object in the very act of grasping it. Moreover, if we were to complete a distinct analysis to the very end, never terminating with a confused concept and therefore producing what Leibniz calls an "adequate" idea, the final step in the analytic process would be to arrive at primitive concepts—concepts that can be analyzed no further and are merely given. But there is therefore nothing to say about primitive concepts—no identifying "marks" by which one can recognize them. One can only point at them, much as with the confused ideas of sensory qualia such as "blue." In that regard it is difficult to distinguish an analysis that ends distinctly from one that ends confusedly. In "General Inquiries About the Analysis of Concepts and of Truth" (1686), Leibniz bites the bullet and includes sensory qualia among primitive simple terms, for the reasons just given. While he isn't entirely happy about classing confused concepts as primitive, he seems to have difficulty coming up with any other kinds.[18]

The alternative to demonstrative knowledge of the kind described above, in which analysis proceeds step by step, is what Leibniz calls intuitive knowledge, in which everything is grasped at once and as a whole. This is the kind of knowing enjoyed by God; human beings can mimic it only with difficulty, if at all. But as Bredekamp points out, confused knowledge likewise grasps everything all at once and therefore anticipates this still-higher, indeed divine form of intuitive knowledge more closely than distinct ideas do.[19] The point is that Leibniz's epistemological ladder is a much more complex structure than at first appears. It doesn't just ascend in orderly fashion from step to step but rather anticipates, folds back on itself, and gets tangled up in sometimes surprising ways. If it is in the end still a hierarchy, it is an inconsistent and self-contradictory one.

This is all to the good, since it installs in Leibniz a form of epistemological hygiene very different from that of Descartes, from whom Leibniz borrows the vocabulary of "confused," "clear," and "distinct" ideas. As Michel Serres points out, Descartes is willing to handle only clear and distinct ideas—ideas that are true without the slightest danger of falsity. Leibniz, by contrast, is happy to entertain ideas that are confused as long as there is any hope of distinctness associated with them. Hence he has no hesitation about consulting the works of poets, romance-writers, historians, artisans, and so forth in search of raw material for investigation.[20]

I began this module by distinguishing between perceptions and ideas in Leibniz's philosophy. I used the phrase "sensible perceptions" at the time, which may have seemed redundant. But there is an additional wrinkle to Leibniz's distinction. As he states in *Principles of Nature and Grace*, a monad's "internal qualities and actions . . . can only be its *perceptions* (that is, the representations of the composite, or of what is external, in the simple), or its appetitions (its tending to move from one perception to another, that is), which are the principles of change."[21] Since this statement is exhaustive—since, that is, monads have nothing *but* perceptions and appetitions, and the latter are just the principle of movement between perceptions—then all forms of thought, including abstract reason, must be implicitly counted as kinds of perception. Leibniz therefore uses the word "perception" in two senses: a narrower one meaning sensible perception and a broader one encompassing the complete array of perceptual and ideational activities of which a human mind is capable. Having distinguished ideas from perceptions in the narrower sense, Leibniz then folds them back into perception in the broader one. Unfortunately, he doesn't have a terminological distinction comparable to that between "apperception" and "perception" to denote when he is using the word "perception" in each of these two senses. And this lack of a terminological distinction feeds a tendency on his part to confuse the two or at least to distinguish them incompletely and inconsistently. In this regard, it is telling that Leibniz employs *object recognition* as the standard with which to judge ideation as either confused or distinct. He thereby assimilates ideas to perceptions even while trying to distinguish them. And of course, the vocabulary of "obscure," "clear," "distinct," etc., that Leibniz employs to characterize different classes of ideas is borrowed from the language of sensible perception.

Section 49 of the *Monadology* states: "A created thing is said to be *active* externally in so far as it has perfection, and to be *passive* towards another insofar as it is imperfect. Thus we attribute *activity* to a monad insofar as it has distinct perceptions, and *passivity* insofar as it has confused ones."[22] Leibniz appears to be using the word "perception" in both its broad and narrow senses here. If we take it to mean sensible perception, then indeed beings capable of distinct sensible perceptions (animals, human beings) are more active than those that are not (plants, inanimate objects). But if Leibniz meant *only* sensible perception, then a lynx would be more active than a human being. He is therefore also using perception in the broader sense, which includes thought. Human beings are more active than lynxes because they are capable of distinct thoughts or ideas in addition to distinct sensible perceptions.

This passage contains not only a metaphysical postulate but, implicitly, a philosophical ethic—one with a Spinozan lilt to it. We are most active when thinking distinct thoughts and operating with distinct concepts, and we are passive when operating with confused ones. By this light, philosophers, mathematicians, scientists, etc., are among the most active of human beings—the ones who most fully actualize the rational capacities of human minds. Those who succumb to the passions or who work mainly with confused ideas are to that degree less active. We might reword Leibniz's dictum in a way that reveals another facet of it without falsifying it: insofar as our perceptions are distinct, *we* are active. And insofar as they are confused, *they* are active in us. Confused perceptions exert the subtle force of the *je ne sais quoi*, affecting us in ways of which we are unaware—ways that can be both inhibiting and generative. Our passivity in the face of confused ideas is not, therefore, necessarily a bad thing, although it can be. In any case, the confused has its own virtues that are as necessary as those of the distinct.

We are all composed of both distinct and confused perceptions; indeed, our individuality is defined by a unique constellation of each, which together constitute our perspective on the universe. Were the philosophical ethic to strive toward distinct thoughts ever somehow taken to completion—that is, were all our thoughts ever to become distinct—we would simply cease to exist, since the marks of our individuation would as well. No worries of that, though. Our storehouse of distinct thoughts and perceptions is necessarily finite, while the number of our confused perceptions is infinite. For this reason, the philosophical ethic I have extracted from Leibniz is reductive and, in fact, too Spinozan. The full ethic would be: yes, strive for ever more distinct perceptions but also cultivate the confused ones. Think philosophically but also train and refine your tastes and your moral sensibilities. Pursue the rational but also take pleasure in the aesthetic, and recognize that they are both ineradicable aspects of your one being.

CHAPTER 17

Philosophy as Aesthetic Object

I will begin by repeating a passage I cited in module 02:

Beautiful truths deserve to be sought out, even when they bring no profit, and [. . .] it is to dishonor them to measure them by the yardstick of our interest.

It is the nature of beautiful things in general, like diamonds and excellent paintings, that they should be valued because of the pleasure that their beauty gives.[1]

We learn a couple of things about Leibniz's understanding of beauty here. First, it is of intrinsic worth. Beautiful things are valued for the pleasure they give apart from their utility. Indeed, their aesthetic value trumps their practical value and is degraded by being measured against it. Second, beauty can be intellectual as well as sensuous. Paintings and diamonds are both material things, and so their beauty partakes of that confused quality that all sensory perception entails. But truth is not a material thing; it is an ideal thing, and yet it can serve as the medium for beauty in a way comparable to that in which paintings and diamonds do. This form of beauty does not involve sensory perception. It attaches rather to thought and is found in things such as mathematical proofs and scientific theories and metaphysical systems. Putting all of this together, Leibniz appears to imply that he is like an artist or diamond-cutter who works with concepts rather than with paint or stones, and that his discoveries are to be valued for the aesthetic pleasure they confer over whatever practical applications they may allow. *Theoria cum praxi* be damned; philosophy is first and foremost an aesthetic object. Making sense of this proposition will require further investigation of several questions. What does Leibniz understand by "beauty"? What, if any, are the distinctive features of intellectual as opposed to sensuous beauty? And how does Leibniz understand his philosophical activity such that it is held to create intellectual beauty?

"We seek beautiful things," states Leibniz, "because they are pleasant, for I define beauty as that, the contemplation of which is pleasant."[2] As his phrasing suggests, beauty is for Leibniz an objective, mind-independent quality of things rather than a subjective state; the subjective correlate of beauty—what we experience in its presence—is pleasure.[3] Moreover, things are objectively beautiful because they exhibit a formal structure of harmony or unity-in-variety: "Now unity in plurality is nothing but harmony [*Übereinstimmung*], and since any particular being agrees with one rather than another being, there flows from this harmony the order from which beauty arises."[4] Elsewhere Leibniz states that "the harmony of things . . . [is] the principle of beauty in them."[5] Beauty is one of the perfections with which God invests the natural order; he "created all things in accordance with the greatest harmony or beauty possible."[6] As a result, "the beauty of nature is so great, its contemplation is so sweet, and the light and good inclination which arise from these bring such glorious fruitage [. . .] that he who has tasted them considers all other delights small by contrast."[7]

The phrase "the beauty of nature" in the passage requires some unpacking. Leibniz has in mind the physical beauty of nature as perceived confusedly by the senses—the blue of the sky, the smell of the forest, the song of a bird, the grandeur of a mountain vista. But he also means the underlying intellectual beauty of nature's design, as revealed by physics, biology, mathematics, and so forth—disciplines that are themselves intellectually beautiful.[8] The natural order created by God thus offers sensory beauties perceived confusedly and intellectual beauties grasped distinctly. God "created all things in accordance with the greatest harmony or beauty possible."[9] Conversely, "of all souls there are none more elevated than those which are capable of understanding the eternal truths, and of not only representing the universe in a confused manner, but also of understanding it and of having distinct ideas of the beauty and grandeur of the sovereign substance."[10] The two kinds of beauty—confused and distinct—work together. Nature produces an abundance of entities whose delightful variety is unified by its underlying lawfulness and thus rendered harmonious:

> *Per variar natura è bella.* But it is like in a song where, despite all the varieties
> of tones, the harmony consists in the agreement or in the consonances, or else

like there is a point of view in the perspective, and like the authors who wrote on the poetic art require the unity of the design in a tragedy. It can therefore be believed that the universe's changes are consistent with the uniformity of the divine action, because the same law of change always subsists.[11]

Just as music consists of a variety of tones that are themselves confusedly beautiful to the ear but are rendered more beautiful still by their being united in the distinct, formal structures of harmony, so nature's confused perceptual variety is rendered more beautiful still by its being unified under physical (and metaphysical) principles. Each of these poles is beautiful in itself and even more so when conjoined.

While disciplines such as mathematics and physics can help illuminate the divine order of the world, it is the task of philosophy to organize their insights into an overarching metaphysical structure, and thus to grasp the intellectual beauty of the whole. And of the available philosophical systems, it is his own (in Leibniz's unbiased view) that shows off God's creation to best advantage:

> Thus no hypothesis can give us a better knowledge of the wisdom of God than can mine, according to which there are substances everywhere which show forth his perfection, being so many mirrors, all different, of the beauty of the universe, nothing remaining empty, barren, uncultivated, and without perception.[12]

By revealing the unifying structures of reality, Leibniz's philosophy allows its harmonious beauty to become apparent. And the structure of Leibniz's philosophy will likewise necessarily be harmonious because the divine order that it illuminates is.

Leibniz frequently compares the created universe to an artwork and God to an architect or painter or sculptor. As we have already seen, this metaphor points to the fact that both divine and artistic creations share a harmonious structure of unity-in-variety. Moreover, the artwork, like nature, exhibits distinct as well as confused elements and is thus a source of intellectual as well as sensuous beauty:

> The pleasures of the senses themselves come down in the end to intellectual pleasures which are known in a confused way. Music can charm us, even though its beauty consists only in the interrelations between numbers, and in

the count, which we are not aware of but which the soul nevertheless makes, of the beats or vibrations of the sounding body, which coincide at certain intervals. The pleasures which sight derives from proportion are of the same kind; and those which the other senses produce will come down to something similar, even though we cannot explain them so clearly.[13]

Just as the pleasure of music involves the apprehension of formal harmony as well as of sound, so the pleasure of painting or sculpture involves the apprehension of proportion, or of abstract, quantitative ratios as well as of colors and shapes. In an important dissertation on Leibniz's aesthetics, Carlos Portales argues that for Leibniz,

> beauty is not only experienced through confused representations, not only derived from sense perceptions and not only sensible. Accordingly, there is also aesthetic experience related to distinct representations, to non-sensible concepts and to the intellect. Furthermore, we will claim that for Leibniz, the experience of beauty is at its best intellectual, grounded on concepts and distinct knowledge.[14]

As Portales shows, the ability to apprehend unity-in-variety is enhanced when the elements of a structure, and thus the structure as well, are grasped distinctly; hence there is a tendency in Leibniz to privilege distinct over confused forms of beauty.

There is a lot to be said for Portales's thesis. In particular, he shows that Leibniz's apparent exaltation of the *je ne sais quoi* does not mean that the viewer or listener should not try to grasp the artwork as distinctly as possible, and thus subject it to intellectual understanding. So, for instance, Leibniz states that "the contemplation of beautiful things is itself pleasant, and a painting by Raphael affects him *who understands it*" (my emphasis).[15] Elsewhere he restates this as: "a painting by Raphael affects him who looks at it *with enlightened eyes*" (my emphasis).[16] The contemplation of the artwork thus clearly involves attempting to behold its intellectual, formal aspects as well as its confused, sensuous ones. The logic of Portales's argument leads him to claim that for Leibniz, "since beauty, as harmony or unity in variety, is a formal structure it is better experienced through distinct ideas and the intellect."[17] Portales assembles an impressive array of evidence in support of this view. But he never quite brings himself to state its logical conclusion: if the distinct is superior to the confused, and if the abstract structures of harmony, which are the essence of beauty, are better grasped distinctly than confusedly, then philosophy must perforce do a better job of representing these structures than the artwork can, since it achieves a higher level of distinctness. In that case, philosophy would not merely be an aesthetic object but the supreme aesthetic object.

Naturally, Leibniz never states anything of this sort, but the logic of his aesthetic theory as construed by Portales seems to imply it. If so, Leibniz participates in the not-so-secret philistinism that often marks philosophy's relation to the artwork, from Plato's banishing of drama from his ideal Republic to Hegel's "end of art" in which philosophy appropriates the artwork's erstwhile work of advancing the development of Spirit.[18] The relation between philosophy and the artwork will therefore require some careful parsing. The first thing to say is that on this, as on so many other issues, Leibniz is not always consistent. Take for instance this letter to Christian Goldbach in which he once again discusses the perception of musical harmony:

> Moreover, I think that the reason for consonance must be sought from the congruity of the beats. Music is a secret exercise of arithmetic where the mind is unaware that it is counting. For, in confused or insensible perceptions, the mind does many things it cannot notice by a distinct apperception. Indeed, those who think that nothing happens in the soul of which it is not conscious are mistaken. Therefore, even if the soul does not realize it is counting, it nevertheless feels the effect of this insensible calculation, that is, the pleasure in consonances resulting therefrom or the vexation in dissonances. For pleasure arises from many insensible congruities.[19]

Here Leibniz appears to privilege the confused over the distinct, asserting that in a confused state, "the mind does many things it cannot notice by distinct apprehension," and also attributing pleasure to insensible rather than distinctly grasped congruities. If the distinct were necessarily more beautiful and pleasurable than the confused, then presumably we could skip the occulted or secret counting involved in musical harmony and achieve higher levels of pleasure just by counting numbers outright. Arithmetic would be aesthetically superior to music, just as philosophy is to the artwork in general. But this can't be Leibniz's point. We must therefore say that while we should indeed try to achieve as distinct a grasp of the artwork as possible by understanding its abstract, formal, and intellectual patterning, there is nevertheless a peculiar kind of pleasure generated by perceiving such patterns confusedly. The artwork presents an internal limit to the process of clarifying perception, even while offering intellectual as well as sensuous forms of beauty, and this grants it a distinctive form of pleasure that cannot be superseded by philosophy.

Moreover, the process of clarifying thought reaches an internal limit even within philosophy itself:

> The most abstract thoughts need some imagination: and when we consider what confused thoughts (which invariably accompany the most distinct that we can have) are, we realize that they always involve the infinite, and not only what happens in our body but also, by means of it, what happens elsewhere.[20]

Completely distinct thought is impossible, even for philosophy, because the philosophical concept, no matter how conscientiously abstracted, contains an ineradicable residue of the confused, the imaginary, and the perceptual from which it originally arose. Moreover, this confused remnant puts us in touch with the infinite, which by its nature can never be grasped distinctly. Leibniz's attachment to the metaphorical image (or so I have been arguing) suggests that eliminating the residue of the confused is not only not possible for philosophy; it is not even desirable. *His philosophy is therefore subject to an inconsistent directive*: grasp things as distinctly as possible and progress toward ever-higher levels of clarity and systematicity. Yet, at the same time, linger in the realms of the confused, which fertilizes thought and which one cannot escape in any case. *Verweile doch, du bist so schön.*

For Leibniz, philosophy and the artwork are in a mutually productive competition. Philosophy exhibits the heights of intellectual beauty that can be achieved by making thought as distinct as possible. The artwork exhibits the beauty of distinct formal structures perceived confusedly, and thereby shows that the internal limit to clarification that is likewise confronted by philosophy is not solely constraining in its effects. That being said, philosophy still provides the descriptive language through which this relationship is grasped, and the saddling of the artwork with "confused" thoughts and perceptions can't entirely remove the implication that philosophy's distinct beauty may be superior. "A confused perception of the distinct" is slightly diminishing to art in the way that Louis Althusser is when he construes art as an ideological critique of ideology.[21]

Leibniz's understanding of nature's harmony as a unity-in-variety has a distinctly baroque inflection insofar as it entails endless variety and endlessly nested complexity. God stuffs every available space with an infinity of entities, each of which is different from all the others (if it were not, it would not exist). The centripetal force of unity must therefore pull against a significant centrifugal force of variation. Nature is densely packed with ornament at every level. Indeed, one of the reasons that Leibniz rejects atomism is that the uniformity of atoms "can have no place in [God's works], for there is no variety or embellishment about them, which is incompatible with the divine architecture."[22] Leibniz's unity-in-variety is not that of a Vitruvian temple but that of Gian Lorenzo Bernini's Baldacchino, which requires shifts in visual scale to move from the shape of the whole to the details that stud and deform every surface. Or it is like a baroque musical score, filled with trills, mordents, appoggiaturas, etc., that threaten to obscure the theme on which they play their variations. The baroque artwork involves a dynamic *tension* between unity and variety, not a facile accommodation (compare Samuel Johnson's description of the metaphysical conceit as "opposites yoked by violence together").

I mention this as a prelude to considering Leibniz's philosophy as aesthetic object—a topic I have been skirting until now. What I mean by this is I have been avoiding a crucial distinction between form and content or rather between philosophy and its referent. When Leibniz speaks of "beautiful truths" in the passage that opens this section or uses the phrase "beautiful discoveries" to describe the results of his work, what exactly is he saying? Is the philosophy itself beautiful or rather the divine order it expounds? The language of "discovery," which Leibniz frequently employs, suggests the latter.[23] In a letter, he claims "to have discovered (*découvert*) a new country in the intelligible world." As the metaphor suggests, the country is a real thing, already objectively there; Leibniz merely stumbles upon it and reveals it to us. His philosophical activity is essentially disclosive: it unveils something beautiful but is not therefore necessarily beautiful itself. Likewise, when he claims that "no hypothesis can give a better knowledge of the wisdom of God than can mine," the wisdom revealed is God's, not Leibniz's. At one level, there is a self-abnegating quality to Leibniz's stance; his philosophy simply mirrors something divinely beautiful. At the same time, the language of discovery or disclosure invests his philosophical claims with the status of objective truths.

And then, of course, the discoverer of an unknown country gets to bask in reflected glory. The country may have existed without him, but the discovery is his. A more pertinent metaphor might be the discovery of a mathematical proof. Once again, the theorem proved is objectively true, and was so even before the mathematician proved it and thereby disclosed its truth to others. But the same theorem can often be proven in multiple ways, and so the proof may be judged for its elegance and brilliance as well as for its efficacy. Indeed, it not infrequently happens that the proof is more dazzling than the thing proven.

God's creation is beautiful because it is harmonious—because, that is, it exhibits a formal structure of unity-in-variety. Leibniz's philosophy is an object of aesthetic contemplation insofar as what it discloses is beautiful. But it might also be intellectually beautiful because the philosophy itself, and not merely what it describes, exhibits the same structure of unity-in-variety. In module 04, we looked at a set of metaphors that Leibniz employed to describe the economy of divine creation. Part of that passage went as follows:

> As to the simplicity of God's ways, it properly relates to means, whereas on the other hand, their variety, richness, or abundance relate to ends or effects. The one should be balanced against the other, as the expenses allowed for a building are balanced against its desired size and beauty. It is true that things cost God nothing, less indeed than it costs a philosopher to invent theories as he constructs his imaginary world, since God has only to make a decree for a real world to be produced; but in regard to wisdom, decrees or theories function as costs in proportion to their independence from each other—for reason requires that multiplicity of hypotheses or principles be avoided, rather as the most simple system is always preferred in astronomy.

Here the principle of variety-in-unity is understood as entailing a multiplicity of effects resulting from a simplicity of means. Just as God derives the variegated abundance of the world from a few basic principles, and thereby invests his creative act with an admirable economy, so the philosopher should derive his metaphysical system from as few premises as possible, thereby investing it with an intellectual elegance that itself confers an aura of validity. Such systems exhibit variety-in-unity and are therefore themselves formally beautiful, apart from the reality they claim to reflect or explain. Tellingly, Leibniz asserts that his "hypothesis" (in the singular) reveals the wisdom of God, thus suggesting that his philosophy too relies on a beautiful economy of means.

The reader will note that the word "system" has crept into my previous paragraph. While not all systems are frugal with their premises, it is hard to imagine the kind of explanatory economy that Leibniz extols in the absence of a system. But of course, the assumption that Leibniz's philosophy is systematic is something I have been trying to question in this study. Spinoza seems a much more parsimonious thinker, spinning an intellectual universe from a few definitions and axioms, while Leibniz exhibits what I have called intellectual sprawl, a product of his habit of endlessly mapping diverse disciplines onto one another. What I would like here to suggest is that the conflict between systemic and anti-systemic tendencies in Leibniz produces a variety-in-unity of a distinctively baroque flavor, exhibiting a dynamic tension between whole and part rather like that of the baroque artwork.

Indeed, we might want to press a bit on the "like" in the phrase "like that of the baroque artwork." What exactly is the difference between the artwork and philosophy as Leibniz construes them? Both enable us to grasp formal orders, the one more confusedly and the other more distinctly. But neither traffics in confused or distinct ideas exclusively. Both are harmonious and therefore beautiful. The differences appear to involve relative positions on a continuum rather than incommensurable kinds of activity. Instead of distinguishing philosophy and art on the confused-distinct axis, then, it might be more profitable to do so on the basis of the kinds of formal order each presents. In the philosopher's case, that order is reality itself, while in the artist's case, it is of the artist's own invention. Here we might consider Leibniz's suggestion, frequently repeated, that novels depict not the actual world but one of the possible worlds that God considered but rejected before realizing ours.[24]

Leibniz lobs the following insult in the course of his testy correspondence with Samuel Clarke:

> Mr. Boyle made it his chief business to inculcate that everything was done mechanically in natural philosophy. But is men's misfortune to grow disgusted in the end with reason itself and to be weary of light. Chimeras begin to appear again, and they are pleasing because they have something in them that is wonderful. What has happened in poetry happens also in the philosophical world. People have grown weary of rational romances, such as were the French *Clélie* or the German *Aramena*; and they have become fond again of the tales of fairies.[25]

Here the infiltration of philosophy by the literary is something to be guarded against as entailing the contamination of reason by fancy and superstition. The target of this brief polemic is—of all people—Sir Isaac Newton, who, I think it fair to say, would *not* have been regarded by most of his and Leibniz's contemporaries as trading in fairy tales, despite his contention (the topic of this local quarrel, and an idea Newton himself was unhappy about) that gravity acts at a distance across empty space. I can't help hearing in Leibniz's tone and his attempt at preemptive rhetorical ju-jitsu a troubling awareness that he, and not the comparatively hard-headed Newton, is the purveyor of fairy tales in natural philosophy—that he, and not Newton, has failed adequately to guard the borders of the scientific against the incursions of the poetic.

In any case, Leibniz's philosophy is harmonious and therefore beautiful by Leibnizian standards, both in its content and in its form. But what are the consequences of this fact? As we have seen, beautiful things—both nature and the artwork—are for Leibniz appropriate objects of *contemplation*; that is, of disinterested aesthetic and intellectual appreciation. Apart from any other purposes they may serve, they are also, and perhaps primarily, to be savored on their own account. Leibniz's philosophy discloses the beauty of God's order and thereby encourages both the piety and the happiness of the beholder. Nevertheless, philosophy is not "for" anything in a strictly utilitarian sense, any more than a painting or a sculpture is. This view might be held to reflect a certain complacency on Leibniz's part. At the same time, it softens, even if it doesn't quite eliminate, the instrumental rationality that characterizes a good deal of seventeenth-century philosophy and which has been subject to critique, from different perspectives, by figures from Carolyn Merchant to Martin Heidegger to Theodor Adorno and Max Horkheimer.[26] Leibniz does not dream of dominating nature in the way that Francis Bacon does; in Carolyn Merchant's view, his attachment to Cartesian mechanism is counterbalanced by a vitalism that "can be construed as antiexploitative."[27] Leibniz's appetite for beauty is unusual among rationalist philosophers of the seventeenth century, in degree if not in kind, and I would suggest that it entails a somewhat different relation to the natural world. Pauline Phemister and Lloyd Strickland have suggested that Leibnizian metaphysics both anticipates and improves upon the "positive aesthetics" of the political scientist Allen Carlson, whose book *Aesthetics and the Environment* (2000) argues that all of nature is beautiful, both sensually and intellectually.[28] While Leibniz's influence on ecophilosophy is more restricted than Spinoza's, and while it might be argued that ecological thought can get along quite well without a metaphysics at all, the fact that Leibniz's aesthetic dimension harbors an ecological potential at least complicates any attempt to reduce his thinking to a form of instrumental rationality.[29]

At the same time, by trying to justify the aesthetic dimension of Leibniz's philosophy by citing its ecological potential, I am myself subjecting it to instrumental purposes, though ones that might well be construed as virtuous. At some level, the aesthetic dimension of Leibniz's thought should be allowed to give pleasure on its own account, whether or not it helps to improve the world, in the same way that we might be allowed to enjoy a painting or a lyric poem without insisting that it improve the world either, other than by merely existing and giving pleasure. Perhaps it is the case that neither poems nor metaphysical systems can make things better. Only we can do that. In savoring something for its own sake or for the pleasure it gives us, we are indulging in momentary selfishness—ignoring larger and more weighty issues for something that benefits no one but us. It is in this sense that I identified Leibniz's emphasis on the aesthetic value of his metaphysics as a sign of possible complacency on his part, though why this charge should be leveled at him rather than at a Caravaggio or a Bernini is an open question. For me, Leibniz is a guilty pleasure and perhaps all the more delectable for that. But in our current climate—political and meteorological—philosophy as such is a luxury good. Perhaps Leibniz's aestheticism helps us keep that in view and not fool ourselves into thinking that it is something other and more useful than that. In any case, if Leibniz does nothing more than make the world a more interesting place, that's no small accomplishment.[30]

CHAPTER 18

Blind Thought

F rom the brilliance of the aesthetic, we now plunge abruptly into the darkness of what Leibniz calls "blind thought" (*cogitatio caeca*). This is the realm of his general characteristic, a lifelong attempt to automate and even mechanize thinking. Like many of his projects, this one never reached fruition but was rather the object of endless tinkering as Leibniz tried to realize a project of vast ambitions with only limited means. While the general characteristic proved inspirational for later logicians and computer scientists, it was for Leibniz a kind of fantasy object onto which he projected certain hopes and dreams regarding thought. My goal here will be to unpack the fantasy.

Basically, the general characteristic was an attempt to perform conceptual reasoning by way of numerical calculation. Concepts would be broken down into a series of constitutive predicates, each of those predicates would be assigned numerical values, and logical operations on the concepts (now represented by a series of numbers) would be conducted by arithmetical operations. The technical details of the system, which will not concern us, evolved over time. In some versions, primitive ideas were to be represented by prime numbers that would retain their identities throughout any arithmetical transformation. In a sense, the distinct identity of prime numbers expressed the identity of distinct ideas. Leibniz experimented with nonmathematical formalisms as well.

The primary quality attached to the general characteristic was infallibility. Since its terms were clearly defined, and its results were the product of arithmetical calculations that could be checked and confirmed, whatever truths the system might spit out could not be challenged, and so controversies of various sorts could be definitively settled:

But to go back to the expression of thoughts through characters, this is my opinion: it will hardly be possible to *end controversies* and impose silence on the *sects*, unless we work all complex arguments to simple *calculations*, [and] terms of vague and uncertain significance to determinate *characters*. . . . Once this has been done, when controversies will arise, there will be no more need of a disputation between two philosophers than between two accountants. It will in fact suffice to take pen in hand, to sit at the abacus, and—having summoned, if one wishes, a friend—to say to one another: *let us calculate* [*calculemus*].[1]

As this passage makes clear, Leibniz did not intend to employ the general characteristic only to produce scientific or philosophical truths but also to settle disputes in law, morality, and religion—areas where emotion, interest, and superstition might otherwise cloud the judgment.

The general characteristic was infallible in part because it worked only with distinctly defined concepts and therefore banished confusion from human thought. In the passage above, the phrase "vague and uncertain significance" points to the confusion that inevitably attends ordinary language and which can be banished only by a mathematical formalism. Instead of being represented by words that have merely an arbitrary relation to concepts and which can also collect fuzziness and unwanted connotations through use, concepts in the general characteristic would be represented by their component predicates; in other words, grasped distinctly. Leibniz compared the general characteristic to the microscope and the telescope, scientific inventions designed to take objects glimpsed only confusedly by the eye because of size or distance and bring them into sharp focus.[2] The general characteristic would invest concepts with comparable distinctness. Of course, we have seen that Leibniz not infrequently contradicts the notion that ideas can ever be purged entirely of confusion, but the general characteristic appears to offer his best hope of doing so. In addition to avoiding fuzziness in the definition of concepts, it promised to avoid the kinds of confusion that result from trying to keep the many steps of a complex demonstration in mind at once. The general characteristic dreamed of removing confusion entirely from thought, which it could do only by removing thought from the mind and handing it over to a formalism that would in effect work by itself and could in theory even be carried out by a machine. Distinct thought would thus remain immune to the obscure currents of microperceptions and microappetitions that suffuse the human mind. Leibniz in effect imagined a computer and designed the first programming language.

The purgation of confused ideas, and with them the danger of prejudices and emotional investments, is further abetted by another characteristic of the general characteristic: its "blindness." By this, Leibniz means the fact that once concepts are reduced to numerical equivalents, arithmetical operations can be performed on those numbers, and logical truths produced thereby, without the operator having any active awareness of the conceptual contents at issue. The formalism simply manipulates numbers; it doesn't trade directly in ideas. And this further ensures the objectivity of results. The operator's own prejudices and emotional investments can't come into play if she doesn't even know or attend to the occulted conceptual content of her calculations.

The blindness of the general characteristic is something that Leibniz borrows from mathematics. When schoolchildren learn long division, they master a formalism that allows them to produce answers without understanding exactly what they are doing.[3] On a more advanced level, Descartes's methods enabled geometric problems to be solved algebraically without attending to the geometric issues involved. But the true triumph of blind thinking in mathematics was Leibniz's invention of the calculus. As Clifford Brown notes:

> [N]o other mathematician, not even Newton, had constructed an algorithmic approach to infinitesimal analysis like Leibniz's. It is not simply the fact that Leibniz's notation dx, dy, $\int y \, dx$ is convenient. Its real advantage is that by manipulating the notation by itself according to simple rules, without much attention to the underlying geometric structure, one is led almost without conscious thought to new approaches and solutions to what had been considered difficult problems. In several cases [. . .] we have seen how Leibniz could give in a few lines solutions to problems that, say, Barrow or Huygens could certainly have also solved, but in several pages of complex argument.[4]

Leibniz's general characteristic was an attempt to extend the "black box" quality of the calculus to thought in general, which is why he sometimes referred to the characteristic as a "universal calculus."

The black box nature of the general characteristic means that it can produce truths without anyone's understanding the exact reasoning behind them. Results would be received as are the utterances of an oracle, their correctness guaranteed by correct arithmetical procedures. By reducing distinct thought to a formalism, the general characteristic in effect hands it off to an automaton or machine. The general characteristic does our thinking for us. Yet this formulation is not quite correct, since what it produces are not thoughts but truths—truths without thought. On the one hand, this bespeaks the fact that we are not to be trusted with truth—that our prejudices and emotions are likely to lead us astray. This gets at the first fantasy level of the general characteristic, which is to cleanse thought of its confused elements. In this respect it completes Francis Bacon's project of banishing the idols of the mind. But its more fundamental fantasy is the opposite of this—if not quite to cleanse thought of its distinctness, at least to transfer the task of working with completely distinct ideas to an external mechanism, so that we don't have to. Presumably, the mind would then be left free to return to its native element, which is a mixture of the confused and the distinct, perhaps to pursue something more creative or pleasurable than grinding its way through a blind mathematical formalism.[5]

Leibniz's general characteristic did not and indeed could not perform as he hoped:

> As impressive as Leibniz's system is, there are still serious problems. Although the logical analysis is correct, to use it satisfactorily one would have to assign characteristic numbers to all concepts in such a way that *all* true propositions satisfy the divisibility criterion and that there is no inconsistency in the numbering system. This would be an enormous job and if accomplished would seem to render Leibniz's method for discovering true arguments pointless, since one would have to know in advance all true propositions and their mutual relationships in order to assign the numbers correctly.[6]

Even putting this (definitive) technical problem aside, the assignment of predicates to concepts would itself surely not escape controversy, especially when impinging on areas such as morality and theology. Leibniz's dream of an infallible technical method for generating truths was just that—a dream.

Significant advances, not only in technology but also in the field of logic, would be required before anything like the development of a working computer could be attempted. But Leibniz's plans for a general characteristic proved inspirational for the logicians who made those advances possible, including George Boole, Gottlob Frege, and Kurt Gödel. Perhaps the most recognizable, if distant, offspring of Leibniz's dream were the early problem-solving programs of the 1950s, such as Theory Logic and the (marvelously if erroneously named) General Problem Solver, developed by Herbert A. Simon, J. C. Shaw, and Allen Newell in 1959. Such programs could, at least in principle, solve problems involving limited, well-defined domains such as symbolic logic, trigonometry, or chess—areas in which Leibnizian "distinct ideas" are available. But such programs would be instantly overwhelmed by anything like a real-world problem. Emulating actual human intelligence would require something more than the serial (if recursive) processing on which the General Problem Solver relied. Connectionist or neural networks would begin to do this work. They would also reintroduce the "black box" quality of Leibniz's general characteristic, since the momentary states of such systems, with their innumerable and subtly weighted connections, cannot be disentangled by an external observer. In effect, these systems work by liquifying (to borrow Hofstadter's terminology) the solid and well-defined concepts on which early programs such as the General Problem Solver relied—in effect, reintroducing Leibnizian "confusion" into the realm of the distinct. Here we are far from the crude number-crunching of Leibniz's characteristic, and yet the cognitive capacities of such systems arise precisely from such number-crunching—both historically and operationally. The digital eliminates the fuzziness and confusion of the analog only to reintroduce it as an emergent property that proves necessary for anything like real cognition. Paradoxically, Leibniz's general characteristic gets the nature of thought wrong in fundamental respects but helps point the way to eventually getting it right.

CHAPTER 19

Dark Leibniz

erhaps no statement by Leibniz is better known or more notorious than his claim that ours is "the best of all possible worlds."[1] Its theological premises are fairly straightforward: if this is *not* the best of all possible worlds, then either God chose to create an inferior one, thereby inflicting more misery on humankind than was necessary, or else his powers proved incapable of carrying out his plans for the best. Therefore God is either not infinitely good or not omnipotent. Other than his conviction that there *is* a God, for which Leibniz can hardly be blamed, it is hard to know what exactly is objectionable here. Yet it has been used to tar Leibniz with a kind of fatuous optimism—as Voltaire did via *Candide*'s Dr. Pangloss. Leibniz's formula is understood to suggest both a blindness to human suffering and a complacent acceptance of the world as it is. Neither of these charges is entirely fair, but they (and the phrase itself) have taken on lives of their own. Among politically minded thinkers even today, Leibnizian optimism provides a good excuse for dismissing him. Leibniz's world supposedly basks in a constant and banal form of moral sunshine: a sort of metaphysical San Diego.

I want to argue that this view of Leibniz is, if not wholly distorting, at least oversimplifying. There are, at the very least, islands of relative darkness in Leibniz. And as I shall go on to argue in module 20, a characteristic form of anxiety pervades his worldview. I am interested both in the fact of darkness in Leibniz's writings and in the fact that this is often overlooked. "Dark Leibniz" echoes the term "dark matter," which supposedly composes most of matter in the universe yet remains steadfastly unobservable.[2] Leibniz's pessimism is likewise oddly occluded from view.

First, I want to exonerate Leibniz from charges of moral blindness: the notion that he simply doesn't see what's wrong with the world, owing either to innate temperament (cf. Ludwig Wittgenstein's "the world of the happy is a happy world") or in response to theologically imposed blindfolds. A sample passage:

> But it seems that this [divine] wisdom, which reveals such economy in each animal or organic body considered separately, has left them afterward to attack each other in the greatest confusion imaginable. A wretched sheep is torn apart by a wolf, a pigeon falls prey to some vulture, the poor flies are exposed to the malice of spiders, and men themselves—what a tyranny they exercise over the other animals, and even among themselves they are more than wolves and more than vultures. What appearance of order is there in all this? Or, rather, since we have agreed on the sovereign wisdom of the Author of things, we must say that he cares not at all for what we call justice and that he takes pleasure in destruction as we take pleasure in hunting the beasts which prey on each other. Individuals must give way; there is room only for the species, some of which subsist through the misfortune of others.[3]

Now, this is spoken by a character named Polidore in a dialogue, and he is answered by his interlocutor, Theophile. But Theophile's reassurances sound somewhat pat by comparison and in any case can't quite match the rhetorical energy of Polidore's objection. This is not unusual for Leibniz. Dystopian visions of widespread suffering are often introduced in a kind of concessive or subordinate fashion, then to be argued away. But these depictions of misery and injustice are often more striking than the attached efforts at consolation. The passage above has mainly to do with the natural order, which it depicts as red in tooth and claw. But the order of divine grace sometimes doesn't fare much better:

> So it is a terrible judgement that God, giving his only Son for the whole human race and being the sole author and master of the salvation of men, yet saves so few of them and abandons all others to the devil his enemy, who torments them eternally and makes them curse their Creator, though they have all been created to diffuse and show forth his goodness, his justice and his other perfections. And this outcome inspires all the more horror, as the sole cause why all these men are wretched to all eternity is God's having exposed their parents to a temptation that he knew they would not resist; as this sin

is inherent and imputed to men before their will has participated in it; as this hereditary vice impels their will to commit actual sins; and as countless men, in childhood or maturity, that have never heard or have not heard enough of Jesus Christ, Saviour of the human race, die before receiving the necessary succour for their withdrawal from this abyss of sin. These men too are condemned to be for ever rebellious against God and plunged in the most horrible miseries, with the wickedness of all creatures, though in essence they have not been more wicked than others, and several among them have perchance been less guilty than some of that little number of elect, who were saved by a grace without reason, and who thereby enjoy an eternal felicity which they had not deserved.[4]

Again, this is not the last word on the matter, and Leibniz is merely collecting objections that others have voiced. He himself rejects double predestination, the eternal torment of the damned, and the damnation of virtuous pagans. But these are beliefs held far more widely, and wielding far more institutional power, than Leibniz's own. The number of pages in the *Theodicy* alone devoted to grappling with them suggests that they are not easily dismissed.[5] And gathering them together into one passage exerts an undeniably powerful effect. Perhaps it is simply the case that theodicy is not an interesting enterprise if the full weight of the task is not felt. But this is a case in which Leibniz's powers as a writer seem to complicate the official optimism of his philosophy.

"The best of all possible worlds" implies that our world is optimal, but not that it is perfect or even not horrible in some ways. It is simply the best that could be created given the constraints implied by Leibniz's criterion of compossibility. Since all entities in the universe compose a total system, and since the good of any one of them may be possible only given a less good state for another (feeding wolves is not a plus for lambs), not everything can enjoy a perfectly happy condition. The point is to find a sequence that provides the best total outcome for the system as a whole, even though this may entail suffering for many. Given the premise of a good, wise, and all-powerful God, the actual world simply has to be the best he could have created, no matter how bad things may appear at any given moment. The problem, for many of Leibniz's readers, is that this belief can turn into a form of retroactive justification. Living the kind of life that Leibniz did, unmarked by radical deprivation or suffering, doubtless made this sort of consolation easier to swallow. And yet it seems to me that the doctrine of the best of all possible worlds is not necessarily a comforting one absent the additional assumption that the actual world is a pretty good one after all. In fact, it is a doctrine that is radically perspectival, if not in content then at least in tone.

To make things dicier still, the fact that this is the best of all possible worlds does not necessarily mean that it is always optimal for human beings. Leibniz rejects "that false maxim [. . .] stating that the happiness of rational creatures is the sole aim of God. If that were so, perhaps neither sin nor unhappiness would ever occur, even by concomitance. God would have chosen a sequence of possibles where all these evils would be excluded. But God would fail in what is due to the universe, that is, in what he owes to himself."[6] Leibniz believes that God does privilege rational creatures. But while we are his prime concern, we are not his *sole* one. Besides ourselves and the plants and animals that populate our world, there are infinities upon infinities of nested microorganisms, each of which has its own differential claim on God's moral attention. Hence the calculus He employs to ensure an optimal world cannot possibly be fathomed by finite beings, and it may not necessarily appear friendly to us.

In addition, Leibniz has more than one criterion for the optimality of the universe. Sometimes he defines it as entailing a maximum of reality or of essence; sometimes he defines it through harmony, or variety-in-unity. And it isn't entirely clear whether these various criteria are complementary or, possibly, competing. In any case, God has metaphysical and even aesthetic concerns to consider in constructing a universe, and not only the maximal happiness of its inhabitants. Perhaps the beauty of a sunset can be purchased only through an increase in pain or ennui somewhere.

All of this raises the question: Given its necessary imperfection, why did God decide to create a universe at all? Why is there something rather than nothing? As Patrick Riley points out, Leibniz's explanations tend to focus more on God's glory than on his goodness. "Substances exist to 'mirror' [God's] perfections, to 'bear witness' to them. [. . .] At best, Leibniz is able to show that the universe as a whole is best, once the decision to create *some* universe has been made."[7] But the logic of that primordial decision is less simple to construe.

The doctrine of the best of all possible worlds would hardly be worth asserting if everything appeared to be in some obvious way optimal. Leibniz therefore chooses the rhetorical approach of vividly depicting the world's faults in order then to try to bring them back under the rule of the best—with mixed results. A particularly interesting example is a long passage in his essay "On the Radical

Origination of Things," which I shall now examine closely in parts. This passage offers a condensed version of some of Leibniz's main theodical strategies, including that of comparing the universe to an artwork. Formally, it provides an instructive instance of what happens when one follows the development of a theme "in motion" across paragraphs.

Following an assertion of the benign order of the universe, Leibniz lists some possible objections. He often distances these by assigning them to someone else—a character in a dialogue, other writers, or in this case the reader ("you"):

> You may object, however, that we experience the very opposite of this in the world, for often the very worst things happen to the best; innocent beings, not only beasts but men, are struck down and killed, even tortured. In fact, especially if we consider the government of mankind, the world seems rather a kind of confused chaos than something ordained by a supreme wisdom. So it seems at first sight, I admit, but, when we look more deeply, the opposite can be established. A priori it is obvious from the principles which I have already given that the highest perfection possible is obtained for all things and therefore also for minds.[8]

To the imaginary reader, the world appears not just badly governed but not governed at all. It is a "confused chaos" where chance rules. So Leibniz must insist first that the universe is ordered, for better or worse. Behind the superficial appearance of chaos stands the reality of law. In accordance with this, one should render judgment not on the basis of empirical evidence but rather on a priori principles that are sufficient unto themselves and cannot be either confirmed or refuted by facts. The doctrine of the best of all possible worlds is logically self-evident and therefore immune to counter-evidence of any kind. (And here we see a first opening for Panglossian satire.)

The passage continues:

> And as the jurisconsults say, it is truly unjust to render a judgment without having studied the whole law. We know but a very small part of an eternity stretching out beyond all measure. How tiny is the memory of the few thousand years which history imparts to us! Yet from such slight experience we venture to judge about the immeasurable and the eternal; as if men born and reared in prison or in the underground salt mines of Sarmatia should think

that there is no other light in the world but the wretched torch which is scarcely sufficient to guide their steps.[9]

Here Leibniz scores an important point, and it is one he will elaborate. Since the universe is an ordered totality, it is unjust to judge it merely on the basis of local evidence, including temporal locality. The few thousand years of history we know is as nothing compared to eternity. Of course, Christians do not regard the world as eternal. It runs its course in a finite amount of time, succeeded by Doomsday and God's eternal reign. So it is unclear whether Leibniz means that the secular mechanism itself will assume a shape that justifies it or whether things will have to be made right after the end of historical time. More than once, he invokes the notion of eternal reward or punishment as a way to balance out the world's inequities.[10] Which leaves open the possibility that the span of worldly time itself does not reveal a redemptive pattern. Elsewhere, he expresses uncertainty about whether the perfection of the world increases, decreases, or oscillates over time.[11]

Regardless, we see too little of the span of the world to judge accurately, a point that Leibniz illustrates with the similes of the prisoners and the slaves in the salt mines. Here he has recourse to his habit of metaphorical clumping: never use just one simile when more than one will do. Ostensibly, both are invoked solely for the weak light that their torches cast. Our vision is like their torches, illuminating only a pathetically small portion of eternity. But it would be easy to come up with other, less charged instances of weak and partial illumination. It is rhetorically odd, given Leibniz's apparent intent to prove this the best of all possible worlds, to invoke images of hapless prisoners and slaves. The interest of these similes resides less in the specific basis of comparison, therefore, than in the subsidiary details. Through these, Leibniz seems determined to depict instances of horrifyingly unjust suffering, since these prisoners and slaves have been "born and bred" in miserable confinement. Someone imprisoned from birth cannot have committed any crime to justify the sentence. The situation indirectly invokes the idea of original sin, which, as we have already seen, Leibniz cites as a problem testing the limits of theodicy. Although a Lutheran, Leibniz is not of Luther's temperament. He does not see us as depraved masses of sinful flesh, fully deserving damnation. He sees us rather as somehow implicated in a crime we did not directly commit. For him the Fall is a *problem*, not a given— something to be explained, not an explanation itself. The salt mine complements the prison by invoking enforced and burdensome *labor*—a primary consequence of the Fall. And since Sarmatia lies beyond the bounds of Christendom, the slaves in its mines are both confined to endless drudgery and potentially excluded from the possibility of salvation. The Sarmatian salt mines involve both an intolerable inside and a hopeless outside.

The similes compare the world as we have known it—that is, the portion visible to us through the entire span of human history—to brutal, unjust forms of confinement. The weakness of our torches—the original basis of the simile—is itself a function and further sign of our debased condition. As Leibniz states, there are lights in the world far brighter than the torch of the prisoner/slave—presumably, he has in mind the sun. The similes indirectly invoke not only the Fall, therefore, but also Plato's Allegory of the Cave, while turning it into a kind of hellscape. All of this hardly seems designed to reinforce confidence in Leibniz's thesis of an optimal universe.

Let us follow the passage as it continues:

> If we look at a very beautiful picture but cover up all of it but a tiny spot, what more will appear in it, no matter how closely we study it, indeed, all the more, the more closely we examine it, than a confused mixture of colors without beauty and without art. Yet when the covering is removed and the whole painting is viewed from a position that suits it, we come to understand that what seemed to be a thoughtless smear on the canvas has really been done with the highest artistry by the creator of the work.[12]

The speed with which we go from mining salt in Sarmatia to viewing a beautiful picture is somewhat head-spinning. As is the transition to an aesthetic defense of the divine order. Beauty is, after all, part of the optimality of the universe, so this is more than an analogy. Smoothing the transition is a continuing focus on constriction: from that of a prison cell to that produced by covering up most of a painting. What this simile makes clear is that Leibniz's perspectivalism has been at work in the series of similes all along. Elsewhere, he compares the apparent disorder of the world to that of the movements of the planets when viewed from the earth—movements that seem random and inexplicable to us but that become orderly and predictable when viewed from the standpoint of the sun.[13] Here it is a matter of zooming out from a confusing welter of detail to take in the design of the whole.

One question this simile poses is who gets to occupy, and thus enjoy, the redemptive perspective that encompasses the painting as the whole. Is it reserved for generations millennia from now, who alone will be granted the privilege of seeing history brought to completion? Will we, who occupy the Sarmatian mine portion of history, get to view it from the ramparts of heaven after the end of time? Will the woman forced to watch her children die of starvation or the man who spent his entire life as a slave mining salt concede upon viewing the shape of history as a whole that it was a pretty good show after all and that they were happy to have played their part in it? Indeed, can anyone at any time really grasp the design of history as totality, given that it is structured in such a way as to account for infinities upon infinities of beings? Isn't it God's eye alone that can take in the entire painting? The divine painter appears to have executed a work that can be appreciated solely by Himself. We are merely messy daubs of pigment composing a beautiful structure.

While I have been extolling Leibniz's focus on aesthetic thought and the art-work throughout this study, it doesn't generally fare well when applied to moral questions or theodical ones. Things become still more problematic in this regard as our passage continues:

> And what the eyes experience in painting is experienced by the ears in music. Great composers very often mix dissonances with harmonious chords to stimu-late the hearer and to sting him, as it were, so that he becomes concerned about the outcome and is all the more pleased when everything is restored to order.[14]

The introduction of dissonance was one of the great formal innovations of baroque music, and Leibniz often employs the concept for theodical purposes similar to these.[15] He likewise notes how the dark, shadowy areas in paintings and the difficult situations in the course of a novel contribute to an improved artistic design.[16] While not enjoyable in themselves, they ultimately enhance aesthetic pleasure.

Leibniz's invocation of musical dissonance does not, therefore, simply trans-late his earlier point about painting into a different artistic medium. No one covers up the majority of a painting in order to enhance their enjoyment when subsequently viewing the whole. The apparent confusion seen when looking at only a tiny fraction of the painting is not part of the artist's design; it is merely the effect of a perspectival shift. But a musical composer intentionally includes dissonance so as to accentuate the subsequent return to harmony. The logic of the simile thus appears to argue that the imperfections of the world are not merely an unavoidable result of the constraints imposed by compossibility but something voluntarily added by the divine artist in order to improve the effect of the whole—to add, as it were, a certain piquancy to the composition. Once more, an aesthetic model pushes theodicy in rather disturbing directions. And we again face the question of the implied auditor of this musical composition— the one who will relish immense quantities of human suffering and death as an enhancement of the design of the whole. Elsewhere Leibniz insists that it is *God's* ear whose pleasure is increased by mixing dissonances with harmonies.[17]

Here is the rest of the passage:

> Similarly we may enjoy trivial dangers or the experience of evils from the very sense they give us of our own power or our happiness or our fondness for display. Or again, in witnessing performances of rope-dancing or sword-dancing [*sauts périlleux*], we are delighted by the very fears they arouse, and we playfully half-drop children, pretending to be about to throw them away for much the same reason that the ape carried King Christian of Denmark, when he was still a baby dressed in long clothes, to a rooftop and then, while everyone waited in terror, returned him, as if in play, to his cradle. By the same principle it is insipid always to eat sweets; sharp, sour, and even bitter things should be mixed with them to excite the taste. He who has not tasted the bitter does not deserve the sweet; indeed, he will not appreciate it. This is the very law of enjoyment, that pleasure does not run an even course, for this produces aversion and makes us dull, not joyful.[18]

It is interesting to speculate about whether Leibniz has entirely lost sight of the theodical context of his argument at this point. If not, there is some difficulty in making the transition from minor evils suffered in an otherwise happy life, or bitter tastes endured before sweet, or momentary states of anxiety and tension that are then relieved, and the justification of the moral structure of the universe. It is worth noting as well that Leibniz has now descended from high art forms to modes of popular entertainment (rope- or sword-dancing) that require skill but perhaps not the same degree of formal mastery or aesthetic depth as painting or baroque musical composition. What I find most striking here, however, is the ape who dangles the infant King Christian of Denmark before returning him "as if in play" to his cradle. If one follows the logic of the analogy, it is clear that this ape stands in for . . . God. The divinity is no longer imagined as an artist but rather as a possibly playful, possibly deranged primate whose motives, such as they are, must perforce remain opaque to us and are not necessarily benign. It is simply the case that we experience a sigh of relief at the spectacle he provides for us, when he decides not to drop the human infant to its death after all (in a kind of simian rewriting of the story of Abraham and Isaac). Things could have turned out much worse, and we are grateful that they did not. In any case, Leibniz's attempt at theodical justification has left us in its closing cadences with the image of a dangerous God-ape as governor of the universe. I would suggest further that the ape might also stand in for Leibniz himself, whose intentions, like those of his imagined deity, have become impenetrable at this point.

I can already hear some philosophical readers exclaim that this is precisely why we should *not* pay undue attention to Leibniz's metaphors, similes, and analogies, and why we should focus rather on his clearly defined and mutually articulated philosophical concepts. What I have been coaxing from a close reading of this passage contradicts Leibniz's well-established opinions, and even what he understands himself to be doing in this very essay. In responding, I'll bracket for the moment the facts that Leibniz's well-formed concepts are themselves sedimented metaphors, and that the preference for one sort of textual evidence over another simply reflects disciplinary habits rather than a convincingly argued approach. Instead, I will claim that attention should be paid to Leibniz's use of figurative language precisely *because* this can unearth unexpected and even unassimilable elements that contradict the presuppositions of the "system." In this case, cracks appear in Leibniz's official mask of optimism. Something anarchic, dark, and unpredictable seems to work its way free when Leibniz is released into the realms of image and figure. Like the chiaroscuro in paintings that, Leibniz insists, improves the composition as a whole, there are shadowy areas in his own thought—veins of darkness that contrast with optimism. Whether these very different elements can be triumphantly synthesized or whether they are the expressions of an underlying and irreducible ambivalence is harder to say. My subject of analysis is Leibniz the monad, gifted with extraordinary zones of clarity but also permeated with confused drives and impulses. There may be no total Leibniz, but a complete one will include shadow as well as light.

In any case, the figurative language of "On the Radical Origination of Things" does not so much contradict the principles of Leibnizian theodicy as throw some of their complexities into vivid relief. Leibniz himself makes clear that the phrase "the best of all possible worlds" does *not* mean "the *happiest* of all possible worlds," though precisely this mistranslation has proven irresistible for most of Leibniz's casual readers. The whole point of Leibniz's doctrine was not to minimize unhappiness but rather to explain its absolute necessity. God could have created a happier world, but only at the expense of impairing its perfection in other respects. What respects, exactly? Lloyd Strickland demonstrates convincingly that the governing criterion for divine creation in Leibniz is a rich, ordered harmony, which includes the harmonies of the physical world and its laws.[19] But harmony, as we have already seen, is for Leibniz also the criterion for beauty. It could be argued, then, that God ultimately chooses aesthetic principles over moral ones in the creation of the world. Leibniz appears to say as much: "Nature preserves the utmost order and beauty . . . there is no reason to think that God, for the sake of some lessening of moral evil, would reverse the whole order of nature."[20] Moreover, as Leibniz also makes clear, God's primary motive for creating the world is not our happiness but "his own joy or love of himself."[21] That rational creatures are created at all, Leibniz states at one point, is mainly so that the harmonious order of nature will not lack "reflection or refraction and multiplication," thereby enriching its complex harmonies.[22] While he sometimes insists that the happiness of rational creatures is a particular concern of God's, Leibniz also paints a very different and hard-to-reconcile portrait of God as self-absorbed artist for whom creatures are mere means for the production of a vast, harmonious composition. It should not be surprising, then, either that Leibniz frequently invokes the artwork in explicating the logic of divine creation or that doing so brings out the more unsettling aspects of his thinking on the topic.

The German theologian Christoph Matthäus Pfaff published in the *Acta Eruditorum* of 1728 a summary of a letter purportedly sent him by Leibniz in which the philosopher admitted that he was only diverting himself in the *Theodicy* and did not take its arguments seriously. An unresolved controversy ensued over whether the letter was authentic (Richard H. Popkin leans slightly toward the view that it is) and, if it was authentic, whether Leibniz was joking to Pfaff when he made those claims.[23] An interesting tangle! Was Leibniz unserious in the *Theodicy*? Was he unserious when he claimed he was being unserious? Or is this someone else's joke, a prankster impersonating Leibniz? Regardless of its ultimate authenticity, this image of a Leibniz amusing himself by playing with some rather weighty theodical matters leads us in a couple of interesting directions. One is back to Leibniz the tinkerer, who experiments or plays with ideas rather than committing himself to definitive formulations. (This would link up nicely with the Montaignesque dimensions of the *Theodicy*, discussed earlier). The other is to that ape in "On the Radical Origination of Things," who diverts himself by dangling the infant King of Denmark off a rooftop. In this case, Leibniz is diverting himself by dangling, not a human infant but divine justice itself.

I invoke the Pfaff episode because it foregrounds something too often overlooked in discussions of Leibniz's theodical writings: their performative dimension. As we have seen, performance—and particularly artistic performance—is central to Leibniz's theodical strategy. We must judge the universe the way we would judge a painting or a musical composition. But how are we to judge Leibniz's own theodical performance? Voltaire had no trouble reaching a verdict; he reacted with derision to Leibniz's claims. And if the letter to Pfaff happens to be a forgery, then Voltaire wasn't the first reader to be inspired to a witty response by the *Theodicy*.

The standard account of the afterlife of the *Theodicy* holds that it was warmly received in the first half of the eighteenth century but that the Lisbon earthquake of 1755 delivered a blow to rationalist optimism, inspiring Voltaire to compose his *Poème sur le désastre de Lisbon* in 1756 and then *Candide* in 1759, both of which made Leibniz their whipping boy. Optimistic theology thereafter fell into disrepute. But as Hernán D. Caro has recently shown, critical responses to Leibnizian optimism appeared in the early eighteenth century as well.[24] The reaction against optimism reaches a kind of philosophical apogee in Schopenhauer's philosophy of pessimism and a literary apogee in Dostoevsky's *The Brothers Karamazov*, where Ivan cites Leibniz in arguing that existence as such is unjustified.[25] The French philosopher and sociologist Georges Friedmann perceptively observed that "Leibnizian optimism is in reality one of the first forms of the modern philosophies of anguish and despair."[26]

The fate of Leibnizian optimism can be chalked up in part to the vagaries of philosophical, cultural, and even geologic history. It can be argued as well that its opponents are often dealing with reductive or vulgarized versions of Leibniz's arguments. But the point is not whether such criticisms of Leibniz are accurate or fair. It is rather why the performance of Leibnizian theodicy proves such an irresistible target. Whatever their philosophical coherence or merit, Leibniz's arguments strike readers as morally callous and naïve. Moreover, there is something powerfully provoking about Leibniz's claim that this is "the best of all possible worlds" that makes it almost impossible not to reflect rather on its imperfections. Leibniz's optimism is insufferable in a way that generates a countervailing pessimism; his light makes us flee to darkness. This is the *performative truth* of Leibnizian theodicy, which not only undoes its own claims but renders any defense of divine justice appear untenable.

Now when I speak of performative truth I do not mean that this necessarily or even likely falls within Leibniz's *intentions*—though the issue of intention is always a complicated one. Performative truth is objective, not subjective. Or rather, it is read off from the subjective reactions of many readers, not from that of the author. Leibniz's genius was to have produced an almost universally repellant form of optimism—one that is therefore productive of pessimism. The close readings I have been doing expose moments when a kind of darkness rises to the surface of Leibnizian theodicy. But these are just the local manifestations of a deeper performative truth that subtends the project as a whole, just as Leibniz's metaphors bring to the rhetorical surface patterns of thought that underlie his intellectual project more generally. When Voltaire mocks Leibnizian theodicy or when Dostoevsky's Ivan employs it to feed his own nihilism, they are in one sense Leibniz's opponents but in another loyally responsive to his performative truth. Like Milton's God, "dark with excessive bright," the sunniness of Leibnizian optimism leaves dark spots in our field of moral vision when we turn away from it and back to the realities of the world.

CHAPTER 20

Things Fall Apart

I have stated several times that, toward the end of his career, Leibniz starts to wonder whether physical bodies may be nothing more than "well-founded phenomena." Strictly speaking, this is not correct. Such speculations actually begin quite early; they merely become more frequent later on.[1] Here he is in 1675:

> But at this point you are right in stopping us for a while and renewing the criticisms of the ancient Academy. For at bottom all our experiences assure us of only two things: first, that there is a connection among our appearances which provides the means to predict future appearances successfully; and, second, that this connection must have a constant cause. But it does not follow strictly from this that matter or bodies exist but only that there is something which gives us appearances in a good sequence. For if some invisible power were to take pleasure in giving us dreams that are well tied into our preceding life and in conformity with each other, could we distinguish them from reality before we had awakened?[2]

"If some invisible power were to take pleasure in giving us dreams": this sounds like something straight out of Descartes's *Meditations*. Only one thing is missing, and that is the epistemological anxiety that attends this possibility for Descartes. This is not because Leibniz somehow convinces himself that corporeal bodies necessarily have, after all, some kind of solid ontological foundation beyond appearances. To the contrary: if he achieves any kind of certainty, it is that the very things that constitute material reality for Descartes—extension

in space, shape, movement, etc.—contain at the very least an irreducible phenomenal element:

> There is never either a globe without inequalities, or a straight line without
> intermingled curves, or a curve of a certain finite nature without a mixture
> of some other one, in the small parts as in the large ones, so that shape, far
> from being constitutive of bodies, is not even an entirely real and determi-
> nate quality outside of thought, and one will never be able to assign to any
> body a certain precise surface, as one could if there were Atoms. And I can
> say the same thing of size, and of motion, namely that these qualities or pred-
> icates partake of the phenomenon, like colors and sounds, and although they
> contain a greater amount of distinct knowledge, they cannot stand up to the
> final analysis any better, and consequently extended mass considered without
> the substantial form consisting only of these qualities is not bodily substance,
> but an entirely pure phenomenon, like the rainbow.[3]

Now, simply declaring imaginary the very things that for Descartes define the
reality of bodies does not mean that Leibniz necessarily also regards bodies as
imaginary. Because for Leibniz, the ultimate reality of bodies resides not in
extension but in *force*. Regardless, it is no small matter to decide that extension,
shape, movement, etc., are merely phenomenal. The initially odd thing is that
Leibniz is not disturbed by this, and that he blithely maintains a kind of skeptical *epoche* or suspension of judgment on the matter more or less indefinitely.

Leibniz's imperturbability is not ungrounded. For one thing, to call something phenomenal does not mean that it is not real. Rainbows and solar parhelia,
his favorite examples of the phenomenal, are real things, although not tangible.
They involve light and physical laws. This is one of the senses in which Leibniz
considers such phenomena "well founded." More generally, phenomena are well
founded when they are internally consistent, both from moment to moment and
among different observers: "Matter and motion are not so much substances or
things as the phenomena of perceivers, *the reality of which is located in harmony of
perceivers with themselves (at different times) and with other perceivers*" (my emphasis).[4] "It suffices for these dreams to be in agreement with one another, and to
obey certain laws, and accordingly to leave room for human prudence and pre-
diction."[5] As long as what we perceive is not an unpredictable dreamscape—as

long as it allows us to make reliable inferences and to agree among ourselves about what we observe—it doesn't really matter whether our perceptions correspond totally (or at all) with whatever is "out there," since the latter is reduced to inaccessible *Dinge an sich*.

Moreover, Leibniz has other, a priori, reasons for thinking that material things exist:

> Again, I am asked why God does not think it enough to produce all the thoughts and 'modifications of the soul,' without these 'useless' bodies, which the soul, it is said, could neither 'move nor know.' The answer is easy. It is that God wanted there to be more substances rather than fewer, and he thought it best that these 'modifications of the soul' should correspond to something outside.[6]

If matter exists, it is not because our senses tell us so but because God's creation possesses a maximum of reality, abundance, and variety, and it will have more of these things if there are real material bodies as well as monadic perceptions. "The more matter there is, the more God has to exercise his wisdom and power."[7] Nevertheless, we can know that matter exists only with a moral and not a metaphysical certainty.[8]

There is one dimension of this issue that Leibniz cannot contemplate with quite his usual degree of equanimity, however. And that is the aggregation problem—the fact that material bodies are merely collections of parts, like piles of stones or logs. As such, a body cannot be an entity, for in Leibniz's view only something simple or unified can have full being. And the one kind of thing that satisfies this criterion is a monad or substance, which is without parts. Hence monads are real but bodies are ontologically lacking because they are aggregates or multiplicities:

> Thus there will never be a body of which it can be said that it is truly one substance. It will always be an aggregate of many. Or rather it will not be a real being, since the parts that compose it are subject to the same difficulty, and since we never arrive at any real being, beings by aggregation having only as much reality as there is in their ingredients.[9]

The ontological formula for a body is not "It exists" but rather "They (i.e., the constitutive parts) exist." Yet this is not right either, since the parts themselves are also aggregates, as are their parts in turn. Every time you think you've reached a foundational unit, it disintegrates in turn into parts. So the correct ontological formula for any given body is not "It exists" but rather "*They do not exist.*" Upon metaphysical examination, bodies dissolve, as it were, into fine sand. Their multiplicity adds up to ontological nullity.

Insofar as bodies do possess reality, this results from the fact that they are ultimately composed of monads, which are unities and not aggregates. But starting from a given body, one never gets to these ultimate foundations, as the above quotation reveals, because an infinity of composites intervenes. And the premise that bodies are composed of monads raises a host of other problems. How do monads, which are not only dimensionless themselves but which do not even exist in space, manage to aggregate themselves into spatially extended bodies? And how are monads aggregated at all, given the fact that they are self-contained and do not interact with one another? What, in other words, is the aggregating principle or metaphysical glue that binds them together? If the aggregated body seems somewhat unreal to Leibniz, this is because it is composed of explanatory deficits. It is a site where not only the metaphysical fabric of the world but also (and perhaps even more threateningly) the internal coherence of Leibniz's thought threatens to tear.

Now when I describe this situation as a source of anxiety for Leibniz, I don't mean to suggest that his writings on the topic are suffused with explicitly anxious affect. But he *worries* the problem, meaning that he sinks his teeth into it and won't let it go. He repeatedly returns to it and attacks it and never produces a sufficient or self-consistent answer. It is his worrying the problem that I take as evidence of worrying *about* it.[10] And to be sure, it represents a pretty large and gaping hole in his metaphysics. The aggregation problem vexes Leibniz's career from early on until the very end.

The aggregation problem divides into two cases, one of which is even thornier than the other. Animal bodies, or corporeal substances as Leibniz sometimes calls them, have a dominant monad that somehow supposedly confers unity on their multiplicity. Inorganic bodies, such as rocks or chunks of metal, lack even that. Or rather, as I suggested in module 10, Leibniz's physics of forces *implies* that even inorganic bodies *should* have dominant monads. But this notion entails obvious difficulties. It seems awkward to suggest that if I split a stone in two (or cut a violin string in two), each half now has its own dominant monad, in which case I have in effect created one by my actions.

But if the aggregation problem is bifurcated substantively by the difference between animal and nonanimal bodies, it is also bifurcated theoretically by the fact that Leibniz offers idealist and realist accounts of each. In the idealist account, bodies are purely phenomenal, while in the realist account, there is something mind-independent that undergirds our phenomenal experience of bodies. The most extensive, rigorous, and illuminating attempt to bring order to this metaphysical tangle is Glenn Hartz's 2007 book-length study, *Leibniz's Final System: Monads, Matter and Animals*.[11] Hartz conducts a wide-ranging survey of Leibniz's often conflicting statements about bodies and the aggregation problem, and he brings the resources of analytic philosophy to bear in order to see if these statements can be corralled into a logically consistent doctrine. I shall proceed here by selectively summarizing some of Hartz's claims, though in doing so I shall be sacrificing a good deal of nuance and detail, and also omitting the supporting evidence. (I recommend Hartz's book to anyone interested in the issue.)

As Hartz argues, the challenge posed by a realist account of bodies has contributed to the predominance of the idealist account in Leibniz scholarship. Elements of the realist account are often admitted only insofar as they are regarded as being compatible with the idealist one. Much of Hartz's book is therefore devoted to rehabilitating the realist account, which, he argues, is far more subtle and self-consistent than is generally appreciated. There is no way to do justice to Hartz's treatment of Leibniz's realist account in a short space. Much of it involves the concept of "rigid embodiment," borrowed and adapted from the work of the British philosopher Kit Fine. Rigid embodiment is, roughly, both a set of relations that renders a thing what it is, and the concept that designates that thing by way of those relations. For Hartz, the relations specified by rigid embodiment are what aggregate separate monads into an object that is perceived as extended. They also allow us to form an accurate (and therefore falsifiable) perception of objects, and thus provide a "sturdy epistemic bridge" between observer and a real external world.[12]

Hartz characterizes Leibniz's realist account as "nothing short of breathtaking" and a "grand philosophical feast" that puts paid to the problems usually associated with it. Then why did Leibniz not adopt it consistently? In Hartz's view, he "did not want to face the full fury of objections lying in wait for anyone who would declare a meaningful relation between knower and reality," and therefore repeatedly tacked back to the idealist account when on the verge of endorsing the realist one. In any case, states Hartz, there is an irreducible "mystery" at the heart of the relation between knower and known,[13] and how this mystery can coexist with a "sturdy epistemic bridge" is an interesting question. Other problems arise. One of the advantages of the realist account as reconstructed in his book, Hartz claims, is that it moots the problem posed by the absence of any known "principle of aggregation" that would organize monads into an aggregated object. The work of this principle, in Hartz's account, is accomplished instead by the concept of rigid embodiment. Yet "the establishing of such relations between substances [by rigid embodiment] is something I never have access to."[14] One wonders whether the explanatory gaps in Leibniz's account have been filled in or merely relocated to a philosophically tonier neighborhood.

Regardless, Hartz views the realist account as successful on its own terms, as is the idealist account on its own terms. The two accounts are incompatible, but each illuminates different aspects of the aggregation problem and thus the underlying truth of the world. Hence the only way to reconcile conflicting textual evidence on the question is to assume a "theory-pluralism" on the part of Leibniz. Idealist and realist accounts offer different "perspectives" on a single truth that cannot be fully expressed by either. (Hartz's general approach is clearly compatible in at least some respects with the perspectivalist approach for which I have been advocating in this book.)[15] It is worth noting, however, that this solution seems to reproduce the formal structure of the Leibnizian aggregated body within the realm of theory. That is, in place of multiple monads that do not interact but somehow combine themselves into an object that undergirds phenomenal perception without being directly accessible to it, we now have multiple theories that do not interact but serve as our ways of perceiving an underlying truth that is likewise inaccessible directly. Is this a solution to the problem or an instance of the problem spreading metastatically to the structure of explanation that tries to master it?

In his poem "Mending Wall," Robert Frost writes:

> I let my neighbor know beyond the hill;
> And on a day we meet to walk the line
> And set the wall between us once again.
> We keep the wall between us as we go.
> To each the boulders that have fallen to each.
> And some are loaves and some so nearly balls
> We have to use a spell to make them balance:
> "Stay where you are until our backs are turned!"

Leibniz loves to describe the aggregated body as if it were a pile of stones. Conversely, the speaker of Frost's poem and his neighbor find themselves confronting a kind of Leibnizian object in their wall, which the winter frosts destroy annually by making the ground swell and tumbling the stones. No matter how often the wall is reconstructed, it keeps falling apart because it is a mere aggregate. (Note that Frost's strong predilection for monosyllables in this poem—e.g., "Where they have left not one stone on a stone"—makes the individual lines and the lyric construct as a whole into a collection of rounded verbal objects that must be carefully balanced.) The two laborers fit stone upon stone as carefully as they can, but then in the end a magical supplement is needed to make the whole cohere.[16] Their "spell" is something between a performative and a prayer, and it is the only mortar they have. Aggregative bodies in Leibniz require something akin to Frost's spell: a magical supplement that isn't magical at all and doesn't really do anything more than express a wish.

In the case of animal bodies, the role of the magical supplement is played by the dominant monad, which supposedly confers unity on the body's constituents. Yet as we have seen, the nature of monadic dominance remains murky, and the very concept appears to clash with other elements in Leibniz's thought. Lacking any consistent or convincing rationale, the "dominant monad" represents little more than a bare assertion in the face of a daunting conceptual problem. Moreover, in his correspondence with the Jesuit theologian Bartholomew Des Bosses, where Leibniz tries to imagine ways in which his theory of monads might make sense of the Catholic doctrine of transubstantiation, the realist account of aggregated bodies comes under considerable pressure, to the degree that the concept of the dominant monad no longer suffices. To explain the "real unity" among the monadic components of a body, Leibniz thus has recourse to a new and unprecedented concept, the "substantial bond" (*vinculum substantiale*), to do what the concept of the dominant monad apparently no longer can. Setting aside the metaphysical niceties of the exchange with Des Bosses (which are fascinating),[17] what interests me is that Leibniz finds himself driven to posit a supplement to the supplement. His earlier "spell"—the invocation of the dominant monad—having lost its potency, he needs additional resources to cement the body together and make a unity out of it.

Leibniz's disintegrative vision finds answering intuitions in the world of painting and visual art. From his own era, the most obvious instance would be the famous composite portraits by Giuseppe Arcimboldo, who depicts human heads and faces formed from juxtaposed images of vegetables, flowers, even fish. In strikingly Leibnizian fashion, these heads are fashioned not from parts but from autonomous, organic wholes (vegetable or animal beings) that are only half-heartedly playing the roles of parts. Some of the intense visual energy of Arcimboldo's compositions derives from the fact that while their constituent entities are in physical contact, nothing apparently glues them together or holds them in place. Their visual heterogeneity is therefore reinforced by a corresponding precariousness of juxtaposition. Lacking a dominant monad that would assign them organic functionality in a human body (the composites testify rather to the *absence* of an accompanying subjectivity or mind in the "heads" they form), they are organized and held together solely by the compositional logic of the portrait itself. In the empty place of a dominant monad, the void of a *trompe l'oeil*.

The work of the contemporary neo-baroque artist Raúl de Nieves, as well as Vik Muniz's "Pictures of Junk," extend this aesthetic into the twenty-first century. In such works, the coherence of representation is constantly collapsing into aggregates of the heterogeneous. Leibniz, of course, endorses a baroque harmony in which a maximum of variety is corralled into unity. But aggregation opens up the prospect of pure, disordered multiplicity—something with which he is less comfortable. That he sees it everywhere and can't formulate a fully convincing remedy is one of the veins of darkness in his work. It is also a prime motive behind his often demoting material bodies to the merely phenomenal.

Of course, material bodies do not spontaneously shatter into an infinity of parts, either in real life or in Leibniz's thought. They generally possess stability and internal coherence. In a sense, aggregation pertains only to the Cartesian dimensions of bodies—their status as extended things positioned in space and time. These are, for Leibniz, relative and therefore phenomenal. Bodies considered in what Leibniz regards as their real aspect, as constellations of active and passive forces, don't appear to raise the specter of aggregation in as dire a fashion. Indeed, force is what holds otherwise aggregated bodies together. Specifically, the passive derivative forces of antitypy, or resistance to penetration, and inertia, or resistance to movement, grant objects relatively firm boundaries and positions. But in making objects solid, these forces also make them inert, mute, and uncommunicative. They are what enable objects to be stacked or piled into a heap—Leibniz's prime image of the aggregate.

We can understand the pile better by opposing it to the fold. The fold allows for variation and thus novelty across scales (folds within folds) but is essentially continuous, and therefore ordered. Combining variation with structure, the fold embodies harmony. The pile, by contrast, substitutes mere contiguity for continuity. Objects in a pile touch at isolated points but are not otherwise connected, and the pile is thus discontinuous and chaotic. It is also relatively homogeneous in that stones or logs or bricks in a pile don't differ interestingly from one another. If harmony is variety reabsorbed into unity, the pile is monotony in a state of disorder: an unbeautiful and unrelieved spatial dissonance. The problem, in a way, is that the objects in a pile are *too* solid. They would have to compromise their antitypy, to begin to liquify and become more permeable, before they could form a continuous order of folds. While the monad makes perceptual contact with the most distant objects in the universe, the objects in a pile ignore one other even though they are right on top of one other.

And as with material objects, so in a sense with intellectual ones. The rhetorical counterpart to contiguity is metonymy, a figure at variance with Leibniz's philosophical practice, which relies instead on metaphor and related figures of similitude. As I have been arguing, Leibniz engages in a continual practice of metaphorical mapping (or conceptual blending) of sometimes distant and heterogeneous discursive areas, and this fuels the generative power of his thought. Moreover, metaphysics by its very nature strives to provide a synthesizing conceptual framework for the totality of human knowledge. The image of the pile or aggregate is thus also an image for knowledge as divided into separate and potentially noncommunicating areas of specialization—something Leibniz is determined to oppose. Leibniz's intellectual dictum: turn every pile into a fold, liquify every solid to the degree that it can bend and thus come into meaningful contact with what is distant—mapping onto or even blending together with other conceptual areas. Sometimes this process is distinct and logically articulated; sometimes it is confused, suggestive, and "writerly." Things are prone to fall apart, and so they must be continually folded together.

CHAPTER 21

The Monad as Event

Alfred North Whitehead

Here we begin a set of modules devoted to figures who carry Leibnizian transdisciplinary thought forward into the twentieth century and beyond—sometimes through direct influence, and sometimes through the spontaneous reappearance of Leibnizian themes and styles of argument. Some of these thinkers release and develop potentials that are merely embryonic or otherwise constrained in Leibniz. All straddle separate disciplines. All leap the barrier separating the sciences from the humanities, and in so doing engage in forms of mapping that display a Leibnizian flavor. All are immensely ambitious and brilliant (if sometimes flawed) thinkers. All enjoy cult followings but have seen their influence limited in part by the fact that they don't fit neatly into established disciplinary boundaries.

Of the four thinkers treated here, the philosopher Alfred North Whitehead is the most difficult to fit into a short module of this kind. His metaphysics is so ambitious in its reach, so complex and so subtle in its workings that it doesn't lend itself to economical summary. And his relationship to Leibniz is by no means simple, either. I shall attempt to sketch in at least some major Whiteheadian themes largely by way of comparison with Leibniz, recognizing at the same time that this way of proceeding will inevitably produce a Leibniz-tinted Whitehead. (But then again, I think he really *is* Leibniz-tinted.) More specifically, I shall compare Whitehead with the version of Leibniz I have been developing in this book.

Before delving into specifics, it is worth noting some general parallels between Whitehead and Leibniz as philosophers. Both are accomplished in mathematics and logic; both incorporate these fields into their metaphysics, along with physics and biology. Both are philosophical cosmologists who attempt to explain the workings of (among other things) the natural world, and who explore the forms of coherence that bind individual entities into a universe. Both balance an interest in matters scientific and mathematical with attention to matters aesthetic. Indeed, both install aesthetic concerns at the very heart of existence. Both assign a place to God in their metaphysics and yet largely insulate him from the world and the world from him. Both make extensive use of analogical mapping as a means of philosophical invention. And both harbor anti-systematic impulses that compete with their systematic ones. In addition to sharing a number of themes and concerns, they also share important elements of philosophical style.

By Whitehead's own account, his knowledge of Leibniz came largely from secondary sources: Bertrand Russell's *A Critical Exposition of the Philosophy of Leibniz* (1900) and Louis Couturat's *La Logique de Leibniz* (1903).[1] The Leibnizian philosophers James Ward (1843–1925) and Rudolf Hermann Lotze (1817–1881) also appear to have influenced his thinking.[2] In *Science and the Modern World*, Whitehead acknowledges that "the basing of philosophy upon organism [i.e., the basis on which Whitehead himself places it] can be traced back to Leibniz."[3] Indeed, Whitehead explicitly describes his own metaphysics as a "theory of monads."[4] Contemporary process philosophers likewise designate Leibniz as an important forebear for Whitehead and process philosophy more generally.[5] At the same time, Leibniz plays an unexpectedly minor role in *Process and Reality*, Whitehead's metaphysical magnum opus, which engages widely with pre-Kantian philosophy but pays little explicit attention to Leibniz compared to figures such as Descartes, Locke, and Hume. Indeed, Whitehead declares in *Process and Reality* that it is Locke, not Leibniz, "who most fully anticipated the main positions of the philosophy of organism."[6] He then announces, just a few pages later, that "The philosophy of organism is closely allied to Spinoza's scheme of thought."[7] But Leibniz drops out as an avowedly primary inspiration. And when he is mentioned there, it is more often than not as exemplifying the dangers posed by a metaphysics of substance rather than one of event. I would argue, however, that Leibniz's informing presence in *Process and Reality* is out of all proportion to his infrequent invocations (the same, I think, is true for Spinoza). Whiteheadian metaphysics can be seen (and has been seen by Deleuze) as a freeing of the evental or processual elements in Leibnizian thought from their confinement in the framework of a substance philosophy.

In what sense is Whitehead's metaphysics a "theory of monads"? For Whitehead, the bedrock components of the universe are what he calls "actual occasions" or "actual entities": " 'Actual entities'—also termed 'actual occasions'—are the final real things of which the world is made up. There is no going behind actual entities to find anything more real."[8] Indeed, actual entities are not merely the most ontologically basic things that exist—they are the only things that exist.[9] But while actual occasions/entities are foundational, they are not things but rather events or processes. An actual entity is the event or process of its own self-constitution from data supplied by other, already-existing entities.

Whitehead describes actual entities as "drops of experience."[10] Elsewhere he employs the term "subject-superject" as a synonym for "actual entity," thus making clear that such entities include a subjective pole. In short, Whitehead is a panpsychist, though his commentators often prefer to describe him as a panexperientialist because the experiences of an actual entity are not "had" by a preexisting subject but rather aim to constitute that subject as a kind of final term via a process Whitehead calls concrescence. Thus we can already see why the Leibnizian monad, as a perceptual process unfolding over time, might offer a template for Whitehead's actual entities. And yet, the differences between the two are as fundamental as the similarities:

> This is a theory of monads; but it differs from Leibniz's in that his monads
> change. In the organic theory, they merely *become*. Each monadic creature is a
> mode of the process of "feeling" the world, of housing the world in one unit of
> complex feeling, in every way determinate. Such a unit is an "actual occasion";
> it is the ultimate creature derivative from the creative process.[11]

Leibnizian monads change, but their existence precedes those changes, which are preprogrammed into them from the start. Whiteheadian actual occasions are, by contrast, a process of becoming that is conditioned by the data they take in but which is by no means predetermined in its course. And where Leibniz speaks of monadic *perceptions*, Whitehead speaks of *feelings* as a way of taking in the external world. The actual entity's relation to the world is therefore primordially affective or emotional rather than perceptual and cognitive. The latter aspects emerge from the former.

But the biggest difference between a Leibnizian monad and a Whiteheadian actual entity is that the former is closed and self-sufficient while the latter is fundamentally open. Whitehead supplies windows for his monads. Indeed, the actual occasion constructs itself by taking or borrowing—as Whitehead puts it, "prehending"—elements from other entities. Some of these prehensions are physical, as when a plant absorbs nutrients from the soil, or an atom takes on an additional electron to become a negative ion, or a philosopher eats a cupcake. Sometimes they are conceptual, as when an actual entity prehends "eternal objects" (something like Platonic forms or universals) from other actual entities, as well as the patternings by which they are harmonized and integrated within them.[12] As Whitehead states, "no individual subject can have an independent reality, since it is a prehension of limited aspects of subjects other than itself."[13] The concrescent entity must decide what to prehend from other objects and what to exclude, and then how to evaluate those prehended elements and integrate them in such a way that they produce a maximum of intense yet harmonious feelings through their patterned contrasts. This process is spontaneous and creative. If the Leibnizian monad is like the performance of a musical score (prewritten by God), the Whiteheadian actual entity is more like the invention or composition of such a score. Or perhaps like an improvisational jazz solo where composition and performance are one.[14]

The process of concrescence aims at producing a subject, and when it does so in a moment of final "satisfaction," the aimed-at subject dies into a "superject" or objective datum for other actual entities to prehend in turn. (It is noteworthy that Whitehead borrows Leibniz's term "appetition" to designate the force that drives concrescence forward.)[15] This language of feeling, prehending, evaluating, and deciding, and of experiencing intensities and satisfactions, appears to assign complex and variegated mental functions to entities that are in many cases nonliving. While Whitehead's use of such terms is not merely metaphorical (he claims), it should be kept in mind that most of these activities are not themselves conscious and do not produce conscious experience. It would admittedly be difficult to say what an atom's "feelings" are when it "decides" to prehend an additional electron. But Whiteheadians deny that this affective vocabulary is simply a matter of anthropomorphic projection and rather regard the human affects as unusually heightened, complex, and conscious versions of more widespread processes.[16]

While Leibnizian and Whiteheadian "monads" differ sharply in their inner constitutions, they give rise to worlds that exhibit some striking similarities. One is that actual entities do not solely prehend other entities that happen to be in their vicinity; they prehend every other entity there is, and so the universe constitutes a totality. "Every item in the universe, including all other actual entities, is a constituent in the constitution of any one actual entity."[17] Even negative pre-hensions, through which an entity decides *not* to incorporate certain aspects of other entities, leave their mark as negations. It is perhaps not surprising that philosophers as ambitiously syncretic as Leibniz and Whitehead should pro-duce visions of a universe that mirror their own intellectual habits of connecting everything to everything else. In the case of Whitehead, the number of actual entities in the universe is apparently finite, though very large, and in that sense he differs from Leibniz. But the fact of universal connection remains. Leibnizian monads are in one sense nothing *but* their perceptions of all the other monads, hence of their interrelatedness to them.

The relations among Whiteheadian actual entities can cause a given entity to become incorporated into larger, more encompassing units:

> An individual entity, whose own life-history is a part within the life-history
> of some larger, deeper, more complete pattern, is liable to have aspects of that
> larger pattern dominating its own being, and to experience modifications of
> that larger pattern reflected in itself as modifications of its own being. This
> is the theory of organic mechanism.[18]

This vision of entities nested within larger ones that "dominate" them directly recalls Leibniz's concept of dominant and dominated monads, only in White-head's case the process of domination is a good deal less equivocal and more directly causal than it is in Leibniz. This process is exemplified in animal bodies:

> The concrete enduring entities are organisms, so that the plan of the *whole*
> influences the very characters of the various subordinate organisms which
> enter into it. In the case of an animal, the mental states enter into the plan
> of the total organism and thus modify the plans of the successive subordi-
> nate organisms until the ultimate smallest organisms, such as electrons, are
> reached. Thus an electron within a living body is different from an electron
> outside it, by reason of the plan of the body.[19]

Again, the image of organic entities nested within others, each level dominat-ing the lower ones, is directly Leibnizian. One point of philosophical interest in this position is that it resists reductionism—the notion that lower levels deter-mine higher ones (so that, for instance, physics would explain chemistry, and chemistry biology, etc.). The only difference between Whitehead and Leibniz is that the process of nesting appears to reach a final term in Whitehead's case and does not go on indefinitely as it does in Leibniz. Whitehead's actual entities act like, and organize themselves in a manner similar to, Leibnizian monads, though they are differently constituted.

Whitehead's world, like Leibniz's, is a perspectival one. Each actual entity has its own, unique point of view on the others, and this point of view is constitutive of its nature, i.e., of the course of its concrescence:

> The things which are grasped into a realised unity, here and now, are not the castle, the cloud, and the planet simply in themselves; but are the castle, the cloud, and the planet from the standpoint, in space and time, of the prehensive unification. In other words, it is the perspective of the castle over there from the standpoint of the unification here. It is, therefore, aspects of the castle, the cloud, and the planet which are grasped into unity here. You will remember that the idea of perspectives is quite familiar in philosophy. It was introduced by Leibniz, in the notion of his monads mirroring perspectives of the universe. I am using the same notion, only I am toning down his monads into the unified events in space and time.[20]

His interest in perspective even leads Whitehead to incorporate projective geometry into his treatment of the extensive continuum, again in imitation of Leibniz.[21] But (once again as in Leibniz) spatiotemporal position is really just a metaphor for something else. In Leibniz, spatial perspective expresses the integrated array of distinct and confused areas within perception, and hence the balance of active and passive forces within a given monad. In Whitehead, perspective is the evaluative process by which elements of the datum are deemed more or less relevant for inclusion in an entity's concrescence. Of course, since entities start from nothing, they have no initial perspective at all; that is supplied by God, with an eye toward novelty and intensity, though an entity's initial perspective does not completely determine the course its concrescence will take.[22] It is more of an initial shove that may ultimately proceed in any number of directions given the contours of the terrain. In any case, spatiotemporal position cannot constitute perspective because Whitehead shares Leibniz's view that space and time are not givens but rather express intermonadic relations that are not themselves intrinsically spatial or temporal: "space and time are simply abstractions from the totality of prehensive unifications as mutually patterned in each other."[23] Space and time are the products of perspective, not the containers within which point of view is defined.

But the perspectival nature of the actual entity complicates the notion that such entities are fully open to the world. Indeed, it complicates any notion of "the" world since every actual entity produces its own version, which it shares fully with no other: "Each actual occasion defines its own actual world from which it originates. No two occasions can have identical actual worlds."[24] Not only do actual entities not share a common world; they do not share their subjectivities. As Whitehead insists, the subjectivizing process of an actual entity is private; only the superject, or the objectified precipitate of the subjectifying process, is public. What actual entities "prehend" are the superjects of other entities, not their subjective poles, and they prehend them in such a way as to produce a unique world shared with no other.[25] Whitehead fits the Leibnizian monad out with something that is not so much a window, then, as a one-way mirror. The subject can look out—indeed, reach out and grab things—but no one can look in. And none of the windows points in quite the same direction as the others, so that the view is different from each one. This maximizes variety, along Leibnizian lines; but it also makes it clearer why Whitehead describes his actual entities as monads. Actual entities are in some respects connected with one another and in other respects closed off.

All that being said, it is not as if subject and superject are unrelated. The pathway of a subject's concrescence involves concern for "the objectification of the subject beyond itself."[26] The process of subjectification exhibits an altruistic element that aims at supplying the world with novel data. Hence, as Judith Jones puts it, "feelings are directed *at a superject and not from a subject*" (emphasis in original).[27] Because the superject is a final cause for the subject ("for the datum is felt with that subjective form in order that the subject may be the superject that it is"),[28] something the subject forms itself in order to be, I would argue that it is also a Leibnizian *expression* of that subject. Each superject crystallizes the feelings, choices, contrasts, syntheses, and intensifications carried out by its subject and thereby expresses it. To take up an earlier metaphor, we cannot know the private feelings of a composer, but we can know the piano sonata that is their superject and that therefore bears an expressive relation to them. As objectified data, superjects allow a mediated, expressive view of the subjects that produced them, guiding the latter through what I have earlier called an "aesthetic detour."

We have been drifting from ontology to perception, and this is another area in which Leibniz and Whitehead exhibit suggestive parallels. In this book, I have been arguing for the minority position that Leibniz unsettles the Cartesian hierarchy of the confused and the distinct. For Leibniz, confused perceptions are central to aesthetic experience, ethics, and various kinds of practical knowledge. But even the philosopher, whose task is to form ideas that are as clear and distinct as possible, finds that confused thought and perceptions (which cannot be entirely scrubbed from distinct ones in any case) "always involve the infinite, and not only what happens in our body but also, by means of it, what happens elsewhere."[29] The confused thereby has a fertilizing effect on philosophical thought. Whitehead does not harbor a concept directly comparable to Leibnizian microperceptions, but he does offer several interrelated ways of thinking the confused and the distinct: causal efficacy versus presentational immediacy, physical versus conceptual feelings, and the vague versus the narrow. Here I shall focus on the first of these and argue that causal efficacy plays a role in Whiteheadian metaphysics comparable to what confused perceptions play in Leibniz.

Since for Whitehead, every actual entity is a part of every other, it necessarily follows that some entities will play larger roles and some smaller in the concrescence of a given entity, and the vast majority will be relegated to a kind of dim background. The name Whitehead gives to this dim background is "causal efficacy." Causal efficacy arises from the early stages of concrescence in which physical feelings mark direct causal connections between entities. By contrast, objects or situations that are brought into clear focus display what he calls "presentational immediacy." Here the term "immediacy" appears to be somewhat ironic, since presentational immediacy is in fact mediated; abstracted from the background of causal efficacy, it turns what was "vague, ill defined, and hardly relevant" in the latter into something that is "distinct, well defined, and importantly relevant."[30] But while presentational immediacy is vivid and clear, it is also "barren" since it is restricted to the temporal present and tends to conceal the connectedness of things, while causal efficacy provides connections between present and past.[31]

Whitehead attempts to convey the experience of causal efficacy in an evocative passage:

An inhibition of familiar sensa is very apt to leave us a prey to vague terrors respecting a circumambient world of causal operations. In the dark there are vague presences, doubtfully feared; in the silence, the irresistible causal efficacy of nature presses itself upon us; in the vagueness of the low hum of insects in an August woodland, the inflow into ourselves of feelings from enveloping nature overwhelms us; in the dim consciousness of half-sleep, the presentations of sense fade away, and we are left with the vague feeling of influences from vague things around us.[32]

The gothic, swampy, almost Lovecraftian tone of this passage will merit comment later on. Here we might note the threefold repetition of "vague," along with "doubtful" and "dim." Vagueness, is, in effect, the effect of multiplicity: not one or two objects but innumerable ones are at work, and this myriad paradoxically creates the impression that the resulting mood, or *Stimmung*, has no concrete, locatable source at all.[33] Causal efficacy conveys the influx of an entire landscape or environment into the self.[34] The terror that Whitehead invokes results not from the presence of a terrifying object but from the absence of any tangible object, and from the threat of dissolving back into an ambient, ill-defined multiplicity. Presentational immediacy, by contrast, preserves the classical subject-object dichotomy: a detached, well-defined observer contemplates a well-defined object. Causal efficacy breaches this relationship on both sides: it infiltrates the detached consciousness of the observer with feelings hovering dimly on the margins of the unconscious, while it replaces the well-defined object with a generalized, vague landscape.

Causal efficacy involves mechanisms that differ radically from those of confused perceptions in Leibniz (who would recoil in some respects from the very phrase "causal efficacy"). But their effects are strikingly similar. In Leibniz, confused perceptions occupy the realm of the *je ne sais quoi*, and thereby a liminal space between the conscious and the unconscious. At the same time, they "involve the infinite; that connection that each being has with all the rest of the universe."[35] Both confused perceptions and causal efficacy enable the subject to grasp the universe as totality. Or rather, it enables the universe as totality to grasp the subject, which is passively influenced by forces it cannot fully grasp or control.

It would not be difficult to list additional numerous, intriguing areas of convergence between Whitehead's and Leibniz's thinking. Chief among these would be the central role played by aesthetic experience in the writings of each philosopher, as well as their respective ways of construing that experience.[36] Another would be the role played by God in their metaphysical systems. But the very brief and partial account I have given thus far of some elements of Whitehead's metaphysical system will suffice to get to my main focus, which is his manner of practicing philosophy, as well as his understanding of the role that metaphysics can play in the twentieth century. It is primarily here, rather than in specific conceptual parallels, that Whitehead demonstrates a way of transmitting and updating a Leibnizian legacy.

Whitehead's interest in pre-Kantian philosophy goes beyond issues of philo-sophical theme and method; the very enterprise of cosmology, which attempts to provide metaphysical underpinnings for everything, including the natural world, is very much a throwback to the seventeenth century. The advances made by the natural sciences since that time had been enabled precisely by the Newto-nian insistence that engaging in metaphysics was not only unnecessary but also positively harmful to scientific progress. Partly in response, metaphysics tended to detach itself in turn from the natural sciences. Whitehead's contemporary Heidegger understood the project of metaphysics in a way antithetical to his, and he viewed the kinds of thinking associated with the natural sciences as the metaphysical enemy. Whitehead, by contrast, imported a very Leibnizian mix of physics, biology, psychology, and mathematics into his philosophy. Despite this, Whitehead also saw some fundamental incompatibilities between scientific and metaphysical ways of thinking, and these help to ground a justification of meta-physics in an age when it might otherwise be seen as superfluous, since science had proven its capacity to progress without philosophical help. For Leibniz, the importance of metaphysics was so self-evident as almost to go without saying; for Whitehead, this is no longer the case, and his response to this situation may also help chart a path for the future of Leibniz's thought.

Whitehead views the vocation of metaphysics as having to do with totality, and that in several senses. One is a totality of knowledge: "It must be one of the motives of a complete cosmology to construct a system of ideas which brings the aesthetic, moral, and religious interests into relation with those concepts of the world which have their origin in natural science."[37] Here Whitehead speaks of "interests" rather than "knowledge," but it is also certainly the case that meta-physics aspires to provide a general framework that will allow for the synthesis of different areas of knowledge as well. Science, by contrast, is hampered by special-ization: as scientific subfields proliferate and develop, they achieve ever-greater things in their delimited areas but increasingly lose the capacity to communicate with one another. The results, in Whitehead's view, are deleterious not just for the sciences but for society and culture as a whole:

> The dangers arising from this aspect of professionalism are great, particularly in our democratic societies. The directive force of reason is weakened. The leading intellects lack balance. They see this set of circumstances, or that set; but not both sets together. The task of coördination is left to those who lack either the force or the character to succeed in some definite career. In short, the specialized functions of the community are performed better and more progressively, but the generalized direction lacks vision. The progressiveness in detail only adds to the danger produced by the feebleness of coördination.[38]

This tendency toward professional specialization has, conversely, "pushed philosophy out of the effective currents of modern life. It has lost its proper rôle as a constant critic of partial formulations. It has retreated into the subjectivist sphere of mind, by reason of its expulsion by science from the objectivist sphere of matter."[39] Science certainly contributes to this problem, but science itself is also just one instance of a more generalized tendency toward professional specialization. (Apparently the crisis of "hyperprofessionalism" is not entirely new.) The role of cosmology then, is to stitch together the fragmented forms of knowledge that modern society produces, and thereby reassert the essential synthesizing function of philosophy.

How to do this? How can cosmology create a synthetic worldview from specialized areas of knowledge? One way involves analogy, or what I have elsewhere identified in Leibniz as metaphorical mapping and conceptual blending. Whereas science proceeds by way of "the strict systematization of detailed discrimination, already effected by antecedent observation," in other words by a Baconian method of induction,

> what Bacon omitted was the play of a free imagination, controlled by the requirements of coherence and logic. The true method of discovery is like the flight of an aeroplane. It starts from the ground of particular observation; it makes a flight in the thin air of imaginative generalization; and it again lands for renewed observation rendered acute by rational interpretation. . . . But the conditions for the success of imaginative construction must be rigidly adhered to. In the first place, this construction must have its origin in the

generalization of particular factors discerned in particular topics of human interest; for example, in physics, or in physiology, or in psychology, or in aesthetics, or in ethical beliefs, or in sociology, or in languages conceived as storehouses of human experience. In this way the prime requisite, that anyhow there shall be some important application, is secured. The success of the imaginative experiment is always to be tested by the applicability of its results beyond the restricted locus from which it originated. In default of such extended application, a generalization started from physics, for example, remains merely an alternative expression of notions applicable to physics. The partially successful philosophic generalization will, if derived from physics, find applications in fields of experience beyond physics. It will enlighten observation in those remote fields, so that general principles can be discerned as in process of illustration, which in the absence of the imaginative generalization are obscured by their persistent exemplification.[40]

What unifies and thereby vivifies otherwise isolated and reified kinds of partial knowledge is imaginative forms of analogical mapping. Physics must be applied to areas beyond physics; a theory of organism must be generalized so that it pertains to entities not regarded as organic; experiential qualities such as feeling, valuation, decision, and intensity are extended to beings not ordinarily felt to have experiences. Whitehead does not abandon scientific rationality *for* imaginative construction but rather attempts to reestablish a balance and interplay between them. In so doing he recaptures a form of Leibnizian "chemical wit"—the ability to grasp unexpected connections across apparently distant realms of experience. Such a procedure aims at producing not only new forms of knowledge but novel kinds of aesthetic intensity. As Steven Shaviro puts it:

> Whitehead presents us with a highly systematized philosophy, and he seeks after "the most general systematization of civilized thought" (1929/1978, 17). But he also insists that, before any work of systematization can even begin, the "primary stage" of philosophy is a process of "*assemblage*" (1938/1968, 2). Philosophical speculation collects the most heterogeneous materials and puts them together in the most unexpected configurations. It is something like the practice of collage in modernist painting or better—to use an analogy not from Whitehead's time, but from our own—it is like a DJ's practice of sampling and remixing.[41]

Like Leibniz, Whitehead exploits the productive tensions that can arise from the interplay between systematizing and anti-systemic impulses. I'm skeptical, however, of his claim that the two can be neatly divided into temporal "stages."

The problem with science, in Whitehead's view, is abstraction. Abstraction is both necessary to the conduct of science and a kind of fatal or at least potentially fatal weakness lodged within it. We have already looked at one form of abstraction, which involves separating knowledge of the natural world and its laws from other kinds of knowledge, and even separating different areas of study within the natural world from one another, as science develops. But there is also another, complementary form of abstraction at work in the way that science selects its data. The empirical facts on which scientific argument relies must be clear, well-defined, and measurable. They must, in other words, consist of perceptions in the mode of presentational immediacy. But as Whitehead argues, presentational immediacy is an abstraction from a broader, deeper, and more ill-defined background of causal efficacy. Hence, in relying on the kind of data it does, science necessarily produces an abstracted, simplified understanding of the entities it studies.

"It is here," writes Whitehead, "that philosophy finds its niche as essential to the healthy progress of society. It is the critic of abstractions. A civilisation which cannot burst through its abstractions is doomed to sterility after a very limited period of progress."[42] The specific role of philosophy with respect to science is to "present an elucidation of concrete fact from which the sciences abstract."[43] Scientific thought is both enriching in some respects and impoverishing in others. Philosophy attempts to rescue the concreteness of things from the abstraction that renders them available to scientific treatment. Of course, Whitehead's philosophy is itself infamously, often frustratingly, abstract—an abstract theory of the concrete (the paradox is merely a superficial one). At the same time, "every philosophy is tinged with the colouring of some secret imaginative background, which never emerges explicitly into its trains of reasoning."[44] Like perception itself, which includes areas of brightly defined presentational immediacy emerging from a dim background of causal efficacy, philosophy itself has a conceptually vivid foreground of logical, systematic argumentation but is also powered by more elusive imaginative forces that grant each particular philosophical approach its own distinctive flavor.

Indeed, for Whitehead, the synthesizing work of philosophy does not mediate solely between different kinds of knowledge, as I suggested somewhat misleadingly above. In the passage where Whitehead states that cosmology "brings the aesthetic, moral, and religious interests into relation with those concepts of the world which have their origin in natural science," I converted "interests" into "knowledge," but that is not quite right. Because philosophy as Whitehead conceives it does not limit itself to the problem of knowledge but addresses itself more broadly to the full range of human (and even inhuman) experience, of which knowledge is just one kind:

> Speculative Philosophy is the endeavour to frame a coherent, logical, necessary system of general ideas in terms of which every element of our existence can be interpreted. By this notion of "interpretation" I mean that everything of which we are conscious, as enjoyed, perceived, willed, or thought, shall have the character of a particular instance of the general scheme.[45]

Elsewhere, Whitehead identifies the ideal of philosophy as "the attainment of some unifying concept which will set in assigned relationships within itself all that there is for knowledge, for feeling, and for emotion."[46] The aesthetic, the moral, and the religious are not merely different domains of knowledge but different domains of experience, each with its characteristic ratios of thought and feeling, presentational immediacy and causal efficacy, distinctness and vagueness. Articulating conceptual thought together with feeling is made easier for Whitehead by the fact that he regards thought as a particular variety of feeling, the latter being the more foundational category. (Just as Leibniz, in a not unrelated fashion, includes conceptual thought under the broader aegis of perception.)

The work of philosophy is, as even the above quotations make clear, primarily conceptual, even if it is handling kinds of experience that are themselves not necessarily or completely conceptual. But as we have seen, philosophy for Whitehead also engages in imaginative, analogical mapping. And this practice rebounds on the philosopher's handling of language: "Words and phrases must be stretched towards a generality foreign to their ordinary usage; and however such elements of language be stabilized as technicalities, they remain metaphors mutely appealing for an imaginative leap."[47] Moreover, even philosophical language that is rendered logically precise still comes accompanied with subliminal associations that cannot be pared away: "a sentence conveys one proposition, while in its phraseology it suggests a penumbra of other propositions charged with emotional value."[48] Given all this, it should not be surprising when Whitehead declares that

"philosophy is akin to poetry."[49] What he means by this will require some explication, however.

I am trying to work toward a description of Whitehead's philosophical style,
but I should admit that I have some trouble coming up with a satisfying or coherent characterization of it. Readers of Whitehead will recognize a distinctive philosophical texture that isn't found elsewhere and isn't always felt to be appealing.
He can be notoriously abstract and also notoriously unclear, though sufficient
time spent marinating in his works will dispel some (not all) of the unclarity.
He is often dry and technical but can also turn "rhapsodic" (as one reader puts
it).[50] Abstract arguments veer suddenly into vivid images or striking epigrams
(e.g., "intensity is the reward of narrowness").[51] Or the prose will become moody
and affect-laden, as in the Lovecraftian passage quoted above. Not many philosophers (and certainly none who are looked upon favorably by their analytic
colleagues) will dare to produce passages such as this:

> It is by reason of the body, with its miracle of order, that the treasures of
> the past environment are poured into the living occasion. The final percip-
> ient route of occasions is perhaps some thread of happenings wandering in
> "empty" space amid the interstices of the brain. It toils not, neither does it
> spin. It receives the past; it lives in the present. It is shaken by its intensities of
> private feeling, adversion or aversion. In its turn, this culmination of bodily
> life transmits itself as an element of novelty throughout the avenues of the
> body. Its sole use to the body is its vivid originality; it is the organ of novelty.[52]

The important thing when reading prose of this kind is to keep in mind that
it was composed by the coauthor of the *Principia Mathematica* and, in its way,
aspires to comparable precision even while bringing a greater variety of writerly
resources to bear.

When Whitehead says that "philosophy is akin to poetry," it is all too easy to
give a deconstructive spin to this pronouncement; i.e., what appear to be conceptual and logical arguments are really just rhetorical or literary performances.
To some degree, I have myself been pursuing a similar line of argument in order
to dislodge the method of reading Leibniz dominant among Anglophone philosophers. We can begin to decode what Whitehead means by his statement, however, by noting that he is in the habit of quoting English-speaking poets in his
work: from Shakespeare, Milton, and Pope, to Wordsworth, Shelley, and Keats,

to Whitman, Tennyson, Arnold, and Clough (he stops short just before the modernist poets of his own day). When he does so, however, it is mainly to attend to their arguments or doctrine, not directly to their rhetorical or literary dimensions or even their aesthetic properties. If philosophy is akin to poetry, this is partly because, for Whitehead, poetry is akin to philosophy in that it can make cogent and succinct conceptual arguments. Poets are therefore worthy philosophical interlocutors. Whitehead can cite them as he cites Hume or Kant. In *Science and the Modern World*, a chapter titled "The Romantic Reaction" contains numerous passages of Romantic poetry, about some of which Whitehead notes: "Both Shelley and Wordsworth emphatically bear witness that nature cannot be divorced from its aesthetic values; and that these values arise from the cumulation, in some sense, of the brooding presence of the whole on to its various parts."[53] Not surprisingly, Whitehead seeks out the Romantic poets to find confirmation of elements of his own philosophy. Here, they anticipate his concept of causal efficacy. But surely, he quotes Wordsworth and Shelley not solely because they invoke or refer to the "brooding presence of the whole" but because they make it powerfully, aesthetically felt as well. The value of poetry is that it makes argumentative foreground and vague background present simultaneously in one unified aesthetic experience. It thus reminds us—by making us feel—that cognition is just another form of feeling, and that even distinct forms of it arise from a vague but looming milieu.

Whitehead includes a great deal of science—including quantum physics and Einstein's theory of relativity—into his metaphysics. But he doesn't declare philosophy "akin" to science. Indeed, it is philosophy's task to repair the damage done, if not by science itself than at least by its preconditions: abstraction and crippling specialization. In attempting to grasp the whole of reality, philosophy is rather akin to poetry. And I would argue that just as poetry does not solely refer to that wholeness but attempts to convey it as aesthetic experience, so Whitehead's philosophical style aims at "poetic" effects: often image and metaphor take over for concept as philosophical medium; imaginative leaps sometimes replace closely reasoned argument; a difficult-to-define mood or tone often arises from the prose; a recurrent murkiness blurs Whitehead's attempts at precision. Philosophy doesn't just have a subject matter different from that of science (by exceeding it in breadth); it is a different experiential domain, with its own, distinctive forms of intensity. As with Leibniz, philosophy is for Whitehead an aesthetic experience; but then again for Whitehead, all experience is aesthetic experience, even that of inanimate things. Leibniz's mixture of the confused and the distinct in his metaphysical writings offers a possible deep antecedent for Whitehead's style, though Leibniz lacks Whitehead's tonal range and is in general more restrained in his use of writerly effects.

My concern, however, is not to demonstrate ad nauseam the number of things Whitehead might have borrowed from Leibniz. Whitehead borrowed from a lot of people; another point of resemblance with Leibniz is the fact that both philosophers are highly syncretic. One can do worse than think of Whitehead's philosophy as itself a concrescence, prehending various philosophical strands and synthesizing them into vivid contrasts productive of intensity. Regardless, I do not think it is wrong to see Whitehead's "theory of monads" as a Leibnizianism for the twentieth century. This involves more than simply repeating Leibniz; it involves releasing and developing potentials that are merely nascent in him. Deleuze employs Whitehead to extract a theory of the event from Leibniz, and he can do so because that theory is indeed there, at least *in nuce*; but it took Whitehead to develop and perfect it, in part by rejecting the philosophy of substance to which Leibniz was still committed. Likewise, Whitehead's prying open of the Leibnizian monad, so that it can have real relations with other monads, was both necessary and fruitful.

Simply to pile up similarities of philosophical position between Whitehead and Leibniz is in effect to reduce them to timeless substances with predicates, mirroring one another. I am more interested in the way Whitehead continues and develops the dynamic of Leibnizian writing, employing metaphorical mappings and conceptual blends to kindle what Schlegel identified as flashes of "chemical wit." What Whitehead takes from Leibniz above all is a certain philosophical *style*, though again, altered to fit a different age. Whitehead's is a Leibnizianism for a modern era in which the status of, and rationale for, metaphysics is no longer secure in the way that it was in the seventeenth century. While Whitehead comes as close as any in modern times to Leibniz's status of "universal genius," that very fact signifies differently in an age of advancing specialization, and one in which the relation between science and metaphysics has fundamentally shifted. Whitehead's is a self-consciously "late" Leibnizianism.

A final perspective on the relation between Leibniz and Whitehead can be gleaned by looking briefly at the latter's emphasis on novelty. Along with "intensity," "novelty" is a kind of final cause in Whitehead—both motive of, and goal toward which, the process of concrescence tends. In Leibniz, by contrast, the concept of novelty does not play a significant role. It is implicit, however, in his insistence on maximal *variety*. The principle of the identity of indiscernibles requires that every entity differ from every other, and clearly this requirement extends over time as well as space. If two identical things cannot exist at the same moment but in different locations, they clearly cannot exist one after the other, either.

Whitehead was no modernist—at least, no obvious one—but his emphasis on novelty resonates with an artistic movement that insisted on the need to "make it new." Whitehead, moreover, saw novelty as not only a metaphysical but a cultural imperative. Societies lacking the adventurousness to continue forging novel ideas and works would, in his view, lapse into staleness and decadence.[54] The optimism of endless innovation is haunted by the fear of entropic decline—another modernist sentiment. Moreover, the endless succession of new entities, one replacing the other, threatens to consign all predecessors, and hence the past as a whole, to oblivion. One of the primary functions of Whitehead's God, therefore, is to serve as a melancholy archivist who preserves all superseded entities in the divine memory. Novelty is thus doubly haunted by the specters of staleness and of loss.

The concept of novelty establishes a relation to Leibniz, even though it is largely absent from his work. But it also invests this Leibnizian potential with affective tonalities that are on the whole alien to Leibniz. Whiteheadian novelty is an example of the very process it describes, at once perpetuating and transforming Leibnizian "variety" into something recognizable yet also markedly different. The pressure of the new is felt in Whitehead's age in a way that it was not in Leibniz's. And it lays down an unavoidable condition for any propagation of Leibniz's legacy. Whitehead can advance the banner of Leibniz only by not being too Leibnizian—by synthesizing him with other thinkers into a set of vivid contrasts productive of new kinds of intensities. It is left to melancholy archivists like myself to trace the Leibnizian leavings in that process.

CHAPTER 22

The Monad as Strange Loop

Douglas Hofstadter

D ouglas Hofstadter has made several brief appearances in this study. But it might prove surprising that he gets a section of his own, and that on a couple of counts. For one thing, Hofstadter's own intellectual standing is complicated. His academic accomplishments in the fields of computer and cognitive science are overshadowed by his work for a general readership. In the field of artificial intelligence—one of his principal concerns—he is more of a visionary gadfly than someone who sets research agendas. He is best known, rather, as the author of a Pulitzer Prize–winning book that has attained a kind of cult status. At the same time, it would be deeply misleading to describe him solely as a popularizer of scientific and mathematical research, though he is a brilliant one. (It is hard to imagine anyone else making the proof of Gödel's incompleteness theorem not only accessible but entertaining to a lay audience.) *Gödel, Escher, Bach: An Eternal Golden Braid*, which will be my principal focus here, is an original, one-of-a-kind work that not only straddles the fields of mathematics, logic, art, and music (among others) but also is itself an artwork of a decidedly "distinct" character. It is as if a Leibnizian aesthetic found its perfect instantiation there.

At the same time, any direct connections to Leibniz would be difficult to trace. In fact, I have not encountered any evidence that Hofstadter has ever cited or even read Leibniz. (He is not, of course, a philosopher, though his work is sometimes of interest to philosophers.) Nor is he a metaphysician or a cosmologist in the manner of Whitehead, which would provide a conducive setting for Leibnizian themes to emerge. But his thinking is, like Leibniz's, deeply grounded in mathematics. And it seeks deep connections between the mathematical and seemingly distant areas, including the aesthetic. Above all, Hofstadter's work draws continuously upon the theory and practice of analogy. He is perhaps the supreme modern practitioner of a Leibnizian "chemical wit" that draws striking, unexpected connections across the most far-flung areas. While not quite a Leibnizian "universal genius," Hofstadter's intellectual interests are impressively wide-ranging in this age of enforced specialization. And his work is, like Whitehead's, a protest against it.

All of this is to say that what Hofstadter carries forward is not so much the matter as the manner of Leibnizian argument. And he renders explicit what is merely implicit in Leibniz's philosophical style, since a ground note of Hofstadter's work is that "*analogy-making lies at the heart of intelligence*" (italics in original).[1] It is also worth noting that in Hofstadter—as in Leibniz but not Whitehead—a commitment to analogical thinking is accompanied by an equally strong commitment to lucidity of expression. One of the reasons that Hofstadter has proven of little interest to literary theorists, I suspect, has to do with his style, which has nothing of the oracular about it. But it is, of course, crucial to his success as public intellectual.

Before engaging with *Gödel, Escher, Bach*, I want to return briefly to *Fluid Concepts and Creative Analogies: Computer Models of the Fundamental Mechanisms of Thought*, published in 1995 and coauthored with other members of the Fluid Analogies Research Group (FARG). *Fluid Concepts* is a series of papers that FARG published in the late 1970s and 1980s, along with forwards for each of the essays and other framing materials supplied by Hofstadter. The goal of FARG was to create computer models of human intelligence, and especially human creativity. This it did by formulating programs designed to solve numerical and alphabetical analogy problems. The most interesting of the projects, a program called Copycat, solved alphabetical analogy problems such as: "Suppose the letter-string **abc** were changed to the letter-string **abd**; how would you change the letter string **mrrjjj** in "the same way"?[2] While there is one fairly straightforward solution (**mrrkkk**), it is not the only possible one, depending on how one interprets the phrase "in the same way." And of course, the trick is to get a *computer* to "interpret" the phrase and produce interesting solutions. The choice of solving analogy problems was chosen (obviously) because of Hofstadter's conviction that analogy-making lies at the heart of intelligence. "Copycat is nothing if not a model, albeit incipient, of human creativity."[3] Copycat enacts a computerized analogy to the human capacity to think with analogies, and thus to be creative. But this analogy must be pitched at the proper level. Hofstadter does not attempt to model the brain's neural networks by means of a connectionist model but rather emulates higher, cognitive functions by way of introducing random, stochastic features into his program.[4] In other words, he tries to model the human mind, not the human brain.

The idea behind Copycat was to surpass the limits of serial programming—which applies strict, formalized rules to solve problems—and thus to get at something like the flexible, intuitive, and experimental dimensions of thought. For this reason, Hofstadter turns to "fluid concepts," which we looked at briefly in module 15. The phrase "fluid concept" itself encodes an analogy between the cognitive structure of concepts and the molecular structure of water; and this is not the only one Hofstadter employs to describe the mechanisms instantiated in his analogy-creating programs. Another is the cytoplasm of a cell:

> All building and dismantling of temporary, puzzle-specific structures takes place in what is called (as in Jumbo [another of FARG's projects]) the *cytoplasm*. This term can be thought of as a synonym for "working memory" or "blackboard"; however, its biological connotations, reflecting some of the key intuitions behind this type of architecture, make it seem preferable. The basic image is that of a living cell, in which multitudes of enzymes (the role of which is played by codelets) are continually at work, inspecting various structures, modifying others, creating or destroying yet others, and so on. The area of a biological cell in which such activity takes place is the cytoplasm. The image is therefore one of distributed, parallel computations, rather than one of serial computation (despite the fact that codelets run one at a time).[5]

To call the term "cytoplasm" a metaphor or analogy runs the risk of oversimplifying the matter by attributing a merely rhetorical or heuristic function to it, whereas Hofstadter implies that ruminating on cytoplasm, as well as on the molecular structure of water, helped produce the conceptual blend from which the inspiration for these programs first emerged. "Metaphor" can carry the connotation of something applied after the fact, whereas for Hofstadter it precedes (and creates) the fact. This is what Copycat is trying to model. It is both the producer and product of analogy.

Of course, what begins as liquified conceptual blend must then be engineered into an actual, working computer program. While coding has its aesthetic dimensions, these arise from an exacting architecture. Just as Copycat itself begins with a stochastic shower of codelets but then, as these begin to converge toward a solution, switches to serial processing, so the very creation of Copycat follows a similar sequence. And what Hofstadter calls "Copycat" I am tempted to call the "Leibniz machine." It has been my thesis in this study that Leibnizian philosophizing involves the attempt to impart a logical, tightly argued, systematic structure to what is essentially an ongoing process of metaphorical mapping and conceptual blending. But, unlike Hofstadter's programs, Leibniz's system never actually "works." It is rather a baroque, Rube Goldberg–ish process subject to endless tinkering (a concept worth pondering in relation to Hofstadter as well, who like Leibniz is an inveterate intellectual tinkerer). Of course, to be fair, the problems Leibniz sets out to solve are a good deal more challenging than those posed to Copycat.

Hofstadter's masterpiece of analogical thinking is, of course, *Gödel, Escher, Bach*. It is not just that his analogies there are often unexpected and witty; they are also sometimes developed at great length and in impressive detail. Perhaps the most memorable occur in the chapter titled "Ant Fugue," named after an illustration by M. C. Escher. The chapter is a philosophical dialogue featuring the recurrent characters Achilles, Tortoise, and Crab in conversation with an anteater. Its topic is an extended analogizing ("mapping," as Tortoise calls it)[6] between the functioning of an ant colony and that of the human brain. Ant colonies exhibit behaviors far more complex and intelligent than those of which any individual ant is capable; likewise, brains exhibit behaviors far more complex and intelligent than those of which any neuron is capable. It is one thing to state the parallel in a single sentence, as I have done. It is another to develop it over a span of twenty-five pages that delve into the social, functional, and informational structures of an ant colony while deepening the analogy to brain function. In another, equally striking instance, Hofstadter constructs an extended, striking isomorphism between the metalanguage of typographical number theory and the biochemical mechanisms of DNA reproduction. This is not merely "chemical wit," as Schlegel would have it, but biochemical wit. Hofstadter permits a certain degree of whimsy to creep into his analogizing (and *Gödel, Escher, Bach* in general) that Leibniz would never allow himself. There is always something a bit guarded if cordial about Leibniz's authorial persona. But Hofstadter's is a distinctly Leibnizian performance regardless.

Other parallels emerge when we turn to the main business of *Gödel, Escher, Bach*. That main business is to offer a mathematical or, rather, metamathematical theory of conscious mind. Basically, Hofstadter attempts to give a mathematical spin to the concept of "emergence" whereby a higher-order phenomenon (consciousness) arises from the complex interactions of lower-order entities (neurons). As Hofstadter argues, "this act of translation from low-level physical hardware to high-level psychological software is analogous to the translation of number theoretical statements into metamathematical statements."[7] The key, in Hofstadter's view, is self-reference or self-reflection: the fact that a Gödelian sentence can be an element of itself. This gives rise to the structure that Hofstadter calls a "strange loop," which in turn makes possible the "I" of conscious thought.

In elaborating a metamathematical model of mind, what is Hofstadter doing but updating the Leibnizian monad? In place of the infinite series, we now have the mapping of one formal system onto another. Adding recursion or self-reflexivity to the mathematics of mind ramps up complexity and even introduces indeterminacy, and thus transcends the limits of Leibniz's more mechanical model. But Leibniz is also the founding progenitor of the very developments in mathematics and logic that Hofstadter brings to bear—as Gödel himself would have been the first to acknowledge. In a different kind of strange loop, one Leibnizian line of thought projects itself into the future in order to meet back up again with another.

Hofstadter is careful to maintain that Gödelian metamathematics offers an *analogy* for mind but is not itself mind. Most Leibnizian commentators would insist that Leibniz likewise offers the infinite series as only an analogy for the monadic law of the series, although, as I have argued, the boundary between "is" and "is like" is usually a porous one for Leibniz. In the view of Hofstadter's critics, maintaining arguments in a perpetual state of analogy leads to vagueness and even evasiveness: a succession of suggestive claims that ultimately prove impossible to pin down.[8] Here is a paragraph in which Hofstadter defends his procedure:

> Does Gödel's Theorem, then, have nothing to offer us in thinking about our own minds? [. . .] I think that the process of coming to understand Gödel's proof, with its construction involving arbitrary codes, complex isomorphisms, high and low levels of interpretation, and the capacity for self-mirroring, may inject some rich undercurrents and flavors into one's set of images about symbols and symbol-processing, which may deepen one's intuition for the relationship between mental structures on different levels.[9]

It is not hard to imagine why some computer scientists might balk at the squishiness of this claim. Thinking about Gödel and consciousness "*may* inject some rich undercurrents and flavors [. . .] which *may* deepen one's intuition." Repeated "mays" aside, the term "undercurrents" returns us to the world of fluid concepts, as in its way does the role of intuition in conducting science.

But Hofstadter is not pretending to formulate a theory of consciousness. Having seen that then-current models in artificial intelligence (AI) are not really leading anywhere, he offers rather a conceptual blend from which a workable model of mind might emerge. Fluid thought must eventually solidify, at least to some degree, just as Hofstadter's computer programs ultimately switch from stochastic to serial processing in the course of a run. But it is not yet time for it to do so. Analogy and intuition still have important roles to play. *Gödel, Escher, Bach* cannot deliver a fully fledged theory of mind, but it can model ways of thinking that may eventually lead to one. This, at least, is the book's wager.

As part of this process, Hofstadter turns to the artwork for inspiration. Both Bach and Escher illustrate what Hofstadter calls "strange loops," which occur "whenever, by moving upward (or downwards) through the levels of some hierarchical system, we unexpectedly find ourselves right back where we started."[10] Escher's endlessly rising staircases and waterfalls that somehow return to the same spot offer a striking visual emblem of the strange loop, which occurs in more conceptual form in Gödel. Hofstadter finds only one musical instance of a strange loop in Bach, and even that has to be massaged a bit before it conforms fully to the concept.[11] Moreover, it is less clear what the phrase "hierarchical levels" means in the context of an artistic or musical composition than it is in some of the scientific and mathematical contexts Hofstadter invokes. But the beauty (or vice, depending on one's perspective) of conceptual blends is that the analogies flowing into them need not necessarily be precise.

The work of Escher resonates provocatively in a Leibnizian context, given his attacks on Albertian perspective. Rather than simply abandoning depth of field for the flatness of the modernist canvas, however, Escher submits it to mathematical and artistic distortion. A work such as *Print Gallery* (figure 22.1), which folds outside and inside into a kind of Klein bottle, can be taken to illustrate the field of view from within a Leibnizian monad as reimagined by Hofstadter's use of metamathematics.

While Bach's work does not offer much in the way of strange loops, it is certainly marked by complex forms of self-reflection and recursion. Hofstadter

employs fugal form throughout *Gödel, Escher, Bach* in order to braid the various strands of his argument together. It is worth noting that both Escher and Bach are vigorously kinetic artists. There is nothing restful about an Escher illustration, which typically sends the eye into perpetual motion—often on a forced march along an endless, impossible loop. The spatial construction of Escher's work thus prompts a temporal movement as well. Meanwhile, Leibniz would have understood Bach's work as mathematics unfolding in time (and perceived confusedly). In this sense, music is an aesthetic counterpart to the monad, whose infinite series of mathematically generated perceptions likewise play out in time.

In *Gödel, Escher, Bach*, the device of philosophical dialogue is also a medium for fugal structure. Each new step in Hofstadter's argument begins with a dialogue, based on Lewis Carroll's "What the Tortoise Said to Achilles" (1895). In Carroll's dialogue, the Tortoise entraps Achilles in an argument about logical inference that gets caught in a recursive pattern and leads to an infinite regress—a logical "strange loop" that is a counterpart to Escher's ever-rising staircases and Gödel's theorem. Hofstadter revives Carroll's two characters and adds others, including (at various points) Zeno, a Crab, an Anteater, a Sloth, Charles Babbage, Alan Turing, and Hofstadter himself. Just about all of these dialogues are given musical titles: Canons, Fugues, Sonatas, etc., thereby drawing an analogical connection between the dramatic interplay of different philosophical positions and the structure of musical counterpoint. Moreover, the topics of the dialogues are then elaborated in more abstract and theoretical form in subsequent chapters, thus establishing more complex kinds of looping and counterpoint, and this is in turn absorbed into still larger sequences of argument. The underlying logic is explained by one of Hofstadter's striking analogies, this time between DNA reproduction and music:

> We have been using this image of ribosome as tape recorder, mRNA as tape, and protein as music. It may seem arbitrary, and yet there are some beautiful parallels. Music is not a mere linear sequence of notes. Our minds perceive pieces of music on a level far higher than that. We chunk notes into phrases, phrases into melodies, melodies into movements, and movements into full pieces. Similarly, proteins only make sense when they act as chunked units. Although a primary structure carries all the information for the tertiary structure to be created, it still "feels" like less, for its potential is only realized when the tertiary structure is actually physically created.[12]

Bracketing for the moment the Leibnizian lilt of "beautiful parallels," here we get a better sense of what Hofstadter means by "hierarchical levels" in music, as we move up from the note to the phrase to the melody and so forth, each higher level demonstrating greater degrees of organization and complexity than the ones below it. *Gödel, Escher, Bach* mimes this musical organization, "chunking" lower levels together into ever-higher and more complicated structures and ultimately forming "one big self-referential loop, symbolizing at once Bach's music, Escher's drawings and Gödel's Theorem."[13]

Not only is *Gödel, Escher, Bach* "one big self-referential loop" but so, in their different ways, are the works of Escher and Bach from which it takes its inspiration. Contrapuntal music is all about internal relations of echoing, inversion, and variation among its four melodic lines. Escher's works likewise depict self-enclosed worlds. *Picture Gallery* makes explicit the fact that the "outside" view offered by the Albertian window is really an inside. Complexity arises, not from the interactions between a formal system and its environment but from self-reflections and recursions of the system upon itself. This inward-turning—and therefore fundamentally monadic—tendency distinguishes Hofstadter's approach from Whitehead's but finds an answering voice in the work of Humberto Maturana and Francisco Varela, to which we shall now turn.

CHAPTER 23

The Godless Monad

Humberto Maturana and Francisco Varela

T he theory of autopoiesis, or self-producing systems, was first formulated in the 1970s and 1980s by the Chilean biologist and philosopher Humberto Maturana, often in partnership with his student Francisco Varela. Its discursive career is a peculiar one. From its home in biology it has spread to fields as far-flung as sociology, law, environmental sciences, information theory, cognitive science, artificial intelligence, business administration, psychology, architecture, and literary criticism.[1] At the same time, it has exerted little influence and attracted little attention within biology itself. This is because it is largely immune to empirical confirmation or refutation and does not lend itself readily to research agendas. Moreover, it entails a radically constructivist epistemology that is foreign to the practical work of scientific research and finds answering voices rather in postmodern theorists such as Jean-François Lyotard and Bruno Latour. Maturana and Varela have a place in this book in part because their work provides a way of rethinking some very fundamental issues in Leibnizian metaphysics. Above all, it enables us to reimagine the "windowless" Leibnizian monad without a need for preestablished harmony and therefore for God. In the theory of autopoiesis, the monad—Leibniz's most visionary and vexing concept—finds a novel, distinctly modern reincarnation.

Maturana and Varela also merit a place here because they are seminal transdisciplinary thinkers. This aspect of their work is not as immediately evident as it is in the case of the other thinkers considered in this book, and that by design. Autopoiesis has philosophical influences running back from Heidegger and Husserl to Descartes, Spinoza, and Leibniz.[2] It is also informed by cybernetics and other fields. And yet, as we shall see, it often presents as self-generated and devoid of outside influences. But this is misleading. The interdisciplinary trajectory of autopoiesis—the fact that it spread to so many fields—provides more telling testimony than does its surface texture.[3]

Autopoiesis is first of all an attempt to define biological life and to distinguish living entities from nonliving ones.[4] For Maturana and Varela (and with a Cartesian echo), "living systems are machines," but machines with a specific kind of organization:

> An autopoietic machine is a machine organized (defined as a unity) as a network of processes of production (transformation and destruction) of components that produces the components which: (i) through their interactions and transformations continuously regenerate and realize the network of processes (relations) that produced them; and (ii) constitute it (the machine) as a concrete unity in the space in which they (the components) exist by specifying the topological domain of its realization as such a network. It follows that an autopoietic machine continuously generates and specifies its components, and does this in an endless turnover of components under conditions of continuous perturbations and compensation of perturbations. Therefore, an autopoietic machine is an homeostatic (or rather a relations-static) system which has its own organization (defining network of relations) as the fundamental variable which it maintains constant.[5]

This is a bit of a mouthful and will require some unpacking. Autopoietic systems consist of components and of processes by which those components are made and remade. The processes of production produce the components that in turn reproduce those same processes and relations of production, in a circular fashion. Put differently, the organism's internal organization generates the components that reproduce this organization. And this circular and homeostatic process constitutes life. Their foundational circularity means that autopoietic systems are also autotelic: "Living systems, as physical autopoietic machines, are purposeless systems."[6] What autopoietic machines make are themselves; they serve no other function.

What counts as an autopoietic machine, and what count as its components? For Maturana and Varela, the one indubitably autopoietic machine is the unicellular organism, and its "parts" are molecular and biochemical, not morphological. They are provisionally willing to allow that multicellular organisms are second-order autopoietic systems, but the relevant components here are individual cells rather than tissues, organs, etc. Things become trickier still when we come to societies of living things, or third-order autopoietic systems. Here

Maturana and Varela part ways, with only the former allowing for social auto-poiesis. More controversially, Maturana has declared that any system exhibiting autopoiesis, including computer models, is alive.[7]

Autopoietic systems are both unified and perpetuated by their internal orga-nization. Before turning to matters Leibnizian, we might note in passing that the theory of autopoiesis intriguingly updates (and conceivably draws upon) Spi-nozist *conatus*, by means of which an entity perpetuates itself through maintain-ing a constant (homeostatic) relation among its component parts. More relevant to our immediate purposes is the image of autopoietic systems nested within larger autopoietic systems, which enables a rethinking of the Leibnizian domi-nant monad. While nested autopoietic systems are allopoietic with respect to the larger system for which they serve as components, they remain autopoietic (and therefore autotelic) with respect to themselves. This, I think, solves the problems with Ohad Nachtomy's notion of monadic dominance as functional subordina-tion, which I examined in module 11.

The closed organizational structure of an autopoietic system, circulating end-lessly in a loop, would seem to impose a kind of perpetual sameness on the organ-ism. But this is not the case. Living organisms are in "a continuous process of becoming without the specification of an end state."[8] While any change so severe that it disrupted an organisms's autopoiesis would lead to its death, the sole con-straint of maintaining its internal organization does not prevent an organism from exhibiting novelty and creativity in its behavior, especially in the case of what Maturana and Varela call "observing systems."[9] As I argued in module 10, the mathematical "law of the series" that determines the becoming of the monad likewise allows for unpredictable novelty.

Autopoietic systems resemble Leibnizian monads primarily though their organizational closure, which entails an informational closure: "Autopoietic machines do not have inputs or outputs. They can be perturbated by indepen-dent events and undergo internal structural changes which compensate these perturbations."[10] Changes within an autopoietic system are determined by the state of the system itself. External entities can "perturb" the system but not spec-ify its reaction. An obvious parallel in Leibniz (which we shall examine more closely later on) would be the way in which a moving body "occasions" the elastic force within a body that it strikes to assert itself. But the change within each body is specified by its own internal forces, not by any causal determination exerted by other bodies.

Informational closure is probably the most striking and counterintuitive element of the theory of autopoiesis. It does not imply that organisms and their environments do not interact. But entities in its environment can only *de*-form an autopoietic system, not *in*-form it. Informational closure is best illustrated by the nervous system, which is not autopoietic (the nervous system does not produce the neurons of which it is composed) but which is organizationally closed. As a result, the nervous system does not represent entities external to itself but rather its own complex internal state: "all that is accessible to the nervous system at any point are states of relative activity holding between nerve cells, and all that to which any given state of relative activity can give rise are further states of relative activity in other nerve cells by *forming* those states of relative activity to which they respond."[11] What our eyes "see," for instance, are not external objects but instead relative states of excitation among the rods and cones in our retinas, and the way that these in turn are propagated through the system as a whole. The nervous system has no way of distinguishing between external and internal states, and thus for it there is no inside or outside. Consequently, "the anatomical and functional organization of the nervous system secures the synthesis of behavior, not a representation of the world."[12]

Autopoietic systems are not quite preprogrammed in the way Leibnizian monads are, but their informational closure nevertheless renders them strikingly monadic. Even in the absence of preestablished harmony, however, such systems do not stumble blindly through the world, to their immediate destruction. Why that is so will require some explication and take us into the epistemological dimensions of Maturana and Varela's thought. We can begin by noting that to an observer, an organism will indeed appear to perceive other entities—often quite accurately—and interact causally with them. This is not an illusion or misperception but rather the artifact of a descriptive domain that includes the organism apprehended as a unity in relation to its environment. Conversely, an observer of the internal workings of the organism will see its autopoiesis operating under conditions of organizational and informational closure. "Anything said is said by an observer," and is relative to its observational domain.[13] Maturana and Varela operate a perspectivalism that is reminiscent of Leibniz's but, if anything, more radical. For Leibniz, a monad simply *is* a unity without parts. For Maturana and Varela, whether an organism is a unity or has component parts depends on the observational domain within which it is located.

Maturana employs a vivid analogy to capture the difference between observational domains as applied to autopoietic systems:

> What occurs in a living system is analogous to what occurs in an instrumental flight where the pilot does not have access to the outside world and must function only as a controller of the values shown in his flight instruments. His task is to secure a path of variations in the readings of his instruments, either according to a prescribed plan, or to one that becomes specified by these readings. When the pilot steps out of the plane he is bewildered by the congratulations of his friends on account of the perfect flight and landing that he performed in absolute darkness. He is perplexed because to his knowledge all that he did at any moment was to maintain the readings of his instruments within certain specified limits, a task which is in no way represented by the description that his friends (observers) make of his conduct.[14]

The pilot who lands by means of instrument readings both recalls and updates the viewer of shadow plays in Plato's Allegory of the Cave.[15] Only, in emerging from the night-shrouded cockpit into the company of his friends, he does not pass from the simulacrum to the real, or the illusory to the true. On the contrary, he remains puzzled by his friends' description of his activities. Both descriptions are equally true: to the friends, as external observers perceiving him in relation to his environment, the pilot landed a plane, while to himself (as internal observer) he adjusted controls in response to instrument readings so as to maintain a kind of "homeostasis" in those readings.[16] In Leibniz, by contrast, one kind of description is truer than another: monads appear (even to themselves) to be perceiving other monads, i.e., to be taking in information from their environments, while in fact the law of the series within them generates these "perceptions." His perspectivalism, which is otherwise quite thoroughgoing, doesn't extend quite this far; epistemology abuts against an absolute ontological bedrock. And yet even this apparent difference points to a deeper underlying parallel. Because in Maturana and Varela, a constructivist epistemology that assigns equal validity to different kinds of observations is somewhat at odds with a definition of autopoietic systems that presents itself as objective and non-perspectival. The latter makes it difficult to avoid saying that organisms merely "appear" to a third-party observer to communicate among themselves but are "in fact" organizationally closed.

In any case, Maturana and Varela's perspectivalism intriguingly parallels an element of Leibniz's philosophy we have not yet discussed: the notion of the "two kingdoms."

> I would maintain that everything can be explained in two ways: in terms of the *Kingdom of Power*, or *Efficient Causes*, and in terms of the *Kingdom of Wisdom*, or *Final Causes*. God governs bodies in the way that a designer governs machines, in accordance with *laws of size or of mathematics*; but he does so for the benefit of souls. And souls, which are capable of wisdom, he governs for his greater glory as citizens, or fellow members of society, in the manner of a prince, or indeed of a father, in accordance with *laws of goodness or of morality*. Though these two kingdoms thoroughly interpenetrate each other, their laws are never confused or disturbed, so that there arises both the greatest in the Kingdom of Power and the best in the Kingdom of Wisdom.[17]

Nature, or the realm of material bodies, operates according to mechanical laws of efficient causality, while the realm of souls operates according to a moral law that answers to final rather than efficient causes. Natural or efficient causality operates "from behind," both temporally and effectually, as one body collides with another or one event causes another subsequent one that reacts to it. Souls or monads or substances, which are by definition isolated from everything else, cannot be subject to efficient causality (since nothing "collides" with them) and instead operate according to a final causality or causality "toward" greater perfection or goodness. And the monad drives forward from one perception toward another by way of appetitions or the law of the series.

The two kingdoms answer to Leibniz's principle of sufficient reason, which insists that everything that happens requires not only a "how" or efficient cause but also a "why" or final cause. Each principle provides a different kind of explanation for events and indeed constitutes what Maturana and Varela would call a "descriptive domain." Moreover, the kingdom of power, or of efficient causality, explains entities as they interact with one another or with their environments, while the kingdom of wisdom, or of final causality, explains the development of entities within their autonomy. Or rather, it divides entities into bodies, which suffer efficient causality from without, and souls, which operate according to their own, immanent laws.

But things are not that simple. *"All the phenomena of nature can be explained solely by final causes, exactly as if there were no efficient cause; and all the phenomena of nature can be explained solely by efficient causes, as if there were no final cause,"* and hence "there are, so to speak, two kingdoms even in corporeal nature."[18] Even events involving natural bodies and their interactions require a "why" as well as a "how," since nothing happens without a reason for Leibniz. Hence final causes operate within the realm of bodies as well as that of souls. Efficient and final causes offer independent and internally sufficient ways of explaining the same event. Except that they really don't, because in the end, there is no such thing as efficient causality, even in the world of bodies:

> It can be said that, speaking with metaphysical rigor, *no created substance exerts a metaphysical action or influence upon another.* For to say nothing of the fact that it cannot be explained how anything can pass over from one thing into the substance of another it has already been shown that all the future states of each thing follow from its own concept. What we call causes are in metaphysical rigor only concomitant requisites. This is illustrated by our experiences of nature, for bodies in fact recede from other bodies by force of their own elasticity and not by any alien force, although another body has been required to set the elasticity (which arises from something intrinsic to the body itself) working.[19]

"What we call causes" is not really causality but concomitance. It appears to the observer that one billiard ball striking another sets it in motion, whereas in fact the motion of the second results from its own elastic force. As in Maturana and Varela, observing an entity in relation to its environment will produce what looks like causal interaction, whereas entities actually follow their own "autopoietic" paths. A closer look at efficient causality reveals it to be a version of final causality. Even billiard balls do not suffer causal interference from without but follow their own paths. Billiard ball B is not set in motion "by" billiard ball A; rather, billiard ball B's elastic force sends it "toward" a given point. Indeed, it is the "towardness" of active elastic force in the bodily world that enables it to express the "towardness" of final cause in the monadic world.

All that being said, the bodily world operates *as if* under the influence of efficient causes. Hence the laws of mechanics accurately describe how bodies of different mass and speed will react upon collision. Not only is it perfectly

acceptable to describe bodies as if they interacted causally, but it would be difficult to make sense of the natural world if one did not employ the laws of mechanics with their assumption of such interactions. But at the deepest metaphysical
level, causal descriptions are not true. Bodies are as autonomous as minds, and
as little susceptible to causal interaction. At most, bodies can occasion the active
force in one another, just as for Maturana and Varela, external bodies can perturb organisms. The operation of autonomous force within bodies gives rise to
"*what we call* cause," just as preestablished harmony gives rise to "*what we call . . .*
communication" between souls and bodies.

Let us now lay Leibniz's two kingdoms and Maturana and Varela's epistemology side by side. Both posit two "descriptive domains" for considering entities.
One places the entity in relation to other entities, and the other considers the
entity as it is in itself. The first allows for causal relations, communication, and
informational transfer between entities; the second posits entities as autonomous and self-enclosed, pursuing an immanent logic and capable at the most of
being "perturbed" but not informed by other entities. Leibniz and Maturana/
Varela depict these two descriptive domains as equally legitimate but also, at the
same time, suggest that only one of these is foundationally true while the other
is an "as if" description. For both it is "as if" entities interact but not ultimately
so. For Maturana and Varela, organisms are in fact and not merely perspectivally autopoietic (if they were not, the theory of autopoiesis wouldn't count for
much), and for Leibniz, monads are in fact preprogrammed and closed to interactions with other entities. Both insist that the world as we observe it—a world
of apparent perception, communication, etc., among entities—is valid relative
only to a particular kind of descriptive domain while the world of autopoiesis/
law of the series is likewise relative to a descriptive domain (i.e., perspectival) but
at the same time, and contradictorily, also somehow objectively true. The two
systems display many of the same features and, as a result, some of the same intellectual tensions and inconsistencies as well. But this is apparently the price to
pay for insisting on informational closure as foundational to living things while
also having to explain a world that does not look informationally closed.

I have been speaking of differently situated observers, but, given the organizationally closed nature of autopoietic systems, it may be wondered where
"observers" are supposed to come from. While such systems do not allow informational input, they do interact with outside entities: photons impinge upon
the retina, sound waves upon the tympanum, etc., and initiate cascades of neural

firings, which are processed according to the circularity of the system. And since this circularity entails repetition, such systems are sensitive to repeated kinds of encounters and learn what "works" in responding to them.[20] In addition, autopoietic systems can learn to respond to their own internal states, at which point abstract thinking becomes possible, and to their own interactions, at which point self-consciousness emerges. The nature of this learning process implies that Maturana's epistemology not only is constructivist and anti-representationalist but also contains significant elements of pragmatism:

> We are used to talking about reality orienting each other through linguistic interactions to what we deem are sensory experiences of concrete entities, but which have turned out to be, as are thoughts and *descriptions*, states of relative activity between neurons that generate new *descriptions*. The question, "*What is the object of knowledge?*" becomes meaningless. There is no object of knowledge. To know is to be able to operate adequately in an individual or cooperative situation.[21]

The basis for evaluating knowledge is not whether it is true or false, or accurate or inaccurate, but rather whether it enables the organism to operate adequately—to survive and, presumably, to flourish. Hence "learning is not a process of accumulation of representations of the environment; it is a continuous process of transformation of behavior through continuous change in the capacity of the nervous system to synthesize it."[22]

Repeated interactions with an environment—including other autopoietic systems—lead to what Maturana and Varela call "structural coupling." The autopoiesis of one organism as it responds to external perturbations provides a source of repeated encounters or perturbations for another organism, such that a shared or consensual domain develops between them even without informational transfer. Maturana and Varela at one point employ the term "braiding" to figure such structural coupling—a suggestive image.[23] Each autopoietic system follows its own self-enclosed line or thread, but the threads get braided or wound together in their progress. (The figure of braiding is, of course, something Maturana and Varela share with Hofstadter.)[24] From this, what looks like communication arises. But again, the thing that binds organisms in a consensual domain is not shared information or representation but shared conditions for continued autopoiesis within a mutually inhabited environmental niche. Even language is, in Maturana and Varela's view, not a medium for informational transfer but one for consensual orientation or enhanced braiding; its function is pragmatic and connotative, not representational and denotative.[25]

For all their many points of convergence, there is one principle, and that a foundational one, on which Leibniz and Maturana and Varela might at first seem to part ways: Maturana's declaration that "cognition is a biological phenomenon and can only be understood as such."[26] Insisting that cognition is essentially embodied—an efflux of the neural system—apparently contradicts Leibniz's view that the monadic realm of perception is nonbodily. And yet, since Maturana defines the biological *as* autopoiesis, to say that cognition is biological is likewise simply to say that it too is autopoietic. Autopoiesis is identified by a certain kind of organization, not by a particular kind of substrate. Both Maturana and Varela, and particularly the latter, explored mathematical and computer models of autopoiesis, and, as I have already noted, Maturana was willing to declare computer models of autopoiesis as living. Moreover, the theory of autopoiesis distinguishes between organization, an ideal entity, and structure, which is the way that organization is instantiated in a given organism. Might it then be permissible to see the bodily structure of a concrete organism as *expressing*, in a Leibnizian sense, the ideality of its organization?[27]

The Leibnizian elements in their thought have not gone unremarked by readers of Maturana and Varela. Perhaps unsurprisingly, however, they themselves never appear to mention this connection and are in general reticent on the question of outside influence. Maturana even published a long article on autopoiesis and the epistemology of science in which he footnotes only other works written by himself.[28] It is unclear whether this was self-conscious performance art or the symptom of a deeply "autopoietic" intellect. Maturana and Varela's own "structural coupling" frayed somewhat over time; while they continued to share some fundamental premises, their work increasingly diverged and was pursued independently by each until Varela's untimely death in 2001. Perhaps the notion of braiding can serve to figure the relation between Maturana and Varela on the one hand and Leibniz on the other. Each party pursues its own path, but these paths get wound together into a consensual domain. Leibniz, Maturana, and Varela are thinkers who not only write about informational closure but also posit their own status as closed. Maturana and Varela are avowedly autopoietic, as they would have to be to avoid contradiction in their writings, and Leibniz is a self-confessed monad. Nevertheless, the one perturbs the others, productively.

CHAPTER 24

The Quantum Monad

David Bohm

The dispute between Leibniz and Sir Isaac Newton over who deserved credit for inventing calculus was not a polite one. Both sides pressed their claims fiercely, and both engaged in some ethically questionable tactics.[1] When the dust had settled, the contest was declared a draw. It is now generally recognized that both parties invented calculus independently. Newton's claims of plagiarism against Leibniz are no longer taken seriously, though Leibniz may have had more than a little help from another mathematician, Isaac Barrow. The ghost of Newton might congratulate itself on the fact that Newton made his discoveries first. The ghost of Leibniz might congratulate itself on the fact that, having been the first to publish his results, Leibniz saw his approach and notation became standard among mathematicians. Even today, we still take derivatives and integrals *à la mode Leibnizienne* while no one employs Newton's method of fluxions.

In the realm of physics, however, there was seemingly no contest at all. Leibniz's practice of mixing physics with metaphysics made for some impressive philosophy, but scientifically it was a dead end. By contrast, Newton's adherence to mathematical descriptions produced a form of mechanics that dominated physics for well over a century and remains the standard in classical situations where neither relativity nor quantum phenomena play a significant role. Scientifically minded college freshmen today learn Leibniz's calculus but Newton's physics. Nevertheless, Leibniz's role in the history of physics is more extensive than this simple dichotomy would suggest. Richard T. W. Arthur provides an impressive list of ways in which Leibniz either foresaw or influenced later developments in physics, from the first law of thermodynamics, to the distinction between kinetic and potential energy, to the notion of a physical field.[2] Isabelle Stengers and Nobel laureate Ilya Prigogine argue that the conceptual language of dynamic systems ultimately came to follow a Leibnizian rather than a Newtonian model, and they ask whether Leibniz "missed" physics or "whether it is not the history of physics that has "missed" Leibniz."[3]

Newtonian assumptions began to be questioned, moreover, beginning in the late nineteenth century, and decisively in the early twentieth. Special relativity and quantum physics produced worldviews very much at variance with Newton's and reduced his results to approximations of a very different reality. Ironically, the more that physics departed from Newtonian assumptions, the more its results became eerily reminiscent of Leibnizian views. This is especially the case in recent decades. Leibniz's vision of the physical world turns out to be not so dismissable after all.

The most obvious, and oft-noted, vindication of Leibniz in modern physics was offered by Einstein's special theory of relativity, which put paid to Newton's belief in absolute space and time. Position and movement, Einstein showed, are relative with respect to non-inertial reference frames—pretty much as Leibniz had argued. More broadly, Einstein reinforced the perspectivalism that lay at the basis of Leibniz's claim that motion and position are relative and largely imaginary. But in fact, the dismantling of absolute space and time had already been initiated by the physicist Ernst Mach, whom Einstein credited with the inspiring the theory of relativity. Mach, who was widely read in philosophy, struck a distinctly Leibnizian note when he observed that "No one is competent to predicate things about absolute space and absolute motion; they are pure things of thought, pure mental constructs that cannot be produced in experience."[4]

By contrast with the theory of relativity, quantum theory, at least in its basics, does not appear to validate Leibnizian thinking. The Planck length may possibly set a lower limit to physical entities, thus refuting Leibniz's vision of ever-smaller, nested bodies. And the dominant Copenhagen interpretation introduces elements of randomness and discontinuity, which likewise contradict fundamental Leibnizian tenets. That being said, some recent theories about quantum foundations offer intriguing echoes of Leibniz's thought. One not-quite-so-recent development—the work of the physicist David Bohm—will be the topic of the current module.

Bohm, who was active from the 1940s up until his death in 1992, is widely regarded as one of the great physicists of the twentieth century. Like Maturana and Varela, however, he was ultimately more influential outside of his chosen field than within it. Doubly a dissident, he was both a committed Marxist at the height of the Cold War and a skeptic toward the Copenhagen interpretation of quantum physics that reigned supreme in the field then and still does now.[5] Together, these had the effect of marginalizing Bohm's theories, which evolved over time, and which were moreover difficult to confirm empirically since their results were necessarily identical to those of the Copenhagen interpretation.[6] Nevertheless, Bohmian mechanics survives even today as a somewhat niche subfield within quantum physics. But Bohm's views have resonated widely with artists, writers, and even spiritual leaders such as Jiddu Krishnamurti and (more recently) the Dalai Lama. This is owing in part to Bohm's manner of doing physics. An avid reader of philosophy, he used it—along with visual art, music, child psychology, and other disciplines—to think through issues in quantum theory that often received mathematical form only later in the process. (One of his first professional accomplishments was a theory of plasma inspired by his notion of an ideal Marxist social order and which today is still regarded as correct.)[7] So not only the matter but the style of his work will be of interest.

Bohm's earliest challenge to quantum orthodoxy involved a revival and elaboration of Louis de Broglie's pilot-wave theory. According to the Copenhagen interpretation, the position and momentum of an elementary particle are undetermined—in effect, a cloud of probabilities described by the Schrödinger wave function—until the particle encounters a measuring device, whereupon the wave function collapses and the particle assumes a definite state. By contrast, pilot-wave theory held that the apparently indeterminate condition of the particle is the product of the observer's ignorance. The particle is actually somewhere all the time, guided in its trajectory through information provided by a so-called pilot wave, in the same way that radio transmissions might guide a boat into harbor, although the boat travels under its own power.[8] Pilot-wave theory purported to provide a deterministic account even for such counterintuitive quantum phenomena as the famous double-slit experiment.

Bohm's version of de Broglie's pilot-wave theory (Bohm called it a "hidden variable theory," then a "causal interpretation," and finally an "ontological interpretation") makes quantum physics more Leibniz-friendly in a couple of respects. For one thing, it maintains that particles are discrete entities that travel along linear, continuous paths through space, not fields of probabilities that discontinuously pop into specific states. Bohm turned the Schrödinger wave function into an objectively real field called the "quantum potential" that exerted a force on the particle and guided it on its way, though for practical reasons the precise path is usually inaccessible to an observer owing to a sensitive dependence on initial conditions. Bohm's approach thereby reduces the strangeness of the Copenhagen interpretation to something that looks much more like classical mechanics, which is one reason it failed to find widespread favor. But it does make quantum physics into something that would look much more recognizable to Leibniz.

In addition, Bohm's theory is nonlocal and holistic. The quantum potential does not diminish in strength over distance, and it reflects the state of the entire system of which a given particle is part. In effect, it connects the state of every element in a system with the state of every other element, even if the "system" is expanded to include the entire universe. Bohm thereby constructs a physicist's version of the Leibnizian intuition that every monad "perceives" every other. As Bohm would put it at a later point in his thinking, "we come to a new general physical description in which 'everything implicates everything' in an order of undivided wholeness."[9] Even more suggestive in this context is a vision Bohm had during a visit to Copenhagen, as recounted by his biographer F. David Peat:

> The vision came to him in the form of a large number of highly silvered spherical mirrors that reflected each other. The universe was composed of this infinity of reflections, and of reflections of reflections. Every atom was reflecting in this way, and the infinity of these reflections was reflected in each thing; each was an infinite reflection of the whole. This image possesses almost mystical connotations in its vividness, and at the metaphorical level at least, it contains the seeds of the concept that Bohm was later to call the implicate order.[10]

It also almost uncannily recalls Leibniz's vision of the universe as an infinity of monads or "living mirrors" that reflect one another—mirrors that are infinite in number and, as I suggested earlier, ought to be understood as spherical.

Another Leibnizian intuition emerges in a line of investigation that Bohm began with a 1954 paper.[11] There he attempts to explain the apparent randomness of quantum movement by positing that particles move in a sub-quantum fluid. As a result, quantum fluctuations are like Brownian motion—a kind of statistical randomness rather than the absolute randomness posited by the Copenhagen interpretation. This once again renders all movements of elementary particles causal. But it also, in Leibnizian fashion, represents space not only as a plenum[12] but also as a fluid one. Moreover, as time went on, Bohm entertained the possibility of sub-sub-quantum levels, and so on, ad infinitum: "all matter contains an infinity of qualitatively different levels, all interconnected."[13] And as with Leibniz, Bohm posited that events on lower levels could surge up and create unexpected effects on higher ones.[14] Moreover, "sub-quantum processes will very probably involve basically new entities as different from electrons, protons, etc., as the latter are different from macroscopic systems."[15] Of course, these sub-quantum entities are not spatially nested within larger ones, as is the case for Leibniz, but they nevertheless offer a striking vision of ever-smaller entities that exhibit variety as one moves from a given level to another.

Already implicit in Bohm's early "hidden variable" theory, but explicit later on, the quantum potential supplies *information* to the particles whose movement it governs, and as a consequence of this, elementary particles have to be reimagined so as to receive and respond to information. This does not lead Bohm to the kind of panpsychism we have seen in Leibniz and Whitehead, but it does assign some internal complexity to these particles. As F. David Peat observes:

> In Bohm's theory the electron is able to "read" and respond to this information [supplied by the quantum potential]. But this means that it is no longer an elementary, structureless "billiard ball" but has considerable inner complexity. Bohm liked to make a somewhat ironical aside to astounded scientists that the electron is at least as complicated as a television set.[16]

We might recall here that Leibniz's objections to atomism involved not just a desire to avoid a lower limit on the size of entities but also an aversion to the monotony entailed by atomism—the notion that everything boils down in the end to relatively featureless, similar building blocks. Likewise, Bohm declares that "nature may have in it an infinity of different kinds of things."[17]

Bohm's thinking continued to evolve in the 1960s and 1970s, resulting in his theory of the "implicate order" as well as his first of many books for a general readership, *Wholeness and the Implicate Order* (Routledge, 1980). Bohm's implicate order further elaborates his causal interpretation of quantum physics while also, in some ways, reversing course, or at least shifting emphasis, with respect to his earlier work. It also both develops and complicates his echoes (intended or not) of Leibnizian metaphysics. In his earlier version of pilot-wave theory, Bohm posited discrete point particles that were guided along their paths by a quantum potential. Now he began to see point particles as not only guided but also created by converging waves in the quantum potential, the result of effects upon that potential by a "superpotential" operating even further behind the scenes. The "explicate order" of the universe we inhabit— composed of particles, energy, time, space, etc.—was now considered to be the secondary product of events in quantum fields—the "implicate order"—that do not appear directly in our world. Eventually, Bohm came to speculate that there were further super-super-quantum potentials, and so forth, potentially ad infinitum, just as earlier there had been a potentially endless series of sub-sub-quantum fluids.

Suggestively, for our purpose, the inspiration for Bohm's implicate order came largely from outside of quantum physics—in fact, from a device he saw demonstrated on a BBC television show:

> A more striking example of implicate order can be demonstrated in the laboratory, with a transparent container full of a very viscous fluid, such as treacle, and equipped with a mechanical rotator that can "stir" the fluid very slowly but very thoroughly. If an insoluble droplet of ink is placed in the fluid and the stirring device is set in motion, the ink drop is gradually transformed into a thread that extends over the whole fluid. The latter now appears to be distributed more or less at "random" so that it is seen as some shade of grey. But if the mechanical stirring device is now turned in the opposite direction, the transformation is reversed, and the droplet of dye suddenly appears reconstituted. . . . When the dye was distributed in what appeared to be a random way, it nevertheless had *some kind* of order which is different, for example, from that arising from another droplet originally placed in a different position. But this order is *enfolded* or *implicated* in the "grey mass" that is visible in the fluid. Indeed, one could thus "enfold" a whole picture. Different pictures would look indistinguishable and yet have different implicate orders, which differences would be revealed when they were explicated, as the stirring device was turned in a reverse direction.[18]

In this analogy or metaphorical mapping, the ink drop stands in for the classical point particle that Bohm originally sought to rescue from the Copenhagen interpretation. Operating the treacle rotor device "enfolds" the drop into the treacle such that it disappears, but the system as a whole preserves the information about the drop's original state such that it can be reconstituted by running the machine in reverse, thereby unfolding the previously enfolded drop.

Bohm did not employ the language of "enfolding" and "unfolding" in a loose fashion. He and his collaborator Basil Hiley gave the terms precise mathematical meanings by way of algebraic topology—a form of mathematics that appealed to Bohm because it could express pure relationship without relying on underlying notions of space and time.[19] It therefore fulfilled a function for Bohm very much like what the *analysis situs* did for Leibniz.[20] Bohm's vision of a universe in a perpetual process of enfolding and unfolding therefore not only expressed a central Leibnizian intuition but also engaged a form of mathematics that would doubtless have appealed to Leibniz.

It should not be surprising, then, that Bohm invokes Leibniz along with Whitehead in *Wholeness and the Implicate Order*:

> In certain ways this notion [of the implicate order] is similar to Leibniz's idea of monads, each of which "mirrors" the whole in its own way, some in great detail and others rather vaguely. The difference is that Leibniz's monads had a permanent existence, whereas our basic elements are only moments and are thus not permanent. Whitehead's idea of "actual occasions" is closer to the one proposed here, the main difference being that we use the implicate order to express the qualities and relationships of our moments, whereas Whitehead does this in a rather different way.[21]

Bohm had a passionate, lifelong interest in philosophy. Exactly how much Leibniz he read is unclear, unlike his more extensive engagement with Whitehead and process philosophy, which unmistakably leave their mark on his understanding of the implicate order.[22] But reading Whitehead is also, as we have seen, a way of imbibing a reconfigured Leibniz, as Bohm seems implicitly to recognize by pairing the two. In the movement from Leibniz to Whitehead to Bohm, we can see how Leibnizian thought is at once propagated and transformed as it passes through historical relay points. At the same time, while the metaphorics of the implicate order are vividly Leibnizian, the ontology to which they give rise is less so than that of Bohm's earlier work. Particles are now the secondary product of a holistic order that is somehow more fundamental and real, rather in the way that Spinozist modes are the outcroppings of divine substance. Indeed, Bohm eventually included consciousness as well as matter into the implicate order, in a fashion that strongly recalls Spinozist attribute-dualism.[23]

In any case, we cannot gauge the extent of Bohm's Leibnizianism by attending solely to the content of his theories; his manner of doing physics is equally important. Bohm exhibits a Leibnizian predilection for intellectual sprawl and metaphorical mapping. Elements of his scientific theories draw upon sources as far-flung as philosophy, painting, and art criticism, the child psychology of Jean Piaget, and Eastern religion.[24] The religious sources sometimes impart a New Age-y flavor to his speculations that attracted a broader public but probably did little to bolster the confidence of his fellow physicists.[25] Bohm's wide reading in philosophy doubtless encouraged his tendency to blur the boundaries between physics and metaphysics, particularly when addressing a general audience. More broadly, Bohm's conviction that a fundamental holism underlies the physical universe encourages an intellectual approach that likewise attempts to synthesize across disciplinary and other boundaries. Like Whitehead, Bohm opposes intellectual fragmentation, and he states that "we can overcome it by using language in a freer, more informal, and 'poetic' way, that properly communicates the truly fluid nature of the difference between relevance and irrelevance."[26]

Bohm repeatedly draws connections between the practice of physics and that of poetry.[27] And as part of this, he insists on the foundational role played by metaphor in scientific thought:

> This notion of a metaphor can serve to illuminate the nature of scientific creativity by equating, in a metaphoric sense, a scientific discovery with a poetic metaphor. For in perceiving a new idea in science, the mind is involved in a similar form of creative perception as when it engages a poetic metaphor. However, in science it is essential to unfold the meaning of the metaphor in even greater and more "literal" detail, while in poetry the metaphor may remain relatively implicit.[28]

In Bohm's thinking, physics, philosophy, art, psychology, linguistics, religion, and other areas form a conceptual blend that is the holistic mental counterpart to the implicate order itself.

As in Leibniz, Bohm's habit of bringing different disciplines to bear on his work results in a pronounced perspectivalism: "One may indeed compare a theory to a particular view of some object. Each view gives only an appearance of the object in some aspect. The whole object is not perceived in any one view but, rather, it is grasped only *implicitly* as that single reality which is shown in all these views."[29] Indeed, the irreducibly perspectival nature of scientific theorizing forecloses, in Bohm's view, the very possibility of achieving a definitive interpretation of nature:

> In this activity, there is evidently no reason to suppose that there is or will be a final form of insight (corresponding to absolute truth) or even a steady series of approximations to this. Rather, in the nature of the case, one may expect the unending development of new forms of insight (which will, however, assimilate certain key features of the older forms as simplifications, in the way that relativity theory does with Newtonian theory). As pointed out earlier, however, this means that our theories are to be regarded primarily as ways of looking at the world as a whole (i.e. world views) rather than as "absolutely true knowledge of how things are" (or as a steady approach toward the latter).[30]

The unavoidably perspectival nature of scientific knowledge, together with the prospect of a potential infinity of superimplicate orders, one behind the other, ensures that the physicist's work is never done. But this is not, for Bohm, a nightmare vision like that of Kafka's parable in which an infinity of gatekeepers bar entrance to the Law. To the contrary, it provides an endless opportunity for improving or at least changing one's theories—a way to remove the threat of a final theory that would end physics in crowning its efforts. In Bohm, that is to say, we return to the figure of the intellectual tinkerer with which we began—a figure in whom the earnest desire to complete his task runs up against the equally powerful urge to extend its pleasures indefinitely.

CHAPTER 25

Afterword

Leibniz in My Latte

Michael Gottlieb Hansch tells the following story about Leibniz: "I remember that once, when Leibniz and I met in Leipzig and were drinking caffe latte, a beverage which he greatly savored, he said that in the cup from which he was drinking there might be, for all we know, monads that in future time would become human souls."[1] It is risky to make too much of a merely reported remark, much less to mine a casual witticism for deep significance. But the whole point of the joke (if Leibniz did indeed make it and if it is indeed a joke) is to invest a quotidian situation with philosophical significance. Leibniz's cup of latte brims with metaphysics as well as monads.

Those monads, by the way, are in a situation not very different from that of the rest of us. The Leibnizian universe is a plenum filled with fluid—thus a kind of immense caffe latte in which we are all suspended. Moreover, given Leibniz's apparent assumption that there exist immense creatures too large for us to perceive, how do we know that we are not ourselves floating in a gigantic cup of latte held by one of them? If the world is fish in ponds in fish in ponds, why not monads in lattes in monads in lattes? But the joke also assumes that Leibniz will shortly imbibe the monads with his beverage, at which point these future human souls will be inside him, either incorporated as dominated monads else or only visiting, shortly to be excreted with his urine. The fantasy of imbibing living human beings is not original with Leibniz. In Rabelais's *Gargantua*, the eponymous giant unknowingly swallows six pilgrims while eating salad; they survive by clinging to his molars. Meanwhile, in *Pantagruel*, the fictional narrator/author Alcofribas Nasier (an anagram of François Rabelais) voluntarily enters Pantagruel's mouth, where he discovers another world with its own sun and moon, and a peasant growing cabbages.

Leibniz entertains the possibility that his latte contains monads that will one day become human souls. But then, why not also monads that *once were* human souls—or rather, still are, though their associated bodies are no longer human? Monads are immortal—created at the commencement of the world and accompanied from the start by a microscopic, "divinely preformed" body, they await their turn to assume human form.[2] And after death, they revert to a microscopic state until they are reconstituted, presumably at the end of secular time. In the meantime, they too might end up in someone's latte.

Monads are immortal because they do not contain parts, and it is therefore impossible for them to suffer dissolution.[3] This is true for animal souls as well as human ones.[4] But in the case of humans there is an additional, theological motive at work: they are to be assigned their appropriate reward or punishment at the Day of Judgment. And for this, it is necessary not only that they be conscious but that they remember what they did in the human world.[5] As we have already seen, Leibniz describes the processes of birth, life, and death as a passing between greater and lesser theaters or theatrical stages.[6] Among other things, this metaphor suggests a degree of continuity underlying what appear to be dramatic changes. But Leibniz also provides a more precise, biological account. Preformed bodies are folded up; conception initiates a process of unfolding by which they move from the microscopic to the macroscopic world. At death they are again enfolded into a fragment of the dying body and so escape its dissolution.[7]

The different "stages" a monad comes to occupy entail different levels of awareness as well as scale. Human spermatozoa, for instance, are monads, but they do not incorporate the powers of human reason until conception.[8] And a mirror reversal of this process appears to occur at death. Sometimes Leibniz describes the postmortem state of the monad as "insensibility," in which the monad is plunged into confused perceptions, which Leibniz compares to sleep or a fainting spell.[9] At other times, however, he describes the effects of death as being less drastic: "generation being apparently only a change consisting in growth, death will only be a change of diminution, making the animal turn back into the nook of a world of little creatures, where it has more limited perceptions, until the order perhaps summons it to resume the stage."[10] Here it is unclear whether the monad's perceptions are "more limited" (*plus bornées*) because they are of lower quality—i.e., more confused—or simply because they are confined to the smaller "nook" (*l'enfoncement*) of its microscopic world. The very fact that Leibniz speaks here of a "world" (*monde*) returns us to some of the considerations

I explored in module 11 regarding dominated monads.[11] Here, as often, Leibniz's positions are not always consistent. The language of theater and of worlds seems to contradict comparisons to sleep or fainting. Above all, the simile in which Leibniz compares death to Harlequin's doffing of one costume to reveal another beneath it (see module 04) reduces dying to a kind of performance on the part of a trickster-figure who cannot ever really be subdued. Here, death is not something passively and inevitably suffered but rather the occasion for a display of elusiveness on the part of the cunning monad, which jettisons its dying body in the same way that the pilot ejects himself from the cockpit of a stricken fighter jet. Just as the movement of the monad's perceptions finds no end or final term, so the monadic body is perpetually in motion, sometimes under its own power and at other times adrift upon the currents of the world.

Leibniz on the life of the posthumous monad recalls Hamlet's speculations on the afterlife of monarchs. The flesh of a dead and buried king, Hamlet surmises, may be eaten by a worm, that worm may be swallowed by a fish, and that fish may be caught and cooked by a man, and hence "a king may go a progress through the guts of a beggar." Similarly, Leibniz says of the monad that escapes from a sacrificed ram that "this little animal that once was a ram might be absorbed by another one, and even make up part of its flesh or its blood, but it will always be another animal."[12] Hamlet, of course, is depicting dead flesh, while for Leibniz, the posthumous monad is both mind and body; and Hamlet's imaginations revel in the afterlife as a space for the *degrading* of the king's body, whereas Leibniz maintains the monad's inherent dignity.

I have argued elsewhere that Hamlet's meditations on the ceaseless transformations attendant upon death are, among other things, a way for Shakespeare to reflect on the literary afterlife of *Hamlet* itself.[13] Likewise, Leibniz's speculations on the posthumous monad may be, among other things, a way of anticipating his own philosophical afterlife. Maybe the defunct, microscopic Leibniz eventually drifted into Alfred North Whitehead's latte (or tea), took up temporary residence in the English philosopher's brain after being imbibed, and, like one of Gabriel Tarde's monarchic monads, exerted an outsized force on Whitehead's thinking. Stranger things have happened (though not much stranger, to be sure).

In a slightly more serious vein, I would suggest that Leibniz's thoughts on the afterlife of the monad reflect his belief that the process of thinking and perceiving is a perpetual-motion machine, one in which the drive to generate ever-new insights and ideas cannot be interrupted even by death itself. One way to imagine perpetuating one's thoughts is to assemble them into an imposing, impregnable system that, like a stone castle, will endure through the ages. Another way is to render those thoughts unfinalizable and elusive—to persist, not as an edifice but as an unending flow, or as Harlequin stripping off one outfit after another. Leibniz, the philosophical tinkerer, may nurture both of those dreams simultaneously: a castle that leaks, or a pond that partly congeals into a school of fish. If you can't outrun Death, at least you can confuse him.

Leibniz's caffe latte remark suggests, moreover, that these perpetual-motion machines are flowing into and out of one another's bodies, and that you can never predict in advance where they are to be found or where their journeys will take them, or even what the effects of being infiltrated by other monads will be. I am reading this situation as an allegory of Leibniz's philosophical afterlife, but one can also take it as a figure for the transdisciplinary flows that drive Leibnizian thinking and the mechanisms of which I have been exploring in this book. These flows are likewise unpredictable. You can never know in advance where a productive analogy will come from, just as you cannot know what monads are floating in your latte. Things infiltrate other things, often by making themselves tiny, so that they can enter unnoticed.

Advocates for a contemporary or living Spinoza often employ a rhetoric of titanism to describe him, making him not only the theorist but also the conduit and even the fount of immense and irrepressible political energies. Leibniz was always more interested in the microscopic or even the infinitesimal than he was in the immense.[14] It is fitting, then, that he imagines the afterlife as a process of nanoization. Fitting too that that afterlife is not so much the evasion as the incorporation of a posthumous state. A microscopic Leibniz (doubtless still sporting a tiny version of his ubiquitous peruke) drifts off into the world and settles into some obscure niche where he continues his monadic existence, generating perception after startling perception endlessly, perhaps shared with an audience assembled around a smaller but for all that no less exquisitely wrought stage.

Acknowledgments

As I've grown older and lost all sense of shame, I've gotten into the habit of emailing scholars I don't know personally and peppering them with questions about matters of interest to me. In a book such as this one, which extends well beyond the bounds of my own expertise, this annoying habit of mine has proven extremely fruitful—for me if not for my selected victims. Everyone on the following list responded graciously to my unexpected inquiries. Some are colleagues from other department at NYU; others are distinguished Leibniz scholars or specialists in early modern philosophy from around the globe; others still are art historians, computer scientists, mathematicians, or physicists. I thank Maria Rosa Antognazza, Richard Cole, Ernest Davis, Vincenzo De Risi, Don Garrett, Mogens Laerke, Louise Rice, Dennis Sepper, Dennis Shasha, Brian Swingle, and Tzuchien Tho. Helpful friends and colleagues I did already know include Sharon Cameron, who alerted me to Wallace Stevens's brief but fascinating remarks on Leibniz; David Hoover, who gave some initial, orienting suggestions regarding cognitive linguistics; and Christopher Wood, who cleared up some obscure details in the image used as illustration 2.2 in this book.

Several friends and colleagues (and one spouse) read chunks of this book manuscript, and in some cases the whole thing, and offered encouragement and/or improving suggestions. I thank Teddy Jefferson, Wendy Lee, Ben Parris, Joanna Picciotto, Steve Shaviro, Clifford Siskin, Alok Srivastava, and Connie You. The anonymous readers for Columbia University Press made valid, helpful criticisms for which I am grateful. Co-teaching a graduate English seminar on Spinoza and Leibniz with Wendy Lee forced me to up my Spinoza game considerably, which had indirect but salutary effects on this book.

I thank Wendy Lochner, my editor at Columbia University Press, for her instant and unwavering interest and faith in this project. Ben Kolstad of KnowledgeWorks Global Ltd. has proven indefatigably helpful, and the graphics people at CUP designed what I personally consider to be a pretty kickass cover.

The philosopher Justin E. H. Smith deserves a paragraph of his own. He is one of those people I emailed out of the blue—in this case, in his capacity as a co-editor of Leibniz's debates with G. E. Stahl. I contacted him about a textual detail in the Latin sentence that forms the basis of module 3 of this book. After some collegial back and forth I sent him a draft of that brief module in case it might interest him. And he responded, quite astoundingly, by asking me to send him the entire book manuscript, which I gladly did. He read it and we then had two Zoom calls of over two hours each in which he offered probing, detailed questions, invaluable bibliographical references, and numerous suggestions. This book has benefited in ways both large and small from his unexampled intellectual generosity and deep expertise. Who on God's green earth volunteers, unasked, to read an entire book written by a complete stranger—from a different intellectual discipline, mind you—and then becomes, in effect, an informal intellectual mentor for the project? Not me, that's for sure. But Justin Smith does. It's a humbling experience, but also an inspiring one, to encounter someone who is clearly a better person than you are.

Notes

ABBREVIATIONS

A Leibniz, G. W. *Sämtliche Schriften und Briefe*. Akademie der Wissenschaften zu Berlin, 1923ff. Cited by series, volume, and page.

AC Maturana, Humberto W. and Varela, Francisco J. *Autopoiesis and Cognition: The Realization of the Living*. Boston: D. Reidel, 1980.

AI Whitehead, Alfred North. *Adventures in Ideas*. New York: Macmillan, 1933.

CN Whitehead, Alfred North. *The Concept of Nature: The Tarner Lectures Delivered in Trinity College*. Canton, OH: Pinnacle Press, 2017.

CP Leibniz, G. W. *Confessio Philosophi: Papers Concerning the Problem of Evil, 1671–1678*. New Haven, CT: Yale University Press, 2005.

DSR Leibniz, G. W. *De Summa Rerum: Metaphysical Papers, 1675–1676*. Translated and edited by G. H. R. Parkinson. New Haven, CT: Yale University Press, 1992.

EDB Bohm, David. *The Essential David Bohm*. Edited by Lee Nichol. New York: Routledge, 2003.

FC Hofstadter, Douglas, and the Fluid Analogies Research Group. *Fluid Concepts and Creative Analogies: Computer Models of the Fundamental Mechanisms of Thought*. New York: Basic, 1995.

G Leibniz, G. W. *Die Philosophischen Schriften von Gottfried Wilhelm Leibniz*. 7 vols. Edited by C. I. Gerhardt. Berlin: Weidmann, 1875–1890.

GEB Hofstadter, Douglas R. *Gödel, Escher, Bach: An Eternal Golden Braid*. New York: Basic, 1979.

LA Leibniz, G. W. *The Leibniz-Arnauld Correspondence*. Translated and edited by Stephen Voss. New Haven, CT: Yale University Press, 2016.

LC Leibniz, G. W. *The Labyrinth of the Continuum: Writings on the Continuum Problem, 1672–1686*. Translated and edited by Richard T. W. Arthur. New Haven, CT: Yale University Press, 2001.

LCC Leibniz, G. W., and Samuel Clarke. *Correspondence*. Edited by Roger Ariew. Indianapolis, IN: Hackett, 2000.

LDB Leibniz, G. W. *The Leibniz-Des Bosses Correspondence*. Translated and edited by Brandon C. Look and Donald Rutherford. New Haven, CT: Yale University Press, 2007.

LDV   Leibniz, G. W. *The Leibniz-De Volder Correspondence*. Translated and edited by Paul Lodge. New Haven, CT: Yale University Press, 2013.

LP   Leibniz, G. W. *Logical Papers*. Translated and edited by G. H. R. Parkinson. Oxford: Clarendon Press, 1966.

LSC   Leibniz, G. W. *The Leibniz-Stahl Controversy*. Translated and edited by François Duchesneau and Justin E. H. Smith. New Haven, CT: Yale University Press, 2016.

LTS   Leibniz, G. W. *Leibniz and the Two Sophies: The Philosophical Correspondence*. Edited by Lloyd Strickland. Toronto: Iter, Inc. and Centre for Reformation and Renaissance Studies, 2011.

MT   Whitehead, Alfred North. *Modes of Thought*. New York: Free Press, 1938.

NE   Leibniz, G. W. *New Essays on Human Understanding*. Translated and edited by Peter Remnant and Jonathan Bennett. Cambridge: Cambridge University Press, 1996.

NS   Leibniz, G. W. *Leibniz's 'New System' and Associated Contemporary Texts*. Translated and edited by R. S. Woolhouse and Richard Francks. Oxford: Oxford University Press, 1987.

PE   Leibniz, G. W. *Philosophical Essays*. Translated by Roger Ariew. Edited by Daniel Garber. Indianapolis, IN: Hackett, 1989.

PPL   Leibniz, G. W. *Philosophical Papers and Letters*, 2nd ed. Translated and edited by Leroy E. Loemker. Dordrecht: Reidel, 1969.

PR   Whitehead, Alfred North. *Process and Reality*, Corrected ed. Edited by David Ray Griffin and Donald W. Sherburne. New York: Free Press, 1978.

PT   Leibniz, G. W. *Philosophical Texts*. Translated and edited by R. S. Woolhouse and Richard Francks. Oxford: Oxford University Press, 1998.

PW   Leibniz, G. W. *Political Writings*, 2nd ed. Edited by Patrick Riley. Cambridge: Cambridge University Press, 1988.

SMW   Whitehead, Alfred North. *Science and the Modern World*. New York: Free Press, 1925.

SOC   Bohm, David and Peat, F. David. *Science, Order, and Creativity: A Dramatic New Look at the Creative Roots of Science and Life*. New York: Bantam, 1987.

T   Leibniz, G. W. *Theodicy*. Translated by E. M. Huggard. Chicago: Open Court, 1990.

WIO   Bohm, David. *Wholeness and the Implicate Order*. New York: Routledge & Kegan Paul, 1980.

EPIGRAPH

The quote from Martin Heidegger comes from *The Principle of Reason*, trans. Reginald Lilly (Indianapolis: University of Indiana Press, 1991), p. 33; the quote from Alfred North Whitehead appears in SMW, p. 7.

PREFACE: LEIBNIZ AMONG THE DISCIPLINES

1. It is true that logicians and computer scientists, including researchers in artificial intelligence, revere Leibniz as a founding figure. But they have no reason to return to his work at this point, whereas Spinoza remains an active resource for thinking.

2. See, e.g., Warren Montag and Ted Stoltze, eds., *The New Spinoza* (Minneapolis: University of Minnesota Press, 1997); and Dimitris Vardoulakis, ed., *Spinoza Now* (Minneapolis: University of Minnesota Press, 2011). See also Antonio Negri, *Spinoza for our Time: Politics and Postmodernity* (New York: Columbia University Press, 2013).

3. Bertrand Russell, *A Critical Exposition of the Philosophy of Leibniz* (London: George Allen & Unwin, 1900); Louis Couturat, *La logique de Leibniz* (Paris: Alcan, 1901).

4. It might here be objected that Spinoza studies, no less than those on Leibniz, have paid considerable attention to the logical structures of his work. My reply is that one key does not fit all locks.

5. See, e.g., Sam Rose, "The Fear of Aesthetics in Art and Literary Theory," *New Literary History* 48 (2017): 223–44.

6. On aesthetics in computer science, see Vikram Chandra, *Geek Sublime: The Beauty of Code, the Code of Beauty* (Minneapolis, MN: Greywolf Press, 2014); and Paul A. Fishwick, ed., *Aesthetic Computing* (Cambridge, MA: MIT Press, 2008).

7. Sabine Hossenfelder, *Lost in Math: How Beauty Leads Physics Astray* (New York: Basic Books, 2018); Ernest Peter Fischer, *Beauty and the Beast: The Aesthetic Moment in Science*, trans. Elizabeth Oehikers (New York: Plenum Trade, 1999); Michael Strevens, *The Knowledge Machine: How Irrationality Created Modern Science* (New York: Liveright, 2020), esp. chap. 10, "The War Against Beauty," pp. 209–38. In *A Beautiful Question: Finding Nature's Deep Design* (New York: Penguin, 2016), the physicist Frank Wilczek makes the very Leibnizian argument that the world is beautiful—indeed, a work of art—because it embodies the most elegant formulations of contemporary physics.

8. For a variety of historical reasons, a systemic treatise of this type and on this subject would not have been a realistic possibility during Leibniz's career. The aesthetic was at an early stage of conceptualization (indeed, the word itself did not yet exist) and would not yet have been considered appropriate subject matter for a treatise—a form that itself was not quite yet the predominant genre for presenting systemic knowledge it would soon become. On the latter point, see Clifford Siskin, *System: The Shaping of Modern Knowledge* (Cambridge, MA: MIT Press, 2016), esp. pp. 81–85 and 92–94. By the mid-eighteenth century, Baumgarten, Herder, and then Kant made the philosophical treatise into the standard form for treating aesthetic theory. The result is that now, through a kind of retroactive historical misprision, Leibniz's not having produced such a treatise can give the false impression that he was not a serious aesthetic thinker.

9. Steve Fuller, "Deviant Interdisciplinarity," in *The Oxford Handbook of Interdisciplinarity*, ed. Robert Frodeman (Oxford: Oxford University Press, 2010), pp. 50–64; Steve Fuller, "Deviant Interdisciplinarity as Philosophical Practice: Prolegomena to Deep Intellectual History," *Synthese* 190 (2013): 1899–1916. I recognize that Fuller is a polarizing figure owing to his very public advocacy of intelligent design as a defensible philosophical position that deserves to be taught in schools. His depiction/exaltation of the deviant interdisciplinarian is at least partly an extended act of intellectual self-portraiture. Nevertheless, I find the concept a useful and compelling one that can be treated in isolation from Fuller's more controversial stances.

10. Fuller, "Deviant Interdisciplinarity as Philosophical Practice," p. 1900.

11. Fuller, "Deviant Interdisciplinarity as Philosophical Practice," p. 1901.

12. Fuller, "Deviant Interdisciplinarity," pp. 52, 50.

13. Fuller, "Deviant Interdisciplinarity as Philosophical Practice," p. 1902; Fuller, "Deviant Interdisciplinarity," p. 50.

14. I feel a least partially justified in doing so because the uses of the term "transdisciplinary" grant it no very clear or consistent meaning. It is more current in the German

and French intellectual worlds, where it is sometimes associated with the cybernetic and structuralist movements. In the Anglophone world it sometimes—but not always—denotes a brand of interdisciplinary work that has some degree of public (i.e., nonacademic) orientation or application. For the origin and semantics of the term, see pp. 8–10 of Andrew Barry and Georgina Born, "Interdisciplinarity: Reconfigurations of the Natural and Social Sciences," in *Interdisciplinarity: Reconfigurations of the Natural and Social Sciences*, ed. Andrew Barry and Georgina Born (New York: Routledge, 2013), pp. 1–56. See also Michael H. G. Hoffman, Jan C. Schmidt, and Nancy J. Neressian, "Philosophy *of* and *as* Interdisciplinarity," *Synthese* 190 (2013): 1857–64, esp. p. 857; and Peter Osborne, "Problematizing Disciplinarity, Transdisciplinary Problematics," *Theory, Culture and Society* 32, no. 5–6 (2015): 3–35.

15. In the case of the interdisciplinary research group, the representatives of individual disciplines do the work of ensuring that their own disciplinary norms are not trampled upon. In the case of the individual interdisciplinary practitioner, this balance depends on a combination of intellectual scruples and the hope of receiving a serious hearing from readers outside of one's "home" discipline. Of course, these norms are often honored more in the breach than in the observance. I am constructing an ideal case here.

16. This is an analytic distinction; the realities of practice are more complicated.

17. See the discussion in Jonathan Kramnick, "Are We Being Interdisciplinary Yet?" in *Paper Minds: Literature and the Ecology of Consciousness* (Chicago: University of Chicago Press, 2018), pp. 17–53.

18. For a superb account, see Siskin, *System.*

19. See, e.g., G. E. R. Lloyd, *Disciplines in the Making: Cross-Cultural Perspectives on Elites, Learning, and Innovation* (Oxford: Oxford University Press, 2009); Donald R. Kelly, "The Problem of Knowledge and the Concept of Discipline," in *History and the Disciplines: The Reclassification of Knowledge in Early Modern Europe* (Rochester, NY: University of Rochester Press, 1997), pp. 13–28; and Simon Schaffer, "How Disciplines Look," in *Interdisciplinarity: Reconfigurations of the Natural and Social Sciences*, ed. Andrew Barry and Georgina Born (New York: Routledge, 2013), pp. 57–81. Schaffer cites Robert Boyle using "discipline" in the modern sense in the mid-seventeenth century (p. 60).

20. See, e.g., Steven Shapin, "Hyperprofessionalism and the Crisis of Readership in the History of Science," *Isis* 96, no. 2 (June 2005): 238–43. Quotations from pp. 239, 238.

21. Shapin, "Hyperprofessionalism," p. 239.

22. Jerry A. Jacobs, *In Defense of Disciplines: Interdisciplinarity and Specialization in the Research University* (Chicago: University of Chicago Press, 2013), p. 127.

23. Fuller, "Deviant Interdisciplinarity as Philosophical Practice," p. 1901.

24. Compare the difference between end-directed forms of knowledge such as *techne* and *phronesis* in Aristotle and the endlessness of *sophia.*

1. LEIBNIZ IN MOTION

1. A 1.2: 719.

2. On Leibniz and early Enlightenment aesthetic theory, see Frederick C. Beiser, *Diotima's Children: German Aesthetic Rationalism from Leibniz to Lessing* (Oxford: Oxford University

Press, 2009); Stephanie Buchenau, *The Founding of Aesthetics in the German Enlightenment: The Art of Invention and the Invention of Art* (Cambridge: Cambridge University Press, 2013); Christoph Menke, *Force: A Fundamental Concept of Aesthetic Anthropology*, trans. Gerrit Jackson (New York: Fordham University Press, 2013); Jeffrey Barnouw, "The Beginning of 'Aesthetics' and the Leibnizian Conception of Sensation," in *Eighteenth-Century Aesthetics and the Reconstruction of Art*, ed. Paul Mattick (Cambridge: Cambridge University Press, 1993), pp. 52–95; and Jeffrey Barnouw, "The Cognitive Value of Confusion and Obscurity in the German Enlightenment: Leibniz, Baumgarten, and Herder," *Studies in Eighteenth-Century Culture* 24 (1995): 29–50.

3. And thereby I distinguish my project from Andrea Gadberry's admirable study on Descartes, *Cartesian Poetics: The Art of Thinking* (Chicago: University of Chicago Press, 2020). Gadberry and I both apply the techniques of literary-critical close reading to early modern philosophy, however, and some of our thematic concerns therefore overlap as well.

4. Compare the theoretical physicist David Bohm's essay "Physics and Perception": "Scientific investigation is basically a mode of extending our *perception* of the world, and not mainly a mode of obtaining *knowledge* about it. That is to say, while science does involve a search for knowledge, the essential role of this knowledge is that it is an adjunct to an extended perceptual process." EDB, p. 66.

5. See Lynn Gamwell, *Mathematics + Art: A Cultural History* (Princeton, NJ: Princeton University Press, 2016).

6. See, e.g., George L. Hersey, *Architecture and Geometry in the Age of the Baroque* (Chicago: University of Chicago Press, 2000).

7. Gottfried Wilhelm von Leibniz, *Opera Omnia*, ed. Ludovic Dutens (Geneva, 1765), 3: p. 437, trans Lloyd Strickland, 2018, http://www.leibniz-translations.com/goldbach1712 .htm.

8. Quoted in Maria Rosa Antognazza, *Leibniz: An Intellectual Biography* (Cambridge: Cambridge University Press, 2009), p. 547.

9. Friedrich Nietzsche, *The Birth of Tragedy and The Case of Wagner*, trans. Walter Kaufmann (New York: Vintage, 1967), p. 22.

10. Leibniz's metaphysical dictum that "It is everywhere as here" is quoted from Anne Maudit Nolant de Fatouville's comedy, *Arlequin, Empereur dans la lune*, and his concept of the dominant monad may well owe something to Cyrano de Bergerac's *Histoire Comique des États et Empires du Soleil*. See Justin E. H. Smith, "Leibniz's Harlequinade: Nature, Infinity, and the Limits of Mathematization," in *Reassessing the Mathematization of Natural Philosophy in the Seventeenth Century*, ed. Geoffrey Gorham, Benjamin Hill, Edward Slowik, and C. Kenneth Waters (Minneapolis: University of Minnesota Press, 2016), pp. 250–73; and Raphaële Andraut, "Leibniz, Cyrano, et le meilleur des corps possibles," *Libertinage et philosophie à l'époque classique*, no. 16 (Paris: Classiques Garnier, 2019), pp. 167–88. See also module 11 of this volume.

11. Martin Heidegger, *The Principle of Reason*, trans. Reginald Lily (Indianapolis: University of Indiana Press, 1991), p. 44.

12. I say *relative* stasis, since the notion that Leibniz's system evolves over time has become a generally accepted premise at least since the publication of Daniel Garber's landmark study, *Leibniz: Body, Substance, Monad* (Oxford: Oxford University Press, 2009). After

Garber it is common to divide Leibniz's system into three chronological stages. I hope to accelerate Garber's notion of a system in slow evolution.

13.   Denis Diderot, *Oeuvres Complètes de Diderot* (Paris: Garnier, 1875–1877), volume 15, p. 473.

14.   Wallace Stevens, *Opus Posthumous*, ed. Samuel French Morse (New York: Alfred A. Knopf, 1972), p. 185.

15.   Ludwik Fleck, *Genesis and Development of a Scientific Fact*, trans. Fred Bradley and Thaddeus J. Trenn (Chicago: University of Chicago Press, 1979), esp. pp. 125–45. See also Robert S. Cohen and Marx W. Wartofsky, eds., *Cognition and Fact: Materials on Ludwik Fleck* (Dordrecht: D. Reidel, 1986).

16.   Fleck's interest is in the ways that institutional, disciplinary, and other collectivities give rise to ways of seeing that not only color but in some sense constitute objects of knowledge. For Fleck, collective styles are at once productive and constraining. Despite his emphasis on the leading role of the thought collective, however, Fleck also acknowledges the power of major individual thinkers to redirect thought styles in significant ways, and also speaks of "the researcher's personal style of thinking." See Cohen and Wartofsky, *Cognition and Fact*, p. 51. That being said, I admit to rubbing against the grain of Fleck's approach by focusing attention on Leibniz's individual thought style and by foregrounding the aesthetic dimensions of style that for Fleck are certainly present but remain largely in the background.

17.   By contrast, in disciplines such as history or biochemistry or political science, the operative aesthetic principles that render a given disciplinary performance satisfying to disciplinary colleagues may remain more implicit and obscure. They generally don't invoke recognizably aesthetic categories such as "beauty." But they nevertheless exist and are productive of pleasure when properly employed and of displeasure or incomprehension when inappropriately violated.

18.   Fleck will not infrequently use artworks, such as medieval paintings, to illustrate the differences in "thought styles" between historical eras.

19.   There are a few exceptions, however. See, for instance, Martin Lengwiler, "Between Charisma and Heuristics: Four Styles of Interdisciplinarity," *Science and Public Policy* 33, no. 6 (July 2006): 423–34. For Lengwiler, however, the term "thought style" pertains mainly to differences in the institutional organization of interdisciplinarity, and so his taxonomy of interdisciplinary "styles" resembles the list of "types" identified in the seminal article by Margaret A. Boden, "What Is Interdisciplinarity?," in *Interdisciplinarity and the Organization of Knowledge in Europe*, ed. R. Cunningham (Luxembourg: Office for Official Publications of the European Communities, 1999), pp. 13–24.

20.   See Karen S. Feldman, *Per Canales Troporum*: On Tropes and Performativity in Leibniz's Preface to Nizolius," *Journal of the History of Ideas* 65, no. 1 (2004): 39–51; Peter Fenves, *Arresting Language: From Leibniz to Benjamin* (Stanford, CA: Stanford University Press, 2001); and Mogens Laerke, "The Problem of *Alloglossia*: Leibniz on Spinoza's Innovative Use of Philosophical Language," *British Journal for the History of Philosophy* 17, no. 5 (2009): 939–53. Feldman and Fenves, in particular, move on from that starting point to acknowledge the rhetorical nature of Leibniz's prose.

21.   For a brilliant, interdisciplinary account of system in the seventeenth and eighteenth centuries to the present, including its role in the formation of modern disciplines, see

Clifford Siskin, *System: The Shaping of Modern Knowledge* (Cambridge, MA: MIT Press, 2016). Siskin does not discuss Leibniz, but his treatment of system as a *genre* of writing rather than merely an idea or ideal is pertinent to this discussion.

22.   For example, PT, p. 279; Frédéric de Buzon, "Double infinité chez Pascal et monade. Essai de reconstitution des deux états du texte," *Les Études Philosophiques* 4, no. 1 (2010): 554, cited in Ohad Nachtomy, *Living Mirrors: Infinity, Unity, and Life in Leibniz's Philosophy* (Oxford: Oxford University Press, 2019), p. 139.

23.   Michel Serres, *Le système de Leibniz et ses modéles mathématiques*, 2nd ed. (Paris: Presse Universitaires de France, 1982), pp. 7–8.

24.   Daniel Garber, "What Leibniz Really Said?," in *Kant and the Early Moderns*, ed. Daniel Garber and Béatrice Longuenesse (Princeton, NJ: Princeton University Press, 2008), pp. 64–78, esp. p. 78; Catherine Wilson, "The Illusory Nature of Leibniz's System," in *New Essays on the Rationalists*, ed. Rocco J. Gennaro and Charles Huenemann (Oxford: Oxford University Press, 1999), pp. 372–88.

25.   Theory mavens will recognize here the formula for fetishistic disavowal, "I know but still." "I know perfectly well that there's no maternal phallus, but still, here it is in the form of this shoe" or "I know perfectly well that there's no Leibnizian system, but still, in my commentary, I will proceed as if there is one."

An interesting middle position regarding Leibniz's writings is adopted by Glenn Hartz in *Leibniz's Final System: Monads, Matter and Animals* (New York: Routledge, 2007). As the book's title suggests, Hartz maintains that what Leibniz produces is indeed a system. Yet he maintains that within this system, Leibniz's idealist and realist accounts of bodies are irreconcilable, and that therefore a "theory-pluralism" is required in approaching Leibniz's writings. I shall have more to say about Hartz's book in module 20 of this one.

26.   Cited in John Whipple, "Leibniz and the Art of Exoteric Writing," *Philosopher's Imprint* 15, no. 35 (December 2015): 1–24, p. 6.

27.   Deleuze's Leibniz is a philosopher *of* variation, but Deleuze does not address or even recognize variation within Leibniz's writings themselves or the evolution of Leibniz's thinking over time. Deleuze's Leibniz is therefore, ironically, more systematic a philosopher than any derived from Anglophone scholarly traditions.

28.   PT, p. 273.

29.   T, p. 364.

30.   See Christian Leduc, "The Epistemological Functions of Symbolization in Leibniz's Universal Characteristic," *Foundations of Science* 19 (2014): 53–68.

31.   PE, p. 204.

32.   Leibniz's primary meaning, of course, is that he can't reference past letters because he doesn't have a draft with him at the time. But I would argue that this does not exhaust the significance of his claim.

33.   LTS, pp. 77–78. See discussion in module 12 of this book.

34.   For an important early chapter in that story, see John Guillory, "Mercury's Words: The End of Rhetoric and the Beginning of Prose," *Representations* 138 (Spring 2017): 59–86.

35.   A full and adequate account of what constitutes the "theory effect" would take us well beyond the boundaries of the present study. Clearly, the distinction between continental

and Anglophone philosophy will not suffice (there are many exceptions on both sides), but I will sometimes employ it as a shorthand here. What constitutes something as "theory" involves a complex mixture of intellectual genealogy, disciplinary gatekeeping, and stylistic features.

36. This is a bit of a simplification. There are distinguished Leibnizians, such as Mogens Laerke, who display an interest in Deleuze. But they are in a distinct minority. See Laerke, "Five Figures of Folding: Deleuze on Leibniz's Monadological Metaphysics," *British Journal for the History of Philosophy* 32, no. 6 (2015): 1192–1213; and Laerke, "Four Things Deleuze Learned from Leibniz," in *Deleuze and* The Fold: *A Critical Reader*, ed. Sjoerd van Tuinen and Niamh McDonnell (London: Palgrave Macmillan, 2010), pp. 1–45. Several of the other essays in that latter volume are by authors housed in philosophy departments.

37. PT, p. 58.

2. TINKERING

1. Bruno Latour, *The Pasteurization of France*, trans. Alan Sheridan and John Law (Cambridge, MA: Harvard University Press, 1988), p. 198. In some respects my quoting of Latour's book is ironic, since he characterizes Leibniz there as a systematic rather than a tinkering philosopher: "There is no preestablished harmony, Leibniz notwithstanding, harmony is *post*established locally through tinkering" (p. 164).

2. See Andre Wakefield, "Leibniz and the Wind Machines," *Osiris* 25, no. 1 (2010): 171–88.

3. For the long and winding story of Leibniz's Guelf history, as well as the other unsuccessful projects mentioned here, see Maria Rosa Antognazza, *Leibniz: An Intellectual Biography* (Cambridge: Cambridge University Press, 2009).

4. For a fascinating account of Leibniz's long and sometimes contentious relations with Ollivier, see Matthew L. Jones, *Reckoning with Matter: Calculating Machines, Innovation, and Thinking About Thinking from Pascal to Babbage* (Chicago: University of Chicago Press, 2016), pp. 56–87.

5. The portmanteau term was apparently coined by Michael Oondatje. See Michele and Robert Root-Bernstein, "Thinkering," Creativity Post, February 18, 2012, https://www.creativitypost.com/article/thinkering. In its ordinary use, the term suggests ways that handling or playing with material objects can catalyze the thinking process, so my restricting it to thought alone is anomalous.

6. LTS, p. 415.

7. Claude Lévi-Strauss, *The Savage Mind* (Chicago: University of Chicago Press, 1966), pp. 16–32.

8. NE, p. 71.

9. See Anne Becco, "Aux sources de la monade: Paléographie et lexicographie leibniziennes," *Les Études Philosophiques* 3 (1975): 279–94; and Carolyn Merchant, "The Vitalism of Anne Conway: Its Impact on Leibniz's Concept of the Monad," *Journal of the History of Philosophy* 17, no. 3 (July 1979): 255–69.

10. John Whipple, "Leibniz and the Art of Exoteric Writing," *Philosopher's Imprint* 15, no. 35 (December 2015): 11.

11. Admittedly, this distinction is likely to seem anachronistic, since philosophy in the Cartesian tradition *includes* natural science and mathematics. Spinoza was at least somewhat conversant with both of these latter. But unlike Leibniz, he made no original contributions to them.

12. Robert Hooke, "Concerning Arithmetick Instruments," printed version in Thomas Birch, *The History of the Royal Society of London for Improving of Natural Knowledge, from Its First Rise* (London: A. Millar, 1757), 3: pp. 86–87. Cited from Jones, *Reckoning with Matter*, p. 65. I take my account of this episode from Jones.

13. LTS, p. 144.

14. See, for instance, Daniel C. Dennett's treatment of engineering, and of biology as engineering, in *Darwin's Dangerous Idea: Evolution and the Meanings of Life* (New York: Simon and Schuster, 1995). Jacques Derrida famously deconstructed Lévi-Strauss's distinction between the bricoleur and the engineer in his essay "Structure, Sign and Play in the Human Sciences," first delivered as a lecture at Johns Hopkins University in 1966 in Derrida's first address to an American audience. For Derrida, there is only bricolage, and so "the engineer is a myth produced by the *bricoleur*." Derrida, *Writing and Difference*, pp. 278–93. Quotation from p. 285.

15. The philosopher of science William Bechtel further muddies the matter by claiming that experimental scientists learn to use advanced forms of equipment such as electron microscopes and ultracentrifuges by "tinkering" with them, i.e., by "physically alter[ing] the instruments or vary[ing] the way they perform . . . [a] procedure." William Bechtel, "Scientific Evidence: Creating and Evaluating Scientific Instruments and Research Techniques," *PSA: Proceedings of the Biennial Meeting of the Philosophy of Science Association* 1990, no. 1 (1990): 559–72. Quotation from p. 560. I thank Alok Srivastava for this reference.

16. See Anne Hartle, *Michel de Montaigne: Accidental Philosopher* (Cambridge: Cambridge University Press, 2003), and esp. chap. 3, "The Essay as Philosophical Form."

17. Christia Mercer, "Prefacing the *Theodicy*," in *New Essays on Leibniz's* Theodicy, ed. Larry M. Jorgenson and Samuel Newlands (Oxford: Oxford University Press, 2014), pp. 13–42. See esp. pp. 20–21.

18. The title of the *New Essays* might seem not to count, because Leibniz is echoing the title of John Locke's *Essay on Human Understanding*; moreover, Leibniz's work is in the form of a dialogue, not an essay as such. And then there is the complex question of what Locke meant by calling *his* work an "essay." Nonetheless, Leibniz's conversion of "essay" to the plural form is noteworthy in this context, as is what the Cambridge editors call the "rambling quality" of the *New Essays* (NE, p. xii).

19. See Mercer, "Prefacing the *Theodicy*," pp. 23 and 38. It is worth noting as well that Leibniz could, like Montaigne, engage in extensive self-revision, producing (for example) no fewer than six drafts of a single personal letter to Sophie, Electress of Hanover. LTS, p. 257.

20. The genre of the essay has a close, complicated, and evolving relation to that of the system. In the late seventeenth century, they were largely posited as antithetical, but that changed over time. See Clifford Siskin, *System: The Shaping of Modern Knowledge* (Cambridge, MA: MIT Press, 2016), esp. pp. 33–34.

21. Of course, even the most businesslike, stringently functional piece of writing will have a style—most likely a correspondingly businesslike and functional one. Style is, in this sense, inescapable. So it might be more correct to say that tinkering provides a space for *stylization*, or for a philosophical style that tends more conspicuously toward the literary.

3. HOW TO READ A LEIBNIZIAN SENTENCE

1. LSC, pp. 326, 327. English translation slightly modified.
2. A 6.4: 1137. In classical Latin, *modificatio* means "measurement." It begins to take on its modern meanings in postclassical times.
3. See Stuart Brown, "Monadology and the Reception of Bruno in the Young Leibniz," in *Giordano Bruno: Philosopher of the Renaissance*, ed. Hilary Gatti (Florence: Taylor and Francis, 2002), pp. 381–403.
4. Arielle Saiber, *Giordano Bruno and the Geometry of Language* (Farnham, UK: Ashgate, 2005), p. 54.
5. See the illuminating discussion of Cartesian optics in Branka Arsic, *The Passive Eye: Gaze and Subjectivity in Berkeley (Via Beckett)* (Stanford, CA: Stanford University Press, 2003), pp. 18–48. See also Dennis L, Sepper, "Figuring Things Out: Figurate Problem-Solving in the Early Descartes," in *Descartes' Natural Philosophy*, ed. Stephen Gaukroger, John Schuster, and John Sutton (London: Routledge, 2005), pp. 228–48.
6. And this is not the only time in the debate with Stahl that he does so. "And the modifications of a merely passive thing, namely, matter or primitive power, are like figures (*quemadmodum figurae*)" (LSC, p. 325).
7. See Robert McRae, *Leibniz: Perception, Apperception, and Thought* (Toronto: University of Toronto Press, 1976), p. 20 and references there.
8. "The Mind consists in a point," A 1.1: 114, quoted in LC, p. xxxv.
9. Note that Leibniz elsewhere employs the same simile yet avoids problems by not using the word "represent" with relation to the vertex. LTS, pp. 151, 386; PT, p. 259.
10. My sincere thanks to Vincenzo De Risi for helping me thrash this out.
11. PPL, p. 545.
12. Stanley Fish, *Self-Consuming Artifacts: The Experience of Seventeenth-Century Literature* (Berkeley: University of California Press, 1972).

4. METAPHORICAL CLUMPING

1. Exceptions include Peter Fenves, *Arresting Language: From Leibniz to Benjamin* (Stanford, CA: Stanford University Press, 2001), pp. 13–79; Karen S. Feldman, "*Per Canales Troporum*: On Tropes and Performativity in Leibniz's Preface to Nizolius," *Journal of the History of Ideas* 65, no. 1 (January 2004): 39–51; Cristina Marras, "The Role of Metaphor in Leibniz's Epistemology," in *Leibniz: What Kind of Rationalist?*, ed. Marcelo Dascal (Dordrecht: Springer, 2008), pp. 199–224; Marcelo Dascal, "Language and Money: A Simile and Its Meaning in 17th Century Philosophy of Language," *Studia Leibnitiana* 8, no. 2 (1976): 187–218; Christopher P. Noble, "On Analogies in Leibniz's Philosophy: Scientific Discovery

and the Case of the 'Spiritual Automaton,' " *Quaestiones Disputatae* 7, no. 2 (Spring 2017): 8–30; G. Mitchell Reyes, "The Rhetoric in Mathematics: Newton, Leibniz, the Calculus, and the Rhetorical Force of the Infinitesimal," *Quarterly Journal of Speech* 90, no. 2 (May 2004): 163–88.

The most extensive and definitive treatment of metaphor in Leibniz is Cristina Marras's excellent book, *Les Métaphores dans la Philosophie de Leibniz* (Limoges: Lambert Lucas, 2017). I unfortunately did not encounter Marras's study until late in the composition of my own. I am pleased that our accounts of Leibnizian metaphor converge on a number of points. I do not, however, share Marras's view that metaphor and analogy must be carefully distinguished. More broadly: Marras sees Leibnizian metaphor as doing important philosophical work that concepts alone cannot accomplish. But this work ultimately accords with and deepens that done by concepts. Metaphor does not, therefore, threaten the coherence of the Leibnizian system but, to the contrary, serves as a kind of epistemological mortar holding it together. My account, by contrast, emphasizes the sometimes unruly behavior of Leibniz's metaphors and their resulting capacity to complicate and even destabilize attempts to construct a system.

2. John Whipple, "Leibniz and the Art of Exoteric Writing," *Philosopher's Imprint* 15, no. 35 (December 2015): 1–24.

3. In the *Specimen Dynamicum*, surely one of his works that leans relatively toward the "esoteric" end of the scale, Leibniz states that he will benefit most from respondents who "can combine power of thought with elegance of style." PT, p. 154.

4. Donald Rutherford, "Philosophy and Language in Leibniz," in *The Cambridge Companion to Leibniz* (Cambridge: Cambridge University Press, 2006), pp. 224–269. Quotation from p. 253.

5. *Herders Sämmtliche Werke* (Berlin: Weidmann, 1877–1913), 33 vols., 8: p. 319; 16: p. 468; 8, p. 178; 23: p. 88. These and other relevant quotations are collected by Vanessa Albus in *Weltbild und Metapher: Untersuchungen zur Philosophie der 18 Jahrhundert* (Würtzburg: Königshausen und Neumann, 2001), p. 108.

6. Peter Firchow, trans. and ed., *Friedrich Schlegel's* Lucinde *and the Fragments* (Minneapolis: University of Minnesota Press, 1991), pp. 191–92.

7. On metaphor as class-inclusion assertion, see Sam Glucksberg, "How Metaphors Create Concepts—Quickly," in *The Cambridge Handbook of Metaphor and Thought*, ed. Raymond W. Gibbs, Jr. (Cambridge: Cambridge University Press, 2008), pp. 67–83, esp. pp. 68–69. On metaphor as experience, see, e.g., George Lakoff and Mark Johnson, *Philosophy in the Flesh: The Embodied Mind and Its Challenge to Western Thought* (New York: Basic Books, 1999); and Mark Johnson, "Philosophy's Debt to Metaphor," in *The Cambridge Handbook of Metaphor and Thought*, ed. Raymond W. Gibbs, Jr. (Cambridge: Cambridge University Press, 2008), pp. 39–52, esp. p. 46.

8. See, e.g., Douglas Hofstadter and Emmanuel Sanders, *Surfaces and Essences: Analogy as the Fuel and Fire of Thinking* (New York: Basic, 2013). It can reasonably be argued that, even granting an ultimate analogical basis, concepts do manage to achieve a high degree of consistency, durability, and autonomy, such that they can be subjected to logical treatment and otherwise handled without reference to their analogical substrate. In my view, however, Leibniz's philosophical practice aims to keep

the analogical nature of concepts in view and thus to maintain them in a relatively fluid state.

9.   Friedrich Nietzsche, "On Truth and Lying in an Extra-Moral Sense (1873), trans. in *Friedrich Nietzsche on Rhetoric and Language* (Oxford: Oxford University Press, 1989), pp. 246–257. Quotation from p. 250.

10.   NS, p. 16.

11.   LDV, p. 127.

12.   PT, p. 116.

13.   A 6.4: 1464, cited and translated in Daniel Garber, *Leibniz: Body, Substance, Monad* (Oxford: Oxford University Press, 2009), p. 66.

14.   For starters, while individual sheep are solids (more or less—see module 15), flocks of sheep are fluids. See Marine de Marcken and Raphael Sarfati, "Hydrodynamics of a Dense Flock of Sheep: Edge Motion and Long-Range Correlations," *arXiv* (February 21, 2020), https://doi.org/10.48550/arXiv.2002.09467. See also Avedis Tchamitchian, "Sheep Fluid Particles in Fast Motion," YouTube, July 8, 2021 [video], https://www.youtube.com/watch?v=OyvBdxE2dxI.

15.   LA, p. 207

16.   LTS, p. 147.

17.   LTS, p. 311.

18.   Tom Stoppard, *Rosencrantz and Guildenstern Are Dead* (New York: Grove, 1967), p. 126.

19.   PT, p. 261.

20.   PT. p. 57.

5. THE MATHEMATICS OF RESEMBLANCE

1.   NS, p. 53.

2.   T, p. 339.

3.   For an excellent discussion of the mathematics of conic sections and their role in Leibnizian metaphysics, see Valerie Debuiche, "La notion d'expression et ses origines mathématiques," *Studia Leibnitiana* 41, no. 1 (2009): 88–117.

4.   The Greek *analogia* can mean mathematical proportion, logical correspondence, and grammatical and conceptual resemblance. The term itself establishes movements among mathematics, logic, and language—establishes, that is to say, analogies among them. It names what it does.

5.   Vincenzo De Risi, *Geometry and Monadology* (Basel: Birkhäuser, 2007), p. 82.

6.   Richard C. Brown, *The Tangled Origins of the Leibnizian Calculus* (Singapore: World Scientific, 2012), p. 180. De Risi describes the *analysis situs* as "a discipline as esoteric as to be the science of just one man" (p. 2). Nevertheless, it anticipated certain elements of modern topology. Hence when the great French mathematician Henri Poincaré published a series of papers in 1895 founding the new mathematical discipline of algebraic topology, he dubbed this new kind of mathematics "analysis situs," with a nod to Leibniz.

7.   De Risi, *Geometry and Monadology*.

8.   PPL, p. 667.

9.   PPL, pp. 254–55.

10. And here I would like to tip my hat to the work of the philosopher, poet, and Leibniz scholar Emily Grosholz, whose writings explore related themes in great depth. See Emily Grosholz, *Great Circles: The Transits of Mathematics and Poetry* (Cham, Switzerland: Springer, 2018); and Emily Grosholz, "Leibniz on Mathematics and Representation: Knowledge Through the Integration of Irreducible Diversity," http://www.emilygrosholz .com/books/productiveambiguity/prodamb_ch8adraft.pdf (accessed November 17, 2022). The latter piece, in particular, raises issues relevant to this study.

6. COGNITIVE MAPPING AND BLENDED SPACES

1. David Chalmers, Robert French, and Douglas Hofstadter, "High-Level Perception, Representation and Analogy: A Critique of Artificial Intelligence Methodology" (1992), reprinted in Douglas Hofstadterand the Fluid Analogies Research Group, *Fluid Concepts and Creative Analogies: Computer Models of the Fundamental Mechanisms of Thought* (New York: Basic, 1995), pp. 169–94. Quotation from p. 187.
2. Gilles Fauconnier, *Mappings in Thought and Language* (Cambridge: Cambridge University Press, 1997), p. 18.
3. NE, p. 485.
4. Cristina Marras, "The Role of Metaphor in Leibniz's Epistemology," in *Leibniz: What Kind of Rationalist?*, ed. Marcelo Dascal (Dordrecht: Springer, 2008), pp. 199–224, likewise applies the categories of cognitive mapping and conceptual blends to Leibniz.
5. Edward C. Tolman, "Cognitive Maps in Rats and Men," *Psychological Review* 55, no. 4 (July 1948): 189–208.
6. See Fauconnier, *Mappings*; Gilles Fauconnier and Mark Turner, *The Way We Think: Conceptual Blending and the Mind's Hidden Complexities* (New York: Basic, 2002).
7. Fauconnier, *Mappings*, p. 1, n. 1.
8. Fauconnier, *Mappings*, p. 9.
9. Fauconnier, *Mappings*, p. 149. The workings of conceptual blends are explored at greater length in Fauconnier and Turner, *The Way We Think*.
10. See Fauconnier, *Mappings*, pp. 166–68 and references therein. See also Fauconnier and Turner, *The Way We Think*.
11. The matter is complicated (slightly) by the fact that Gilles Deleuze and Felix Guattari advance their own concept of "mapping" in *A Thousand Plateaus: Capitalism and Schizophrenia*, trans. Brian Massumi (Minneapolis: University of Minnesota Press, 1987), pp. 12–13, and contrast it with "tracing." While they do not use the term in the same way Fauconnier does, their conception is not incompatible with his. And many of Deleuze's valorized terms—folding, mapping, rhizome, nomadism, etc.—have at least a vague kinship with one another.
12. PPL, p.281.
13. PPL, p. 284.
14. Ludwik Fleck, *Genesis and Development of a Scientific Fact*, trans. Fred Bradley and Thaddeus J. Trenn (Chicago: University of Chicago Press, 1979).
15. See Michel Serres, *Le système de Leibniz et ses modèles mathématiques*, 2nd ed. (Paris: Presse Universitaires de France, 1982).

16.   NE, pp. 144–45.

17.   See Alessandro Becchi, "Leibniz, the Microscope, and the Concept of Preformation," *History and Philosophy of the Life Sciences* 34, no. 1 (2017): 3–23. Becchi claims that preformationism is where Leibniz got the concept of the fold in the first place, or at least that preformationism "entails" such a concept (p. 21). On preformationism and Leibniz, see also Justin E. H. Smith, *Divine Machines: Leibniz and the Sciences of Life* (Princeton, NJ: Princeton University Press, 2011), pp. 165–96.

7. CHEMICAL WIT

1.   *Friedrich Schlegel's* Lucinde *and the Fragments*, trans. and ed. Peter Firchow (Minneapolis: University of Minnesota Press, 1991), pp. 191–92. I was alerted to the connection among Leibniz, Schlegel, and chemical wit by the work of a fellow literary reader of Leibniz, Daniel Tiffany. See Tiffany, *Infidel Poetics: Riddles, Nightlife, Substance* (Chicago: University of Chicago Press, 2009), p. 102; and Tiffany, "Club Monad," *Romantic Circles*, https://romantic-circles.org/praxis/philcult/tiffany/tiffany.html (accessed November 19, 2022).

2.   Samuel Johnson, *The Lives of the English Poets*, vol. 1, ed. Roger Lonsdale (Oxford: Clarendon Press, 2006), p. 200.

3.   Firchow, *Friedrich Schlegel's* Lucinde, p. 221.

8. PERSPECTIVE

1.   See Javier Echeverria, "Recherches inconnus de Leibniz sur la géometrie perspective," *Leibniz et la Renaissance. Studia Leibnitiana* 23 (Supplement, 1983): 191–201; Javier Echeverria, "Leibniz, interprète de Desargues," in *Desargues et son temps*, ed. Jean Dhombres and Joël Sakarovitch (Paris: Blanchard, 1994), pp. 283–93; and Valérie Debuiche, "Leibniz's Manuscripts on Perspective," HAL archives-ouvertes, April 17, 2014, https//hal.archives-ouvertes.fr/hal-00984117.

2.   Erwin Panofsky, *Perspective as Symbolic Form*, trans. Christopher S. Wood (New York: Zone Books, 1991), p. 31. It is worth noting that during the baroque period, the unreliability and distorting properties of vision were becoming increasingly evident from a scientific perspective. To Galileo, for example, true vision could be achieved only by the mathematically perfect instrument of the telescope, not the fallible and distorting eye. See Ofer Gal and Raz Chen-Morris, *Baroque Science* (Chicago: University of Chicago Press, 2013), pp. 16, 53, 93–95. On the ability of scientific instruments (and method) to restore fallen vision to its lost, prelapsarian clarity, see Joanna Picciotto, *Labors of Innocence in Early Modern England* (Cambridge, MA: Harvard University Press, 2010).

3.   Panofsky, *Perspective*, p. 63.

4.   James Elkins, *The Poetics of Perspective* (Ithaca, NY: Cornell University Press, 1994).

5.   But see Laura E. Herrera Castillo, "Die Perspektiv als künstlerische Technik und metaphysisches Konzept in der Philosophie von G.W. Leibniz," *Studia Leibnitiana* 48 (2016): 223–44.

6.   Deleuze, *The Fold: Leibniz and the Baroque*, trans. Tom Conley (Minneapolis: University Of Minnesota Press, 1993), p. 20.

7.   NS, p. 56.

8.   LDB, pp. 241–43.

9.   LC, p. 61.

10. LA, p. 203.

11. NS, p. 110.

12. For a revealing study of the variety of animal sensoria, see Ed Yong, *An Immense World: How Animal Senses Reveal the Hidden World Around Us* (New York: Random House, 2022).

13. PT, p. 263. See also LA, p. 203, where the beauty of God's workmanship ensures that substances "don't get in one another's way."

14. PPL, p. 487.

15. For "the view from everywhere" (a play on Thomas Nagel's "view from nowhere"), see Michaelis Michael, "Cubism, Perspective, Belief," in *Philosophy in Mind: The Place of Philosophy in the Study of Mind*, ed. Michaelis Michael and John O'Leary-Hawthorne (Dordrecht: Springer, 1994), pp. 243–76. It is worth noting that Leibniz comes up in Michael's discussion.

16. LC, p. 229.

17. Michel Serres, *Le système de Leibniz et ses modèles mathématiques*, 2nd ed. (Paris: Presse Universitaires de France, 1982), p. 661.

18. NE, p. 294.

19. LDB, p. 233.

20. PE, p. 91.

21. Panofsky, *Perspective*, p. 27.

22. PT, p. 268.

23. NE, p. 135.

24. On painting and rhetoric, see Michael Baxandall, *Giotto and the Orators: Humanist Observers of Painting in Italy and the Discovery of Pictorial Composition, 1350–1450* (Oxford: Oxford University Press, 1971).

25. NE, p. 258.

26. NE, p. 404.

27. Elkins, *Poetics*, p. 141.

28. Elkins, *Poetics*, pp. 143–44.

9. EXPRESSION

1.   The principal treatment of expression in Leibniz is Vincenzo De Risi's magisterial study, *Geometry and Monadology: and Philosophy of Space* (Basel: Birkhäuser, 2007). Deleuze's *Expressionism in Philosophy: Spinoza*, trans. Martin Joughin (New York: Zone, 1992), argues that Leibniz and Spinoza are distinguished from each other principally by way of their divergent understandings of expression, even while the concept of expression unites them in an anti-Cartesian project.

2.   PPL I, p. 207.

3.   PPL I, p. 208.

4.   LA, p. 241.

5.   LDV, p. 267.

6. NS, p. 106.

7. Robert McRae, *Leibniz: Perception, Apperception, and Thought* (Toronto: University of Toronto Press, 1976), p. 20 (my emphasis).

8. LDB, p. 45.

9. G. W. Leibniz, *Philosophical Writings*, ed. G. H. R. Parkinson (London: Dent, 1973), pp. 176–77. Cited in J. A. Cover and John O'Leary-Hawthorne, *Substance and Individuation in Leibniz* (Cambridge: Cambridge University Press, 1999), p. 100.

10. LA, p. 115.

11. Michel Serres, *Le système de Leibniz et ses modèles mathématiques*, 2nd ed. (Paris: Presse Universitaires de France, 1982), p. 60.

12. LDB, p. 269.

13. PT, p. 275.

14. NE, p. 77.

15. Vincenzo De Risi, *Geometry and Monadology*, pp. 297–436. Leibniz's notion anticipates current speculation that spacetime may emerge from the bulk entanglement of particles. See. e.g., Brian Swingle, "Spacetime from Entanglement," *Annual Review of Condensed Matter Physics* 9 (2018): 345–58; ChunJun Cao, Sean M. Carroll, and Spyridon Michalakis, "Space from Hilbert Space: Recovering Geometry from Bulk Entanglement," (2016), arXiv:1606.08444; Mark Van Raamsdonk, "Building Up Spacetime with Quantum Entanglement" (2010), arXiv:1005.3035.

10. HOW TO BUILD A MONAD

1. Leibniz usually reserves the term "mind" for human beings. But monads are mental entities as opposed to bodily ones.

2. "I maintain that all the Souls, Entelechies or primitive forces, substantial forms, simple substances, or monads, whatever name one may apply to them, can neither spring up naturally nor perish." T, pp. 360–61. Cited (from another edition) in John Whipple, "The Structure of Leibnizian Simple Substances," *British Journal for the History of Philosophy* 18, no. 3 (2010): 393.

3. Strictly speaking, Leibniz says that monads *have* perceptions, not that they *are* perceptions. Later in this module, we will get to the question of what it is that is "having" perceptions. Here, though, we might note that in some circumstances, "has" is awfully close to "is." New York City *has* five boroughs, but in another sense it simply *is* those five boroughs.

4. There is some debate about whether Leibnizian perceptions are indeed instantaneous or whether they are of brief temporal duration. See the discussion in Richard T. W. Arthur, *Monads, Composition, and Force: Ariadnian Threads Through Leibniz's Labyrinth* (Oxford: Oxford University Press, 2018), pp. 269–89.

5. "Appetite is in truth nothing other than the tendency toward new perceptions." LSC, p. 327.

6. See Michel Serres, *Le système de Leibniz et ses modèles mathématiques*, 2nd ed. (Paris: Presses Universitaires de France, 1982), pp. 289–394.

7. PT, p. 60.

8. Obviously, a complete listing of Alexander's predicates would have to include more than life events: physical characteristics, psychological dispositions, habits, relations, etc.

9. At least in the case of human beings, haecceity rests on an infinite richness of determinations. But Leibniz also explores the case of what we might call "bare haecceity" in the case of two identical eggs, indistinguishable even to an angel, that are distinguished solely by the fact that one of them is this one and the other is that (CP, p. 103). On the role of Scotistic "bare, colorless haecceities" in Leibniz, see J. A. Cover and John O'Leary-Hawthorne, *Substance and Individuation in Leibniz* (Cambridge: Cambridge University Press, 1999), p. 278. Leibniz criticized the very notion of haecceity in his early *Disputatio Metaphysica de Principio Individui* (1663), and so it is interesting to see him revive the term later on. See Lawrence B. McCollough, *Leibniz on Individuals and Individuation: The Persistence of Premodern Ideas in Modern Philosophy* (Dordrecht: Kluwer, 1996), pp. 51–69.

10. This confusion of "has" and "is" takes us back to note 3 in this module.

11. "For God wills those things that he perceives to be the best and, likewise, the most harmonious; and he selects them, so to speak, from the infinite number of all the possibles. What, therefore, is the ultimate basis of the divine intellect? The harmony of things. And what is the ultimate basis of the harmony of things? Nothing. For example, no reason can be given for the fact that the ratio of 2 to 4 is that of 4 to 8, not even from the divine will. This depends on the essence itself, i.e., the idea of things." CP, p. 3. And again: "It is therefore the nature of things themselves which produces their sequence, prior to all decisions; God chooses only to actualize that sequence, the possibility of which he finds ready-made." NS, p. 188. One might well respond, of course, that something akin to this is at work in Spinoza.

12. Leibniz, PT, p. 58. Compare T, p. 277.

13. Compare a 1715 letter to Nicholas Remond: "But just as there are certain outstanding points in a geometric curve which are called summits, bend points, points of return, or some other thing, and as there are curves which contain an infinity of them, even so there must be conceived in the life of an animal or a person times of extraordinary change which do not fall without the general rule—as the distinctive points of a curve can be determined by its general nature or its equation." PPL, p. 658.

14. LDV, p. 289.

15. See, e.g., A 7.4: 241, 80; A 3.9: 275, 567.

16. Leibniz, A 6.3: 326, translated in Ohad Nachtomy, *Living Mirrors: Infinity, Unity, and Life in Leibniz's Philosophy* (Oxford: Oxford University Press, 2019), p. 30.

17. Upon reviewing the evidence, Whipple concludes that substance, primitive force, and the law of the series are identical for Leibniz. "The Structure of Leibnizian Simple Substances," pp. 390–95. Nachtomy admits that the way Leibniz conjoins primitive force and the law of the series is "not entirely clear" (p. 33).

18. A 2.1: 342–56. For a discussion, see Oscar M. Esquisabel and Federico Raffa Quintana, "Leibniz in Paris: A Discussion Concerning the Infinite Number of All Units," *Revista Portuegesa de Filosofia* 73 (2017): 1319–42.

19. See Samuel Levey, "Leibniz on Mathematics and the Actually Infinite Division of Matter," *Philosophical Review* 107, no. 1 (January 1998): 49–96, esp. 76–77.

20.   "I say 'No' to anyone who . . . imagine[s] that there is a substantial form in a piece of rock or in any other inorganic body. For vital principles belong only to organic bodies." PPL, p. 586.

21.   "All solids seem, if I might say in passing, to be informed with a mind of some kind" (LC, p. 47). Nachtomy states that Leibniz holds a "panorganic view that all beings are ultimately living beings" (Nachtomy, *Living Mirrors*, p. 140).

22.   NE, pp. 144–45 (II:11). Leibniz actually compares the *brain*, not the mind, to a vibrating string, but then insists that something analogous to this vibration occurs in the mind.

23.   PT, pp. 162–63.

24.   In case the reader hasn't already noticed, I am cheating in one respect because the harmonic series does not specify a temporal series or *succession* of actions on the part of a violin string. In this case, the terms of the harmonic series are deployed simultaneously and overlaid one on the other in an interference pattern. More on the relation between mathematical and temporal sequence in a bit.

25.   In an exception to Stahl, Leibniz declares that "the laws of souls are the laws of appetites" (LSC, p. 321). Unfortunately, it is not clear whether Leibniz is using the objective or subjective genitive here. Is he saying that there is a law that governs appetition (and thence the soul) or simply that appetition governs the soul? Other moments in the exchange with Stahl (pp. 301–3) extend the uncertainty about how Leibniz understands appetition by identifying it with appetite in the more usual sense.

26.   Game designers will rightly take umbrage at this formulation. My point is simply to say that computer games do not derive all their features from one master algorithm. Recent game design includes "systemic gaming" with internal entities able to detect and interact with one another, thereby producing events unscripted by the game designers and what is called "emergent gameplay." But this move toward spontaneity, while it makes for more interesting and lifelike games, moves us in the opposite direction from Leibniz, for whom not only every event in the game but every response in the gamer must be prescribed. That being said, the interconnectivity of entities in the world of the systemic game bears a suggestive resemblance to the mutual accommodation of entities in the Leibnizian world via compossibility. As does the proto-awareness of even nonliving entities within the game world. For a brief introduction to systemic gaming, see the YouTube video "The Rise of the Systemic Game," https://www.youtube.com/watch?v=SnpAAX9CkIc. I thank Cliff Siskin for this reference.

27.   One usually speaks of "playing" a video game, and the verb is useful in conveying a sense of active engagement, decision-making, etc., whereas "viewing" or "perception" suggests passivity. Life is a game we play, earnestly. But the term is misleading in this context insofar as it suggests that, while the game itself is programmed, we (the players) are spontaneous and free. In the Leibnizian universe, both the game of life and the playing of it is programmed, though in such a way as to produce the impression of freedom and spontaneity in the players. This module will engage the topic of Leibnizian freedom and determinism later on.

28.   See, for instance, David J. Chalmers, *The Conscious Mind: In Search of a Fundamental Theory* (Oxford: Oxford University Press, 1996), pp. 281–310; Russell Blackford and Damian Broderick, eds., *Intelligence Unbound: The Future of Uploaded and Artificial Minds*

(Chichester: Wiley, 2014). For the so-called Bostrom argument, see Nick Bostrom, "Are You Living in a Computer Simulation?," *Philosophical Quarterly* 53, no. 211 (2003): 243–55. Giulio Tononi's theory of mind as "integrated information" has been attracting some attention of late. See, e.g., Giulio Tononi, "Integrated Information Theory," *Scholarpedia* 10, no. 1 (2015): 4164. Terrence W. Deacon mounts a powerful critique of the computational theory of mind in *Incomplete Nature: How Mind Emerged from Matter* (New York: Norton, 2013), esp. pp. 494–504.

29. On a less facetious note, the impossibility of finding such an algorithm (because it would be infinite) brings up interesting issues related to randomness and algorithmic incompressibility.

30. For a sampling of views, see the essays in Hector Zenil, ed., *A Computable Universe: Understanding and Explaining Nature as Computation* (Singapore: World Scientific, ca. 2013). See also Hector Zenil, "The World Is Either Algorithmic or Mostly Random," *arXiv* (September 10, 2011): 1109.2237v1, https://arxiv.org/abs/1109.2237.

31. Stephen Wolfram, *A New Kind of Science* (Champaign, IL: Wolfram Media, 2019).

32. See, e.g., T, p. 277. See also passage cited in Benson Mates, *The Philosophy of Leibniz: Metaphysics and Language* (Oxford: Oxford University Press, 1986), p. 147.

33. Alfred North Whitehead, *Process and Reality, Corrected Edition*, ed. David Ray Griffin and Donald W. Sherburne (New York: Free Press, 1978), p. 344.

34. Nachtomy, *Living Mirrors*, pp. 174–75.

35. See Kyle Sereda, "Leibniz on the Concept, Ontology and Epistemology of Number" (unpublished PhD dissertation, University of California, San Diego, 2017), https://escholarship.org/uc/item/8fg3gopv. It is often assumed that because Leibniz regards numbers as relations, his nominalism declares them unreal. See, e.g., Mates, *The Philosophy of Leibniz*, p. 173. Sereda critiques this position on pages 70–77.

36. See, e.g., T, 3: 334, pp. 326–27.

37. For Quine, Putnam, and Gödel, and for a helpfully orienting survey of modern debates about mathematical realism, see chap. 1 of Penelope Maddy, *Realism in Mathematics* (Oxford: Oxford University Press, 1992), pp. 1–35. For a critical discussion of Badiou's *Being and Event*, see Ricardo L. Nirnberg and David Nirnberg, "Badiou's Number: A Critique of Mathematics as Ontology," *Critical Inquiry* 37 (Summer 2011): 583–614. As the authors claim, "for Badiou those set-theoretical objects, those multiplicities, are not only real, they are the *only* real, the only objects that *are*, the only basis for ontology" (p. 584).

38. See Gabriella Crocco, "Gödel, Leibniz and 'Russell's Mathematical Logic,'" in *New Essays on Leibniz Reception*, ed. Ralf Krömer and Yannick Chin-Dran (Basel: Springer, 2012), pp. 217–56, esp. pp. 250–54.

39. NS, p. 123.

40. PPL, p. 221. G VII, p. 184.

41. There is good reason to think that Leibniz identified active force with the law of the series. See Cover and O'Leary-Hawthorne, *Substance and Individuation in Leibniz*, pp. 222–23 and 227.

42. LDV, p. 135.

43. In some respects it might be more accurate to describe the algorithm as a formal cause.

44.   "While maintaining that souls, or monads, 'act according to the laws of final causes,' Leibniz is clear that appetitive forces are genuinely efficacious, in bringing about changes in a monad's states. His point, therefore, is not that monadic states do not *act* as efficient causes of subsequent states but that those actions cannot be *explained* by appeal to the laws of efficient causation that govern the actions of bodies. Rather, changes within the monad are produced by forces that act according to the 'laws of final causes.' " Donald Rutherford, "Leibniz on Spontaneity," in *Leibniz: Nature and Freedom*, ed. Donald Rutherford and J. A. Cover (Oxford: Oxford University Press, 2005), pp. 156–80. Quotation from p. 166.

45.   A 6.3: 326 and G 4: 518, both cited in Cover and O'Leary-Hawthorne, *Substance and Individuation in Leibniz*, p. 107. The authors conclude that the law of the series "is the substance, its own Haecceity" (p. 227).

46.   John Whipple makes a convincing case that, at the most fundamental ontological level, monads are the "law of the series" that sequences their perceptions. I have merely given a mathematical twist to this position. See Whipple, "The Structure of Leibnizian Substances," pp. 379–410. In this I am preceded by L. E. Loeb in *From Descartes to Hume* (Ithaca, NY: Cornell University Press, 1981), who suggests that the law of the series is analogous to a mathematical formula. A similar notion is explored by Ohad Nachtomy in *Possibility, Agency and Individuality in Leibniz's Metaphysics* (Dordrecht: Springer, 2007), pp. 70, 243–44. Whipple, in response, is careful to insist that "these are *only analogies*" (p. 386 n. 16). Obviously, the current module is devoted to imagining what it would take to see the law of the series as, quite literally, a mathematical series; and this book as a whole is devoted to overturning the "only" that all too often attaches to analogies in the minds of philosophers.

47.   More recently, the physicist Max Tegmark has claimed that mathematics does not just describe reality but constitutes it. See Max Tegmark, *Our Mathematical Universe: My Quest for the Ultimate Nature of Reality* (New York: Penguin, 2015).

48.   John Archibald Wheeler, "Information, Physics, Quantum: The Search for Links," PhilPapers, https://philpapers.org/archive/WHEIPQ.pdf (accessed November 21, 2022).

49.   Wheeler, "Information, Physics, Quantum," pp. 314, 315.

50.   See quotations in Lloyd Strickland, *Leibniz Reinterpreted* (London: Continuum, 2006), p. 24.

51.   See De Risi, *Geometry and Monadology: Leibniz's Analysis Situs and Philosophy of Space* (Basel: Birkhäuser, 2007), p. 271: "In most writings, Leibniz seems to account for the passing of time by a change in monadic properties, thus definitely assigning substances (or their modifications) to the sphere of diachronic succession. In other writings, especially his late ones, Leibniz seems on the contrary also to embrace a radical phenomenalism relative to time. Thus (by following the same reasoning he has applied to space) he seems to think that monads are outside any temporal order, while only their phenomenal manifestations occur in time." So, for instance, LDV, p. 267: "time is the order of inconsistent possibilities." "Leibniz is alive" and "Leibniz is dead" are inconsistent possibilities. Time allows both to be true by way of succession.

52.   He pursues this theme at greatest length in the *Theodicy* but also in a series of shorter essays.

53. Immanuel Kant, *Gesammelte Schriften*, ed. Akademie der Wissenschaften (Berlin: Georg Reimer [later De Gruyter], 1910–), 5: p. 97. Cited on p. 228 of Sean Greenberg, "Leibniz Against Molinism: Freedom, Indifference and the Nature of the Will," in *Leibniz: Nature and Freedom*, ed. Donald Rutherford and J. A. Cover (Oxford: Oxford University Press, 2005), pp. 217–33.

54. "In strict metaphysical language, we are perfectly independent of the influence of all other created things." NS, p. 19. And again: "According to me the soul and the body are directed (you say) by an effective antecedent cause to do everything that they do; where then is freedom? I reply that they are directed to do what they do only by their own natures—the soul freely and from choice, in accordance with real or apparent good or bad, and the body blindly, in accordance with the laws of motion." NS, p. 188.

55. GEB, p. 692. Admittedly the purport of this is more Spinozan than Leibnizian.

56. GEB, p. 713.

57. A 6.4: 1658; PPL, p. 407–9.

58. Despite the discovery in Leibniz's day of formulas for calculating such well-known irrational numbers as π or $\sqrt{2}$, the proportion of irrational numbers that are calculable is vanishingly small. In fact, if you were to point at random at the real number line, the chances of selecting a number that is calculable—i.e., algorithmically compressible—is zero. See Gregory Chaitin, *Metamath!: The Quest for Ω* (New York: Pantheon, 2005). Leibniz might well have imagined that all irrational numbers could be calculated, and this would comport with his view of the world as essentially ordered. But this is not the case. Chaitin, notably, invokes Leibniz repeatedly in the pages of *Metamath!*, and views him (mistakenly) as a philosopher of randomness on the basis of an unfortunate misreading of a passage in the *Discourse on Metaphysics*.

59. In the case of π, actually, a formula was eventually discovered that allows calculation of an *n*th term without having to calculate the intermediate terms. But this did not occur until centuries after Leibniz's death.

60. See also NS, pp. 83–84, where Leibniz compares the soul to a parabolic function, which, while remaining unchanged itself, produces different curvatures over different segments.

61. See PE, p. 28. See also "Leibniz's Theories of Contingency" in Robert Merrihew Adams, *Leibniz: Determinist, Theist, Idealist* (Oxford: Oxford University Press, 1994), pp. 9–52.

62. See Patrick Riley, *Leibniz' Universal Jurisprudence: Justice as the Charity of the Wise* (Cambridge, MA: Harvard University Press, 1995), pp. 13–21.

11. MONADIC POLITICS

1. Gottfried Wilhelm Leibniz, *Leibniz: Political Writings*, 2nd ed., ed. Patrick Riley (Cambridge: Cambridge University Press, 1988).

2. LA, p. 157.

3. Justin E. H. Smith explores relations between metaphysical and political domination in Leibniz and relates these to Leibniz's views on slavery in *Nature, Human Nature, and Human Difference* (Princeton, NJ: Princeton University Press, 2015), pp. 176–80.

4. Cyrano de Bergerac, *Other Worlds: The Comical History of the States and Empires of the Moon and Sun*, trans. Geoffrey Strachan (London: New English Library, 1976), pp. 153–57. For

critical discussion, see Justin E. H. Smith, "Leibniz's Harlequinade: Nature, Infinity, and the Limits of Mathematization," in *The Language of Nature: Reassessing the Mathematization of Natural Philosophy in the Seventeenth Century*, ed. Geoffrey Gorham et al. (Minneapolis: University of Minnesota Press, 2016), pp. 250–73. See also Raphaële Andraut, "Leibniz, Cyrano, et le meilleur des corps possibles," *Libertinage et philosophie à l'époque classique* 3 (2019): 167–88.

5.   Bertrand Russell, *A Critical Exposition of the Philosophy of* Leibniz, 2nd ed. (London: Allen and Unwin, 1937), p. 148; Robert Merrihew Adams, *Leibniz: Determinist, Theist, Idealist* (New York: Oxford University Press, 1994), pp. 285–88.

6.   Brandon Look, "On Monadic Domination in Leibnizian Metaphysics," *British Journal for the History of Philosophy* 10, no. 3 (2002): 379–99; reference to pp. 385–86.

7.   Look, "On Monadic Domination," pp. 387–88.

8.   Look, "On Monadic Domination," p. 392.

9.   Ohad Nachtomy, *Possibility, Agency, and Individuality in Leibniz's Metaphysics* (Dordrecht: Springer, 2007), pp. 227–29.

10.   The closest Leibniz comes to endorsing item 4 in the list is the following sentence contained in a reply to G. W. Molanus's essay "The Soul and Its Nature" and included in a letter to the Electress Sophie dated June 12, 1700: "However, since it is a matter of *unities of substance*, it must be the case that there be some force and perception in the unities themselves, for without that there wouldn't be any force or perception in anything which is formed from them, which can only contain repetitions and relations of what is already in the unities." LTS, p. 199; G VII, p. 552. This sentence is somewhat murky, but it might indeed be construed to mean that the perceptions of component monads are somehow aggregated in the dominant monad. Pairing perception with force strengthens this possibility, since forces can indeed be aggregated. But a couple of things stand in the way of this reading. First, Leibniz makes it clear elsewhere that dominant monads are created separately by God. They do not emerge from the aggregate of monads they dominate. Second, it is unclear how perceptions, as Leibniz understands them, could conceivably be aggregated. If Leibniz really believed that the perceptions of dominant monads aggregate those of their component monads, this is a point he would have trumpeted loudly and often, not squirreled away in an insert to a single letter.

11.   LDB, p. 257.

12.   Nachtomy, *Possibility*, pp. 227–28.

13.   LSC, p. 331.

14.   Leibniz describes the worm as "requisite," but earlier in the letter he distinguishes the requisite from the substantial. The worm is requisite because "its existence is in fact required by the order of nature" (LDB, p. 301). What Leibniz means by this isn't entirely clear. He *could* mean that the worm is necessary for the existence of its host, but that seems unlikely. Perhaps he is leaving the door open for an as-yet undiscovered function. More likely, though, he simply means that worms are requisite to the natural order as a whole rather than to the host. If they were not requisite in this larger sense, they would not exist. But their reason for being could simply be the general one of packing as many perspectives as possible into nature rather than one of functionality within the animal they inhabit.

15. Maria Rosa Antognazza, *Leibniz: An Intellectual Biography* (Cambridge: Cambridge University Press, 2009), p. 558.

16. PPL, pp. 512–13.

17. LC, p. 49; DSR, p. 27.

18. PE, p. 290. This does not mean that they necessarily *do* think (though it also doesn't mean that they don't), but only that nothing about them (presumably some lack of complexity) would render them structurally incapable of thought.

19. LC, p. 338.

20. See "On the Secret of the Sublime, or On the Supreme Being," in LC, pp. 45–53.

21. NS, p. 214. Against this, one might quote the following: "God governs minds [i.e., human minds] as a prince governs his subjects, or rather as a father looks after his children; whereas he deals with other substances as an engineer handles his machines" (NS, p. 13.) Yet engineers do not supply machines with "worlds."

22. Leibniz writes to Des Bosses that "it is naturally represented or expressed most perfectly in the internal phenomena of any monad whether it itself is an ingredient requisite of a body that any other monad dominates; and if the body of any worm is a part of the human body, this could be read in the soul of the worm, to be sure, in accordance with the natural course of things" (LDB, p. 303). But the fact that this function is expressed in the worm's soul does not mean that it is necessarily apparent to the worm. Examining the genome of the bacteria in our microbiome would reveal the basis of qualities that allow them to perform their useful functions, but this would hardly be apparent to the bacteria. Their natures simply harmonize with ours. In general, monads are not aware of the ways they have been engineered so as to be compossible with other monads. The case of dominant and dominated monads is simply a special instance of the general rule of compossibility.

23. Compare Spinoza's description of a "little worm living in the blood" in a letter to Oldenberg. *The Collected Works of Spinoza*, ed. Edmund Curley, 2 vols. (Princeton, NJ: Princeton University Press, 2016), 2: p. 18.

24. LTS, pp. 77–78. Compare Cyrano de Bergerac, in arguing for the absurd results of denying the reality of the vacuum and allowing for a plenum (as Leibniz does): "For it would be ridiculous to believe that when a fly pushes a parcel of air aside with its wings, this parcel makes another recoil in front of it, and this second one yet another, and that in this manner the agitation of a flea's little toe produces a lump on the other side of the world!" Cyrano de Bergerac, *Other Worlds*, p. 58.

25. Leibniz may be taking a leaf from Pascal's book. Pascal famously observed that the slight elongation of Cleopatra's nose changed the history of the world (see module 14), and in his brief history of the English Civil War, he wrote that "Cromwell was about to ravage the whole of Christendom: the royal family was lost, and his own family was set to be forever powerful, except for a tiny grain of sand that lodged itself in his urethra." Cited and translated in Richard Scholar, *The Je-Ne-Sai-Quoi in Early Modern Europe: Encounters with a Certain Something* (Oxford: Oxford University Press, 2005), p. 169.

26. LC, p. 251.

27. LA, p. 263.

28. T, sec. 35, p. 94.

29. PW, p. 71. See Patrick Riley, *Leibniz' Universal Jurisprudence: Justice as the Charity of the Wise* (Cambridge, MA: Harvard University Press, 1995), pp. 13–21.

30. See Sergio Tonkonoff, *From Tarde to Deleuze and Foucault: The Infinitesimal Revolution* (London: Palgrave Macmillan, 2017); and Bruno Latour, "Gabriel Tarde and the End of the Social," in *The Social in Question: New Bearings in History and the Social Sciences*, ed. Patrick Joyce (London: Routledge, 2002), pp. 117–32.

31. Gabriel Tarde, *Monadology and Sociology*, ed. and trans. Theo Lorenc (Melbourne: re. press, 2012), p. 10.

32. Tarde, *Monadology*, p. 60.

33. Tarde, *Monadology*, p. 28.

34. Tarde, *Monadology*, p. 28.

35. Tarde, *Monadology*, p. 9.

36. Tarde, *Monadology*, p. 40.

37. See Tarde, *Monadology*, pp. 39–40.

38. Tarde, *Monadology*, p. 45.

39. Tarde, *Monadology*, p. 37. See also Latour, "Gabriel Tarde and the End of the Social," p. 7.

40. Tarde, *Monadology*, p. 37.

41. See Tarde, *Monadology*, pp. 39, 43.

42. Tarde, *Monadology*, p. 47.

43. Tarde, *Monadology*, p. 13.

44. Tarde, *Monadology*, pp. 46–47.

45. Tarde, *Monadology*, p. 61.

46. Tarde, *Monadology*, p. 27.

47. Tarde, *Monadology*, pp. 34–35.

12. THE MIND-BODY PROBLEM

1. Baruch Spinoza, *Ethics*, trans. G. H. R. Parkinson (Oxford: Oxford University Press, 2000), p. 166.

2. Spinoza, *Ethics*, p. 118.

3. For a critical history of these debates and a proposed solution, see Noa Schein, "The False Dichotomy Between Objective and Subjective Interpretations of Spinoza's Theory of Attributes," *British Journal for the History of Philosophy* 17, no. 3 (2009): 505–32.

4. For a recent critical account of these, see Karolina Hübner, "Spinoza on Intentionality, Materialism, and Mind-Body Relations," *Philosopher's Imprint* 19, no. 43 (October 2019): 1–23.

5. Antonio Damasio, *Looking for Spinoza: Joy, Sorrow, and the Feeling Brain* (New York: Harcourt, 2003); Adrian Johnson and Catherine Malabou, *Self and Emotional Life: Philosophy, Psychoanalysis and Neuroscience* (New York: Columbia University Press, 2013).

6. Even this formulation is inexact, since for Leibniz, the extension of bodies is a secondary and somewhat imaginary quality. Leibnizian dualism rather involves the distinction between primary and derivative force, the former acting in a mental realm, the latter in a bodily one.

7. NS, p. 26.

8. A 6.4: 1367, cited and translated in Daniel Garber, *Leibniz: Body, Substance, Monad* (Oxford: Oxford University Press, 2009), pp. 196–97.

9.   David J. Chalmers, *The Conscious Mind: In Search of a Fundamental Theory* (New York: Oxford University Press, 1997), p. 94.

10. See Chalmers, *The Conscious Mind*, p. 94 n. 1. Daniel Dennett makes repeated use of the philosopher's zombie in *Consciousness Explained* (Boston: Little, Brown, 1991).

11. We can complete this spooky scene by adding Thomas Nagel's bat. See Nagel, "What Is It Like to Be a Bat?," *Philosophical Review* 83, no. 4 (October 1974): 435–50.

12. PPL, p. 207.

13. LC, p. 333.

14. PE, p. 33.

15. LC, p. 311.

16. LDB, p. 255. And yet, Leibniz also asserts the opposite. See LDV, p. 267. This sort of inconsistency is not uncommon.

17. See the discussion in Richard T. W. Arthur, *Monads, Composition, and Force: Ariadnean Threads Through the Leibnizian Labyrinth* (Oxford: Oxford University Press, 2018), pp. 69–84.

18. See the correspondence and other materials included in NS.

19. See Chalmers, *The Conscious Mind*, and Galen Strawson et al., *Consciousness and Its Place in Nature: Does Physicalism Entail Panpsychism?*, ed. Anthony Freeman (Exeter, UK: Imprint Academic, 2006).

20. Strawson et al., *Consciousness*, pp. 12–24. One of the reasons the brain-body problem appears intractable to philosophers of mind such as Chalmers and Strawson is that they pose it in reductive ways. For a more scientifically sophisticated and promising account, see Terrence W. Deacon, *Incomplete Nature: How Mind Emerged from Matter* (New York: Norton, 2011).

21. NE, p. 67.

22. Chalmers, *Conscious Mind*, pp. 293–97.

23. For the latter, see, e.g., Godehard Bruntrup and Ludwig Jaskolla, eds., *Panpsychism: Contemporary Perspectives* (Oxford: Oxford University Press, 2016); and Michael Blamauer, ed., *The Mental as Fundamental: New Perspectives on Panpsychism* (Frankfurt: De Gruyter, 2011).

24. See Strawson, *Consciousness*, pp. 10–12; and Chalmers, *Conscious Mind*, p. 154.

25. See, e.g., David Chalmers, "The Combination Problem for Panpsychism," in Bruntrup and Jaskolla, *Panpsychism*, pp. 179–211.

26. Strawson, *Consciousness*, p. 54.

13. MICROPERCEPTIONS

1.   LC, pp. 59–61.

2.   See, e.g., Michel Serres, *Le système de Leibniz et ses modèles mathématiques*, 2nd ed. (Paris: Presse Universitaires de France, 1982), pp. 206, 208–9.

3.   NE, p. 54.

4.   PT, pp. 260, 269. The consciousness of perceptions actually takes two forms for Leibniz. Sentience is the awareness of the perceived object and is something of which both animals and human beings are capable. Apperception is the awareness of perception, including the role of the "I" as perceiving subject. In a sense, it is the becoming-aware of perspective.

5.   NE, p. 54.

6.   NE, p. 103.

7.   NE, p. 238.

8.   Robert B. Brandom, "Leibniz and Degrees of Perception," *Journal of the History of Philosophy* 19, no. 4 (October 1981): 447–79. Quotation from p. 466. See also Robert McRae, *Leibniz: Perception, Apperception, and Thought* (Toronto: University of Toronto Press, 1976), pp. 43–46.

9.   NE, p. 114. Cf. NE, p. 76, where Philalethes/Locke states that it "seems to me a contradiction to say, that there are truths imprinted on the soul, which it perceives . . . not," and Theophilus/Leibniz replies "if you have that prejudice, I am not surprised that you reject innate knowledge." Both of these quotations directly contradict McRae's claim that "Leibniz's is plainly not a storehouse theory of memory. There is nothing being permanently deposited in the soul, no impressions are left on it" (McRae, *Leibniz*, p. 46).

10. Of course, this notion of memory as writing should not be taken to imply that the soul is Lockean—a notion that Leibniz is careful to reject. For Leibniz, the soul onto which perceptions are inscribed or impressed is irregular and, as it were, already written on.

11. The Derridean echoes in this sentence are fully intended.

12. Sigmund Freud, *Beyond the Pleasure Principle*, trans. James Strachey (New York: Norton, 1961), p. 28.

13. Sigmund Freud, *General Psychological Theory: Papers on Metapsychology* (New York: Macmillan, 1963), pp. 207–12.

14. See Jacques Derrida, "Freud and the Scene of Writing," in *Writing and Difference*, trans. Alan Bass (Chicago: University of Chicago Press, 1978), pp. 196–231.

15. NE, p. 55.

16. H. D. P. Lee, ed., *Zeno of Elea: A Text, with Translations and Notes* (Cambridge: Cambridge University Press, 1936), p. 108.

17. LSC, pp. 301–3.

18. See Norman Sieroka, *Leibniz, Husserl, and the Brain* (Basingstoke, UK: Palgrave Macmillan, 2015), p. 86 and references there, including NE, pp. 192–93.

19. NE, p. 57.

20. NE, p. 165.

21. NE, p. 56.

22. NE, p. 94.

23. NE, pp. 77–78.

24. PPL, p. 634.

14. THE *JE NE SAIS QUOI* AND THE LEIBNIZIAN UNCONSCIOUS

1.   Jacques Rancière, *The Aesthetic Unconscious*, trans. Debra Keates and James Swenson (Cambridge: Polity Press, 2010).

2.   NE, p. 55.

3.   See Richard Scholar, *The Je-Ne-Sais-Quoi in Early Modern Europe: Encounters with a Certain Something* (Oxford: Oxford University Press, 2005).

4. PPL, p. 291. Compare PT, p. 76: "When I can recognize one thing among others without being able to say what its differences or properties consist in, my knowledge is *confused*. In this way we sometimes know *clearly*, without being in any way in doubt, whether a poem or a painting is good or bad because there is a certain *je ne sais quoi* which pleases or offends us."

5. PPL, p. 115.

6. See Scholar, Je-Ne-Sais-Quoi, pp. 199–200.

7. See Scholar, Je-Ne-Sais-Quoi, pp. 10–11; and Nicolas Cronk, *The Classical Sublime: French Neoclassicism and the Language of Literature* (Charlottesville, VA: Rookwood Press, 2002), pp. 51–76.

8. Blaise Pascal, *Pensées*, ed. Philippe Sellier (Paris: Bordas, 1991), p. 32. Cited and translated by Scholar, Je-Ne-Sais-Quoi, p. 166.

9. Jacques Lacan, *Écrits: A Selection*, trans. Bruce Fink (New York: Norton, 2002), p. 115.

10. René Descartes, *Oeuvres*, ed. Charles Adam and Paul Tannery, 11 vols. (Paris: Vrin, 1964–1976), 5: pp. 57–58.

11. William Shakespeare, *Hamlet*, ed. Ann Thompson and Neil Taylor (London: Methuen, 2006).

12. NE, p. 178.

15. MIND IS A LIQUID

1. In this section I will be treating the terms "liquid" and "fluid" as if they were synonyms, which they are not, strictly speaking. Fluids include gases and plasmas as well as liquids. "Fluid" is thus a hypernym for "liquid."

2. LC, p. 331.

3. PPL, p. 473.

4. "Now if it is possible for everything to be a plenum, then everything will be a plenum, for it is absurd for any place to be left useless in which there could be an infinity of creatures." LC, p. 247. Cf. LC, p. 45.

5. LTS, p. 347.

6. LC, p. 246.

7. PPL, p. 157.

8. PPL, p. 407.

9. NE, p. 151.

10. LDB, p. 9. Cf. LDV, p. 11: "And so, however small a body may be, there is a much subtler fluid surrounding and permeating it, from which the elasticity of the body comes."

11. LC, pp. lxxxvi–lxxxvii.

12. LC, p. 185

13. PPL, p. 279.

14. "Nothing is absolutely solid or fluid, and everything has a certain degree of solidity and fluidity." PT, p. 173.

15. DSR, pp. 35–37.

16. LC, p. 47.

17. On oceans, liquidity, knowledge, and conceptual blending in Leibniz, see Cristina Marras, "The Role of Metaphor in Leibniz's Epistemology," in *Leibniz: What Kind of*

Rationalist?, ed. Marcelo Dascal (Dordrecht: Springer, 2008), pp. 199–212; and Cristina Marras, *Les Métaphores dans la Philosophie de Leibniz* (Limoges: Lambert Lucas, 2017), pp. 38–67.

18.   Steven Mithen, *The Prehistory of the Mind: The Cognitive Origins of Art, Religion and Science* (London: Thames and Hudson, 1999).

19.   Douglas Hofstadter and the Fluid Analogies Research Group, *Fluid Concepts and Creative Analogies: Computer Models of the Fundamental Mechanisms of Thought* (New York: Basic Books, 1995).

20.   FC, p. 2.

21.   FC, pp. 2–3.

16. THE CONFUSED AND THE DISTINCT

1.   Robert McRae, *Leibniz: Perception, Apperception, and Thought* (Toronto: University of Toronto Press, 1976), p. 36.

2.   PPL, pp. 291–92.

3.   This at least is Leibniz's premise. There are things one might say about the color blue to try to differentiate it from the others. One might call it the "coolest" or the "calmest" color. But this method of differentiation is fuzzy and unreliable.

4.   Here and elsewhere in this section, I am drawing on the very clarifying article by Steven M. Puryear, "Was Leibniz Confused About Confusion?," *Leibniz Review* 15 (2005): 95–124.

5.   See the discussions in Margaret Dauler Wilson, *Ideas and Mechanism: Essays on Early Modern Philosophy* (Princeton, NJ: Princeton University Press, 1999), pp. 322–35 and 336–52. Wilson argues that Leibniz is himself confused about the difference between confused perceptions and confused ideas—a claim that Puryear, in "Was Leibniz Confused about Confusion?," tries to refute.

6.   LTS, p. 220.

7.   LTS, p. 152.

8.   NS, p. 166.

9.   T, p. 198.

10.   NE, pp. 186–87.

11.   NS, p. 117.

12.   Horst Bredekamp, *Die Fenster der Monade: Gottfried Wilhelm Leibniz' Theater der Natur und Kunst*, 2nd ed. (Berlin: Akademie Verlag, 2008), p. 92, quoting A 7.1: 598.

13.   Bredekamp, *Die Fenster der Monade*, p. 93.

14.   See Richard C. Brown, *The Tangled Origins of the Leibnizian Calculus* (Singapore: World Scientific, 2012), p. 176, citing Louis Couturat, *La logique de Leibniz* (Paris: Alcan, 1901), p. 62ff.

15.   See note 12.

16.   Heinrich Wölfflin, *Principles of Art History: The Problem of the Development of Style in Later Art*, trans. M. D. Hottinger (Mineola, NY: Dover, 1950), pp. 18–72 and 196–225.

17.   PPL, p. 292.

18.   LP, pp. 51–52.

19.   See Bredekamp, *Die Fenster der Monade*, pp. 106–115.

20. Michel Serres, *Le système de Leibniz et ses modèles mathématiques*, 2nd ed. (Paris: Presses Universitaires de France, 1982), p. 119.

21. PT, p. 259.

22. PT, p. 274.

17. PHILOSOPHY AS AESTHETIC OBJECT

1. LTS, p. 415.

2. PPL, p. 137.

3. On the objectivity of beauty, see Carlos Portales's doctoral dissertation, "Leibniz's Aesthetics: The Metaphysics of Beauty" (PhD diss., University of Edinburgh, 2019), pp. 16–17, https://era.ed.ac.uk/bitstream/handle/1842/35712/Portales2019.pdf?sequence =1&isAllowed=y). I will be engaging with Portales's important dissertation throughout this module.

4. PPL, p. 426.

5. A 6.1: 499, cited in Portales, "Leibniz's Aesthetics," p. 48.

6. A 6.4: 2804, cited in Portales, "Leibniz's Aesthetics," p. 149.

7. PPL, p. 428.

8. See Herbert Breger, "Die mathematisch-physikalische Schönheit bei Leibniz," *Revue internationale de philosophie* 48 (1994): 127–140.

9. A 6.4: 2804, quoted in Portales, "Leibniz's Aesthetics," p. 149.

10. LTS, p. 152.

11. LTS, pp. 117–18.

12. PPL, p. 348.

13. PT, p. 265.

14. Portales, "Leibniz's Aesthetics," p. 159.

15. PPL, p. 422.

16. LTS, p. 179.

17. Portales, "Leibniz's Aesthetics," p. 183.

18. See Arthur C. Danto, *The Philosophical Disenfranchisement of Art* (New York: Columbia University Press, 1986). One comes away from Danto's book with the impression that he regards the Hegelian disenfranchisement as at least partially justified.

19. Leibniz, *Opera Omnia*, ed. Ludovic Dutens (Geneva, 1765), 3: p. 437, trans. Lloyd Strickland, 2018, http://www.leibniz-translations.com/goldbach1712.htm.

20. NS, p. 117.

21. Louis Althusser, "A Letter to André Daspre," in *Lenin and Philosophy and Other Essays*, trans. Ben Brewster (New York: Monthly Review Press, 1971), pp. 221–27.

22. NS, pp. 218–19.

23. See, e.g., G 3: 336.

24. PPL, p. 263; PE, pp. 29, 100.

25. LCC, p. 63.

26. Carolyn Merchant, *The Death of Nature: Women, Ecology, and the Scientific Revolution* (San Francisco: Harper and Row, 1980); Martin Heidegger, *The Principle of Reason*, trans. Reginald Lilly (Bloomington: University of Indianapolis Press, 1991); Theodor W. Adorno

and Max Horkheimer, *Dialectic of Enlightenment*, trans. John Cumming (New York: Herder and Herder, 1972).

27.   Merchant, *The Death of Nature*, p. 283.

28.   Pauline Phemister and Lloyd Strickland, "Leibniz's Monadological Positive Aesthetics," *British Journal for the History of Philosophy* 23, no. 6 (2015): 1214–34.

29.   On Spinoza, Leibniz, and ecological thought, see Pauline Phemister, "Leibniz and Ecology," *History of Philosophy Quarterly* 18, no. 3 (July 2001): 239–58; and Pauline Phemister, *Leibniz and the Environment* (New York: Routledge, 2016). Heidegger is the principle figure who attempts to tar Leibniz with the brush of instrumental rationality, citing principally Leibniz's principle of sufficient reason. For responses, see Renato Cristin, *Heidegger and Leibniz: Reason and the Path* (Dordrecht: Springer, 1998); and Hans Ruin, "Heidegger and Leibniz on Sufficient Reason," *Studia Leibnitiana* 30, no. 1 (1998): 49–67.

30.   On the interesting as an aesthetic category, see Sianne Ngai, *Our Aesthetic Categories: Cute, Zany, Interesting* (Cambridge, MA: Harvard University Press, 2012).

18. BLIND THOUGHT

1.   A 6.4: 912–13, cited in Maria Rosa Antognazza, *Leibniz: An Intellectual Biography* (Cambridge: Cambridge University Press, 2009), p. 240.

2.   PPL, p. 261.

3.   See Richard C. Brown, *The Tangled Origins of the Leibnizian Calculus* (Singapore: World Scientific, 2012), p. 187.

4.   Brown, *Tangled Origins*, p. 174.

5.   Leibniz wrote with regard to the benefits of his calculator that "it is unworthy of excellent men to lose hours like slaves in the labor of calculation, which could safely be relegated to anyone else if the machine were used." David Eugene Smith, *A Source Book in Mathematics* (New York: Dover, 1959), p. 181.

6.   Brown, *Tangled Origins*, p. 162.

19. DARK LEIBNIZ

1.   T, sec. 168, p. 228.

2.   Some recent research suggests that dark matter may not exist after all. See Kyu-Hyun Chae et al., "Testing the Strong Equivalence Principle: Detection of the External Field Effect in Rotationally Supported Galaxies," *Astrophysical Journal* 904, no. 51 (2020), https://iopscience.iop.org/article/10.3847/1538-4357/abbb96. Regardless, I will insist on the existence of dark Leibniz.

3.   PPL, pp. 217–18.

4.   T, p. 126.

5.   There is also the problem that Leibnizian metaphysics, and particularly his notion of the "preprogrammed" monad, seems to imply a predestinarian theology. His attempts to avoid this conclusion are far from convincing, as are his theodical strategies in general. Leibniz is in the unenviable position of having to refute not only his theological opponents but also, in some sense, himself.

6. T, p. 192.

7. Patrick Riley, *Leibniz' Universal Jurisprudence: Justice as the Charity of the Wise* (Cambridge, MA: Harvard University Press, 1996), p. 50.

8. PPL, p. 489.

9. PPL, p. 489.

10. See PPL, p. 564; and CP, p. 7.

11. LTS, pp. 112–13.

12. PPL, p. 489.

13. LTS, pp. 152–53.

14. PPL, pp. 489–90.

15. See Carlos Portales, "Leibniz's Aesthetics: The Metaphysics of Beauty" (PhD diss., University of Edinburgh, 2019), pp. 24–25.

16. See Portales, "Leibniz's Aesthetics," pp. 62–66.

17. CP, p. 49.

18. PPL, p. 490.

19. Lloyd Strickland, *Leibniz Reinterpreted* (London: Continuum, 2006).

20. G 6: 168, quoted in Strickland, *Leibniz Reinterpreted*, p. 143.

21. A 6.4: 2804. Quoted in Strickland, *Leibniz Reinterpreted*, p. 106.

22. A 6.1:138, quoted in Strickland, p. 106.]\

23. Richard H. Popkin, *The History of Scepticism: From Savonarola to Bayle*, Revised and expanded ed. (Oxford: Oxford University Press, 2003), p. 268 and endnotes on pp. 371–72.

24. Hernán D. Caro, *The Best of All Possible Worlds: Leibniz's Philosophical Optimism and Its Critics, 1710–1755* (Leiden: Brill, 2020). See also Lloyd Strickland, "The Reception of the *Theodicy* in England," Manchester Metropolitan University, https://e-space.mmu.ac.uk /601330/2/The%20Reception%20of%20the%20Theodicy%20in%20England%20 %28final%29.pdf (accessed November 26, 2022).

25. David Scott defends Leibnizian theodicy against Ivan's critique in "On the Crassness of Leibniz's Metaphysics," *Review of Metaphysics* 70, no. 2 (December 2016): 311–37.

26. Georges Friedmann, *Leibniz et Spinoza*, 2nd ed. (Paris: Gallimard, 1962), p. 22. Quoted in Scott, "On the Crassness of Leibniz's Metaphysics," p. 333 n. 57. Scott remarks that "Friedmann's perspicacity is as devastating as it is convincing."

20. THINGS FALL APART

1. There is an extensive literature on the question whether Leibniz is an idealist and, if so, when he becomes one. For an important recent contribution arguing that he continues to believe in external reality, see Richard T. W. Arthur, *Monads, Composition and Force: Ariadnean Threads Through Leibniz's Labyrinth* (Oxford: Oxford University Press, 2018). For a strong phenomenalist reading of the late metaphysics, see Vincenzo De Risi, *Geometry and Monadology* (Basel: Birkhäuser, 2007).

2. PPL, pp. 153–54.

3. LA, p. 253.

4. LDV, p. 307.

5. LC, pp. 243–45.

6.   NS, p. 49.

7.   LCC, p. 8.

8.   PPL, p. 364.

9.   LA, p. 149.

10.   One might reasonably ask how I distinguish between the anxiety-induced activity of *worrying* a problem and the pleasure-filled activity of *tinkering with* it. From the outside, they look rather similar. In this case, the determining factor is the presence of a threatening conceptual abyss. Which is not to say that worrying cannot shade off into tinkering, and vice versa. Indeed, I have already offered Leibniz's invention of the *vinculum substantiale*, one of his attempts to mend the body problem, as an instance of tinkering.

11.   Glenn Hartz, *Leibniz's Final System: Monads, Matter and Animals* (New York: Routledge, 2007).

12.   Hartz, *Leibniz's Final System*, p. 128.

13.   Hartz, *Leibniz's Final System*, p. 129.

14.   Hartz, *Leibniz's Final System*, p. 131. Hartz may well mean that the actual relations in the object are inaccessible while the concept of them is not. Here the "bridging" work of rigid embodiment may come into play. But after finishing Hartz's book, I still have no concrete idea of how monads can be aggregated.

15.   I believe that Hartz's clean distinction between "theory-pluralism" and "truth-pluralism," however, ought to be placed under pressure, though it may in the end be defensible. For Hartz, admitting a truth-pluralism would undermine the project of philosophy as such. See Hartz, *Leibniz's Final System*, pp. 18–23.

16.   In his article "Leibniz's Phenomenalisms," Glenn Hartz likewise describes the unifying work of the dominant monad as "magic." Glenn Hartz, "Leibniz's Phenomenalisms," *Philosophical Review* 101, no. 3 (July 1992): 541.

17.   See Brandon C. Look and Donald Rutherford's introduction in LDB, pp. xv–lxxix.

21. THE MONAD AS EVENT: ALFRED NORTH WHITEHEAD

1.   Jean-Pascal Alcantara, "G. W. Leibniz (1646–1716)," in *Handbook of Whiteheadian Process Thought*, 2 vols., ed. Michel Weber and Will Desmond (Boston: De Gruyter, 2013), 2: p. 298.

2.   See Pierfrancesco Basile, *Leibniz, Whitehead and the Metaphysics of Causation* (New York: Palgrave Macmillan, 2009), pp. 32–62.

3.   SMW, p. 155.

4.   PR, pp. 80.

5.   See, e.g., Nicholas Rescher, *Process Metaphysics: An Introduction to Process Philosophy* (Albany: State University of New York Press, 1996); Nicholas Rescher, "Process Philosophy and Monadological Metaphysics," in *On Leibniz:* Expanded ed. (Pittsburgh: University of Pittsburgh Press, 2013), pp. 369–78; and Charles Hartshorne, "Whitehead and Leibniz: A Comparison," in *Contemporary Studies in Philosophical Idealism*, ed. John Howie and Thomas O. Buford (Cape Cod, MA: Charles Stark, 1975), pp. 95–115.

6.   PR, p. xi.

7.   PR, p. 6.

8. PR, p. 18.

9. "Finally, the reformed subjectivist principle must be repeated: that apart from the experiences of subjects there is nothing, nothing, nothing, bare nothingness." PR, p. 167. Eternal forms, the only things apart from actual entities, are potentials rather than actuals.

10. PR, p. 18.

11. PR, p. 80.

12. Whitehead says that eternal objects are "Platonic Forms, the Platonic Ideas, the medieval universals." FR, p. 32, cited in Basile, *Leibniz, Whitehead and the Metaphysics of Causation*, p. 108.

13. SMW, p. 151.

14. I thank Steve Shaviro for this last suggestion.

15. "Appetition is immediate matter of fact including in itself a principle of unrest, involving realization of what is not and may be" (PR, p. 32).

16. I would argue that Whitehead's version of panpsychism is as unconvincing as the others I discussed in module 12.

17. PR, p. 148. The "including" in this sentence might be confusing, since Whitehead insists elsewhere that nothing exists aside from actual entities, and so it is unclear what else could be "included." He probably has in mind eternal objects, which are potentials rather than actualities.

18. SMW, pp. 106–7

19. SMW, p. 7.

20. SMW, pp. 69–70. The same concept is given more technical expression in *Process and Reality*: "An actual entity achieves its own unity by its determinate feelings respecting every item of the datum [i.e., every element of its world]. Every individual objectification in the datum has its perspective defined by its own eternal objects with their own relevance compatible with the relevance of other objectifications" (PR, p. 154).

21. See Elizabeth M. Kraus, *The Metaphysics of Experience: A Companion to Whitehead's* Process and Reality (New York: Fordham University Press, 1997), pp. 151–2, 160.

22. PR, p. 67: "This initial phase [of a concrescence] is a direct derivate from God's primordial nature. In this function, as in every other, God is the organ of novelty, aiming at intensification."

23. SMW, p. 71.

24. PR, p. 210. Cf. PR, p. 25: "the meaning of the phrase 'the actual world' is relative to the becoming of a definite actual entity."

25. I recognize that my way of stating this might seem to break the subject-superject apart into two separate entities, which would violate Whitehead's views. The subjective and superjective dimensions of an actual entity are rather different facets of one thing. Whitehead sometimes appears to assign them a temporal sequence, with the superject as the aim and product of the subjectifying process. I find it helpful to imagine the two rather along the lines of Spinozist attributes, but even this may involve tying them too closely to a substance-based ontology. At PR, p. 30, Whitehead describes subject and superject as "two descriptions" of an entity, and that may be the best way to think of them.

26. Cited in Judith A. Jones, *Intensity: An Essay in Whiteheadian Ontology* (Nashville, TN: Vanderbilt University Press, 1998), p. 61.

27. Jones, *Intensity*, p. 61.
28. PR, p. 233.
29. NS, p. 117.
30. PR, p. 172.
31. Alfred North Whitehead, *Symbolism: Its Meaning and Effect* (New York: Fordham University Press, 1985), p. 23.
32. PR, p. 176.
33. Whitehead's account of vagueness is inconsistent or at least variable. On the one hand, he assigns vagueness as a quality attaching to all causal efficacy and hence necessarily experienced by subjects. But he also describes vagueness as the active *relegation* of data to an irrelevant background on the part of a concrescence so that it may elevate a narrow band of data to a vivid foreground. (AI, p. 260. Cf. Jones, *Intensity*, p. 37.)
34. Alain Badiou similarly claims that for Leibniz, "nothing is ever isolated from the all-encompassing murmuring of being." Alain Badiou, *Deleuze: The Clamor of Being*, trans. Louise Burchill (Minneapolis: University of Minnesota Press, 2000), p. 35.
35. NE, p. 55.
36. By far the best and most sophisticated account of Whiteheadian aesthetics is Steven Shaviro's book, *Without Criteria: Kant, Whitehead, Deleuze, and Aesthetics* (Cambridge, MA: MIT Press, 2009). But Judith A. Jones's *Intensity* is also invaluable for anyone wanting to ponder the relationship between Whitehead's aesthetic and Leibniz's, though Leibniz is not an explicit topic in the book.
37. PR, p. xii.
38. SMW, p. 197.
39. SMW, p. 142.
40. PR, p. 5.
41. Shaviro, *Without Criteria*, p. 147.
42. SMW, p. 59
43. AI, p. 146.
44. SMW, p. 7.
45. PR, p. 3.
46. CN, p. 14.
47. PR, p. 4.
48. CN, p. 18. Whitehead's category of "proposition" is not limited to the ordinary notion of logical propositions but articulates what he calls physical and conceptual feelings in ways that are not always conscious.
49. MT, p. vii.
50. Basile, *Leibniz, Whitehead and the Metaphysics of Causation*, p. 126.
51. PR, p. 112.
52. PR, p. 339.
53. SMW, pp. 87–88.
54. See, e.g., AI, p. 258: "The Chinese and the Greeks both achieved certain perfections of civilization—each worthy of admiration. But even perfection will not bear the tedium of indefinite repetition. To sustain a civilization with the intensity of its first ardour requires more than learning. Adventure is essential, namely the search for new perfections."

22. THE MONAD AS STRANGE LOOP: DOUGLAS HOFSTADTER

1. FC, p. 63.
2. FC, p. 238.
3. FC, p, 308.
4. FC, p. 293.
5. FC, pp. 138–39.
6. GEB, p. 324.
7. GEB, p. 709.
8. See, e.g., reviews by Jonathan Lieberman, untitled review, *Journal of Philosophy* 77, no. 1 (January 1980): 45–52; H. H. Pattee, untitled review, *International Studies in Philosophy* 15, no. 1 (1983): 87–88; and especially Judson C. Webb, untitled review, *Journal of Symbolic Logic* 48, no. 3 (September 1983): 864–71.
9. GEB, p. 707.
10. GEB, p. 10.
11. GEB, pp. 10, 717–19.
12. GEB, p. 525.
13. GEB, p. xiii.

23. THE GODLESS MONAD: HUMBERTO MATURANA AND FRANCISCO VARELA

1. See references in Pablo Razeto-Barry, "Autopoiesis Forty Years Later: A Review and Reformulation," *Origins of Life and Evolution of Biospheres* 42 (2012): 544–45. See also John Mingers, *Self-Producing Systems: Implications and Applications of Autopoiesis* (New York: Springer Science + Business Media, 1995), pp. 1–3, 119–201.
2. For Heidegger and Husserl, see Mingers, *Self-Producing Systems*, pp. 100–10. *Autopoiesis and Cognition*, which is my main concern here, presents a less overtly transdisciplinary texture than that exhibited by the other writers featured in this book.
3. And this texture is itself variable. My discussion will focus largely on *Autopoiesis and Cognition*, the most canonical presentation of Maturana and Varela's theories and perhaps also the one that most strongly suggests a self-generated system. But in other, less theoretically formal works, such as *The Tree of Knowledge: The Biological Roots of Human Understanding* (Boston: Shambhala, 1987), the transdisciplinary roots of their thinking are more patently displayed.
4. In this regard their work has been surpassed—and, in some respects, elaborated upon—by Terrence W. Deacon. See Deacon, *Incomplete Nature: How Mind Emerged from Matter* (New York: Norton, 2012).
5. AC, pp. 76, 78–79.
6. AC, p. 86.
7. Mingers, *Self-Producing Systems*, p. 45.
8. AC, p. 36.
9. AC, p. 51.

10.   AC, p. 81.

11.   AC, p. 22.

12.   AC, p. 22.

13.   AC, p. 8.

14.   AC, p. 51.

15.   He also anticipates elements of John Searle's "Chinese room" thought experiment.

16.   It might be objected that while the pilot only makes adjustments in response to instrument readings, and thus operates entirely within the sphere of the cockpit, with no direct information about the outside world, the instruments themselves are gathering quite accurate information about their environment, and that without this, the pilot would surely have crashed.

17.   PT, p. 164.

18.   A 6.4: 1403 and A 6.4: 1367, cited in Daniel Garber, *Leibniz: Body, Substance, Monad* (Oxford: Oxford University Press, 2009), p. 258. Garber's discussion of the two kingdoms (pp. 255–66) is characteristically lucid and helpful.

19.   PPL, p. 269.

20.   AC, p. 27.

21.   AC, pp. 52–53.

22.   AC, p. 45.

23.   AC, p. 131.

24.   In their book *The Tree of Knowledge*, Maturana and Varela employ M. C. Escher's *Drawing Hands* to illustrate the recursive nature of autopoiesis (pp. 24–25). Whether this is an oblique nod to Hofstadter is unclear.

25.   AC, pp. 30, 57, 120.

26.   AC, p. 7.

27.   One problem with such a notion is that while organization is generic, structure is specific. All human beings share the same autopoietic organization while each individual incarnates it in a unique structure. Organization alone would therefore fail to capture, in ideal form, the *individuality* of each living creature. Its expression of its body would be incomplete, and it could therefore not quite serve as a monad for its body. Despite this, I don't think the relevance of Leibnizian expression should be dismissed out of hand.

28.   Humberto R. Maturana, "Reality: The Search for Objectivity or the Quest for a Compelling Argument," *Irish Journal of Psychology* 9, no. 1 (1988): 25–82.

24. THE QUANTUM MONAD: DAVID BOHM

1.   For a concise account, see Brian E. Blank's (highly unfavorable and informative) review of Jason Socrates Bardi, *The Calculus Wars: Newton, Leibniz, and the Greatest Mathematical Clash of All Time* (New York: Basic, 2007) in *Notices of the American Mathematical Society* 56, no. 5 (May 2009): 602–10.

2.   Richard T. W. Arthur, *Monads, Composition, and Force: Ariadnian Threads Through Leibniz's Labyrinth* (Oxford: Oxford University Press, 2018), pp. 295–96.

3.   Ilya Prigogine and Isabelle Stengers, "Postface: Dynamics from Leibniz to Lucretius," in Michel Serres, *Hermes: Literature, Science, Philosophy*, ed. Josue V. Harari and David F.

Bell (Baltimore, MD: Johns Hopkins University Press, 1982), pp. 137–55. Quotation from p. 139.

4. Ernst Mach, *The Science of Mechanics*, trans. Thomas I. McCormack (Chicago: Open Court, 1919), p. 229.

5. For an account of some leading dissidents from the Copenhagen interpretation (including Bohm), see Adam Becker, *What Is Real: The Unfinished Quest for the Meaning of Quantum Physics* (New York: Basic, 2018). And for many-worlds theory in particular (perhaps the most widespread alternative to the Copenhagen interpretation), see Sean Carroll, *Something Deeply Hidden: Quantum Worlds and the Emergence of Spacetime* (Boston: Dutton, 2019). A useful general survey of quantum physics from a philosophical perspective is Jim Baggott, *Beyond Measure: Modern Physics, Philosophy, and the Meaning of Quantum Theory* (Oxford: Oxford University Press, 2004).

6. Bohmian mechanics is not entirely unsusceptible to testing, however, and in fact, a recent experiment claims to have verified some aspects of it. See Dylan H. Mahler et al., "Experimental Nonlocal and Surreal Bohmian Trajectories," *Science Advances* 2, no. 2 (February 19, 2016), https://advances.sciencemag.org/content/2/2/e1501466. The experiment disconfirms the so-called ESSW paper that had been thought to present insoluble problems with Bohm's views: Berthold-Georg Englert et al., "Surrealistic Bohm Trajectories," *Zeitschrift für Naturforschung A* 47, no. 12 (1992): 1175–86.

7. See F. David Peat, *Infinite Potential: The Life and Times of David Bohm* (New York: Basic, 1996), p. 67.

8. Bohm offers this illustration in SOC, p. 90.

9. WIO, pp. 196–97.

10. Peat, *Infinite Potential*, p. 186.

11. D. Bohm and J. P. Vigier, "Model of the Causal Interpretation of Quantum Theory in Terms of a Fluid with Irregular Fluctuations," *Physical Review* 96, no. 1 (October 1954): 208–16.

12. "It may be said that space, which has so much energy, is *full* rather than empty." WIO, p. 242.

13. See Peat, *Infinite Potential*, pp. 138–39.

14. See Peat, *Infinite Potential*, p. 141.

15. WIO, p. 135.

16. Peat, *Infinite Potential*, p. 297. Cf. SOC, p. 89.

17. EDB, p. 13.

18. WIO, pp. 188–89. For Bohm's encounter with this device on a TV show, see F. David Peat and B. J. Hiley, *Quantum Implications: Essays in Honour of David Bohm* (London: Routledge and Kegan Paul, 1987), p. 40.

19. Peat, *Infinite Potential*, pp. 210–11, 240, 242.

20. Indeed, as I noted in module 05, note 6, Henri Poincaré, the inventor of algebraic topology, referred to it as *analysis situs*.

21. WIO, p. 263.

22. See Peat, *Infinite Potential*, pp. 187n. and 272; also, WIO, p. 61.

23. See, e.g., EDB, p. 116: "So we do not say that mind and body causally affect each other, but rather that the movements of both are the outcome of related projections of a common higher-dimensional ground."

24. On Bohm and painting, see Peat, *Infinite Potential*, pp. 232–40. On Bohm and Hegel (a principle philosophical interest after he renounced Marxism in 1956), see Peat, *Infinite Potential*, pp. 155–57, 179–81. On Bohm and Piaget, see Bohm, "Physics and Perception," EDB, pp. 39–77. On Bohm and linguistics, see WIO, pp. 34–60. On Bohm and Krishnamurti, see Peat, *Infinite Potential*, pp. 195–200, 223–31, 284–85, 298–300.

25. That being said, Bohm was hardly the only theoretical physicist to perceive connections between his field and Eastern religion, particularly Buddhism. Fritjof Capra's successful book *The Tao of Physics: An Exploration of the Parallels Between Modern Physics and Eastern Mysticism* (Berkeley, CA: Shambhala Press, 1975) inspired a slew of imitators, such as Gary Zukav, *The Dancing Wu Masters: An Overview of the New Physics* (New York: HarperOne, 2009). To what degree such books are Orientalist fantasies I do not feel qualified to say. Here again, though, Leibniz's interest in Chinese philosophy seems to point the way. See Gottfried Wilhelm Leibniz, *Writings on China*, trans. and ed. Daniel J. Cook and Henry Rosemont, Jr. (Chicago: Open Court, 1994).

26. WIO, pp. 43–44.

27. See, e.g., WIO, pp. xvi, 43–44, and 71.

28. SOC, p. 33.

29. WIO, p. 10.

30. WIO, p. 6.

25. AFTERWORD: LEIBNIZ IN MY LATTE

1. Michael Gottlieb Hansch, *Godefridi Guilielmi Leibnitii Principia Philosophiae, More Geometrico Demonstrata* (Frankfurt and Leipzig: Petri Conradi Monath, 1728), p. 135. Quoted in Benson Mates, *The Philosophy of Leibniz: Metaphysics and Language* (Oxford: Oxford University Press, 1986), p. 204.

2. On Leibniz's theory of divine preformation, see Justin E. H. Smith, *Divine Machines: Leibniz and the Sciences of Life* (Princeton: Princeton University Press, 2011), esp. pp. 165–96.

3. LTS, pp. 39, 100, 347.

4. LTS, pp. 105, 286.

5. LC, pp. 317–18.

6. I cannot help wondering whether Leibniz's frequent recourse to the figure of passing between larger and smaller stages doesn't in part reflect his own experience of traveling from the relative cultural backwater of Hanover to live in Paris and then, against his will, being summoned back again.

7. LTS, pp. 275, 285.

8. Smith, *Divine Machines*, p. 186.

9. LC, p. 317; LTS, pp. 285–86.

10. LA, p. 205.

11. Compare the following: "But there still remained the even bigger question as to what becomes of these souls or forms on the death of the animal or the destruction of the individual organized substance. This question is all the more difficult, because it seems hardly reasonable that souls should remain, useless, in a chaos of confused matter. This led me to decide in the end that there is only one view that can reasonably be taken,

which is that not only is the soul conserved, but so also is the animal itself and its organic mechanism; although the destruction of its cruder parts has made it so small as to be as little perceptible to our senses as it was before its birth." But if the soul of the individual is preserved in recognizable form, along with a miniaturized body, that body must look rather like the original one, since the body expresses the soul. (It is much smaller, true, but recall that for Leibniz, size matters less than shape.) Moreover, the soul of the deceased will remain "useless" not only if its *body* is a "chaos of confused matter" but also if its ambient *world* is comparably disordered.

12. LAC, p. 237.

13. See Richard Halpern, *Eclipse of Action: Tragedy and Political Economy* (Chicago: University of Chicago Press, 2017), pp. 154–58.

14. "Observatories have been founded for watching the stars, whose structures are spectacular and demand great apparatus, but telescopes are far from being as useful and from revealing the beauties and varieties of knowledge which microscopes reveal." PPL, p. 566.

Index